"WE ARE JEWS AGAIN"

Modern Jewish History
Henry Feingold, *Series Editor*

Select titles in Modern Jewish History

Assimilated Jews in the Warsaw Ghetto, 1940–1943
Katarzyna Person

Bundist Counterculture in Interwar Poland
Jack Jacobs

The Children of La Hille: Eluding Nazi Capture during World War II
Walter W. Reed

The Downfall of Abba Hillel Silver and the Foundation of Israel
Ofer Shiff

Judah L. Magnes: An American Jewish Nonconformist
Daniel P. Kotzin

Leaving Russia: A Jewish Story
Maxim D. Shrayer

"Silent No More": Saving the Jews of Russia, the American Jewish Effort, 1967–1989
Henry L. Feingold

Will to Freedom: A Perilous Journey through Fascism and Communism
Egon Balas

"We Are Jews Again"

Jewish Activism in the Soviet Union

Yuli Kosharovsky

Translated by Stefani Hoffman

Edited by Ann Komaromi

With a Foreword by Joshua Rubenstein

Syracuse University Press

On the cover: Refuseniks celebrate Succot with Israeli sportsmen in Lunts Meadow outside Moscow, 1975. *First row*, seated, from left: Anatoly Sharansky, Zeev Shakhnovsky, Ephraim Rosenstein (child), Yuli Kosharovsky. *Second row*: Isakhar Aharoni, Michael Bronstein, Menachem Berkowitz, Shlomo Fried. *Back row*, standing: Rami Miron, unidentified, Solomon Stoliar, Zeev Rom, Vladimir Slepak, Maria Slepak, Vitaly Rubin, Lev Gendin, Oksana Iablonsky. Collection of Inna and Yuli Kosharovsky.

Syracuse, New York 13244-5290

First Edition 2017
17 18 19 20 21 22   6 5 4 3 2 1

∞ The paper used in this publication meets the minimum requirements of the American National Standard for Information Sciences—Permanence of Paper for Printed Library Materials, ANSI Z39.48-1992.

ISBN: 978-0-8156-3500-0 (hardcover)   978-0-8156-3519-2 (paperback)
978-0-8156-5400-1 (e-book)

Library of Congress Cataloging-in-Publication Data

Names: Kosharovskiĭ, I͡Uliĭ, author. | Hoffman, Stefani, translator. | Komaromi, Ann, editor.

Title: We are Jews again : Jewish activism in the Soviet Union / Yuli Kosharovsky ; translated by Stefani Hoffman ; edited and with an introduction by Ann Komaromi ; with a foreword by Joshua Rubenstein.

Description: First edition 2017. | Syracuse, New York : Syracuse University Press, [2017] | Series: Modern Jewish history | Includes bibliographical references and index. | Description based on print version record and CIP data provided by publisher; resource not viewed.

Identifiers: LCCN 2017014308 (print) | LCCN 2017014992 (ebook) | ISBN 9780815654001 (e-book) | ISBN 9780815635000 (hardcover : alk. paper) | ISBN 9780815635192 (pbk. : alk. paper)

Subjects: LCSH: Zionism—Soviet Union. | Jews—Soviet Union—Biography. | Refuseniks—Biography. | Political prisoners—Soviet Union—Biography. | Dissenters—Soviet Union—Biography. | Civil rights—Soviet Union. | Kosharovskiĭ, I͡Uliĭ.

Classification: LCC DS149.5.S6 (ebook) | LCC DS149.5.S6 K68 2017 (print) | DDC 305.892/40470904—dc23

LC record available at https://lccn.loc.gov/2017014308

Manufactured in the United States of America

This book is dedicated to those who devoted their lives to our freedom:

Enid Wurtman, Stuart Wurtman, Glenn Richter,
Michael Sherbourne, Adele and Joel Sandberg, Pamela Cohen,
Connie and Joseph Smukler, Shirley Goldstein, Lynn Singer,
Irene Manekofsky, Barbara Stern, Lana and Bernie Dishler,
Sir Martin Gilbert, Jeffrey Tigay, Shirley and Alan Molod,
Marvin Verman, Frank Brodsky . . .
and hundreds of others.

Contents

Illustrations

Foreword

DURING THE LATE 1960S, when Leonid Brezhnev was the preeminent leader of the Soviet Union, the Kremlin repudiated the more relaxed policies of Nikita Khrushchev, who had been deposed in October 1964. Brezhnev tightened censorship over cultural expression and historical inquiry, and moved away from criticism of Joseph Stalin and his murderous regime. And when Warsaw Pact forces invaded Czechoslovakia in August 1968, the crushing of the Prague Spring ended any hope that Communist Party officials were open to reforming the system from within. Disheartened by the regime's harsher policies, several grassroots movements arose among disparate groups of Soviet citizens who were determined to press for their rights. Crimean Tatars wanted to return to their traditional homelands from where Stalin had forcibly removed them in 1944. Ukrainian nationalists tried to defend their cultural legacy and national rights against a system of enforced Russification. Liberal-minded activists challenged the regime's monopoly of information control, exposing both the abusive kangaroo courts that failed to follow the country's constitution and criminal codes and the difficult conditions in the labor camps for convicted political prisoners. At the same time a network of Jewish activists began to demand the right to emigrate to Israel, eventually becoming the best organized and most successful movement among the various streams of dissent. By the time Leonid Brezhnev died in November 1982, the regime, in spite of its repressive instincts, had permitted more than a quarter million Jews to leave. And when the Soviet Union collapsed in 1991, the Soviet Jewish emigration movement had already triumphed: nearly eight hundred thousand Jews had emigrated, an astonishing and altogether unforeseen result of their struggle.

Soviet Jews lived a paradoxical life. A half century after the revolution that brought the Bolsheviks to power in 1917, a significant majority of Soviet Jews had cultivated a profound devotion to the Russian language. Cut off from access to books on Jewish history or religion, they made Russian culture the source of their cultural and moral education. In her essay "Do I Feel I Belong to the Russian People?" the human rights activist Larisa Bogoraz, who had been born and raised by Jewish parents, expressed a common dilemma among Soviet Jews:

> Who am I now? Who do I feel myself to be? Unfortunately, I do not feel like a Jew. I understand that I have an unquestionable genetic tie with Jewry. I also assume that this is reflected in my mentality, in my mode of thinking, and in my behavior. But this common quality is as little help to me in feeling my Jewish identity as similarity of external features—evidently a more profound, or more general, common bond is lacking, such as community of language, culture, history, tradition; perhaps, even, of impressions, unconsciously absorbed by the senses: what the eye sees, the ear hears, the skin feels. By all these characteristics, I am Russian.
>
> I am accustomed to the color, smell, rustle of the Russian landscape, as I am to the Russian language, the rhythm of Russian poetry. I react to everything else as alien.[1]

But even as the country's Jews assimilated into Russian culture, history and the regime itself never allowed them to forget their origins. The Holocaust, during which the Nazis killed as many as two and a half million Jews throughout German-occupied Soviet territory, destroyed almost half of the country's Jewish population, leaving a traumatic burden that the survivors were barely permitted to publicly mourn once victory was achieved. Educated to accept assimilation yet not permitted to forget their origins, they could not mourn the Nazis' Jewish victims as Jews. And during the postwar years, "the Black Years of Soviet Jewry," Stalin targeted the leading voices of Yiddish culture, executing writers, poets, and journalists or shipping them off to labor camps. Soviet Jews came to believe that they had no future as Jews in Soviet society. While they could work, often in prestigious positions within the country's cultural, scientific, and industrial institutions, they had to live with the discomfort related to the effects of an identity they could not shed, however much they appeared to assimilate. As for leaving the country and making a life elsewhere, the very idea seemed unimaginable.

Several events in the late 1960s, however, prompted a shift in their attitudes. The Six-Day War of 1967 generated a broad and deeply felt identification with Israel's fate. And when Israel defeated Arab armies that had been supplied by the Kremlin, Soviet leaders launched a hysterical, anti-Zionist campaign whose sharp, ugly, anti-Jewish images reinforced discrimination against Soviet Jews in areas of education and employment. A half century after the revolution, in which many Jews had sided with revolutionary forces to create a new, promising, utopian order for Russia, a new generation of Jews "considered that the Jews had spilled enough of their blood on alien fields and altars in return for which they had received stark ingratitude and renewed antisemitism."[2] As the refusenik Boris Ainbinder recalled, "I was completely disillusioned with the Soviet Union. I understood that it was almost impossible to change anything here and that it was not my task to try. They didn't want us there, we were alien, let them deal with it."[3]

As *We Are Jews Again* makes clear, for almost all the Jewish activists the demand to leave was the culmination of a process of self-renewal. They always knew their internal passports recognized that they were of Jewish nationality, but once individual Jews decided they would apply to emigrate, the process led them to explore Jewish history and Jewish linguistic and religious traditions. Now they insisted on their right to mourn their martyrs, whether they rested among the millions of Hitler's victims on Soviet soil or suffered as bearers of Yiddish culture and therefore Jewish identity who had disappeared among the hundreds of literary, artistic, and cultural figures in Stalin's last years.

The emigration activists pursued a single, seemingly achievable demand—to leave the country—along with the associated goal of developing Jewish national culture within the constraints of Soviet society. These goals were still limited in contrast to the human rights movement's sweeping goal of wide-ranging civic and legal reforms. While the demand to emigrate may have seemed less threatening to Soviet officials in a superficial sense, for a regime that had always refused to acknowledge its mistakes the dream of leaving was a contagious threat that the Kremlin could not be expected to tolerate. That it eventually did and allowed hundreds of thousands of Jews to leave for Israel and the West—even as it singled out an unpredictable proportion of would-be emigrants for reprisal, refusing their applications to leave and forcing them into a form of legal and civic purgatory—was a testament to the movement's defiance and the regime's surprisingly flexible response.

We Are Jews Again vividly describes how they managed to live as Jews independent of how the Kremlin preferred them to behave. Even as tens of thousands would emigrate in a given year, there were always families who faced refusal. These "refuseniks," as they came to be called, found themselves thrust into a civil no-man's-land. Deprived of their professional work, socially isolated, increasingly dependent on the solidarity of other refuseniks and their dissident allies, along with foreign tourists, they set off on a journey of self-discovery. To pursue the right to leave as Jews, the emigration activists found themselves initiating several related activities. Organizing Hebrew classes, scientific seminars, meetings with foreign tourists and dignitaries, demonstrations on the streets and in Communist Party and government offices, and insisting on fair trials for arrested colleagues and solidarity with Prisoners of Zion[4]—all required the exercise of rights that the regime was not going to willingly recognize. Yuli Kosharovsky was one of those refuseniks. Trained in radio-electronics engineering, at one point in his career he found work in a highly sensitive field: developing a guidance system for missiles with nuclear warheads. After he applied for an exit visa in 1971, he spent the next eighteen years "in refusal," giving him the opportunity to be an active participant in the Jewish emigration movement. As he conducted these detailed interviews in Israel with other former refuseniks, he compiled a remarkable, intimate account of their common struggle: how they organized a wide array of activities under the noses of a repressive and ever-suspicious regime. Their creativity continues to astonish. My favorite was the time they pulled together Hebrew classes on a beach in the

Crimea, inviting families to vacation together as if they were doing nothing more than enjoying the sunny weather at the seashore. The regime thought it could stifle them forever. These Jewish activists gathered their strength. By standing up to the regime, they regained their voices and their history.

Joshua Rubenstein

Author's Acknowledgments

I WOULD LIKE TO EXPRESS my profound appreciation to the people and organizations who helped me write this book. I am grateful to all those who shared their memories and thoughts with me and who gave me access to their personal archives, including those whose interviews are excerpted in the text: Pavel Abramovich, Mark Azbel, Boris (Baruch) Ainbinder, Vladimir Aks, Mikhail Babel, Yosif Begun, Dina Beilin, Mikhail Beizer, Irina Brailovsky, Viktor Brailovsky, Mikhail Chlenov, Vladimir Dashevsky, David Drabkin, Yuli Edelstein, Eliyahu Essas, Veniamin Fain, Evgeny Finkelberg, Roza Finkelberg, Sara Frenkel, Viktor Fulmakht, Zeev Geizel, Mikhail Grinberg, Lev Gorodetsky, Alexander Ioffe, Grigory Kanovich, Yakov Kedmi, Mikhail Khanin, David Khavkin, Anatoly Khazanov, Alexander Kholmyansky, Vladimir Kislik, Boris Kochubievsky, Dov Kontorer, Valery Krizhak, Mark Kupovetsky, Edward Kuznetsov, Alexander Lerner, Alexander Lunts, David Maayan (Chernoglaz), Ida Nudel, Mikhail Nudler, Israel Palhan, Moshe Palhan, Pinhas Polonsky, Viktor Polsky, Vladimir Prestin, Dan Roginsky, Inna Rubin, Zeev Shakhnovsky, Maria Slepak, Vladimir Slepak, Natan Sharansky, Aron (Arkady) Shpilberg, Lea Slovin, Alexander Smukler, Vitaly Svechinsky, Aba Taratuta, Lev Ulanovsky, Igor Uspensky, Inna Uspensky, Ilia Voitovetsky, Leonid Volvovsky, Alexander Voronel, Nina Voronel, Shmuel Zilberg, and Yosif Zisels.

I thank the organizations who made available important documents and other materials: Nativ (Israel); Vaad (Russia); the Association "Remember and Save" (Israel); the National Coalition Supporting Eurasian Jewry, formerly National Conference for Soviet Jewry (USA); the Union of Councils for Soviet Jews (USA); the Student Struggle for Soviet Jewry (USA); the

Central Archive of the History of the Jewish People (Israel); and the Public Council for Soviet Jewry (Israel).

I would like to express my sincere thanks to Israel and Ann Shenkar for their invaluable help in research and for making available their wide collection of materials.

I thank the organizations, foundations, and private individuals who provided or helped secure grants for this research and for the writing of the book over many years: the Legacy Heritage Fund, Israel Shenkar, Shirley and Leonard Goldstein, Adele and Joel Sandberg, Dan Mariaschin and Irving Silver of B'nai B'rith, the Shtraks-Smukler Family Foundation, the National Coalition Supporting Eurasian Jewry, Bernie Dishler, Enid Wurtman, Glenn Richter, Henry Gerber, Connie and Joe Smukler, and Marvin Verman.

I want to express my gratitude to my first readers and critics, the members of my family: Inna Kosharovsky, Leonid, Anna, Galina, and Michal Kosharovsky.

I acknowledge with gratitude Dina Beilin, Mikhail Chlenov, Elena Dubiansky, Yakov Kedmi, Vladimir Mushinsky, Vladimir Prestin, Inna Rubin, Natalia Segev, Alexander Smukler, Vitaly Svechinsky, and Ilia Voitovetsky for valuable comments and help with the manuscript.

My special thanks go to Enid Wurtman, who provided invaluable help with research and mobilization of support for the project. Without her faithful and selfless assistance, the book would not have been written.

Yuli Kosharovsky

Editor's Acknowledgments

IT WAS MY GREAT HONOR to become acquainted with Yuli Kosharovsky while he was finishing work on his monumental four-volume history of the Jewish movement in the Soviet Union, *My snova evrei* (We Are Jews Again). I had come to Israel for research on Soviet Jewish activism, documenting the uncensored press known as samizdat and interviewing activists who had been involved with the journals. Yuli was not directly involved with producing samizdat journals, but he had been a leader in other areas and he was working on a history of the movement. Yuli and his collaborator Enid Wurtman opened my eyes to aspects of the Jewish movement in the Soviet Union I had not heard about elsewhere: in particular, they helped me to appreciate the relatively high level of organization characterizing much of the activity. Yuli convinced me of how important Hebrew study was to the movement. Practically every person who became active in the Jewish movement in the 1970s or later started with Hebrew study. For most, Hebrew classes provided an introduction to Jewish studies and an opportunity for entry-level engagement for those who felt drawn to Jewish activities. Some came to Hebrew classes with a simple desire to spend some of their time in refusal among people who would not treat them like second-class citizens. Through study and the socializing that went along with it, many of them came to view Israel as their future home.

The personalities of successful Hebrew teachers in the movement were legendary. Yuli had been one of those popular teachers, infecting students with his enthusiasm and boundless energy. Yuli worked at the center of the Jewish movement for many years, sharing his passion with Hebrew students and teachers and helping realize initiatives developed by others.

Beginning with his teaching in the USSR and through many years of work up to his publication of a history of the movement, Yuli never stopped seeing his mission in terms of consciousness-raising among Jews.

Yuli's collaborator Enid Wurtman exemplified similar qualities, although she started from a different place. Enid and her husband, Stuart Wurtman, became engaged with the issue of Soviet Jewry in the United States. Their lives were changed by traveling to the Soviet Union and meeting Yuli and other refuseniks, whom they first encountered in November 1973. In 1977 Enid and her family pulled up roots and made aliya like the Soviet Jews they sought to help. After moving, Enid continued to help refuseniks as part of the Public Council for Soviet Jewry in Israel. Yuli and his family were finally able to make aliya in 1989, approximately twelve years after the Wurtmans' aliya, and in Israel the two continued working together. I had a chance to see them in their shared office. Yuli worked on his seemingly endless interviews, fueled by his natural energy and benefiting from the large network of friends and acquaintances among former refuseniks and highly placed Israeli officials. Enid patiently tracked down dates, names, and documents, drawing on her own rich set of connections, developed over many years of activism. Enid shared her extensive knowledge and contacts with all kinds of scholars. It was humbling to learn that I came to her for help and advice after people such as Yuli and the eminent historian Martin Gilbert, who had also asked Enid for research support. I am one of many who are not only indebted to Yuli and Enid, but profoundly inspired by their generosity. They helped me understand what a commitment to "*Klal Yisrael*" means.

Yuli died in an accident on the first day of Passover in 2014, and his unexpected loss came as a tremendous blow to all who knew and loved him. Yet his work continued thanks to a number of scholars and friends who believed in its unique value. I was privileged to be asked to join the work after Stefani Hoffman had translated materials selected by Yuli for an English edition. Yaacov Ro'i also brought his years of expertise in the field to bear on this project. Both of them shared significant help and advice. They read the entire edited manuscript and provided detailed comments and suggestions. Stefani Hoffman shared valuable thoughts about the "ordinary heroes" of the movement, and she edited my often-awkward formulations, the result of shortening segments and condensing information into one volume. Yaacov Ro'i had further observations and insights about facts and sources that no one else could have provided.

In addition, my other debts to historians and former activists are many. I owe thanks to people including Pavel Abramovich, Mordechai Altshuler, Gal Beckerman, Yosif Begun, Mikhail Beizer, Irina and Viktor Brailovsky, Mikhail Chlenov, Zakhar Davydov, Jonathan Dekel-Chen, Avital Ezer, Veniamin Fain, Alexander Frenkel, Viktor Fulmakht, Anatoly Khazanov, Anna and Boris Lifshits, Yosef Mendelevich, Benjamin Nathans, Vladimir Prestin, Yosef Radomyslsky, Joshua Rubenstein, Anna Shternshis, Liudmila Tsigelman, Elie Valk, Alexander and Nina Voronel, Sima Ycikas, Leonid and Mira Zeliger, Natasha and Shmuel Zilberg, Dina Zisserman, the Euro-Asian Jewish Congress staff including Leonid Raitsen and Pavel Zhuravel at the Archive, Veniamin Lukin and the staff at the Central Archive for the History of the Jewish People, and Aba and Ida Taratuta and Edward Markov with the Association "Remember and Save," which has done a tremendous amount to document this history.

I benefited from funding from the Social Sciences and Humanities Research Council of Canada and the Victoria College Research Grant program for work on this project.

Throughout the long period of work on sources, biographical notes, and edits, Enid Wurtman continued to be supportive with the reams of material she and Yuli had collected. Alexander Smukler demonstrated his appreciation of Yuli and his work by supporting this project in moral and practical ways. Joshua Rubenstein kindly agreed to lend his voice to the project. If this edition succeeds in conveying to the English reader the tremendous scope and careful detail of Yuli's massive and marvelous history, thanks are due to these people and others who worked on the project, including all the remarkable men and women represented in Yuli's interviews.

Ann Komaromi

Note on the Text and Russian Names

YULI KOSHAROVSKY wrote the main text of chapters 2–5, drawing on the extensive interviews he conducted with former activists. For this edition, the editor has condensed the text in those chapters from the original and slightly adapted the language to create consistent third-person narration, apart from the quoted interviews and Kosharovsky's personal recollections. The editor has expanded footnotes and provided sidebar notes with the English reader in mind.

Russian names have been transliterated according to a modified Library of Congress system (e.g., –ii is rendered –y; and Ia-, Io-, and Iu- at the beginning of first names are Ya-, Yo-, and Yu-). Women's last names ending in a feminine form—Badanova, Beilina, Kosharovskaia—have been normalized in this text to the masculine form—Badanov, Beilin, Kosharovsky—for ease of identification. A few well-known names have been adopted in their accepted English form: these include Sharansky (not Shcharansky); Edelstein (not Edelshtein). In some cases the transliteration from Hebrew has been adopted, including Hava (not Khava); Eliyahu (not Eliagu); Mordecai (not Mordekhai); Pinhas (not Pinkhas); Palhan (not Palkhan).

Diminutive forms of names appear frequently because of the informal and friendly tone of interviews and reminiscences. Occasionally, people who are older or occupy a position of some significance are referred to more formally by name and patronymic, for example, Inna Moiseevna or Ester Isaakovna. Following is a list of some names appearing in the text, beginning with the standard spelling, followed by their diminutive or informal forms:

Alexander – Alik, Sasha
Anatoly – Tolia, Tolik
Andrei – Andriusha
Anna – Ania
Arkady – Arik
Boris – Boria
Efim – Fima, Fimka
Elena – Lena
Evgeny/Evgenia – Zhenia
Galina – Galia
Gennady – Gena
Grigory – Grisha
Ilia – Iliusha
Leonid – Lyonia
Lev – Lyova
Liubov – Liuba
Mikhail – Misha, Mika
Natalia – Natasha
Olga – Olia
Pavel – Pasha
Petr – Petia
Semyon – Syoma
Sergei – Seryozha
Valentin – Valia
Valery – Valera
Veniamin – Venia
Viacheslav – Slava, Slavik
Viktor – Vitia
Vitaly – Vilia
Vladimir – Volodia, Vlad, Vladik
Yakov – Yasha
Yisrael – Srolik
Yuli – Yulik
Yuri – Yura

Some activists took a Hebrew name in refusal, and some adopted a Hebrew name in Israel. These activists include:

Mark Blum = Mordecai Lapid
David Chernoglaz = David Maayan
Vladimir Dashevsky = Zeev Dashevsky
Vladimir Geizel = Zeev Geizel
Yakov Kazakov = Yakov Kedmi
Leib Khnokh = Arye Khnokh
Anatoly Sharansky = Natan Sharansky
Arkady Shpilberg = Aron Shpilberg
Ernst Trakhtenberg = Moshe Palhan
Leonid Volvovsky = Ari Volvovsky

PART ONE

History from the Ground Up

1

Soviet Jews
Making History

ANN KOMAROMI

THE LIBERATION OF SOVIET JEWS is a gratifyingly heroic phase of Jewish history in the late twentieth century. Soviet Jews accomplished something remarkable: they resurrected their Jewish identity from what had been a "valley of dry bones" after the destruction of Jewish life under Stalin. External factors facilitated this renaissance. Foremost among them, Israel's Six-Day War in 1967 provided a powerful impulse for the revival of a Jewish national identity in the Soviet Union. Soviet Jews described Israel's victory as a decisive event for the transformation of their consciousness.[1] Moreover, the post-Holocaust cry of "*Am Yisrael Chai!*" (The Jewish people lives) resounded around the world as a rallying cry for the cause of Soviet Jewry,[2] who faced discrimination and potential spiritual—though rarely physical—death as Jews in the post-Stalin USSR.[3] Jews abroad could with good reason feel proud of their role as midwives assisting the rebirth of Soviet Jews. Many Western Jews, burdened by the memory of the Holocaust and facing the more subtle challenges of affluence and assimilation in the 1960s, were seeking means for attaining their own spiritual renewal. As a result, in Western countries Jewish students, housewives, and other community members flocked to the streets to contest the power of the "Red Pharaoh" and demand that Soviet authorities "Let my people go."[4] This new struggle for liberation differed from the fights for revolution and Zionism that had mobilized Jewish communities in the early twentieth century.[5] The postwar struggle was not less dramatic, however. Moreover, its achievements were undeniable. By 1991 almost a million Soviet Jews had immigrated to Israel.

As we look back, however, the drama of the struggle for Soviet Jewry that gripped Western imagination should not obscure the more prosaic desires and day-to-day struggles of the refuseniks and activists in the Soviet Union.[6] In addition, that drama should not prevent us from acknowledging the complexity of the forces that came together to make the mass emigration of Soviet Jews possible. In Western countries, and particularly in the United States and Great Britain, the cause of Soviet Jewry fit into Cold War narratives as a fight against the Soviet Union and the revolution's failed promises. It thus helped American Jewish communities demonstrate their pro-American loyalties. Nevertheless, most Soviet activists and their supporters resisted overtly anti-Soviet rhetoric, because it was not strategically effective for dealing with Soviet authorities.[7] The cause of Soviet Jewry appealed to Western Jews in another way: it allowed them to support Israel's growth by promoting the aliya (emigration to Israel) of Soviet Jews, without in most cases undertaking aliya themselves. Beginning in the late 1990s, Nehemiah Levanon's publications revealed the extensive and mostly clandestine efforts of the Israeli Nativ Bureau to mobilize and guide Western efforts to put pressure on the Soviet government to ameliorate their treatment of Jews and allow free emigration.[8] The tensions between grassroots and establishment Jewish organizations over how best to aid Soviet Jews are relatively well known by now. Far less widely known is the story of the Soviet Jewish activists themselves. This is why Yuli Kosharovsky's work is so valuable: his memoirs and interviews provide a series of firsthand accounts of how the Soviet Jewish refuseniks bravely faced many challenges and how the Soviet Jewish movement developed. These accounts abound in personality, drama, and prosaic yet telling details. Kosharovsky led the effort to remember and record this history by initiating and coordinating the collective efforts of a huge range of fellow refuseniks and activists, whom he interviewed. In this way he continued playing the role he filled as an important behind-the-scenes coordinator of the Jewish movement in the Soviet Union.[9] Kosharovsky's history sheds significant light on the internal organization of the Soviet Jewish movement, including formerly secret initiatives such as the coordinating committee Mashka and the Cities Project to support Hebrew teaching in various provincial cities around the USSR.[10] He gives us a view from the inside. Kosharovsky's interviews bring to life the voices of those Elie Wiesel had once famously called "the Jews of Silence." By the 1970s and 1980s, these Jews were decidedly "Silent No More."[11]

Many of those familiar external factors from Israel and the West facilitating the Soviet Jewish movement and push for aliya appear meaningfully integrated into the lives and efforts of Soviet Jewish activists in Kosharovsky's history. There were also internal Soviet factors that include but are hardly limited to the pressure exerted by Soviet authorities on the refuseniks and activists. This introduction aims to provide additional context for the struggle of Soviet Jews by highlighting the view from among the Soviet grassroots activists. As in Kosharovsky's history, here the government leaders remain present, but they yield center stage to the activists, and it is the activists' voices we hear.

Making history in the late Soviet period had to do with becoming active citizens and developing alternative forms of historical imagination. This became possible following Khrushchev's denunciation of Stalin's crimes in 1956; after that event, and with momentum building in the mid- to late 1960s, groups began to connect with one another and to disseminate their independent views relatively widely.[12] Like the activists of the Jewish movement, the rights activists (also referred to as the democrats), many unofficial Baptists, Crimean Tatars, and independent poets of Leningrad, among others, became part of a growing, pluralized network of dissidence and independent culture. There was some overlap among groups, and occasional pooling of resources and strategies. The groups remained distinct, however, with cultural and educational activities particular to each community and relatively separate channels for spreading information. Each group conceived of an alternative history appropriate to its particular public. These groups changed history, not because Soviet Jews or rights activists brought down the Soviet Union, but because they helped create new historical models within the minds and hearts of people. Soviet Jewish activists were heroic because they wrote their own alternative history.

The highly publicized rights movement in the Soviet Union forms one significant backdrop for the development of the Jewish movement and other forms of dissidence and independent culture around this time. The rights movement got its start with the case of writers Yuli Daniel and Andrei Siniavsky.[13] Arrested in the fall of 1965, the two writers were put on trial in February 1966 for publishing works abroad without permission and under pseudonyms. Siniavsky published under the very Jewish name Abram Terts (Tertz), although he had no Jewish roots.[14] Yuli Daniel was of Jewish origin, although his satirical short stories, published under the name Nikolai Arzhak, did not feature specifically Jewish themes.[15] Daniel's wife, Larisa Bogoraz, became active with Siniavsky's wife, Maria Rozanov, on behalf of the imprisoned authors, pioneering the strategy of writing open letters to Soviet officials that were circulated in the uncensored Soviet self-publishing system known as "samizdat." Samizdat entailed the informal production and circulation of texts, usually in typescript form, and it included works from abroad that one could not obtain in the USSR: poetry by modernist-era greats such as Osip Mandelshtam, Boris Pasternak, and others, which had never been published or had gone out of print in the Soviet Union; open letters, petitions, and appeals; original essays and literary works; and bulletins and extracts from the émigré press began to be shared among people in the Soviet Union and between foreigners and Soviet citizens. Rights activist Vladimir Bukovsky, who helped organize a demonstration demanding openness in the proceedings against Daniel and Siniavsky, described the transformation this way:

> Throughout Moscow, office typewriters worked overtime, clicking out—for the pleasure of the typists or for their friends—the poetry of Gumilyov, Mandelstam, Akhmatova, and Pasternak. It felt as if everyone were gingerly straightening numbed limbs after ages of sitting still, of people trying to twiddle their fingers and toes and shift position as their bodies pricked with pins and needles. It seemed there was nothing to keep them sitting still any longer, but they had lost the habit of moving and had forgotten how to stand on their own two legs.
>
> The rebirth of culture in the Soviet Union after half a century of plague recapitulated all the stages in the development of world culture: folklore, epic, tales passed from mouth to mouth and from generation to generation, songs by troubadours and minstrels, and finally

prose—novels, dissertations, philosophical treatises, topical articles, open letters and appeals, journalism.[16]

Bukovsky's memoirs demonstrate that the Jewish national revival occurred in the midst of what many perceived as a "rebirth of culture" and a renewal of Soviet public life more generally. It also makes clear the basic conceptual model for history employed by Soviet rights activists. Bukovsky adapted the Hegelian philosophy of history with its stages of world culture from the official Marxist-Leninist philosophy of the Soviet Union. He turned that official version on its head: his "half a century of plague" and rapid post-Stalin recapitulation of the stages of progress represent a dissident history.[17] Bukovsky's account generalized the model that had been used by Soviet citizens for decades as they repurposed Hegelian and Marxist philosophy and metaphors in their own private accounts of lives overrun by history and the Soviet state.[18]

Other dissidents and activists developed more specific alternative histories. For the Jewish movement, Israel replaced the Soviet state as the subject of their history, one that infused the struggle for repatriation to Israel with profound meaning. This particular orientation shaped a distinct Soviet Jewish public identity and a historical narrative that was not (like the Hegelian narrative) supposed to be shared by all Soviet citizens alike. Alexander Voronel exemplified the choice some Jewish activists made. In his samizdat memoirs, Voronel traced his trajectory from youthful member of an opposition group, one of many that—as his memoirs helped reveal—existed even under Stalin, in the period 1945–52. At that time, these student groups, inspired by tales of the revolutionary underground preceding the establishment of the Soviet Union, did not know of the existence of other groups and were quickly suppressed.[19] In the prison camps, Voronel benefited from the special care extended to him by fellow Jewish prisoners. Back in Moscow in the late 1960s, Voronel, a physicist, became close to the circles to which Siniavsky and Daniel belonged. Despite the respect and friendly affection he had for his friends among the rights activists, including Andrei Sakharov, Voronel chose a different path. Around 1971, he read the story of Yosef Mendelevich's efforts to produce the Jewish samizdat journal *Iton* (two issues, 1970) and the repression he subsequently endured, and for Voronel this proved to be "the call of destiny, the word from heaven."[20] He founded the samizdat journal *Evrei v SSSR* (Jews in the USSR, 1972–79). This highly regarded journal employed personal accounts and other means to address Soviet Jews where they were—many were not yet ready for aliya. They were groping for a Jewish identity in the midst of a Soviet culture that often marked that identity as negative and offered no support for its development.[21] Thus personal histories, featured in the journal's rubric "Who Am I?" served in this context as a springboard for a national Jewish consciousness.[22] Voronel counted on the fact that fellow Soviet Jews' reflections on the topic would help readers gain insight and "make the choice between Russian and Jewish identity." Indeed, he claimed, the journal "legalized for the 'Soviet' Jew the very concept of Jewishness."[23] This and other Jewish educational materials and activities initiated by activists (as illustrated by the description of the cultural movement in Kosharovsky's account)[24] were designed to help more Soviet Jews become prepared for aliya.

Voronel's samizdat journal filled a niche with those Soviet Jews in the center of the Soviet empire who were more assimilated than Jews in the recently annexed western territories or in the southern and southeastern areas.[25] However, the most broadly effective samizdat publication for creating an alternative Jewish consciousness centered on the history of modern Israel was surely Leon Uris's novel *Exodus* (1958). *Exodus* circulated in several different samizdat translations and adaptations, and it had a bombshell effect on Soviet Jews, "transforming" them overnight into Zionists.[26] The novel's appeal certainly had something to do with its portrayal of muscular Jews building a country and defending it. This depiction directly countered negative Soviet stereotypes of cowardly Jews who shirked military service.[27] It also resonated with the surge of pride among Soviet Jews associated with the victory of the Six-Day War. Uris's novel was kitschy, to be sure, but it was also extremely effective at capturing the minds and hearts of Soviet Jewish readers and helping them imagine a national alternative to the Soviet state.

In their attempts to conceive of their own national alternative to the Soviet state, Jews of the post-Stalin era were like other groups in the Soviet Union. Lithuanian dissidents similarly developed their own alternative history and identity. The occupation of Lithuania and the history of resistance formed part of their alternative history.[28] So did local geography and folklore for clubs like "Ramuva," which put out an unofficial journal of the same name for a short while from 1969 to 1971. Similar youth clubs formed in the late 1960s "no longer stressed Lithuania's occupation, but rather sought to revive and restore to life old traditions, festivals and songs, encourag[ing] interest in the country's history, the cultural heritage and the language."[29] Such clubs exploited the possibility for organizing in universities and becoming semi-independent. In addition, the Catholic Church in Lithuania served as a source of alternative authority and identity, as well as a supporting unofficial infrastructure for producing and circulating samizdat publications. For many Lithuanians, an alternative history (and possible future) depended on the preservation of ties to its past, with religion playing a central role.[30]

Samizdat journals and other periodical editions provide a good indication of the maturity of alternative public groups in the Soviet Union in this period.[31] By this measure, the Lithuanians and the Jews had highly developed dissident publics, with thirty-two Lithuanian periodicals attested and twenty Jewish editions of this type—significantly more than other groups.[32] Jewish activists and Lithuanians had strong ties to the rights activists in Moscow. Even while they developed their own distinctive identity, they borrowed tactics from the rights activists and benefited from amplification of their demands in rights activist publications such as the samizdat bulletin *Chronicle of Current Events*. However, there were other factors at play in the success of these groups.

While its initial impulse and constant guiding light came from Israel, the Jewish dissident public had a multifaceted identity that—as in the Lithuanian case—drew significant sources of strength from tradition and religion. For example, in the first Jewish samizdat journal, *Iton* (Newspaper), no. 1, 1970, published like practically all Soviet Jewish samizdat in Russian, an item on the "New Prime Minister of Israel" (Golda Meir) shared the pages with an essay on "Purim and Pesach" by Yosef Mendelevich.[33] Mendelevich linked the two holidays through the trajectory of the Jewish people from slavery to freedom. Mendelevich discussed biblical texts and traditional holidays to reveal their resonance for the present audience. At the end of the piece he provided readers with the dates in the secular calendar for Purim and Pesach in 1970.[34] The journal *Tarbut* (Culture), nos. 1–13, 1975–79, also regularly provided the dates for Jewish holidays in the back of its pages. *Tarbut* featured more articles than *Evrei v SSSR* on Jewish religious traditions and observance.

The desire for another way of organizing time according to a different sacred calendar and history appeared in various ways throughout Soviet dissident and alternative culture. Tatiana Goricheva and Viktor Krivulin led a religious and philosophical seminar in Leningrad, beginning in 1976. Goricheva wrote about the potential of the Orthodox Church calendar to create an alternative to the "homogeneous monotonous grey" of unsanctified time.[35] The samizdat journal that came out of their seminar, *37* (nos. 1–21, 1976–81), featured important poetry by independent Leningrad writers who looked back to the repressed heritage of Modernist poetry and its ties to biblical culture. Poems by Elena Shvarts, such as "Moses and the Bush in which God Appeared," and by Viktor Krivulin, including "The Approach of the Visage" with its opening phrase "The one who navigated across the Egyptian darkness . . . ," indicate the highly serious interest in using biblical themes to gain a new perspective on history among members of the so-called "Petersburg school."[36] The destruction of culture associated with the establishment of a postrevolutionary order constituted an important theme for Leningrad literati writing for samizdat.[37] However, martyrdom and a struggle with the Soviet state mattered less than the independent renewal of culture in the contemporary moment. Original writing in *37* and the chronicle of alternative cultural events found at the back of most of its issues testified to that renewal. Krivulin wrote about Joseph Brodsky and another Leningrad poet of this generation, Leonid Aronzon (like Brodsky, also of Jewish origin), as important predecessors for the revival of an independent literary culture. Aronzon, although he was not as well known internationally as Brodsky, and despite his tragic early death, exerted more of an influence on contemporary poetic development, as Krivulin and many of his milieu believed.[38]

Those involved with the Petersburg school of unofficial poetry had few if any ties to the Jewish national movement, but they shared with the Jewish movement a creative relationship to local history and geography, including the highly significant Leningrad/Petersburg cityscape, which forms an important topos of Russian literature.[39] Among the Jewish activists of Leningrad, Mikhail Beizer led excursions devoted to local Jewish history and brought to life lost aspects of the city's past. Apropos of a building on Dzerzhinsky Street that had housed the early revolutionary police (the Cheka) from late 1917 to spring 1918, Beizer recalled Isaac Babel's story "The Road" ("Doroga"). In that autobiographical story, Babel described arriving, frozen and hungry, in Petrograd in December 1917 and being welcomed by the Cheka, with whom he was given work.[40] Beizer demonstrated how Soviet history, literature, and architecture could be decoded to tell alternative Jewish stories.

As part of his excursions, Beizer also talked about the Preobrazhensky (Transfiguration) Cemetery near Leningrad, with its important Jewish section.[41] He described Abram Varshavsky's burial vault combining Moorish and pseudo-Russian elements. To provide context for this person, Beizer cited Osip Mandelshtam's recollection of a childhood visit to the synagogue in his memoirs *The Noise of Time*. Mandelshtam remembered "two top-hatted gentlemen, splendidly dressed and glossy with wealth, with the refined movements of men of the world, touch the heavy book, step out of the circle and on behalf of everyone, with the authorization and commission of everyone, perform some honorary ritual, the principal thing in the ceremony. Who is that? Baron Ginzberg. And that? Varshavsky."[42] The narrator appears alienated from these wealthy high-society Jews and from the "highly honored and important act" they perform. The memoirs of Mandelshtam, as an outstanding modernist poet of Jewish origin, were likely to be familiar to the typical educated Jew of Leningrad in Beizer's time, although such readers would most likely have felt even more removed than Mandelshtam did from the Jewish society figures and the ritual in the synagogue he described. Beizer noted that the inscription on Varshavsky's gravestone was in Russian written in Hebrew characters from left to right, reading, "To the Memory of Abram Moiseevich Varshavsky."[43] This inscription—as the architecture of the burial vault—suggests the particular features of Jewish memory in the Soviet Union. The transmission of that memory was neither uninterrupted nor pure. Semantic markers (the Moorish style, Hebrew characters) that signify

"Jewishness" in such an instance also suggest the fragility of a connection attenuated under the pressure of the surrounding culture and context. Beizer's account demonstrates how such traces contained also a potential for the recovery of Jewish memory and links across time for those willing to dig into the historical materials and learn to read them anew.

Participants in the Jewish history seminar were not partisans of superficial nostalgia; they devoted themselves to learning and researching historical links, producing scholarly articles that circulated in the samizdat publication *LEA* (Leningrad Jewish Almanac), nos. 1–19, 1982–89. Alexander Frenkel, who attended later sessions of the seminar, went with Mikhail Ryvkin to research Jewish graves and monuments to the Jewish Holocaust victims in small towns of the former Belarusian and Ukrainian republics. They found that although local residents had oral knowledge that "they shot Jews" there, the monuments mentioned only "Soviet citizens" as victims of the Nazis. In the town of Nevel, just north of the border of the Belarusian republic, they found gravestones with strange five-pointed stars. It turned out that the Jewish residents, forbidden to carve a six-pointed Magen David (Star of David) on these stones, came to a compromise with local authorities, who allowed them to carve a five-pointed star. In a photograph, the star looks obviously deformed, like a Magen David with the bottom point removed.[44]

Another impulse from the outside helped spark an interest in local geographies and the Jewish heritage of which some evidence still remained: Elie Wiesel's book on Hasidic masters, *Souls on Fire*, became popular in Jewish samizdat. Wiesel quoted the legendary last words of the Maggid of Mezeritch: "Keep together, stay united, always." He followed those words with his own commentary on what these *tzaddikim* (righteous men) could mean to contemporary Jews: "through all of them we are linked to the most fervent moments of Jewish imagination and Jewish soul; without them our history would be poorer, much poorer, for it would be a dreamless history, devoid of nostalgic legend."[45] That world was gone, but Wiesel's book helped sensitize Soviet Jews to the fact that they had access to the places where it had existed, and that they might yet track down and preserve the traces that remained. Excursions led by Ilia

Dvorkin to towns in the former Pale of Settlement, including Medzhybizh (Medzhibozh), Chernivtsi (Chernovtsy), Lyubavichi, and other towns mentioned by Wiesel, began in 1982. The excursion participants gradually became more research-oriented, studying Jewish folk art, taking pictures and collecting oral histories from the few remaining survivors. They imagined themselves to be following in the footsteps of S. Ansky, who conducted his ethnographic expeditions in the same territory between 1911 and 1914. Unlike Ansky, however, this group no longer knew Yiddish.[46]

If the revival of Yiddish language, like the memory of the Holocaust on Soviet territory and the Jewish life that formerly existed in the Pale of Settlement, offered a way for Soviet Jews to connect to their roots, the study of Hebrew—which was more widely pursued within the movement—offered a connection to a national and local Jewish past with clear implications for a future in Israel. Yuli Kosharovsky was a leading Hebrew teacher. Because the opportunities for learning Hebrew in the Soviet Union were almost nonexistent, the production of Hebrew textbooks formed a huge part of Jewish samizdat, with highly developed networks for copying the texts.[47]

The first issue of the collection *Ivrit* ([Hebrew], no. 1, 1978) contained materials related to the one-hundredth anniversary of the revival of Hebrew as a spoken language. The issue—in Russian—opened with a quote from Ben Yehuda, "Am ehad—safa ahat. Iegudi, daber ivrit!" (One people—one language. Jews, speak Hebrew!) The collection connected the rebirth of Hebrew as a modern living language to its ancient roots and to contemporary Russian with its segment on "Thousand-Year-Old Roots" (biblical aphorisms in Russian). The editor of *Ivrit*, Pavel Abramovich, quoted Ben Yehuda in his preface to underscore the indispensable character of this language study:

> Ben Yehuda wrote that national development is impossible without a return to Hebrew as the single language of Jewish religion, literature and everyday conversation. Ben Yehuda insisted, "We have a language in which we can write and which now we may speak if only we want to do so." Ben Yehuda's basic idea that a national renaissance of Jewry

> should begin with the revival of Hebrew seemed controversial, even paradoxical, one hundred years ago. After all, at that time many Jewish public leaders advocated "linguistic assimilation" for Jews. Ben Yehuda began his struggle practically alone, but as a result of his struggle over many years a movement for "a living Hebrew" gained adherents in many different countries.[48]

Without dwelling on the Soviet suppression of Hebrew as a "bourgeois" and "nationalist" language, Abramovich's remarks suggested the significance of Ben Yehuda's "struggle" for the revival of the language to the contemporary fight to resurrect the Jewish national spirit and language in the Soviet Union. Paradoxically, it may have been the official Marxist/Leninist insistence on the importance of a national language and territory (both of which it was said Jews did not possess in modern times) that helped stoke the enthusiasm of Soviet Jews for Israel and the Hebrew language. Vladimir Lenin showed himself to be faithful to Karl Marx's writings when he treated Jews as not a nation but a historical remnant, who persisted as Jews only because of anti-Semitism. Lenin wrote about the language of Russian Jews (Yiddish) as a jargon, and he dismissed their supposed territory, the Pale of Settlement, as not a legitimate national territory.[49] Thus it may come as no surprise that many Soviet Jews in the post-Stalin era felt the crucial importance of Hebrew language for connecting them to Israel and to the Jewish people.

The text of a speech at the First Conference of Hebraists, in Moscow, May 1917, by Haim Nahman Bialik, "Jews and Hebrew" (*Evrei i ivrit*), reprinted in *Ivrit*, brought back the history of discussions of Hebrew on Russian territory. At the same time, the samizdat journal featured contemporary voices and personal stories in the section "Why I Started Studying Hebrew." Alexander Ostronov wrote,

> I myself grew up in an assimilated Jewish family where the adults sometimes said something in Yiddish but only so that the children would not understand (this seems to me a typical picture of Jewish families in Moscow in the 1950s, and not only in Moscow). Naturally neither at school nor at home did anyone ever talk about Hebrew or Jewish history.

> I had no idea what a synagogue was. I lacked the least bit of understanding of Jewish holidays. The turning point only came when I was studying in university and I happened to see several volumes of the *History of the Jews* by Heinrich Graetz. As a result, I found out about a lot of things and understood more. Only then did I experience an awakening of the so-called national feeling. So, of course, after a short time I began to study Hebrew. Now Hebrew is not only a means of communication for me—it is a means of self-expression, providing a way to draw closer to the priceless cultural achievements of our Jewish people over its four-thousand-year history.[50]

The segment recalls the rubric "Who Am I?" from *Evrei v SSSR*. Such individual stories personalized the history that was being recovered and renewed by those Soviet Jews who experienced a resurgence of their national consciousness. Many Soviet Jewish readers, even if they were in refusal, were not active in the national movement. For them, such accounts modeled a different way of making sense of their lives and recognizing the common bonds shared with other Soviet Jews in light of a larger historical perspective. That horizontal axis of bonds formed among individual citizens could replace the imagined attachment to the Soviet state as prime mover of history.

Kosharovsky's history of the movement continues that practice of giving a privileged place to the individual account. Kosharovsky did not simply record the history of a Jewish revival; he performed it with dozens of interlocutors, doing again what so many of them had done back in the Soviet Union as they read, speaking and writing a new story about themselves and their connection to the Jewish people. Kosharovsky's work on this history represented a logical continuation of his efforts as a Hebrew activist in the Soviet Union. After eighteen years of refusal spent in tireless service to the movement, Kosharovsky arrived in Israel and spent a large portion of the next twenty-five years gathering information and recording conversations with his fellow former Soviet activists and their supporters. He was not entirely unique. The job of citizen-historians in the Soviet Union and the moral load associated with such work had been famously exemplified by Alexander Solzhenitsyn, who spoke to scores of fellow and former prisoners to document the Stalin-era prison-camp system in *The Gulag Archipelago.*

Solzhenitsyn's example inspired others, including the amateur historians responsible for the samizdat historical collections *Pamiat* (Memory), nos. 1–5, 1976–81. This group had nothing to do with the notorious anti-Semitic group of the same name.[51] Led by Arseny Roginsky (another rights activist with Jewish origins), with the participation of Yuli Daniel's son Alexander, along with Sergei Dediulin and others, the group associated with the collection *Pamiat* sought to recover aspects of Soviet history that had been lost on the basis of documents and testimony from ordinary citizens. Roginsky confessed that he and other members of the Pamiat group "found it difficult either to polemicize or to agree with" the idea around which Solzhenitsyn's work was built:

> Alexander Isaevich claims that there once was a real Russia, and then suddenly Bolsheviks fell from the sky and conquered the innocent soul of the Russian people. . . . We did not wish to enter into any historiosophical debate and regarded as our task the presentation of facts, commented facts. Already in the first issue, we published documents by an intellectual with liberal democratic (Cadet) views, an Orthodox monarchist, a Socialist, and a loyal Communist; we were convinced that only from this polyphony could the truth emerge.[52]

Roginsky was speaking about an earlier phase of twentieth-century history, but a similar polyphony made itself heard in the late Soviet period. It was within that polyphony that the activists of the Jewish movement raised their voices too.

Kosharovsky's history of that movement illustrates in a striking way what samizdat in that post-Stalin era made possible: samizdat facilitated an important epistemological shift, whereby historical information could be generated not only by institutions and credentialed experts, but also by citizen-historians.[53] Liudmila Alekseev's history of dissidence, based on the facts collected in the samizdat rights bulletin *Khronika tekushchikh sobytii* (Chronicle of Current Events), represents one outstanding example of an independent history of the post-Stalin era.[54] Kosharovsky's history of the Jewish movement complements that view in an important way: although Alexeyeva had covered the Jewish movement among others, her account was shaped by a universal (and unifying) discourse of human rights. By introducing the voices of many individual Jewish activists, Kosharovsky's history altered the texture of history of dissent in this period, demonstrating the possibility of a real polyphony of views within a pluralized independent public in the late Soviet Union.

Kosharovsky's history of the Jewish movement offers its own internal variety by presenting a wide range of views from his various interviewees. Together with American-Israeli activist Enid Wurtman, Kosharovsky assembled a significant collection of materials that includes many dozens of interviews and photographs, as well as journals, bulletins, and reports from a wide variety of organizations created in North America, England, and Israel to support Soviet Jewry. A substantial selection of these materials can be found in Russian and English on Kosharovsky's website.[55] The Association "Remember and Save" established by Aba Taratuta is another significant example of citizen-historian activism, one built on the foundation of Aba and Ida Taratuta's work with other Jewish refuseniks in the Soviet Union.[56]

Kosharovsky's history reveals that in addition to the dramatic cases of persecution, suffering, and heroic advocacy that made news at the time, the Jewish movement in the Soviet Union depended also on the bedrock of people who devoted themselves to building Jewish identity and community in more prosaic ways. Often they did this through long years of refusal, quietly but stubbornly insisting on the lawful right to emigration and Jewish culture. Soviet Jews participated in and ran seminars for scientists; they mounted seminars on Jewish culture and history; they pursued Jewish education and worked hard to make it available to adults and children; they organized and participated in holiday gatherings and outdoor events. Many of them simply sought a "normal" Jewish life.[57] Most of the activists thought or came to believe that such a life would be in Israel. A few, like Mikhail Chlenov (see chapters 4 and 5 of this book), were determined to establish legal Jewish life in the USSR. However, the legacy of this movement—including the contributions of these immigrants—exists on three continents.[58] The history that Soviet Jews wrote has become part of our shared Jewish history. Kosharovsky's account, featuring the many and varied voices of Soviet Jews who were "Silent No More," greatly enriches our understanding of their role in creating that recent, stunning chapter of history.

PART TWO

Voices of the Movement

2

Beginnings

Formative Experiences in Prison

The period from the second half of 1948 until March 1953 has been justly described in terms of the "black years" of Soviet Jewry.[1] On Stalin's secret orders, the chairman of the Jewish Anti-Fascist Committee (JAC), the actor Solomon Mikhoels, was killed in a staged accident in Minsk on January 13, 1948. At the beginning of 1949 dozens of Jewish public and cultural figures were arrested. In January 1949 another major anti-Semitic campaign was initiated against "rootless cosmopolitans." Jews were targeted, fired from jobs, and in many cases arrested.[2] The so-called "Doctors' Plot" described in the official Soviet press involved the arrest of doctors who had supposedly poisoned high Party officials: the overwhelming majority of the doctors were Jewish. As part of the events not reported in the press, one date stands out: on the night of August 12, 1952, thirteen Jewish writers, intellectuals, and artists were shot.[3]

Among the thousands of Jews arrested during this period were members of the group Eynikeyt (Unity),[4] including one of its leaders, Meir Gelfond from Zhmerinka.[5] He and others including Mikhail Margulis and Vitaly Svechinsky—who belonged to a different unofficial group in Moscow—served terms in prison but emerged to mentor others and help lead a new Zionist movement. This new generation of Zionists met and learned from Zionists of previous generations in Soviet prisons.

Svechinsky talked about his prison experience in this period:[6]

KOSHAROVSKY: *Why were you arrested?*

SVECHINSKY: We wanted to escape to Israel. The War of Independence was being waged there. We were nineteen years old. We planned to cross the border in the south, across the Charokh River. It's a whole story.

KOSHAROVSKY: *Did you admit your guilt?*

SVECHINSKY: The three of us were arrested and we admitted our guilt. But the authorities wanted to expand the circle. They needed to arrest around ten to twelve, but they came up against a wall. They threatened us and subjected us to petty physiological discomforts. Then they threatened us with the torture prison at Sukhanovo, which was truly terrible.

KOSHAROVSKY: *What was your sentence?*

SVECHINSKY: Not bad, a "tenner."[7] We were lucky.

KOSHAROVSKY: *How did it go?*

SVECHINSKY: It depended. At the beginning, it was very difficult. The winter of 1951–52 was harsh, the camp regime was awful, but the main thing was there was nothing to eat. I was assigned to earth-digging work, which is very strenuous. Even people in good health reached the end of their tether there. I was a gymnast with third-level ranking, I had no complaints about my health before that, but I declined very quickly. My organism required sustenance but there wasn't any. We had to work an exhausting ten-hour day in the frost and there was no place to take shelter. I very quickly became a "goner."

Jews saved me. I had a camp father, Natan Zabara, a Yiddish writer.[8] And there was also a fellow, Irma Druker, God bless his memory. They didn't do the general hard work. In the convoy garrison, they served in the kitchen, chopped wood, paved. In general, they performed light service work. The cook would bring them something to eat from the kitchen. Natan would collect cereal in a jar and bring it to the zone. That was very dangerous because people were frisked before entering the zone, but he did it so artfully he was not caught. Thus, every evening I was able to receive a portion of cereal and this saved me.

KOSHAROVSKY: *Was the second year easier?*

SVECHINSKY: It was easier. We learned a bit about how to survive, how to behave. We "sniffed things out" as they say in camp. We learned how to endure both hunger and cold, which was already a lot. Then Fimka Spivakovsky and I went to the camp director's weekly reception hours and told him that Fimka graduated from the economics faculty of Kharkov

University and could do something besides striking the earth and that I was a third-year architectural student and could work in that field. This camp happened to have a planning *sharashka*.[9] Two or three weeks later, I was summoned and told that I would be transferred there. At first I worked the night shift. It was difficult because my fingers couldn't bend to hold the pencil, but with time, I got the knack of drafting. I designed various officers' homes and a residential settlement and this work was, of course, a lot better.

Following Stalin's death in early 1953, during the period of relative liberalization known as Khrushchev's "Thaw," Jews, like other Soviet citizens, began meeting informally in cities all over the Soviet Union to talk about previously taboo topics. The majority of Soviet Jews still hoped that, with the end of the anti-Semitic campaign, they could integrate into the surrounding society. Others no longer saw their future in the Soviet Union. Having learned the lessons of the war and Stalinist repressions, they thought of repatriation to Israel.[10] Israel and everything related to it were the main topics in the nationally minded groups. Those with knowledge of Yiddish, Hebrew, or English would listen to the *Voice of Israel* (*Kol Yisrael*) broadcasts and provide information to others. Although the regime began to jam broadcasts in Yiddish in 1954, those in Hebrew and English were accessible on shortwave radio practically throughout the Soviet Union and on a medium wavelength in the Caucasus and Black Sea coastal area. The station of the *Voice of Israel for the Diaspora* (*Kol Tsion lagola*) informed Soviet Jews of the various sports competitions in the USSR in which Israeli sportsmen took part. The extent of a Jewish presence at these competitions and the crowds waiting for the Israeli sportsmen at intermediary stops on the way to Moscow testify to the fact that a considerable segment of the Jewish population was listening to the Israeli broadcasts.[11]

Some people approached representatives of the Israeli embassy despite the risk it entailed: the Israeli delegation was under constant surveillance. At the meetings, embassy workers would distribute printed material on cultural and historical topics and Hebrew textbooks, which Soviet Jews had been lacking for many years. The local population submitted requests, for example, "to simplify the Hebrew in the Israeli radio broadcasts so that more people could understand them."[12] Hundreds of Soviet Jews from various cities took part in gatherings of Zionist groups and circles, which were being revived. The first wave of arrests of members of such groups in 1955–56 affected about one hundred people, the majority of whom were later freed.[13]

Open activity included attendance at the Sixth World Festival of Youth and Students, which took place in Moscow in July–August 1957. Tens of thousands of Jews came to see the Israeli delegation in the relatively liberal atmosphere prevailing at the festival.[14] In the period between the Youth Festival and the Six-Day War, Zionist activity in the USSR gradually broadened in scale. Ties with the Israeli embassy grew closer, and there were more frequent meetings with Jewish tourists from abroad and with Israeli delegations who came for scientific conferences, symposia, sports competitions, or exhibitions. More books began to arrive in various ways. Western radio broadcasts also played an important role. In sum, the Iron Curtain lifted a bit and information about the life of Soviet Jews reached the West, while information about Israel and the Jewish diaspora penetrated into the USSR. The synagogue regained an important place in Jewish life. The area near it became a natural meeting place for Jewish youth. In that area they were able to meet foreign tourists or members of foreign delegations, who did not miss the opportunity to attend services in a Soviet synagogue on the Sabbath.

In this context, older groups of nationally oriented Jews continued to operate in Moscow, Leningrad, Gorky, Kiev, Kharkov, Rostov-on-Don, Baku, Riga, Vilnius, and other cities, and new groups arose. The members would meet to discuss events in Israel, to study the Hebrew language and Jewish history, and to disseminate knowledge that would facilitate the awakening of a Jewish national consciousness.[15]

The regime was dissatisfied with the growth of the Zionist movement but it had to take into consideration the pressure from leading Western leftists, including members of the Communist parties of Italy, France, and Canada. The measures to suppress the Zionist movement were harsh but limited. At the beginning of 1957 Kiev Zionists Baruch Vaisman,

Meir Draznin, Hirsh Remennik, and Yakov Fridman were arrested and charged with Zionist activity and with keeping and disseminating anti-Soviet material. Draznin received a ten-year sentence, Remennik got eight, and Vaisman and Fridman received five years each. In Riga the activists Yosef Shnaider and Yuri Kogan were arrested on charges of listening to Israeli radio broadcasts and slandering the Soviet Union in letters to relatives in Israel. In Odessa Zolia Katz was arrested and, after a yearlong investigation, he was sentenced to eight years of imprisonment for hostile nationalist propaganda.[16]

In Moscow in April 1958, Dora, Shimon, and Baruch Podolsky and Tina Brodetsky and her stepfather, Evsei Drobovsky, were arrested. In December of that year, David Khavkin, a member of a Moscow group, was arrested. Zionist activists in other cities were also arrested. All received prison terms.

David Khavkin spoke about his imprisonment:[17]

KOSHAROVSKY: *How many years did you get?*

KHAVKIN: Five years of general regime.

KOSHAROVSKY: *Was it hard?*

KHAVKIN: No. On the contrary, it was the most interesting time in my life. I met very interesting people there and remain friendly with them to this day.

KOSHAROVSKY: *Were there Zionists there?*

KHAVKIN: Yes, there were Zionists and ordinary Jews who under our joint influence also became Zionists.

KOSHAROVSKY: *Did you stay in the "family," David?*

KHAVKIN: Yes, this was natural in political camps. When a group would arrive from a transport, the Lithuanians would meet the Lithuanians, the Ukrainians would meet the Ukrainians, and the Jews would meet the Jews.

KOSHAROVSKY: *Was there enmity among the "families"?*

KHAVKIN: On the contrary, we maintained rather good relations with the Ukrainian nationalists and the Lithuanians. They attended our holiday celebrations and we theirs.

KOSHAROVSKY: *Did Boria Podolsky serve time with you?*

KHAVKIN: Yes, and also his father. His mother was in the women's camp. He was totally skinny in camp, like an Auschwitz prisoner. And other prisoners would keep watch to see when he was alone and defenseless so they could beat him up. I was beside myself with anger.

KOSHAROVSKY: *Were there any other Zionists there?*

KHAVKIN: David Mazur, Tina Brodetsky, and Anatoly Rubin. Tina was arrested in the same case with the Podolskys.[18] Boria was seventeen years old at the time and she was a little over twenty.

KOSHAROVSKY: *Did you serve the full term?*

KHAVKIN: No, my case was reviewed at the request of my mother, who was very ill. In the course of the review, the article under which I was charged was changed. The new article carried a term of up to three years, but I had already been imprisoned longer than that so I was released after the review.

KOSHAROVSKY: *Did you go to live at the 101-kilometer marker?*[19]

KHAVKIN: No, at first I went to Odessa because it was a Jewish city where the first Zionists lived. But I didn't remain there long. I traveled often to Moscow and stayed with friends or with my sister. After a year, I spent almost all my time in Moscow. My father put in a request, explaining that they were elderly people and it was hard for them to manage alone. Finally I obtained a residence permit.

KOSHAROVSKY: *Did you return to the synagogue and sing there again?*

KHAVKIN: And how—after my release, everything began for real. Until my arrest, I was much more cautious.

At the start of the 1960s, the Jewish national movement lacked generally acknowledged leaders, organizational structures, or forums for discussing basic issues. It was a movement born of circumstance and necessity that developed without discipline or instigation, evolving from isolated cells. Those who had the courage and ability to express their views and establish links with other cells, with foreign tourists, and with the Israeli embassy became the new activists.[20]

In that early period, Riga Zionists played a central role in the expansion of the Jewish national movement. They included Yosef Shnaider, who returned to Riga after his imprisonment in 1958. Yitzhak Egelberg, arrested in 1959, continued his activity after his release. David Zilberman and David Iafit were active and joined later by Gesia Kamaisky, Boris and Lea Slovin, and Mark Blum. Clandestine Hebrew study in Riga took place. German (Yirmiyahu) Branover, a physicist who became active in scholarly and religious publishing in Israel, began his Zionist activity in Riga.[21] In the middle of the 1960s, a new youth group was formed that included Boris Druk; his wife, Rivka; and her brother Yosef Mendelevich. They rented a dacha in a Riga suburb and began to study Judaism and other Jewish topics as preparation for future emigration. Using a second-hand typewriter that they had purchased, they also disseminated typed excerpts from books they had obtained.[22] Shnaider maintained contacts with groups in Vilnius, Leningrad, Kiev, and Moscow. The durable links forged while serving terms together in camps or prisons played an important role in these contacts.

Prisoners of Zion Yosef Khorol and Meir Gelfond created a similar network. Khorol moved to Riga in 1958. Gelfond obtained a permit to reside in Moscow after he married a Muscovite in 1959. Like Shnaider, Khorol and his friends translated, adapted, and copied material that was then given to Gelfond for distribution in Minsk, Kiev, Moscow, and the Urals.

Babii Yar

The Babii Yar ravine in Kiev became infamous as the site where the Nazi Einsatzgruppen shot the most people. More than 33,000 Jews were assassinated at Babii Yar on September 29–30, 1941, with tens of thousands of others shot there in subsequent weeks. The Soviet government refused to acknowledge the particular nature of the Jewish tragedy. A monument erected by Soviet authorities in 1976 made no mention of Jewish victims. The silence about Jewish victims at Babii Yar, contested by individual Soviet writers and composers, became emblematic of a taboo on Jewish topics, including the Holocaust, throughout the late Soviet period and until perestroika.

On the twentieth anniversary of the Nazi massacre of Jews at Babii Yar in Kiev, Evgeny Yevtushenko published his famous poem "Babii Yar"

(1961), which resonated for readers as a powerful, sincere protest. Its words tore apart the dense web of anti-Semitism that enfolded Soviet public consciousness. A year later Dmitry Shostakovich composed his Thirteenth Symphony, basing an aria on Yevtushenko's verses. Soviet Jews began a campaign for the erection of a monument at Babii Yar. Fifteen years later, in 1976, the government finally erected that monument, but it lacked any mention of the mass shooting of Jews. Similarly, the Jews of Vilnius petitioned for the building of a monument and fence around the mass grave of thousands of murdered Jews at Paneriai. A monument with an inscription in Yiddish had been set up after the war, but the authorities destroyed it in 1952. Later, an official monument was placed at Paneriai, but it also failed to mention the Jewish victims.

In the 1960s the mass grave of 38,000 Jews at Rumbula outside of Riga became a gathering place for Jews. In April 1963, on the eve of the twentieth anniversary of the Warsaw ghetto uprising, Riga Jews Zalman Baron, David Garber, and Mark Blum brought an obelisk-shaped board to this site. Having received permission to clean up and maintain the site, Riga Jews flocked there in greater numbers. In the fall of 1963, about eight hundred people went there to commemorate the anniversary of the massacre of Riga Jews at Rumbula. It gradually became a legitimate meeting spot, where thousands would gather on the two anniversaries, arriving not only from Riga, but also from Vilnius, Leningrad, Kiev, Moscow, and other cities. None of those who assembled there had any doubts: these meetings were dedicated to the struggle for repatriation to Israel.[23]

The tours of Israeli artists who arrived in the framework of cultural exchange programs turned into demonstrations of solidarity. They invariably performed to full houses. Israeli singer Geula Gil was the most popular, giving three concerts each in Moscow and Riga and one each in Vilnius and Leningrad in the summer of 1966. People stood in line all night for tickets. Sports competitions in which Israelis participated were also very popular. No one questioned why the Israelis had so many fans. Film festivals in Moscow in 1963 and 1965 acquainted viewers with Israeli films and themes. Thousands saw the film *Kibbutz* and they saw the film *The Glass Cage,* which dealt with the Eichmann trial and the Holocaust.[24]

Two Israeli exhibitions in 1966 on the agricultural machinery and poultry industries provided occasions to meet with Israeli representatives. The Israeli pavilion at the agricultural fair in Moscow in the spring became a meeting place for Jews from all over the Soviet Union. The regime could not prevent Israel from participating in the events, but it was extremely disturbed by the evidence of Soviet Jews' massive manifestations of solidarity with the State of Israel. It reacted by intensifying anti-Israel propaganda and arresting several people.

Among the active Zionists in Kiev were Anatoly Feldman, Nelli Gutin, Evgenia Bukhin, Emanuel Diamant, and Anatoly Gerenrot. They translated articles about Israel, Judaism, and anti-Semitism into Russian and disseminated them. The Kiev group was in contact with activists in Riga. In Leningrad in the fall of 1966, a group was formed with the goal of fighting assimilation and studying Hebrew. The group included Grigory Vertlib, Ben-Tsion Tuvin, Hillel Butman, Solomon Dreizner, and Arkady Shpilberg. They opened their first Hebrew study group at the beginning of 1967 at a skiing area near Leningrad. By the spring of 1967, the group had grown to fifteen people.[25] Anatoly Rubin played an important role in the revival of Zionist activity in Minsk. Arrested in 1958 and sentenced to six years of imprisonment, he continued his Zionist activity after his release. In Georgia the Orientalist Gershon Tsitsuashvili played an active role in the Zionist revival.

Eitan Finkelshtein initiated the Zionist movement in Sverdlovsk. At the end of the 1960s, he moved to Vilnius, hoping that it would be easier to emigrate from there. He had contacts in Moscow and other cities. He sent a large quantity of samizdat material to Sverdlovsk and did it so ably that the local KGB did not know about the existence of Zionists in Sverdlovsk until open protests were organized in 1970.[26]

Personal Recollections: Origins and the Awakening of a Jewish Consciousness

KOSHAROVSKY: I was born into an assimilated family.[27] The Kosharovsky family came from the shtetl of Kosharovka, in the Pale of Settlement, some ten kilometers from Chernobyl and one hundred kilometers to the north of the Ukrainian capital, Kiev.

My parents, Mikhail Nisonovich Kosharovsky and Sima Markovna Galinsky, were married in 1937 in Kiev, in their final year of studying paper production. In 1938 my older brother Daniel was born there. I was born six months after the Soviet Union entered World War II. I was born after we reached our destination in the settlement of Novaya Lyalya. My younger brother Leonid was born there a year and a half later. My parents' profession entailed living in small workers' settlements because paper production was very destructive for the environment. There were practically no Jews in these locations.

After the war, my father was sent from one factory to another because of the need to rebuild destroyed enterprises. The entire family thus led a nomadic life. My two brothers and I attended high school in four different towns, which deprived us of a chance to develop childhood friendships and a natural feeling for a homeland. We did not really experience anti-Semitism because my father had an important position as chief engineer and the enterprises provided a livelihood for almost the entire adult population of these towns.

My parents tried to inculcate in us an interest in the exact sciences. They encouraged us to study and to participate in school and club activities. They did not discuss Jewish topics at home and, as was common, they would switch to Yiddish only when they didn't want us to know what they were talking about. My first serious encounter with Jewish matters occurred in 1956, when I was fifteen years old. The newspapers were excoriating Israel for its "aggression against Egypt." My father was gloomy and taciturn and my mother tried to protect his peace and quiet. We children were engrossed in our own problems and, honestly speaking, I did not fully understand what connection there could be between Israel and our town and us.

Father decided to end his manufacturing career in the year that I finished high school. He moved to the Sverdlovsk Design Institute and then went to teach at the Polytechnic Institute in Sverdlovsk, a large industrial city on the eastern slope of the Ural Mountains. He worked for many years there as a lecturer, the head of the Forestry Department, and secretary of the institute's Party organization.

I graduated in 1964 from the Ural Polytechnic Institute in Sverdlovsk with a master's degree in aircraft electronics. I was assigned a job at an automation research institute in the same city. The institute dealt with the development of a guidance system for long-range ballistic missiles with nuclear warheads. This was a Soviet strategic weapon and the institute was tops in its field.

This was the period of the strategic arms race with the United States, and we were encouraged in every way. A creative atmosphere reigned in the laboratory. I soon felt that I had landed in a prestigious place. Evidently my father's impeccable reputation and my own achievements in school and institute had played a role in my assignment. The Jews in this institute had a good reputation. They headed the majority of the laboratories and they were treated with respect. A magnificent touring club functioned under the auspices of the institute, and I enjoyed going on trips with coworkers. I continued to engage in boxing, which I had enjoyed as a student. On a trip in 1965, I met an attractive woman named Sonia who became my wife.

The Six-Day War turned my life upside down. Was it because of the pressing anxiety before the war, the feeling of impotence, or the fear of another Holocaust? I cannot forget it. I wanted to cry out in the streets. The authorities were gloating. Everything that I had been taught fell apart. I couldn't understand anything and for the first time I began to feel that the country in which I was living was my enemy.

During the weeks just before the war and during the war itself, I couldn't think of anything else. I remember being struck by the remarks of one television commentator who declared that Israel was an alien body in the Middle East that had no chance of survival and it was necessary to become reconciled to its disappearance. Not that I knew a lot about Israel, but people who had survived the Holocaust found refuge there and the commentator gloated over the possibility that fate was preparing yet another horrible catastrophe for them.

On the first day of the war, Soviet papers reported that the Arabs had downed seventy-two Israeli planes and on the second day something similar, and I began to think: My god, how many planes does Israel have, for how many days will their supply suffice? Soviet propaganda patently rejoiced at the Arabs' successes. On the third day, unable to bear the Soviet malice, on the roof of our five-storied building I set up a large antenna aimed in the direction of the jamming station in order to reduce the interference, and I listened to the "Voices" (foreign radio stations) all night long.[28] Israel, it turned out, was winning, and Soviet propaganda changed its tone. On the third day, the state that only two weeks ago had been sentenced to death by the Soviets became a "brazen aggressor." This clumsy but venomous propaganda, like the Nazi propaganda, affected part of the local population, arousing anti-Semitic instincts.

Yet the switch was so drastic and the lie so blatant that many refused to believe it. I matured several years in one day. I never before felt so strongly that I was a Jew as at that moment. I never before felt so acutely that the country in which I was living and for which I labored was an enemy of my people. The Six-Day War helped reveal this terrible truth.

For whom was I working?

Later, it became clear that the USSR had prepared the Arab countries for war against Israel. The Soviet Union had almost no doubt about the outcome: equipped with Soviet arms, their clients ought to be victorious. Victory by the Arab countries would also solve the problem of the loyalty of Soviet Jews, making them more industrious and less demanding of rights. Even if the outcome was not decisive, then the Arabs would still need to purchase Soviet arms and seek economic and political support from the USSR. No one foresaw a total defeat. In the aftermath of this defeat, the Soviet leadership lapsed into hysteria, which it tried to conceal with clamorous and primitive anti-Israeli propaganda. For me, however, the victory was a triumph, as it was for other Jews and for many Russians.

The contradictions that I encountered kept me in a state of constant tension. At night I would listen to the "Voices," and in the day I would "serve my time" at work.

Once something strange, almost mystical, happened that left a profound mark on me. It occurred when, deep in thought, I was walking along a noisy street and my head was buzzing from lack of sleep. Suddenly everything around me vanished, it became quiet, and the passersby and cars disappeared. A bright light illuminated my consciousness and I saw with piercing clarity who I was, where I was going, and what I wanted. I knew that this was not a fantastic trick, that I was seeing my path. It was a divine beacon to my atheistically educated soul.

I don't know how long this lasted, but then once again the street became noisy and the cars were moving.

That moment ended all doubts.

Until my departure, another long twenty-two years would pass. It would be difficult and hard to endure because of fear, pain, and exhaustion. There would be children who would grow up in the midst of all this.

At the most difficult moments, I would return in my mind to that spark of consciousness, to that clarity, and my strength would return.

I began to seek out like-minded people. New questions fired my mind and I thought it would not be fair to demand answers from my parents. They had experienced the cruelest times. They had lived under Stalin and gone through World War II. A great fear of the all-powerful regime had been implanted in their hearts.

We grew up in a different period and we were not as intimidated. Khrushchev's struggle against Stalin's personality cult and Brezhnev's struggle against Khrushchev's personality cult had already passed. Now it was the time of Brezhnev's personality cult. Jokes about the old men in the Kremlin circulated openly throughout the country and people were not arrested because of them.

We grew up and matured without any particular respect for the regime and without any special fear of it. The obligatory study of Communist Party history that was adapted to suit each new leader, the study of Marxism-Leninism, and exams on the subject were perceived as an unnecessary, formal burden and a total waste of time.

The apparatus of suppression, however, still functioned well: dissidents were arrested and it was dangerous to stick out too much or to go against the constantly changing Party line. I did not go against the stream. Until the Six-Day War, technology satisfied me completely and I tried not to delve too deeply in the contradictions and absurdities of the regime although it was more than tempting to do so.

My father had told me, "In the field of technology, inconvenient questions don't exist. It's better if you occupy yourself with technology and avoid doing anything foolish." That conversation determined my academic preferences. I no longer considered the humanities a worthy field of study because it required thinking in a particular way and avoiding painful questions. Technology absorbed me completely until the Six-Day War. The war helped me understand that I had become a technologically educated slave.

Why was I wasting my life? I did not understand anything about life other than technology. I wanted to leave but could not. It was unbearable to be in the Soviet Union but I was forced to remain. My interest in technology waned and was replaced by an interest in Jewish issues and the search for a way of leaving for Israel.

I was drawn to Jews. Not that I had earlier shunned Jewish companionship but now I sought it purposefully. I began to attend Jewish get-togethers and birthday parties. At one of them in the apartment of Sasha Gurovich, I met some medical students and we began talking. We agreed for starters to look for material on history, culture, and language. Since there wasn't anything in Russian, we decided to head for the library of foreign languages.

The three of us went in and registered, as was required, listing the year of birth, address, place of study or work, nationality, and something else and sat down with the catalogs. A few hours later we requested Shapiro's Hebrew-Russian dictionary.[29] No doubt we were the first to order this book because the librarian looked at us with a long, studied gaze. They brought the book and we were able to leaf through it in the reading room.

The library visit had unexpected consequences for the medical students. They were summoned to the personnel department, which in Soviet institutions was usually operated by officials linked to the KGB, for a conversation about unhealthy nationalist interests and about Hebrew, which is spoken only in Israel. Under threat of expulsion, they were warned about the inadmissibility of Zionist activity within the walls of the institute. The warning about a possible expulsion was also conveyed to their parents. The students were thoroughly intimidated and our first group dissipated without having taken shape.

At work, I had access to second-level secret information: this came with a three-year ban on contacts with foreigners or on trips abroad. A month after the Six-Day War, I applied to leave my place of work, but it took half a year in order to obtain permission. I understood that I would not be allowed to leave the country right away and that it might take three years or more to stick out the quarantine. During all these years, I would have to support my family, raise my children, and prepare as much as possible for life in Israel.

In 1968 my father died very suddenly. I always respected and somewhat feared him. His life and unexpected death reflected the bitter and sad irony of Jewish diaspora fate. He lived all his life as a Russian—which he wanted—and devoted all his talent to Russia, but he died as a Jew. Before leaving for vacation that summer, he left orders for repair work in the Forestry Department. When he returned, he saw that his orders had not been carried out. He gave the administrative manager a dressing down in the Russian manner—he knew how to do this. The latter retorted to father, "You Jews, you yourself go on vacations, you rest, and then you return and you drink the blood of us Russians with renewed vigor."

Two days later he had a massive heart attack.

Father was given a state funeral. The coffin with the body was placed in the foyer of the institute. We stood near the coffin and people passed by. Then the cortege of dozens of cars set off to the cemetery.

At my grandfather's insistence, it was a Jewish cemetery and a Jewish rite. Kaddish was recited. My father was wrapped in a shroud and lowered into the grave without a coffin. It was a well-tended Jewish cemetery with stone gravestones, metal fences, and tall trees. Next to it was a Russian cemetery with crosses, birch trees, and low fences.

After they set up the gravestone, Sonia and I went to put the grave in order. Just then, an inebriated party of eight people emerged from the Russian cemetery. "Look at those Jews," one of them called out. "When they're alive, they suck our blood and after death, look at the mansions they build." They stopped about ten meters from us and began to taunt us with anti-Semitic jokes. I was filled with anger and humiliation.

"Go away, he just buried his father," Sonia cried out. "Well, now let's put the little Yid next to his papa," wheezed one of them in a sailor's vest and he moved toward us. Sonia stood in front of me, but I pushed her aside, knocking her over. My ears were ringing, a red haze covered my eyes, my hair stood on end, and my hands merged with the shovel. A savage cry burst forth from my throat: "Two will lie with me!"

Then something unexpected happened. They stopped suddenly. Fear froze on their faces mixed with astonishment. "Well, you know, chap, yes, we didn't mean anything bad." One of them stepped forward and extended his hand in reconciliation. "Yes, forgive us." I couldn't separate my hand from the shovel. They hurried away and for some time I heard, "Forgive us, fellow."

I leaned over toward the gravestone and slowly slid to the earth. Weakness and emptiness washed over my body and I began to shiver. It took me a week to recover. From that time, I think, Sonia understood conclusively that I must not stay in that country. Everything moved in one direction.

After leaving the automation institute, I found work in a civilian enterprise, the Institute of Hygiene and Professional Illnesses, in the laboratory of medical electronics. The noted academician Vladimir Rozenblat established the laboratory. It was his "baby"—it developed instruments that were used in studying how people function in real, at times extreme, situations, for example, sportsmen during training, or workers engaged in dangerous professions.

Several technicians and engineers, some of whom were able specialists, worked in the laboratory. Although I was given the position of chief engineer, my salary was less than a third of what I had been earning in the automation institute. In order to compensate me some way for the loss of income, Rozenblat offered me additional work repairing and modifying the apparatus in the institute. I willingly agreed and did not regret it. Almost all of the institute's laboratory directors were Jews. I established good relations with my coworkers.

Doctor Rozenblat had over twenty graduate students. Two graduate students were already working on dissertations in our lab. Rozenblat suggested that I join them. His proposal was phrased in his peculiar style: "Yuli Mikhailovich, you have a pretty good chance of becoming a candidate of science [the equivalent of a doctorate in the West] in three years. There is a very interesting topic. You have a week to take the graduate exams in electronics, a foreign language, and Marxism-Leninism, without, of course, taking time off from your work obligations. If you can do this, you will be most worthy of becoming one of my graduate students. If not, it's also not so terrible. You can remain an engineer. Any questions?"

Work in science? Now? My first impulse was to refuse politely but that kind of proposal was a great honor; people waited in line for years to work with Rozenblat. If I refused, people might suspect me of "bad" intentions. In conversations about Israel, I had already managed to reveal something about my views. But I still had to live somehow for a minimum of another three years. And when all was said and done, what was I losing? If I was already destined to spend several more years in Russia, then I would spend that time usefully. I did not hesitate long—I had no questions.

Over half a year passed after my move to "civilian status" before I sought my first serious Zionist-oriented contact. It turned out to be Valery Kukui, who lived two hundred meters from me. Then Boria Edelman appeared, and Liuba Zlotver. In the winter of 1968–69 we would meet in the evenings, walk along the frozen Sverdlovsk streets, and talk and talk.

On Saturdays we started to meet at the home of Boria Edelman. Kukui then invited me to his home. He had an abundance of samizdat, more than I had ever seen. He watched silently while I avidly selected old journals, typescript books, brochures, and postcards. I wasn't much interested in the democratic movement samizdat but I happily took the old Jewish journals and the new one, *Iton*,[30] which had been produced on thin onionskin paper. I also found at his place the Russian-language Hebrew instruction manual of Shlomo Kodesh.[31] It was new and apparently had been lying untouched for quite a while. "Take it, I don't have time for that now," Valera said. On enthusiasm alone, I managed to get through eight lessons but I was unable to advance further without outside help.

It seemed to me that Hebrew study could be seen as preparation for our departure and it would add content to our Saturday meetings. The group welcomed the idea and attendance rose noticeably. At first we would discuss the latest news, and then Edelman would serve a meal with wine and cognac. After this, having rested a bit, we would turn to studying Hebrew. Everyone was equipped with pens and notebooks and industriously copied down the new material. As there were no textbooks, there was no homework. I must admit that at no other time did I prepare for the lessons so diligently, working out how and what I would say down to the last details. It was a happy time with the feeling that we were all one family.

Almost half a century has passed since then and each of us has gone his own way. Some managed to leave the USSR quickly; others were detained for many long years, and some endured prisons and labor camps. One was more successful in Israel while another one less so. We continue to keep in touch, however, and when one of us marries off a child or grandchild or celebrates an anniversary or other family occasion, the group gets together. We have our common memories and things to dream about together. But at that time, we faced harsh ordeals.

The Six-Day War

The links between the various groups inside the USSR, the preparation and dissemination of uncensored literature, and the establishment of contacts abroad led to the gradual consolidation of the Jewish movement. Attempts by the Soviet authorities to crush these national strivings were unsuccessful. The Six-Day War, which took place June 5–10, 1967, initiated a new phase in the Jewish national movement.[32]

Hundreds of thousands of Soviet Jews turned to their radios, trying to break through the Soviet jamming to hear the Western "Voices."

"Voices": Foreign Shortwave Radio Stations

The "Voices" (Russian: *Golosa*), stations Soviet citizens could catch on shortwave radios, included the *Voice of America, Radio Liberty,* the BBC Russian service, *Deutsche Welle,* and *Kol Yisrael.* Many Soviet citizens owned shortwave radios in this period, and the "Voices," with programming in Russian or easy English or Hebrew, provided independent news about world events. Western governments supported the stations, and the Soviet government made attempts to jam the transmissions, although they lessened or ceased the jamming efforts in certain periods because of international pressure.

For the Jews, the victory signified much more than simple heroism: it became a watershed in contemporary Jewish history, allowing Jews once again, this time positively, to acknowledge their common national fate. It also helped them realize that this fate was now linked to the State of Israel. For many, the Six-Day War became a turning point in their national consciousness: it changed not only how they perceived Israel but also how they perceived themselves.

Yosif Begun recalled his early attitudes and the effect of the Six-Day War:[33]

BEGUN: I grew up with a split soul. On the one hand, I understood that I was a Jew and that was burdensome to me. On the other hand, at home a reverential attitude toward Jewishness reigned—it was important for my mother. I was in a state of constant duality. At the beginning of the second grade, when the teacher listed each pupil's nationality in her register, I found this a terribly humiliating procedure. When she called on me, I couldn't get myself to say that I was a Jew. I said that I was Belorussian. And for some time, it was recorded in her book that I was Belorussian. I was terribly embarrassed. If at the time, when I was still in the dark about many things, I could have become Russian, I probably would have. When I began to understand where things stood, that sensation passed. By the Six-Day War, I was already a proud Jew, and that war helped me make up my mind to leave.

Boris Ainbinder answered a question about the impact of the war:[34]

KOSHAROVSKY: *How did the Six-Day War influence you?*

AINBINDER: I was completely disillusioned with the Soviet Union. I understood that it was almost impossible to change anything there and that it was not my task to try. They didn't want us there, we were alien, let them deal with it. On the other hand, there was a country where Jews were living. Of course, there was euphoria after 1967.

The Fifth Line of the Passport

The fifth line (or point) of the Soviet passport and other official identity documents listed nationality as a required category. At the age of sixteen, Soviet citizens received their first passports and could at that time choose the nationality of either parent if their nationalities differed. The fact that Jews after the Second World War had practically no official access to Jewish culture or Jewish institutions, yet were often required to list their nationality as Jewish—with all the implications for discrimination in educational, employment, and other opportunities that implied—is one of the reasons Soviet Jews became acculturated but not integrated.

The Six-Day War transformed many Soviet Jews in a fundamental way. It was overwhelming: the sense of anxiety and triumph, the propaganda, and the revelation of Jewish strength. The surrounding milieu began to change: the anti-Jewish jokes disappeared. Others began to look at Jews differently and Jews began to look at themselves differently. Being Jewish was no longer a mark of Cain but rather a distinction. The fifth line listing nationality on the Soviet identity card magically switched from a negative to a positive and became a source of inner joy and pride for some Jews. The process developed rapidly, accompanied by a colossal burst of national energy. Thousands of passionate advocates of a Jewish national revival pushed off from this starting line, gradually finding each other and those who had started earlier on a Jewish nationalist path.

The anti-Israeli and anti-Semitic propaganda continued to upset Jews, but it betrayed the impotence of the Soviet leadership in a situation of its own making: just as the entire world perceived Israel's victory as a victory for the West, so too it saw the Arabs' defeat as a defeat of the Soviet Union.

Yakov Kedmi (formerly Kazakov) discussed his dramatic response to the war and the difficulties he encountered in seeking to emigrate from the USSR:[35]

KOSHAROVSKY: *On June 13, just after the end of the Six-Day War, you declared that you renounced your Soviet citizenship.*

KEDMI: On June 11, the day after the Soviet Union severed diplomatic relations with Israel—on that day I severed my relations with the Soviet Union.[36]

I had been thinking about the letter for around two months. I had submitted my documents for an exit visa by February 1967. The authorities repeatedly rejected my application, and I understood that I could get nothing out of them by the usual methods. I began to think of alternatives. The events of the Six-Day War acted merely as a catalyst. I had already considered the idea of renouncing my citizenship earlier.

KOSHAROVSKY: *Had anyone applied for an exit visa in Moscow before you did in February 1967?*

KEDMI: Until that time, only those who had relatives in Israel had applied. Otherwise, the authorities would not accept the application. It worked in the following way: people turned to OVIR first via acquaintances or relatives to clarify whether or not to apply.[37] That's how it was done in the Baltic states, for example. As far as I know, no one before me had applied in Moscow. Those who did not have relatives in Israel didn't apply at all. The logic was simple: they only attempted what had a chance of success. Otherwise, why bother? Under the Soviet regime, people learned not to stick their necks out for no reason.

KOSHAROVSKY: *Did you have relatives in Israel?*

KEDMI: No one. It all started when I dropped in, or rather, burst into the Israeli embassy. Like all Soviet citizens, I was sure that I would not be permitted into the embassy. But I was nineteen years old. I jumped past the guard and he didn't manage to grab me.

KOSHAROVSKY: *Did you know anyone from the embassy staff?*

KEDMI: No, I didn't know anyone.

The embassy worker asked me, "What do you want?" I answered, "I want to go to Israel. How can I do that?" "Do you have anyone in Israel?" he asked. "No one." Then he said, "There are no precedents. I don't know how you can do it. We, of course, would accept you according to the Law of Return. But how will you get permission from the Soviet authorities? It's unlikely that we'll be able to help you in any way."

I asked what the official procedure was. He explained that I had to apply to OVIR but that was unrealistic because I did not have any relatives who could send me an invitation. Then he added, "You know, if you are serious, come back in a week and we'll talk some more." I said to him, "Fine, what do you have about Israel?" "What do you want?" he asked. "Hebrew textbooks and material about Israel," I said. He collected all kinds of booklets for me and I put them in my pockets.

KOSHAROVSKY: *When was that?*

KEDMI: February 19, 1967.

When I came again, I took the Israeli document and went to OVIR. I filled out an application and appended the document from the embassy stating that if I received an exit visa from the Soviet Union, Israel was prepared to receive me. That document was truly necessary. According to international conventions on emigration, a state that allows you to leave must have the assurance that you have a place to go to. At first I attempted to submit documents at the district OVIR, but they did not accept them. Then I went to the municipal OVIR, but they didn't take them there either. They said, "Bring an invitation from relatives."

They next summoned me to the All-Union OVIR and began to threaten me with real intimidation. This continued until I realized that it wouldn't work and I had to seek some other method. Then I began thinking that I probably would have to renounce Soviet citizenship. Right after they announced the break in diplomatic relations with Israel, I went to the reception room of the Supreme Soviet. According to law, it is the organ that decides issues of citizenship.

KOSHAROVSKY: *Yasha, had anyone before you renounced citizenship?*

KEDMI: No. I entered the large reception hall. People were sitting and submitting applications. Based on conversations I had with them, the majority of petitions were from relatives of prisoners who were requesting a pardon. I wrote my petition to the Presidium of the Supreme Soviet and made four copies by hand. I put the original in an envelope and handed it in through the little window and then went to the Israeli embassy to leave a copy.

KOSHAROVSKY: *What happened next?*

KEDMI: Nothing special. I continued to study and work. I was summoned again to OVIR for a conversation with the same comrades in civilian dress (i.e., KGB workers). They repeated that my visa request had been rejected and they began to threaten me. They said that normal people do not renounce citizenship and that I could be sent to an insane asylum or to another equally unpleasant place. I said, "You have the power. If you think that you can do it, do it. You try your method and I'll try mine." Then they said, "What if we take you into the army?" "What have I got to do with your army?" I asked. "After all, I already renounced my citizenship. There is only one army in the world in which I am ready to serve and that is the Israeli army." They asked, "And what if there is a war with China tomorrow?" At that time, there was tension along the border with China over the Damanski Island in the Amur River. "I sympathize," I said, "but that's your problem, it's none of my business." They asked, "You won't go to the army?" "Not to fight the Chinese for you," I said.

KOSHAROVSKY: *You were already studying in correspondence courses. They could simply draft you.*

KEDMI: There was a law then that granted an exemption from army service even for correspondence or evening studies. In fact, the law was in effect until a student went from his current institute to another one, but I didn't know that then. I wrote a statement resigning from the Komsomol in connection with my renunciation of citizenship and departure for Israel. They expelled me at a general meeting and reported this to my workplace and institute. Just at that time, I had passed an exam on the first part of political economy. They explained that I would not succeed in passing the second part. They stated it directly: "Either you leave on your own or we'll fail you on the exams." The Soviet regime is careful to assure that everything looks just and civilized. I then applied to the Polytechnic Institute's correspondence courses division. They accepted me and everything was fine. I wasn't aware that from that moment, they could draft me.

I had the feeling that whatever would be would be. Suddenly help came from an unexpected source. In August 1968 the Soviets sent troops into Czechoslovakia. This meant that they stopped demobilizing soldiers and started a new mobilization at the same time. Soon it turned out that the army had more people than it could handle. Consequently, in September, after I had received a third notice, they called off the mobilization.

Unexpectedly, the mobilization was delayed to the spring of 1969, while earlier, in December 1968, my letter was published in the *Washington Post*.[38]

KOSHAROVSKY: *That became your visa.*

KEDMI: On December 31 I had an attack of appendicitis and was operated on. The next morning, my mother came and said that a friend's grandfather was listening to the *Voice of Israel* broadcast and they mentioned my name and some kind of letter. "What does that mean?" she asked. I answered, "It means that I shall travel to the east—the Middle East or the Far East" [the Far East meant prison camp].

KOSHAROVSKY: *Was this letter also published in Israel?*

KEDMI: In Israel it was published as a reprint from the *Washington Post*. After my return from the hospital, I went downstairs to get the newspaper and found an envelope with an invitation to appear at the OVIR office. When I came to the Dutch embassy for the exit visa, they told me, "You are our first case of granting a visa from Moscow."

KOSHAROVSKY: *On the international level, the Jews were inconvenient for them. All they wanted to do was to leave, and it was necessary either to imprison them in sight of the whole world or let them go.*

KEDMI: I said, "Either try me or let me go." They apparently decided that a trial would be more damaging. They saw what happened in the trial of Galanskov and those of other dissidents.[39] It was impossible to grab me without attracting notice after I had left my mark everywhere. Holding an open or semi-open trial as they were wont to do would focus American Jewry's attention on the problems of Soviet Jewry, attention that did not exist at a broad level at that time. It would mean presenting the issue in a most unfavorable light, declaring to the entire world that there are young people who want to leave the Soviet Union and are not permitted to do so. This was not like the later Sharansky case;[40] it was not a matter of conveying information. Nor was it connected to the dissemination of some kind of literature. There was no hook on which to hang a case. I calculated that after they had weighed everything, they would reach the correct conclusion.

Kedmi's path was striking. A growing number of Soviet Jews dared to follow him in openly challenging the system and utilizing the Western media. Kedmi's way was successful but it was not suitable for everyone. One needed certain qualities in order to carry it off successfully. Luck played no small role in his fate. Had the attempt to draft him succeeded, he could have been stuck in the Soviet Union for years. Nevertheless, Kedmi's breakthrough showed that the boundaries of the possible in the Soviet Union had expanded beyond what was previously imaginable. Kedmi revealed the Soviet Union's sensitivity to an open and public struggle for freedom of emigration, a right which in the West was taken for granted.

Another early Zionist, Boris Kochubievsky, was born into an assimilated Jewish family in Kiev that experienced all the vicissitudes of a difficult and troubled period. He was twenty-five years old when the poet Evgeny Yevtushenko published his famous poem "Babii Yar" about the site where Boris assumed his father had been shot. He was thirty years old when the Six-Day War broke out. Many were offended by the flip-flops of Soviet propaganda on the eve of and after this war but very few had the courage to stand up and loudly declare, "I disagree."

At that time, almost all large enterprises held mass meetings. The Party speaker would present the official viewpoint denouncing Israel, a prepared resolution would be put to the vote, and its unanimous acceptance would be reported to the higher-ups as evidence of universal popular approval of the Party and the government's policy. That was the ritual. Boris refused to follow the ritual. "I disagree," he declared, "and I want it to be written in the protocol. Israel was not an aggressor. This war was its defense against complete physical destruction." The secretary of the Party organization demanded an immediate halt to this "anti-Soviet speech," but Kochubievsky could no longer stop. He was subsequently condemned at a trade union committee meeting and asked to leave the factory, "preferably voluntarily." In May 1968 Kochubievsky wrote an appeal, "Why I am a Zionist," that was widely disseminated in samizdat. In it, he wrote about persistent anti-Semitism: "This is not how things should be! That decisiveness and that belief distinguish our generation from those that preceded us . . . Jews understand more and more clearly that the road to Auschwitz is paved with Jewish silence and submission . . . The leaders of the Soviet Union have made Zionism anathema. That is why I am a Zionist."[41]

On the anniversary of the Nazi massacre, in 1968, the authorities decided to seize the initiative and organize an official memorial meeting. The speakers condemned "Israeli aggression" and spoke in the most general terms about the Fascists who had murdered Soviet people at Babii Yar. They did not mention the Jews. A friend told Boris about a conversation that he overheard between two participants at the meeting. "What is happening here?" asked one. "Here the Germans murdered a hundred thousand Jews," replied the other. "Too few," the first one reacted. Boris seized on this remark: "They talk that way because on this day and in this place they condemn 'Israeli aggression' and don't say a word about the fact that they murdered Jews here." A man who turned out later to be a provocateur immediately approached him. "Not only Jews were killed here," declared the provocateur. "But only Jews were killed because they were Jews," retorted Boris. A conversation started that later was reproduced in detail in a charge against Kochubievsky.[42]

On December 5, 1968, Kochubievsky was arrested and charged on the basis of Article 187-1 of the Ukrainian Criminal Code for orally disseminating known fabrications defaming the Soviet state and social order. He was incriminated for speaking at a meeting of the radio factory and union committee, for the conversation with the provocateur at Babii Yar, for conversations at OVIR, and for his appeal. Kochubievsky was convicted and sentenced to three years of corrective labor.

Boris Kochubievsky talked about how they pressured him to accept a deal:[43]

KOCHUBIEVSKY: They very much did not want to charge me on the basis of a "political" article. At the investigation, they tried to persuade me: "Look, you have a few minor criminal cases. Admit any one of them and you'll leave the courtroom a free person." If I had agreed, I probably never would have been freed.

At the trial I told them that I was not anti-Soviet. There was no basis to condemn me for that. And with all my heart, I wished the Ukrainian people another five hundred years of Soviet rule.

Kochubievsky served his term, was released on December 5, 1971, and received an exit visa to Israel. The difference in the fate of two Zionist activists, Kedmi and Kochubievsky, confirmed the belief of Western Jewish organizations in the power of public opinion. If Kochubievsky's case had caught the West's attention before his arrest, then instead of landing in prison he might have gone directly to Israel as Kedmi did.

Jewish and Zionist activism began long before the Six-Day War, but it became more intense after it. The effect of the Six-Day War might not have been so strong if it had not exposed the Soviet regime's attitude toward Israel and the Jews, manifested most blatantly in the clamorous anti-Israel propaganda. Many found it morally unbearable to listen to this daily manifestation of the regime's hostility while continuing to work for the Soviet state.

Before the Six-Day War, separate groups were already engaged in preparing and disseminating uncensored texts. After the war, the number of such groups rose sharply and they began to cooperate with one another. The Jewish population's distrust of the official media became more widespread. The movement for a Jewish national revival began to acquire a broader social base.

The processes of awakening and becoming active developed differently in various regions in accordance with local conditions and traditions. In some places, they were limited to listening to the foreign "Voices" and reading uncensored texts. In the Baltic republics, which as non-Soviet territories retained Jewish cultural and social institutions until World War II,[44] groups actively engaged in preparing and disseminating samizdat and even in publishing their own journals and newspapers. In the Caucasus and Central Asian republics, many Jews were prepared to drop everything and leave for Israel, seeing this as the fulfillment of the messianic prophecy.[45]

Moscow was the nerve center of the national revival. In the period from 1967 to the early 1970s, many activists there already possessed experience, commitment, and the benefits of networking in the Soviet corrective labor camps.[46] After David Khavkin's return from the Mordovian prison camps, he renewed his Zionist activity. He played a role in facilitating gatherings near the synagogue, encouraging the practice of singing and dancing outside the synagogue on the holiday of Simhat Torah, a tradition that lasted many years.[47] Khavkin participated in copying and disseminating Jewish songs, spreading information about Israel, providing instruction in Jewish dances, and organizing Hebrew teaching. Possessing unique energy and physical strength, Khavkin succeeded in attracting people and instilling in them a feeling of pride in their nation. While imprisoned, Khavkin acquired new friends with whom he continued to maintain close contact after his release.

Khavkin's fame spread far beyond the Moscow limits: it was to Khavkin that Ruth Aleksandrovich brought the young Riga activists for advice and guidance. It was to Khavkin that Vladimir Mogilever, Solomon Dreizner, and Hillel Butman would come from Leningrad for consultation and sharing of ideas. Schooled with other dissidents in the labor camps, Khavkin stressed legalism and the right to emigrate under the Soviet Constitution and international law. Knowing that he was under continual surveillance by the KGB, Khavkin perfected surreptitious techniques and was always careful not to overstep the limits that would lead to his entrapment and harm the movement.[48] When Khavkin left for Israel in September 1969, more than five hundred people accompanied him to the airport. After Khavkin's departure, the apartment of Vitaly Svechinsky became the natural meeting place and center of Jewish activity.

Samizdat

Soviet "samizdat" (a neologism meaning "self-published") was a system of uncensored production and circulation of texts that developed after Stalin. People usually produced samizdat using typewriters and photographic cameras. Samizdat included literature, open letters, informational guides, textbooks, journals, and bulletins, among other materials.

These included works published decades previously or published in the West and unavailable in Soviet editions. They might be works by a Soviet author that either could not pass censorship or simply would not be published officially in the Soviet Union. "Tamizdat" (publishing "over there," in the West) provided a way to get materials into print that were not published in the USSR. Samizdat readers shared tamizdat editions that had been smuggled into the USSR for clandestine circulation.

Vitaly Svechinsky shared some details about activity in Moscow and his role there:[49]

KOSHAROVSKY: *What did you undertake after your return to Moscow in 1955?*

SVECHINSKY: First, I began to look for my former acquaintances in Moscow. Thanks to my old camp ties, I found many former *zeks* (a Russian abbreviation for prison or labor camp inmates)—Jews and non-Jews—and noticed many interesting things going on. I was struck most of all by the amount of samizdat. Whole books were being copied at night, secretly, and handed from one to the other. A colossal amount of literature appeared that touched the heart directly. Samizdat affected people like a refreshing elixir. People woke up from a stupor, and they understood where and how they were living, what they had become, and who they were.

KOSHAROVSKY: *Do you recall something from the works of that time?*

SVECHINSKY: I was impressed by *The Sources and Meaning of Russian Communism* by Nikolai Berdiaev.[50] After that, I read everything by Berdiaev that I could get my hands on. Then there was Vladimir (Zeev) Jabotinsky—his essays, *Feuilletons.*[51] When I read them, I was stunned. That collection became my primer. It contained so much truth, wisdom, strength, energy, and courage that we choked up. These were not feuilletons but powerful essays that you can read even now and find meaningful. I typed them at night. There were excerpts from Pinsker's "Auto-emancipation,"[52] and some translations from Hebrew, prepared by Meir Gelfond's group.[53] At first I encountered the non-Jewish movements: Crimean Tatars, Baptists, and democrats. Among them were my camp friends such as Vitia Krasin and Petr Iakir. I knew Petr Grigorenko,

Ilia Gabai, Andrei Amalrik, Pasha [Pavel] Litvinov.[54] I used to frequent their homes.

KOSHAROVSKY: *How did you resolve the issue of your relationship with the democrats?*

SVECHINSKY: I debated with them. I tried to prove to Iakir that what they were doing was very good but Iakir's place was not there. Sara Lazarevna, Iakir's mother, attacked me: "What are you doing! Isn't it enough that he is tied in with the democrats, who oppose the Soviet regime? You want to foist Jewishness on him as well so he would go to jail for two articles at once?"

I was well acquainted with Tolia Iakobson and Nadia Emelkin,[55] who defended Volodia Bukovsky.[56] I knew Volodia very well. I was astonished when he got out of prison and right away, without any break, became very active. It turned out that he wrote an academic paper on psychiatric prison hospitals and smuggled it out to the West. This attracted considerable attention and he again landed in prison. I saw all this and understood well what was going on.

KOSHAROVSKY: *Did you see yourself more as a Jew than a dissident?*

SVECHINSKY: When the trials of Ginzburg, Galanskov, Dobrovolsky, and Lashkov began in January 1968,[57] a letter made the rounds, and, as Lyonia Vasilev used to say,[58] "As an honest person, I signed it." This letter became known as the Letter of the 170. I calculated that about 70 percent of the signatories were Jews.

KOSHAROVSKY: *How did you get to Zionist circles?*

SVECHINSKY: Khavkin was the first serious person who did something in the situation of 1967–68. In the summer of 1968 I went to Kiev to my spiritual father Natan Zabara, who had brought me gruel when I was imprisoned in camp. I loved him. He was like a father to me. Zabara said, "I want to introduce you to some young Jews here. Perhaps you can be helpful to them." "What kind of young Jews?" I asked. "They come to me and I teach them Hebrew and this and that," he said.

KOSHAROVSKY: *He taught Hebrew in Kiev in 1968?*

SVECHINSKY: Yes. He was a Yiddish writer.[59] Natan introduced me to [Anatoly] Gerenrot, Zhenia Bukhin, Koifman, Amik (Emanuel) Diamant—the whole group. They invited me to the forest where they sang

Israeli songs, danced, and played music. A hora! I almost went crazy. There was nothing like that in Moscow. There was one ex-prisoner among them, Alik Feldman, with whom I found a common language. I watched all this and I was simply filled with envy. "Kiev is something!" I said to Alik. "I don't see anything like this in Moscow." He told me, "I'll give you the phone number of my friend from camp. His name is David Khavkin."

Upon my return to Moscow, I called Khavkin and I went over to meet him. Just before this something very interesting happened. Fimka Spivakovsky arrived from Kharkov and announced, "We are just sitting here but Riga is going to Israel!" "What are you talking about, what Israel?" I asked. "Under Stalin the old people also left; so what? What does Riga have to do with it?" "No," said Fima, "the Riga OVIR has begun to accept documents! Lida told me." He was friendly with my friend Lida [Lidia, also called Lea] Slovin; they were together in evacuation during the war and went to school together. And Fima and I went to OVIR.

I went up to the little window. A woman was sitting there. I said, "I came to ask a question." She said, "Go ahead." I asked, "Tell me, can I submit documents for departure to Israel?" She looked at me, studying me, paused, and then said, "You may." And at that point, I was speechless. I came to my senses, and I asked, "What do I need for that?" "An invitation from Israel," she said. "An invitation from whom?" I asked. "Well, it could be from an acquaintance of yours, or from a relative, or from a neighbor," she said. You hear, that's how she was talking! "So an invitation doesn't have to be from a mother or father or an immediate relative?" I asked. I was thinking, maybe I didn't hear her right. "No, it's not obligatory," she said. "What else do I need besides an invitation?" I asked. "You need to assemble many documents," she said in a businesslike manner. "When you start, we'll tell you everything in detail. They will take your documents but that still does not mean that you will receive an exit visa. After all, you are asking whether you can submit documents for an exit visa. I am telling you that you may." I asked, "Tell me, how long ago did this happen? It wasn't this way earlier." I still couldn't believe my ears. "Yes, it's about two or three weeks," she said.

That's it! The next day, I went to Khavkin. There was a small circle of former Prisoners of Zion: Lyonia Rutshtein, Meir Gelfond, Lyonia

Libkovsky, who always had his guitar—we loved his songs—and Khavkin himself. It was a group of about forty people and it grew. We would go out of town together on [Israeli] Independence Day.

KOSHAROVSKY: *What did you do on an everyday basis?*

SVECHINSKY: We made samizdat, printed textbooks; we were very busy organizing Hebrew classes.

KOSHAROVSKY: *How did you produce samizdat?*

SVECHINSKY: By photographic copying and on electric typewriters on thin onionskin paper: we inserted twenty pages at a time and struck the keys as hard as we could. For photographic copying, we used a rapid developing agent and dried the photos on newspapers. It all went quickly. Khavkin was a specialist.

KOSHAROVSKY: *How did you solve the problem of our Jewish suspiciousness? After all, you expanded, new people arrived.*

SVECHINSKY: That is a very good question. In Moscow we thought that almost nothing needed to be kept secret. At that time, we didn't even think about it particularly. We worked openly and were not afraid of stool pigeons. It was a feeling that this was our way, our proper path, there was no turning us back. It was an amazing feeling.

KOSHAROVSKY: *Were you in contact with the Hebrew teachers? With Moshe Palhan?*

SVECHINSKY: In our day there was Moshe Palhan, Hava Mikhailovna (Edelman), and Izrail Borisovich Mints. He had lived in Israel, then wound up in Russia because he was a very strong believer in communism. Then, naturally, he served a prison term and when he came out, he was already a normal person.

Professor Mikhail Zand was then participating in underground activity such as translating and composing samizdat texts in cooperation with Meir Gelfond.

KOSHAROVSKY: *What kind of texts?*

SVECHINSKY: Cultural ones. I remember that they put out the translation of the book *Makor.* It combined archaeology with Zionism, a very good publication. Meir had a network of typists and intellectuals working on the texts. It was powerful samizdat.

KOSHAROVSKY: *They say that he was a very nice person.*

SVECHINSKY: Meir was not only a nice person. He also had a golden heart, including with regard to everything connected with health or the hospital. If, God forbid, anyone had a health problem, he was there to help. He was a person full of love, open, lively in a childlike way. He was a clever person and an acute political commentator.

KOSHAROVSKY: *You rather quickly became a center of Zionist activity in Moscow.*

SVECHINSKY: That was much later on. It took four years of "slaying dragons" with no end in sight. And this life, it simply drained me completely. I worked, not paying attention to anything and then later, in the end, I felt that I had overstrained myself. It affected my entire life after that. It even hindered me from finding my bearings in Israel, rather strongly hindered.

KOSHAROVSKY: *You weren't afraid?*

SVECHINSKY: There was no fear. On the contrary. I didn't have the normal routine life of a Soviet citizen: study, marriage, papa, mama, kindergarten, school, institute, bureaucratic job. I didn't have this. Life followed a different course. I was in harness from the time that they came for me at night and took me from my bed, from 1950. Like Drabkin and Khavkin, I felt that I had to answer for everything—who would do it if not I?

KOSHAROVSKY: *A feeling of a mission?*

SVECHINSKY: A feeling of a mission, a vocation. We submitted [visa applications].

KOSHAROVSKY: *The reason for the refusal?*

SVECHINSKY: For almost everyone it was for "inexpediency." No one seriously expected any visa. On the other hand, it blew our cover and life began in earnest.

Democrats

The democrats, more properly known as rights activists (*pravozashchitniki*), were the best-known of the Soviet dissidents. The rights movement got its start on December 5, 1965, at a demonstration to demand openness in the judicial proceedings against authors Yuli Daniel and

Alexander Siniavsky. Physicist Andrei Sakharov and his wife, Elena Bonner, were perhaps the best known activists in a loosely organized movement that included many people of Jewish origin.

David Drabkin was six to seven years older than Khavkin and Svechinsky, which was a considerable difference in those years. Drabkin belonged to a rather rare category of early Zionist leaders who never spent time in prison. David Drabkin talked about Jewish life and activity in the 1950s:[60]

KOSHAROVSKY: *You finished the institute at a problematic time.*

DRABKIN: Yes, they didn't want to give me a job in Moscow but in the end, I managed to find a position at the Moscow Electric Lamp Factory. It was a special place. An overwhelming number of the product engineers and general drafting directors were Jews.

KOSHAROVSKY: *In 1952, strange things were happening all around.*

DRABKIN: We, too, were expecting dismissals. In 1953, however, we were expecting deportation. But our director did not want to fire the Jews. He called in sick and stayed in the hospital in the hope that this anti-Jewish wave would subside. He sat out Stalin in that way, and the Jews in the factory were not fired. When they declared that the doctors (those falsely accused in the so-called Doctors' Plot, 1953) were not guilty, the factory's director of supplies, a Jew, gathered all of us Jews together and he hugged and kissed us.

KOSHAROVSKY: *When did Israel begin to attract you?*

DRABKIN: When I was four years old. We were living at a dacha and under us, on the first floor, lived a family that suddenly disappeared somewhere. I asked mama where they went and she said that they had left for Palestine and that Palestine was the Jewish land. That was in 1927. I already knew that I was a Jew. And I stored away the idea that if I am a Jew then I should also live in Palestine.

KOSHAROVSKY: *When did you undertake the first practical steps?*

DRABKIN: When I considered that there was a real chance to leave. This occurred, in essence, after the Six-Day War when someone told me that OVIR was beginning to accept documents.

KOSHAROVSKY: *How did you connect with Moscow Zionist circles?*

DRABKIN: Someone at work said that I should go to the synagogue on the holiday of Simhat Torah. I am not a religious person but I went. I saw people there behaving in a way that fit my notion of how Zionists should behave. They were singing and dancing Jewish dances. I met David Khavkin there. He is a straightforward and sincere person and a genuine Zionist, something for which he had already spent time in prison.

Through Khavkin, I met other Zionists who had served time even before him: Svechinsky and his friends. There were also many from the democratic movement among Svechinsky's friends. I was afraid of mixing with the democrats because their activity was considered interference in internal Soviet affairs. They arrested people for that. I also met Jews who had been imprisoned for economic crimes—accountants and managers of small black-market enterprises.[61] They were also Zionists by inclination.

Economic Crimes

From July 1961 to August 1963, there were dozens of trials for economic crimes around the USSR. Many convicted received the death penalty, and of those so sentenced, well over half were Jewish. News of the death sentences and the high percentage of Jews receiving them provoked outrage in the West. Among those speaking out against the sentences were the British Board of Deputies president Sir Barnett Janner, the American National Association for the Advancement of Colored People (NAACP), and a group of North American trade union leaders. The American Jewish Committee prepared a petition to Khrushchev signed by leading scholars and clergymen urging repeal of the death penalty for economic offenses, and Bertrand Russell expressed concern over the issue in his open letter to Khrushchev. The harsh sentences for economic crimes helped push Soviet Jewry onto the agenda of Western intellectuals and groups.

KOSHAROVSKY: *There was an interesting group that gathered in your factory, including [Vladimir] Slepak; [Viktor] Polsky; and [Vladimir] Prestin's wife,*

Elena. I heard a lot about your "tourist packages" [a joking reference to group vacations; see below].

DRABKIN: I organized this group. They came to me because they knew that I was a person who would go to Israel. It was well known, including among the Russians. The Russians thought that even though I was a strange fellow, it was natural for a Jew to try to go to Israel, and they viewed those Jews who didn't indicate any interest as bad, scheming, selfish, and as acting that way because it was to their benefit.

KOSHAROVSKY: *You want to say that for a Russian patriot, Jewish patriotism seemed natural?*

DRABKIN: I think that it's quite possible that I learned patriotism towards one's people and country from the Russians.

KOSHAROVSKY: *What did you do in the group?*

DRABKIN: I read them the Bible (Tanakh). My approach was based on the Tanakh: "Let my people go," said Moses. He didn't make any demand to change or "democratize" Egypt. He didn't want anything from Egypt. "Let my people go," and nothing more. I also didn't want anything else. But I didn't say this to them directly. They would not have understood. The second parallel between Egypt and Moscow is the Passover seder. I organized a Passover seder at my home and this became a tradition. We would read the Haggadah, drink the cups of wine. A huge number of people used to come; the house was full.

KOSHAROVSKY: *Who was included in your group?*

DRABKIN: Slepak, Libkovsky, Lena Prestin, Polsky, with their families. We used to travel together on vacations. Our conversations were on Jewish and Zionist topics.

KOSHAROVSKY: *Did you know Hebrew?*

DRABKIN: No, I studied it industriously. We would read the Tanakh in Russian. I would clarify some issues with the older men who had studied in a heder.[62] Later I got hold of the textbook for Hebrew study *Elef Milim*.[63]

KOSHAROVSKY: *How did you obtain printed material?*

DRABKIN: Until the break in diplomatic relations [in 1967], we usually would take material from the Israeli embassy staff, in the synagogue. Together we managed to translate *Exodus*. I did it with Polsky and Prestin.

***Exodus* by Leon Uris**

Leon Uris's novel *Exodus* (1958), about the founding of the State of Israel, was by many accounts the most popular fictional work in Jewish samizdat. Various Russian versions circulated in samizdat, either translations in full (at more than six hundred pages!) or shortened versions. *Exodus* portrayed Jews as people of action, as proud and compelling Jewish heroes, similar to those found in other translated fiction popular in samizdat, including Howard Fast's *My Glorious Brothers* and André Schwarz-Bart's *The Last of the Just*. Such portrayals helped dispel stereotypes about Jews prevalent in the USSR, and they resonated profoundly with Soviet Jewish readers.

KOSHAROVSKY: *Did you know Meir Gelfond?*

DRABKIN: Of course. He was very cautious.

KOSHAROVSKY: *Did you have links with other cities?*

DRABKIN: I knew a lot of people from Riga, the David Zand family and the Garber family. The Garbers would stay at my place when they came to Moscow. We had a connection with Georgian Jews. Yakov Iakobashvili was one of the outstanding people there. The Georgian Jews were able to sign up a large number of people. Once I complained to Iakobashvili that in Moscow, we weren't able to collect more than a few dozen signatures (for petitions). He said to me, "I'll send you at least five hundred," and he did. I knew some other Georgian Jews too: Papatishvili, Mikhail Menasherov. They would come and stay with me. We had a link with David Chernoglaz in Leningrad—now he is called Maayan—and with Ruth Aleksandrovich in Riga. She would also give me open letters and collective petitions.

KOSHAROVSKY: *And how did your letters make it abroad?*

DRABKIN: Through foreign correspondents. The correspondents were friendly with Yasha Kazakov's (Kedmi's) father; they found him interesting. I would ask him when his next meeting would be, then I would come over and hand him the letters. I also utilized the Swiss embassy. It was helpful that my wife knew German so well. A Jew named Yona Ettinger, who was a UN translator in Europe, visited me at home. He took a pack of letters and gave me the phone number of the Swiss embassy in case it would be necessary to transmit some material. When I had accumulated many letters I would go there. Later I used the channel again and again. That I did without Svechinsky.

KOSHAROVSKY: *You, of course, remember the famous "Letter of the 39" in response to the press conference of "official" Jews in 1970. There were some hot disputes at the time of its signing.*

DRABKIN: That letter was signed in my home. My signature came first. After that, it was easier for others to sign because they trusted me. Chalidze wrote the letter. I opposed mixing together democrats and Zionists. Indeed, my approach was, "Let my people go." On a personal level, I had nothing against Svechinsky, but our approaches were different. He was linked to the democrats and was friendly with Iakir. Of course, that gave him connections but Iakir was too personally harmed by the Soviet regime, which had shot his father. Earlier, I had been working in Irkutsk and couldn't write the letter myself, but, after all, everyone in the Jewish national movement ought to be Jews. That's how it was in Riga and in Leningrad. Why should it be different here?

KOSHAROVSKY: *You didn't have to live long in refusal.*

DRABKIN: But I managed to feel it. When a person would submit documents, often his or her close relatives would break off contact, leaving the individual in the society of exclusively like-minded people. The whole application process was accompanied by the loss of acquaintances and relatives for whom he or she seemingly ceased to exist. That person was not invited anymore to birthdays or holidays.

On March 27, 1971, David Drabkin received an exit visa.

VKK: The All-Union Coordinating Committee

Zionist groups arose in many locations in the Soviet Union. In addition to the major cities of Leningrad and Moscow, Zionists were active in places such as Kiev, Kishinev, Odessa, Novosibirsk, and Tbilisi. Activists gradually contacted each other and exchanged opinions on the forms and methods of struggle and intensified the exchange of samizdat literature. This literature went from Riga to Leningrad, Moscow, Minsk, and other cities, from Vilnius to Sverdlovsk, from Leningrad to Kishinev, and from Moscow to Kiev, Riga, Leningrad, Novosibirsk, and Sverdlovsk.

Moscow was a clearing house for samizdat distribution. Some books and printed material, including Leon Uris's novel *Exodus*, were produced simultaneously in a few places. The quality of the translations and of the production work and the scope of samizdat distribution varied greatly. The movement was ripe for more effective coordination and division of labor.

In the summer of 1969 Svechinsky convened activists from several cities in Moscow and proposed creating some kind of coordinating group. Vladimir Mogilever and Solomon Dreizner arrived from Leningrad; Elie Valk and Boris Maftser came from Riga; and Efim Spivakovsky represented Kharkov. Svechinsky was the Moscow representative. There were also people from Kiev, Minsk, and Tbilisi. Two items on the agenda were the exchange of information and the signing of collective letters of protest. Mogilever and Dreizner suggested setting up a formal all-Russia Zionist organization, but the other participants reacted coolly to the idea. Zionist leaders who had been through prisons and labor camps were not eager to create a rigid organizational structure. They preferred flexible ties that were suitable for coordinating certain spheres and solving common problems without a formal leadership. This kind of vague body was, indeed, created at a meeting that took place in the forest near Moscow from August 16 to 17, 1969. It was called the All-Union Coordinating Committee, known in Russian by the initials VKK (Vsesoiuznyi koordinatsionnyi komitet).

Svechinsky recalled some details of the organization:[64]

KOSHAROVSKY: *Who initiated the VKK?*

SVECHINSKY: Some people who considered themselves—I would not say leaders—activists gathered informally at Meir Gelfond's apartment. Lyonia Rutshtein, David Khavkin, Meir himself, and Karl Malkin were there.

KOSHAROVSKY: *Karl Malkin was a Hebrew teacher.*

SVECHINSKY: Malkin was not only a teacher. He was responsible for the links between cities.

KOSHAROVSKY: *You already divided up functions?*

SVECHINSKY: Yes. We decided that something needed to be done and sent the word to all the cities: Riga, Vilnius, Kharkov, Kiev, Leningrad, Odessa, Novosibirsk, even Orel, where there was Karl Frusin. Everyone came on his own account. We met secretly in the forest near Moscow and put sentries at a kilometer's distance. Our gathering received the name the All-Union Coordinating Committee (VKK). There was no list of participants but we knew who they were. We decided many matters there. We assigned responsibility to people in each city for various spheres such as samizdat and we established intercity links. This work required money, material, paper, an exchange of literature, and other tasks. Samizdat represented a large part of our work. Karl Malkin was responsible for it in Moscow and [Yosef] Mendelevich in Riga. Boria Maftser also worked actively in Riga. Perhaps it was even foolish, but we weren't suspicious. Those who had financial problems were given money, not for trips but for work. At that time, we already had a public fund that was rather solid.

KOSHAROVSKY: *Was this from overseas help?*

SVECHINSKY: Not yet. That began later. In the meantime, we collected money from the public. Khavkin sold copies of *Exodus* for ten rubles. I said to him, "David, aren't you ashamed to take ten rubles from a Jew?" But he said, "Let them pay. Let them read and pay." We also got money from the Georgian Jews. They had millionaires who gave us rather large donations. We were very careful in dealing with money.[65]

The Leningrad underground organization arose earlier than the Moscow one and was much more organized. However, the VKK was a Moscow initiative. Svechinsky continued to fill in details about the organization:[66]

KOSHAROVSKY: *The problem of leadership didn't arise in Moscow?*

SVECHINSKY: You know, no. We never had that kind of problem.

KOSHAROVSKY: *In your time there were several recognized leaders: Khavkin, Drabkin, Gelfond, Mikhail Zand, you. How were your mutual relations?*

SVECHINSKY: Vanity and the thirst for personal success were not characteristic of the movement at this stage because of the danger of repression.

KOSHAROVSKY: *After Khavkin received a visa, did you become a leader?*

SVECHINSKY: It's hard to say. I know only that I expended an enormous amount of effort on the movement. Before Khavkin's departure everyone gathered at his place on Serpukhov Street. It was a kind of recognized headquarters to which people flocked. After his departure, I announced that everyone could come to our apartment. Khavkin's departure was a sensitive moment for us: I was afraid that people would disperse and it would be difficult to bring them back together. Everyone began to come to me and it was very difficult for my wife: our place turned into an open house. Just at the time our daughter was born and our son was nine years old—and all this together.

I remember one time that we gathered in the forest for Israel Independence Day. I think that Viktor Polsky was there and even photographed it. When we assembled, we saw policemen and people in civvies looming at about fifty meters from us, officially in sight, without hiding. Nevertheless, we hung out the Israeli flag. The women began to get upset and the public at large did too. It was rather unpleasant. I understood that it was necessary to dispel this uncertainty despite having the police and KGB all around. I could not do this now but then it was different. I got up and said, "In [the labor] camp, we had a saying: 'We don't need any imposters. I'll be the brigadier.' Now listen, I want to say something." And I began to speak about Independence Day, about the Jews and what it means, and so forth, and the KGB men were listening and the policemen were listening.

About a year later, when I was summoned to the Lubianka prison to testify in the case of Ruth Aleksandrovich and other Riga activists—I am running ahead here in the matter of leadership—the investigator placed a paper on the table, labeled "Particular determination of the investigative board of Riga and the Riga region." This paper stated that the case concerning the VKK headed by Vitaly Svechinsky should be dealt with in a separate criminal investigation. The investigator said to me, "You see, you have everything ahead of you, Vitaly Lazarevich."

KOSHAROVSKY: *The ordinary prosecutor's office decided such things?*

SVECHINSKY: At one time, the State Security Committee (KGB) had its own prosecutor's office but Khrushchev canceled this and gave the State Security a dressing down so that it had already lost its power around that time and was forced to turn to the separate state prosecutor's office.

The subordination was maintained, nevertheless, because there were certain people in the prosecutor's office who dealt only with State Security matters.

KOSHAROVSKY: *What about the methods of conducting interrogations? In the Stalin period, the investigators were able to drum out of anyone whatever they wanted. What about in the 1970s?*

SVECHINSKY: Really, there is no comparison. In our time—and I was arrested in 1950—an investigator could come and sock you in the mug. And they shot at me from a TT pistol [a police officer's personal weapon] in order to intimidate me. At the beginning of the 1970s, this was already a different KGB. Of course, it was easier for me than for the others. When the fellows were summoned for interrogations, I understood how hard it was for them because it was still the KGB after all, and they didn't know any other. I went around like a big shot because I knew. I had already been through this grinder, I already had knowledge, and not because I was really such a hero.

KOSHAROVSKY: *How were decisions made in the VKK?*

SVECHINSKY: It did not take a lot of time. Someone would make a proposal and if everyone agreed, that was it. Good proposals passed quickly and questionable ones were not debated for long. The main thing was to act. It was a wonderful time. The idea was to establish links and organize coordination among Jews of various cities. It was the best project of my life. I am an architect and have drafted many projects, but this was the best. The KGB, of course, manipulated the VKK. When arrests began, many testified, particularly Maftser. He wrote four volumes naming people and details.

KOSHAROVSKY: *Did they also drag in Elie Valk?*

SVECHINSKY: He was summoned as a witness. He had heart problems, but he stood there like an old partisan.

KOSHAROVSKY: *Valk didn't break down?*

SVECHINSKY: What are you talking about? Iliusha [Elie Valk] is our joy. Vladik Mogilever proposed calling our organization the VKK. I wasn't very happy with the name. It sounded too typically Soviet: "All-Union" and "Committee," but it was approved. Later the KGB was already in full swing. This VKK worked well—it did a lot.

KOSHAROVSKY: *After you received a visa, did Viktor Polsky replace you?*

SVECHINSKY: He replaced me after our departure.

KOSHAROVSKY: *You handed matters over to him, somehow "anointed" him to the leadership?*

SVECHINSKY: I worked together with him, but no one handed anything over to anyone.

The second meeting of the VKK took place from November 8 to 9, 1969, in Riga at a specially prepared dacha. Those present included Vitaly Svechinsky (Moscow), Anatoly Gerenrot (Kiev), David Chernoglaz (Leningrad), Gershon Tsitsuashvili (Tbilisi), Arkady Shpilberg, Boris Maftser (Riga), and others. The participants reported on the state of Zionist activity in their locale and decided to publish a periodical collection called *Iton* ([Hebrew for Newspaper] 1970, nos. 1–2). The editorial board was to include representatives from Moscow, Riga, and Leningrad. Its task was to select the material and edit it. The publication was supposed to be produced in turn in each of the above cities. At the meeting at Basia Levin's apartment on November 9, the participants decided which addresses and telephones would be used to obtain the necessary literature and information.

The first meeting of the *Iton* editorial board took place in Leningrad on January 10, 1970. Yosef Mendelevich and Boris Maftser in Riga, Lev Korenblit and Viktor Boguslavsky in Leningrad, and Karl Malkin in Moscow contributed to the preparation of *Iton*. Meir Gelfond from Moscow was responsible for printing and distributing the publications.[67]

Vitaly Svechinsky clarified further details of their activity and circumstances:[68]

KOSHAROVSKY: *Do you think that the KGB knew about the VKK before the hijacking case?*

SVECHINSKY: They would have found out anyway because they knew about the Leningrad Zionist organization. We also knew well all the members of the Leningrad committee.

KOSHAROVSKY: *Had any of the Leningrad people served terms before this?*

SVECHINSKY: Not one of them. They paid their dues. They were divided into groups of three and five so that others would not suffer if someone was arrested—they followed all the rules of the underground.

KOSHAROVSKY: *Did Eitan Finkelshtein take part in this?*

SVECHINSKY: Eitan was very active and vital; he was everywhere.

KOSHAROVSKY: *And when did the younger ones—Slepak, Polsky, Prestin, Abramovich—join in?*

SVECHINSKY: Around 1969. Everyone became involved via Slepak. He had such a hospitable home. This was also connected later to the petition campaign.[69]

Coordination within the VKK itself was rather flexible. At each meeting, representatives from one of the five cities were entrusted with organizing the next meeting. Those who came to the meeting comprised the next VKK. The final meeting took place in Leningrad on June 13–14, 1970, at which time the Zionist groups of Minsk, Vilnius, and Kishinev became full-fledged members of the VKK.[70]

At the time, the movement leaders could only speculate to what degree the KGB knew about the activity of the VKK. Published documents today show that the KGB was familiar with the VKK by the middle of 1970. KGB chairman Yuri Andropov reported to the Communist Party of the Soviet Union (CPSU) Central Committee on May 17, 1971, about the consolidation between 1969 and 1970 of an "underground Zionist party," the "so-called All-Union Coordinating Committee."[71]

Andropov, of course, exaggerated with regard to the "underground Zionist party." The concept of an underground party presupposes the articulation of clear political tasks for changing the existing order, the existence of a program, an organizational structure, and the observance of conspiratorial rules. This was not the case for the VKK. The Jews, whose goal was to leave the Soviet Union, were not striving to change the existing order. It was the rights activists who were interested in domestic reform.

The VKK was not nor did it try to become the sole Zionist party of the Soviet Union. VKK members held the most varied views on the development of the movement. Whereas the Leningrad and Kiev groups sought an organized structure and discipline, other groups considered that unsuitable.[72] Neither side succeeded in convincing the other.

The coordination, nevertheless, produced serious practical results. Tasks were allocated to those who could best handle them. Riga and

Leningrad activists took on the publication of the journal, which was dispatched to activists in various cities. They copied it and disseminated it further. Participants in the summer camps, which were open to all, were primarily young people who knew of their existence and could afford to come. Samizdat reached a new qualitative and quantitative level.

The VKK's most important achievement consisted of making the transition to open forms of struggle, to public protests, and to the mobilization of international society. A group of activists in Moscow began to issue a periodical journal, *Iskhod* (Exodus, nos. 1–4, 1970–71) that published open protest letters and documents related to judicial and extrajudicial harassment. Svechinsky gathered the material, while Viktor and Alia Fedoseev edited it and composed the journal. Alia's mother, Dora Koliaditsky, typed the issues, and Yasha Ronenson was in charge of storing and distributing them. After the Fedoseevs and Svechinsky emigrated, Isai Averbukh dealt with producing the journal. According to Svechinsky, this journal became a Jewish *Chronicle of Current Events*.[73]

Prior to the actions of Yasha Kazakov and Boris Kochubievsky, it was not accepted practice in Jewish circles to defy the authorities openly or to ensure that such a challenge would be widely publicized abroad. The wave of national pride after the Six-Day War and the revulsion evoked by Soviet propaganda provided a strong impetus for some activists to undertake the challenge. The emigration that began in 1968 and the support extended to the movement by the West imparted a feeling of strength to a considerably broader circle of activists.

Svechinsky spoke also about the relationship of Jewish activists to activists of the rights (democratic) movement:[74]

SVECHINSKY: When we were denied an exit visa in 1969, it seriously affected our mood.[75] We gathered at Meir Gelfond's apartment in Sokolniki in Moscow to discuss whether to continue with the samizdat or start some new form of activity. At that time, I was already very familiar with the democratic movement and the democrats' self-sacrifice. I knew the Crimean Tatars.[76]

KOSHAROVSKY: *The authorities dealt even more harshly with them than with the Jews.*

SVECHINSKY: Yes, they didn't waste time on niceties with them—they gave it to them right in the mug, off to the punishment cell, and on to the labor camp. Who could intercede for them in the West? Who needed them? I said then, mainly to Meir although Khavkin was there also but he didn't express his opinion because he already had a visa and was getting ready to leave, "Guys, it's impossible to continue living this way. We must emerge from the underground. We must write letters and get published in the Western press." Khavkin supported me because his whole nature was drawn to open activity.

KOSHAROVSKY: *Was this in accordance with the example set by the democrats?*

SVECHINSKY: It was the example of the democrats, Baptists, and others. The first one to do so was Yura Maltsev, with whom we were friendly. He wrote a letter in 1965: "I cannot live in this country whose government I despise."[77] He was immediately sent to an insane asylum but international public opinion was marshaled to get him out. Demonstrations began and he was released. That was the first harbinger, in 1965.

KOSHAROVSKY: *But you were connected to the democrats. You probably did not participate in their undertakings, however.*

SVECHINSKY: No, I did participate, following Jabotinsky's tenets. I am his faithful and grateful pupil. According to him, we should not ignore a progressive movement. We ought to participate but within measure and we shouldn't violate this proportionate response. There should not be a situation in which Jews constitute 1 percent of the country's population but comprise 75 percent of the signatories to letters in defense of the democratic dissidents Ginzburg, Galanskov, Dobrovolsky, and Lashkov.[78]

I said, "Guys, people are already freely expressing their opinion, Amalrik's work has already been published,[79] the *Chronicle of Current Events* is coming out although in samizdat, and Valery Chalidze, whom I know very well, invites all the democrats over on his birthday."

Petr Iakir joked with Chalidze on that account, "Valera, if your ceiling would collapse, Russia would be spared from the democratic movement for the next decade." Everyone was there, including Chalidze's friend Boris Isaakovich Tsukerman. Those two physicists fulfilled the function of lawyers. Chalidze had already openly put out a samizdat collection with his address, telephone number, and name on it, and we were still playing games.[80] It was time to get out into the open. I said, "It's disgraceful that we're this way."

Then Meir jumped up; he couldn't sit still any longer. It was the first time that we started cursing. He yelled, "You adventurer, you want Jewish blood, you want us to get arrested, you want to cut down our movement at the root! We just got started, we've assembled a few dozen Jews around us and you want to destroy everything." He knew how to speak well. He raked me over the coals—it was terrible.

For the first time in my life, however, I started to object and said, "Meir, I won't argue with you. You are right. Maybe not everyone ought to do that, but those who want to should do so. Let's divide up: I'll be group *alef* and you will be group *bet*. We won't socialize together and if we need to communicate, then only via a public telephone or an intermediary. I shall be *treif* (nonkosher) and you'll be *kosher*. Period." Khavkin supported me and we decided on this plan and dispersed. But this idyll lasted only about three months. Then everything got mixed up together.

There's a whole story connected with our first letter. David Drabkin wrote it in September 1969. Later he began to write well and his letters circulated at the synagogue, but this first letter was awful. It was just five to six lines: "We do not understand the Soviet regime's reason for forcibly detaining us in this country," he wrote. And then he thought it was a great discovery to refer to Auschwitz. In short, we edited the letter. Drabkin made a big fuss, but he corrected it.

This was the so-called "Letter of the 10."[81] When he left, Khavkin contrived to carry it out of the country in the picture tube of his television. Of course, at that time, he was frisked in a thorough manner. After an hour, when the frisk had not yet ended, I shouted to Tina Brodetsky that all the signatories to the letter should run home and clear out any incriminating material from their apartments. I didn't know at the time where he had hidden the letter. I thought perhaps it was in the buckle of his pants as we had often discussed, but he had a better idea; he hid it in the television tube. I thought that if they found the letter, they would see all our names and would go immediately to carry out searches in our apartments. Therefore we had to safeguard them quickly.

Later, when I began to tell David Khavkin what a commotion his search had caused among those who came to bid him farewell, he smiled and said unhurriedly, "I was thoroughly 'stuffed.' It was not only the television picture tube; I also took out the insides and stuffed a dozen condensers. They searched me for two days and didn't find anything."

Other letters and documents of the Soviet Jewish activists reached the foreign press by different means, as Svechinsky explained:[82]

KOSHAROVSKY: *How did you contact the foreign correspondents?*

SVECHINSKY: The Jews had periodic meetings with the correspondents. Drabkin and Khavkin somehow managed to meet them, but we lacked the reliable, durable connection that the democrats had. As soon as something happened to them, it immediately became known in the West. I urged Petr Iakir, "Petia, do a good deed for the Jewish movement. After all, you're a Jew, Petia!" "You son of a gun," said Petia, "Okay, I'll introduce you to a correspondent. Meet me this evening at the Mayakovsky subway station."

I came to the subway stop and saw Petia; his wife, Valiusha; Viktor Krasin, of course; and a tall, foreign-looking fellow in a stylish fall coat. Petia, as always, was a little tipsy. "Here, let me introduce you," he said, pointing to me, "A Jew, their leader. And this one," he said, pointing to the foreigner, "Adam Kellett-Long, the representative for Reuters in the Soviet Union. Good luck." We walked together down Kalyaevskaya Street to the apartment where correspondents were living.

Kellett-Long was very interested in me because he hadn't met with any Jews yet, and this was a hot topic for New York Jews and for Americans in general. He had already met Tatars and (democratic) dissidents and evangelists, even Volga Germans, but no Jews. We talked the whole way. I told him all about our movement, whether there were many young people or older ones, what was happening with regard to emigration and anti-Semitism; in short, about everything. He posed intelligent questions. Near his house, we exchanged telephones and addresses and parted. Then we began to speak over the phone. He called me and I called him freely. Kellett-Long introduced me to the *Washington Post* correspondent Frank Starr and we became quite friendly. He was simply a wonderful person. I often visited him in America and stayed there. We did something good in connection with the well-known television interview when they assembled the "court" Jews: Bystritsky, Raikin, and General Dragunsky were there.[83]

KOSHAROVSKY: *And Raikin participated?*

SVECHINSKY: Yes, it was obligatory. I remember how he participated. He was dragged out to the stage as if he were a marionette; he looked at the floor, mumbled something, and left the stage as if he had a heart problem. Bystritsky sat like the heroine Aksinia from the novel *Quiet Flows the Don,* nodding her head as if she wanted to say, "What nonsense this is, what is this Israel, what is this?" It was shameful! A terrible thing! It was 1970. After that, Chalidze phoned me and said, "Vilia, I couldn't sleep all night because of you. I wrote a text. If one of you is willing to sign it, I'll be happy." I ran over to him and took the text. It seemed splendid to me then, and until this day I think it is an excellent text. Valera cared a lot about our safety. From the legal point of view, the text was irreproachable. It became known as the "Letter of the 39."

KOSHAROVSKY: *Why did he do that?*

SVECHINSKY: Why not? After all, we were in touch. Chalidze sympathized with us a lot. He is a very intelligent person and understood very well what the Jewish movement was and what the Jews represent in the history of mankind. He didn't need to be convinced.

We signed the letter at Drabkin's place. He thought that I wrote it, but I didn't want to lie and I said that Chalidze wrote the letter. To this day, I don't know how I got out of there alive. Drabkin was hopping mad. He screamed that I was betraying the Jewish people, I was going to the goyim, we were again going to them for help as if they would save us. What a disgrace! He screamed fiercely. I calmed him down and said, "Look, this is a very respected person who wrote this. Thanks to such people, we have raised our voice. These people set an example for us. He shares our pain and of his own will feels compelled to write a letter for our Jewish cause without asking or demanding anything, but he will be happy if as many people as possible sign it—and that is his compensation."

Drabkin consented, and I think he signed first. Another thirty-eight people signed the letter. It worked out well. The next day we met Frank Starr near the old Moscow circus. We went down the steps and into the circus courtyard so that if I succeeded in conveying the letter to him, it would be in his hands, not mine. Frank, after all, had immunity—he couldn't be stopped on the street and frisked. The correspondents understood this very well and at meetings they would propose, "Well, quickly, give it to me and then we'll talk." I arranged my own press conference for Frank and explained everything.

We also sent a copy to Leonid Zamiatin, the Soviet spokesman,[84] but he, naturally, did not respond to us. We, therefore, considered ourselves free to publish it wherever possible. Frank glanced over the letter, evaluated its worth, and said, "Onward, fellows, stand firm." Marik Elbaum and I left, grabbed a taxi, and spent one and a half rubles of public money on this matter. Usually we were not such big spenders, but we didn't know whether or not we were being followed, and it was easier to check in a taxi. We verified that no one was following us.

In the morning Ester Isaakovna Eizenshtat phoned me: "Vilia, I listened to our letter! How could it be? After all, it seems like I just signed it, and it is already being broadcast on *Radio Liberty*. It's a kind of a miracle." "They have a speedy way of sending things," I said, "teletypes . . ."

David Drabkin's signature on the letter was indeed the first. It was followed by the signatures of Lev Freidin, Boris Shlaen, and Dora Koliaditsky. Among the signatories were Tina Brodetsky, Vladimir Prestin, Vladimir and Maria Slepak, Leonid Libkovsky, Vitaly Svechinsky, and Yosif Kazakov. The signature of the noted democrat, poet, and mathematician Julius Telesin concluded the list. It was number forty. The "Letter of 39" was thus really a "Letter of 40" but Telesin's signature was added after the letter had been sent abroad.

Svechinsky described the drama that attended some of the activity:[85]

SVECHINSKY: It was an era of petitions. Next was the "Letter of 25," followed by letters from Riga, Kiev, Kharkov, and Vilnius. Then Meir Gelfond phoned me, berated me in prison-camp style, and said afterwards, "What are you doing? You are robbing me of my comrades in the most scandalous way. You have left me all alone."

We met and decided that the epoch of samizdat had ended and an open struggle would begin, at least on the level of the printed word.

Then Frank Starr introduced me to an astonishing person, the correspondent of the Norwegian paper *Aftenposten blat*, Per Hege, who became my friend. Later he visited me in Haifa and stayed at my place. One time he got into trouble because he got caught sending Solzhenitsyn's material to the West. At that time, there was a rule that if the correspondent of any newspaper was expelled as persona non grata, then that newspaper was not permitted to have representatives in Moscow. They would punish the newspaper, which, as we know, is a commercial enterprise. But Per somehow was not expelled from the USSR, and he forwarded hundreds of sheets of material for me. The problems of Soviet Jewry became well known and there was a wave of petitions. Housewives began to write letters of protest about how they were insulted or that they had a granddaughter in Israel and hadn't seen her for a long time. And he took it all, the poor guy.

KOSHAROVSKY: *When did the regime start putting on the pressure?*

SVECHINSKY: Sometime in April 1970, I was going to work at Moszhilproekt [the state architectural design office], which is near the Lubianka prison on Kuibyshev Street. I was on a trolleybus and turned around: there was the familiar mug of Iakir's KGB tail. Petia once pointed him out to me. I thought to myself that this time, apparently, he's after me. I looked out the window: a series of Volga cars was following the trolley—four—tailing but not demonstratively. They accompanied me to my place of work. When I went out to dine, they were still waiting there. In the evening, they accompanied me home—that is, this was round-the-clock tailing. Then I came down with flu and stayed home for three days. When I left the house to go to the clinic, a woman was following me. This continued for two and a half months until June 15, 1970, when they arrested people in connection with the airplane hijacking plot. I met with Per Hege during this time that I was being tailed. I managed to break away from them with the help of a few tricks in the subway. I exited at the Mayakovsky station and my handsome Per was standing there in striped red-and-white gaiters, a beret on his head, and some crazy jacket. He was visible a kilometer away. "Per, you fine fellow, you really stand out!" I said. "Why, are you embarrassed?" he asked, smiling. "I was being tailed but I managed to get away," I said. "Well, all in vain," smiled Per, "look over there, they followed me all the way."

I look and see a KGB agent standing openly and brazenly looking at us with his car waiting there. "Your belly is really protruding!" noted Per, who didn't stop smiling. "Well, yes," I answered somewhat anxiously, "I'm completely stuffed. Let's get into the car fast."

We got into the car and he headed for the Belarus train station while I unloaded all my material and put it under the seat. The tails were following us. The light was red but Per continued on the red across the entire Belarus Square whereas the tails were reluctant to run the light and stopped. Driving very fast, he went to Dynamo, where he made a right turn and tossed me into a snowdrift. I ran to my friends to drink coffee and he proceeded on with all the material. I remember that he was a big adventurer, my Per. Sometimes my heart simply skipped a few beats.

Those labeled the "Jews of Silence" by Elie Wiesel thus began to acquire a voice,[86] gradually gaining confidence and strength. This voice of protest evoked a broad response in the West among those who were fighting for Soviet Jews' emigration. Freedom of emigration and the cultural rights of national minorities had long been a generally accepted norm in the enlightened world; therefore, information received from activists harmed the Soviet propaganda campaign abroad and frequently put the Soviet leaders in an awkward position.

No one at the time could predict the consequences of these actions for the activists themselves: would it become a lucky ticket for emigration or a cause for retribution against those who disturbed the peace? Perhaps they would encounter a blank wall. In any case, the transition from underground samizdat to open protest was difficult to stop.

Jews became bolder about signing collective declarations. The small stream quickly turned into a powerful torrent of appeals, letters, petitions, and declarations. They went from every corner of the Soviet Union to Israel, international organizations, the American Congress, and political and social figures in the West. Even when sending appeals to official Soviet bodies (the general prosecutor, the interior minister, the administrative organs of the Central Committee, the chairman of the Council of Ministers, the Presidium of the Supreme Soviet, the general-secretary of the CPSU Central Committee, and so forth), the activists took care that copies of the documents reached the West. Sometimes this was the sole point of the appeal. The torrent gathered strength together with the growth of emigration and public support from abroad.[87]

The Hijacking Attempt and the Leningrad Trials

Many activists of the Zionist movement in the Soviet Union switched to open protest against the regime's emigration policy in 1969. They expected their supporters in the West to do the same. Around 1970 the conditions seemed suitable: the opposition organization grew quantitatively and qualitatively, the potential for détente increased internationally, and the Soviet Union acceded to pressure from the West and did not react to open protest with massive repressions. By the end of 1970 the Leningrad hijacking trial marked a watershed after which the Jewish establishment in the West joined the open struggle.

Although the authorities began issuing a limited number of exit visas at the end of 1968, the amount was inadequate to meet the demand. In 1968 a total of 231 people left the country, and in 1969, 3,033 people.[88] This small stream served the regime's interest of getting rid of the active Zionists and troublemakers who had raised their heads after the Six-Day War. Instead of tamping down the interest in emigration, however, these measures only whetted the appetite for it by demonstrating that departure was possible.

Not surprisingly, therefore, some hotheads among the activists sought to leave by circumventing the border control. People testified about various plans: crossing the border with Finland, escaping in an air balloon, or even hijacking a submarine. An activist from Rostov (now a professor at Ben Gurion University of the Negev) considered swimming to Turkey. These plans, as a rule, terminated at the preparatory stage because of the high risk and extreme complexity of carrying them out. But not all plans ended that way.

One of the attempts to cross the border illegally by hijacking an airplane was destined to mark a turning point in the struggle for freedom of emigration.[89] The idea belonged to Mark Dymshits, a former military pilot, who understood that he could not obtain permission to leave the ordinary way. Mark had a difficult life: at the age of fifteen he lost his parents during the wartime blockade of Leningrad and was sent to an orphanage. Although he suffered in full measure from state and everyday anti-Semitism of the Stalin period, he was not broken.

Knowing firmly that his place was in Israel, he harbored the idea of escape for many years. Aware that he could not realize his plan alone, he looked for companions. He found them after meeting Hillel Butman.[90] Butman became fired up with Mark's idea to hijack an airplane, but doubts remained because the risk was enormous. After lengthy preliminary conversations with Dymshits, Butman decided to discuss the issue with the committee of the Leningrad organization. The majority of the committee hesitated. Butman found encouragement in the fact that no one immediately objected. Dymshits subsequently began to explore various options for accomplishing the plan while Butman began to select participants. In February 1970 Butman traveled to Riga, where his only close acquaintances were Arkady Shpilberg and Silva Zalmanson. Silva and her husband, Eduard Kuznetsov, both dreamed of leaving the country as quickly as possible. This represented a second fateful acquaintance. By April 1970 Butman had already selected about forty candidates for the planned action.

Decisions of the committee of the Leningrad organization were binding on all only if they were adopted unanimously. At the first discussion, only two of the five committee members who were present voted for the plan: Butman himself and Anatoly Goldfeld. The others did not want to participate but promised to help if the project were implemented. Gradually, however, their attitude changed from cautiously positive to cautiously negative and then to sharply opposed. Solomon Dreizner cooled to the idea. Goldfeld stopped speaking about his participation and influenced others toward rejection of the proposal. Vladimir Mogilever spoke out against it. In April 1970 the Leningrad organization held a conference at which its program and charter were discussed. David Chernoglaz, with Mogilever's support, spoke out against the proposed operation as one that could result in arrest of the members and cessation of all the organization's activities.[91]

David Maayan (formerly Chernoglaz) discussed the unfolding of events:[92]

KOSHAROVSKY: *Were you strongly opposed to the operation from the start?*

MAAYAN: Not completely. At first, the idea made a strong impression on me. It was striking and at first glance seemed very attractive. I didn't reject it outright.

KOSHAROVSKY: *How do you explain your sharp speech at the conference?*

MAAYAN: At that time, I already understood the problematic aspect of the operation, as did Mogilever. The authorities most likely knew about the organization's existence and activity; thus, the risk was too great. Moreover, we didn't form the organization for this kind of activity. We had other tasks and interests. The discussion at this expanded meeting, the likes of which did not occur before or afterward, represented a last desperate attempt to stop Butman. The idea was to play for time, let the idea run its course, to dissuade him or let him talk himself out of the idea.

The conference participants who heard about the idea for the first time were upset. Noting that according to the new charter, decisions of the conference were binding on everyone, Butman declared that he would leave the organization in the case of a negative decision and he would carry out the deed. It was then decided to return the discussion of the issue to the committee. Butman stuck to his guns although he was already beginning to be troubled by doubts. Finally, at one of the meetings, Grisha Vertlib threw him a life preserver: "Let's ask Israel. We'll do what they say." Everyone agreed, and the day of reckoning was delayed to everyone's satisfaction.

The answer from authorities in Israel was categorically negative. Butman submitted to the verdict, reported this to the other candidates for Operation "Wedding" (the code name for the plan), and withdrew from their group. Far from all of the participants, however, were willing to renounce the idea. Mark Dymshits, Eduard Kuznetsov, and Yosef Mendelevich became the driving force behind the operation. Even when Kuznetsov suggested delaying the plan for a year, the cool-headed resoluteness of Dymshits and the group's determination to try their luck prevailed.[93]

On June 15, 1970, twelve Jews, most of whom were from Riga, attempted to hijack a plane. They planned to fly to Sweden and from there to Israel. They targeted a small, twelve-seater AN-2 plane that flew a route from Leningrad's Smolny airport to the town of Priozersk, near the Finnish border. The hijacking group bought up all twelve tickets for the flight. However, they did not manage even to board the plane. They were all arrested on the tarmac.

Edward Kuznetsov recalled that day:[94]

KUZNETSOV: As someone who had already served time and not being the stupidest person on the planet, I understood, of course, that it was a hopeless affair. We had sixteen participants.[95] In order to reach this number, it was necessary to speak with hundreds of people. Those who rejected the idea were not obligated to keep the secret and they gossiped and whispered. Even those who were involved in the plan talked—human nature is such that a person can't keep quiet—whether to a friend or a lover. A leak was inevitable.

KOSHAROVSKY: *Why did you go for it despite everything?*

KUZNETSOV: My situation was rather complex. I had just served a seven-year sentence for dissident activity and was under administrative supervision.[96] I was being followed. If I was even minimally active, they would lock me up for practically nothing. Thus, for me, the issue was whether I would be arrested for a deed or simply for no reason.

I pride myself on the fact that at the time, I already perceived the trend that later led to détente. I was in contact with important figures. They believed in an old theory: "We understand that everything is collapsing, that they are all scoundrels, but decent people need to join the party and change everything from the inside." At the same time, these people understood that the economic situation was disastrous. The Soviet Union was ripe for détente, that is, in exchange for hard currency, grain, know-how, and all the rest, the regime was prepared to backtrack on some issues. It wasn't clear on which issues they would be willing to backtrack; perhaps, if we pressured them on the issue of emigration, they would make concessions. That was approximately my thought and I guessed right.

The regime, of course, drove us into a corner. People applied for exit visas several times and received refusals, and they did not have a ray of hope left: there was no work for them and they had been driven out of the institutes. A group of people assembled around us that wanted action, not discussions. They harbored certain illusions about me, thinking, "he's experienced, he knows how it's done." But, in fact, what did I understand? [Boris] Penson [a participant in the hijacking plan] expressed our group's shared feeling about the regime: "Let them arrest us because afterward we'll probably be released." We acted out of a sense of hopelessness.

Looking at things soberly, I knew that they would lock us up. But if it was done quietly, we could be tried behind closed doors and no one would know about it. It was important for us that there be a scandal and in this respect our interests coincided with those of the KGB. It was also important for them to create a commotion with our arrest in order to point out: "Look at these supposed fighters for freedom of emigration! In fact, they are just ordinary bandits."

The team of "hijackers" had been tailed closely. Already in April 1970, KGB chairman Yuri Andropov reported to the Central Committee of the CPSU that the Leningrad Zionist organization together with Riga nationalists was planning a secret operation.[97] Subsequent to the June 15 arrests, the trial took place from December 15 to 24, 1970. The scenario and the outcome of this performance had been determined in advance. On December 21 the court announced the verdict. Kuznetsov and Dymshits received the most extreme punishment: the death sentence. In view of the circumstances of the case—the plan was not carried out and there were no consequences—the sentence seemed monstrously cruel. Other defendants received long sentences ranging from ten to fifteen years of imprisonment. After the death sentences, the doubts of activists were dispelled: the cause of Soviet Jews who wanted to leave was a just cause.

Protest letters from Soviet activists were read aloud on Israeli radio. There were many of them; Andrei Sakharov and Valery Chalidze were among those rights activists who spoke up on the issue. Spanish leader Francisco Franco subsequently repealed the death sentence of six Basque terrorists on December 30, 1970. To those sympathizing with the Leningrad defendants, this seemed like a wonderful coincidence. They waited, holding their breath: would the regime now come to its senses? Golda Meir sent Franco an emissary asking him to repeal the death sentence. He did.

On December 31, 1970, the death sentences of Dymshits and Kuznetsov were commuted to fifteen years imprisonment for each. Soviet Zionists were proud and happy. They reveled in the victory in which, it seemed, they had played some role.[98]

The death sentences were commuted but people continued to suffer in the wake of the initial trial. Soviet authorities unleashed a wave of repressions accompanied by a powerful propaganda campaign. The repressions encompassed Leningrad, Riga, Kishinev, Odessa, Sverdlovsk, and Bendery (Bender, Moldova). A second Leningrad trial targeting the underground Zionist organization took place May 11–20, 1971. Among those sentenced, Hillel Butman received ten years, Mikhail Kornblit seven years, and Vladimir Mogilever four years, while Solomon Dreizner, Lev Korenblit, and Viktor Boguslavsky received three years each. The delay in conducting the second Leningrad trial and the other trials was, apparently, evoked by a desire to let the wave of protests subside. Moreover, the KGB had learned their lesson that trials against Jewish activists would attract the West's careful scrutiny and evoke sustained protests. Moscow, therefore, took direct control of the trials into its own hands, which were gentler than those of the Leningrad authorities. Overseas protests had taken on such an unprecedented scale that the very term "Leningrad Trial" became a synonym of cruelty and injustice. The regime thus decided not to link the trial against the underground Zionist organization to the "hijackers."

In the course of the year preceding the second Leningrad trial, the security services carried out dozens of searches and summoned hundreds of people for interrogations. Leningrad was purged broadly, deeply, and thoroughly. After the two Leningrad trials, Zionist activity in the city died down for several years.

Interrogations and arrests took place in Riga as well. On June 15, 1970, three people from Riga not related to the "hijacking" case were subjected to searches: Arkady Shpilberg, Boris Maftser, and Ruth Aleksandrovich. Interrogations followed the searches. The KGB summoned dozens of Jews as witnesses. They were asked to give testimony about the "anti-Soviet activity" of the suspects and to confess to their complicity. Boris Maftser and Arkady Shpilberg were arrested on August 4, 1970. On October 7 Ruth Aleksandrovich was arrested, ten days before her scheduled marriage to

Isai Averbukh in a Riga synagogue.[99] Mikhail Shepshelovich, active in samizdat activities, was arrested on October 15. On September 28, 1970, the case of Maftser and Shpilberg was separated from the "hijacking" case. All four, Maftser, Shpilberg, Averbukh, and Aleksandrovich, were accused of conducting anti-Soviet agitation and propaganda, and Maftser and Shpilberg were also charged with anti-Soviet organizational activity.

Aron (Arkady) Shpilberg talked about his roots and his path to activism and the Riga trial:[100]

SHPILBERG: My father was a Zionist. I first heard "Hatikvah" from him.

KOSHAROVSKY: *So you matured early?*

SHPILBERG: Our homeroom teacher at school was also the secretary of the [Communist] Party organization. When the "doctor-wreckers" were arrested in 1953, he informed us, fifteen-year-old schoolchildren, that agents of the espionage organization Joint had infiltrated everywhere and there was no doubt that they were among us, too.[101] There was one more Jew besides me in the class.

KOSHAROVSKY: *When did you become an activist?*

SHPILBERG: Only after meeting David Chernoglaz in 1964. We began to form Jewish groups. When we heard that people from Riga were leaving the country, we decided to go there and take a look. From a friend, I got the address of a fellow named Mark Blum and I went there. This Riga fellow played an important role in my life. He gave me a tape cassette with Hebrew songs, told me about the various directions of activities, and explained how to celebrate Jewish holidays. Sometime later a girl came to do training in Leningrad and brought me books by Dubnov from Blum. She later became my wife. We subsequently succeeded in exchanging a room in Leningrad for an apartment in Riga, and in October 1967 we moved there. Our decision was influenced not only by family circumstances but also by the fact that there was a small amount of immigration to Israel from Riga.

KOSHAROVSKY: *Did you know about the "hijackers" before your arrest?*

SHPILBERG: No. No one told me directly about it. At that time, I already had a daughter and my wife was in the ninth month of a second pregnancy.

KOSHAROVSKY: *Did you teach Hebrew?*

SHPILBERG: I found out that Shapiro's Hebrew dictionary appeared at the kiosk in the Electro-Technical Institute. That was in 1966. I had already received Shlomo Kodesh's handbook from Blum. I was later sent on a work assignment to Moscow, where an old Jew gave me several Hebrew lessons. After my return to Leningrad, I began to teach, but not in Riga where there were people on a higher level. I didn't see ulpans there; that was customary in Leningrad.

KOSHAROVSKY: *What were the charges against you?*

SHPILBERG: At first, treason, that is, as if I also participated in the hijacking attempt, but then I was charged with anti-Soviet activity.

KOSHAROVSKY: *Did you try to establish a branch of the Leningrad organization in Riga?*

SHPILBERG: I neither tried nor considered it right to create a formal organization. Why help the Soviet "justice system"? Even without an organization, we were very active.

KOSHAROVSKY: *But in Leningrad, you were a member of the organization?*

SHPILBERG: In Leningrad, I didn't oppose it.

KOSHAROVSKY: *You paid membership dues.*

SHPILBERG: What does "membership dues" mean? In Riga we also collected money but it isn't necessary to call this dues: we needed it for our activity. We had to buy paper and typewriters. All this was done in Riga. Moreover, Riga provided literature for Leningrad and other places. In Riga there were people who were willing to work selflessly. Many of them, unlike those in Leningrad, did not have a higher education but they were remarkable people.

KOSHAROVSKY: *Yes, I remember, in Sverdlovsk, the samizdat was also from Riga. Did you have your own group?*

SHPILBERG: Yes.

KOSHAROVSKY: *How many people?*

SHPILBERG: Let's say that I collected dues from four people.

KOSHAROVSKY: *What happened during the investigation?*

SHPILBERG: For ten days, I refused to testify at all. Then, when they began to read me the testimony of Dreizner and Maftser, I began to testify about what they already knew. For example, not long before my arrest, I sent a letter to Brezhnev that was published in the West. They asked whether it was mine. "Yes," I said, "and now, too, I still think the same way." All the material against me was based on my activity in Riga because I had left Leningrad in 1967.

The items in the charge against Shpilberg compiled by the KGB deputy head Viktor Chebrikov included participation in the preparation and dissemination of Leon Uris's book *Exodus*. It was claimed that Uris's novel defamed Soviet policy. Authorities charged Shpilberg with distributing the pamphlet *For the Return of the Jewish People to the Homeland,* and they cited him for receiving copies of *Iton,* no. 1, and *Iton,* no. 2, which supposedly contained slanderous fabrications regarding the domestic and foreign policy of the Soviet Union.[102] Shpilberg was charged with Article 65, which in the Latvian criminal code corresponded to the Russian republic's Article 70, for anti-Soviet agitation and propaganda.[103]

Around the Soviet Union in 1970–71, there were many other cases of inflated charges based on supposedly slanderous or anti-Soviet statements and reading material. One case involved librarian Reiza Palatnik in Odessa. On December 1, 1970, Palatnik was arrested and charged with disseminating fabrications of a slanderous nature that defamed the Soviet state and social order. She defiantly asserted her innocence at her trial in June 1971.[104] In Sverdlovsk, following the arrest of Valery Kukui and Yuli Kosharovsky for sending a letter protesting the Leningrad trial sentences, a press campaign was mounted against them.[105] Kosharovsky was detained and told his activities surpassed slander, approaching the more serious Article 70, for anti-Soviet agitation and propaganda. Kukui had it worse: he was tried in June 1971 and sentenced to three years.

According to the regime's plan, the wave of judicial persecutions was supposed to destroy the movement's organizational structure, intimidate activists, and diminish the level of pro-emigration feelings. The extrajudicial harassment that encompassed an even broader circle of people pursued the same goal. The effect, however, was contrary to expectations. The judicial persecutions and accompanying propaganda campaign created an atmosphere of distrust and permissiveness toward the Jews, which was utilized not only by the KGB but also by all kinds of rogues, careerists, and anti-Semites. It was sufficient to whisper confidentially "to the right person" that someone was planning to emigrate or had fallen in with a Zionist band and his career was finished. One could inform on a Jewish person and that person would be worked over by KGB operatives. No Jewish person felt secure under such conditions, which intensified rather than reduced pro-emigration attitudes. An even more striking metamorphosis occurred among Zionist activists. The numerous foreign organizations supporting Soviet Jewry regarded these people as real-life heroes. The courage and dignity with which those arrested conducted themselves during trials, the numerous appeals by activists to Western public opinion, and the release of a segment of the movement's leadership had their effect: the strength and scope of the protests in the West increased sharply.

Striving for détente and Western technologies, the Soviet Union was vulnerable to overseas criticism. Thanks to powerful Western support, the persecuted pariahs of Soviet society began to acquire a form of "international immunity." Quickly realizing what force was restraining the repressive services' punitive sword, Zionist activists tried with all their might to inform their friends and supporters abroad about the regime's illegal actions. The KGB had to take this into account.

Anti-Zionist trials were not conducted in Moscow at the end of the 1960s or the first half of the 1970s. At the same time, a significant group of Moscow activists succeeded in obtaining exit visas. Consequently, people began to regard activism in Moscow as a kind of trampoline for emigration, which facilitated the flourishing of Zionist activity at the beginning of the 1970s.

In Riga, a former Zionist center, the activists' ranks were considerably thinned by the departure of several activists, and in Leningrad as well as Riga the severe judicial and extrajudicial persecutions took their toll. A large number of people, some of whom were barely connected or not connected at all to Zionist activity, suffered. As a result, activism was associated with harsh prison terms and other harassments, and the level of activity declined in those places. These were not the only factors that led to the transfer of the center of Zionist activity to Moscow in the 1970s.

1. Early Prisoners of Zion, Dubrovlag labor camp, Mordovia, 1960. Front row, left to right: Dov Sperling, David Khavkin, Yosef Shnaider. Collection of Joseph Schneider, Yuli Kosharovsky archives.

2. Refuseniks in Sverdlovsk in 1972. Left to right: Leonid Zabelyshensky, Mark Levin, Yuli Kosharovsky. Collection of Enid Wurtman.

3. Yuli Kosharovsky, Moscow, 1973. Yuli Kosharovsky archives.

4. At the Summer Universiade, Moscow, August 1973, refuseniks Bella Palatnik and Dov (Dmitry) Ramm, their children Shoshana and Arie, and Bella's mother, Bronia Liokumovich, bravely hold up a sign with SHALOM in Hebrew to welcome the Israeli delegation. Collection of Avital and Natan Sharansky.

5. Hebrew teachers, Moscow, 1972. Standing, left to right: Baruch Ainbinder, Dan Roginsky, Israel Palhan, Anatoly Libgober, Zeev Shakhnovsky, Mikhail Goldblat, Aleksei Levin. Seated, left to right: Sergei Gurvits, Leonid Ioffe, Zeev Zolotarevsky. Collection of Dan Roginsky, Yuli Kosharovsky archives.

6. Seeing off Marianna and Boris (Baruch) Ainbinder, along with Valentina and Dan Roginsky from Moscow, 1973. Boris and Dan were early Hebrew teachers in Moscow who transmitted news of the refuseniks abroad. Association "Remember and Save."

7. Refuseniks celebrate Yom Ha'atzmaut, Israel Independence Day, in Viatki Woods near Moscow, 1974. Collection of Enid Wurtman.

8. Aliya activists in Moscow, 1975. Front row, left to right: Vitaly Rubin, Anatoly Sharansky, Ida Nudel, Alexander Lerner. Second row: Vladimir Slepak, Lev Ovsishcher, Alexander Druk, Yosif Beilin, Dina Beilin. Collection of Avital and Natan Sharansky.

9. Refuseniks meet with Israeli sportsmen in Lunts Meadow, 1975. Standing, left to right: Zeev Shakhnovsky, Menachem Berkowitz, Maria Slepak, Alexander Lunts, Vladimir Slepak. Seated: Anatoly Sharansky. Collection of Enid and Stuart Wurtman.

10. Refuseniks and Israeli sportsmen celebrate Succot together in Lunts Meadow, 1975. Inna and Igor Uspensky collection, Association "Remember and Save."

11. Avital Sharansky and Elie Wiesel address a Soviet Jewry program in a Montreal synagogue, November 1975. Avital made a passionate appeal on behalf of her husband, Anatoly Sharansky, who was enduring harassment by authorities in the Soviet Union. Collection of Avital and Natan Sharansky.

12. Yuli Kosharovsky, Inna Kosharovsky, and Leonid (Ari) Volvovsky in Moscow, enjoying an evening of Hebrew song with musicians and refuseniks. Hanukah, 1975. Collection of Inna and Yuli Kosharovsky.

13. Ida Nudel and Dina Beilin wearing necklaces with Jewish symbols hidden among the beads designed by Bobbie Morgenstern for distribution to Soviet Jews. Moscow, October 1976. Collection of Enid Wurtman.

14. Yuli Kosharovsky, founder of the unofficial Engineering Seminar for refuseniks, on the left, with seminar participant Igor Abramovich. Moscow, October 1976. Collection of Enid Wurtman.

15. Inna Kosharovsky, Enid Wurtman, and Yuli Kosharovsky with Yuli's Hebrew teaching aids. Moscow, October 1976. Collection of Enid Wurtman, Yuli Kosharovsky archives.

16. Aliya activists in Moscow, October 1976. Front row, left to right: Yosif Beilin, Dina Beilin, Enid Wurtman. Back row, left to right: Yuri Berkovsky, Rita Beilin, Anatoly Sharansky, Leonid (Ari) Volvovsky, Ida Nudel. Collection of Enid Wurtman.

3

Context and Strategies

New Leadership in Moscow

The first worldwide Jewish conference devoted to the issue of Soviet Jewry was convened in Brussels from February 23 to 25, 1971, two months after the first Leningrad hijacking trial. More than fifteen hundred people representing Western Jewish communities from thirty-eight countries met in Brussels.[1] Participants in the conference included politicians David Ben-Gurion and Menachem Begin and intellectuals Saul Bellow and Elie Wiesel along with many other distinguished guests. Soviet Jewry was represented by recent arrivals from the Soviet Union, including Vitaly Svechinsky. At the Brussels Conference, world Jewry declared its unconditional support for its brethren in the USSR whose efforts to bring about a national revival brought on cruel reprisals.

The First Brussels Conference

The First Brussels Conference of 1971 had great importance as an international forum for bringing together Western Jewish communities and groups concerned about Soviet Jewry after the Leningrad hijacking trial. Soviet authorities' intense campaign of anti-Zionist propaganda in response to the announcement of the conference suggested their sensitivity to such an endeavor. The conference also highlighted, however, the challenges attending this solidarity: Nativ, which organized the conference, did not welcome the participation of New York firebrand Meir Kahane, who arrived unannounced to promote his program. The detention and expulsion of Kahane from Belgium aroused controversy among the attendees. The anodyne proposals of the conference organizers for quiet diplomacy and designing a symbol for the movement could not compete with Kahane's scandal. The tension highlighted issues that would continue to complicate relations between the established organizations and Western grassroots activists.

The attention of the West compounded problems the regime encountered in corralling Jewish national activists. As we saw in chapter 2, in the first years after the Six-Day War, experienced Zionists, many of whom had survived arrests, interrogations, camps, and prisons, played the primary role in leading a Jewish national revival. Influenced primarily by the Holocaust and by the creation of the State of Israel, and having witnessed the intensified anti-Semitism that ensued, these Zionists had lost all faith in Soviet ideals and feared neither the regime nor informers. They generally did not seek to establish a formal leadership or centralized management nor did they favor rash or risky operations, as they had felt on their own flesh the high price to be paid for such endeavors. Uncompromisingly dedicated to the cause, they strove to transmit their passion and experience to an expanding circle of activists.

In light of the prominence and authority that many of these initial leaders of the Jewish national revival had acquired in the West, it was simpler for authorities to let them go. This would "permit the elimination of nationalistically inclined individuals and religious fanatics who exert a harmful influence on their surroundings," as KGB chairman Yuri Andropov and Foreign Minister Andrei Gromyko explained in a written report to the CPSU Central Committee.[2]

From 1969 to 1971, the families of dozens of veteran activists from the Baltics received exit visas, including the Slovin, Garber, Valk, and Shperling families. In the fall of 1969, David Khavkin, the Moscow "Moses," left the country. At the beginning of 1971, Vitaly Svechinsky arrived in the West in time to attend the First Brussels Conference on Soviet Jewry. David Drabkin, Meir Gelfond, and Mikhail Zand left the USSR and immigrated to Israel in the spring and summer of 1971. The arena was cleared for a new generation of leaders. Three people immediately stood out among the Moscow activists: Viktor Polsky, Vladimir Slepak, and Vladimir Prestin. Alexander Lerner and Alexander Voronel later joined their ranks.

Viktor Polsky, who was already more than forty years old at the time, possessed clear leadership qualities. Tall, sporty, and very articulate, he attracted people to himself.

Viktor Polsky discussed his experiences and the role he played:[3]

KOSHAROVSKY: *From what institute did you graduate?*

POLSKY: The Moscow Engineering and Physics Institute. I received my diploma on December 11, 1952.

KOSHAROVSKY: *What a date you picked! The very height of the campaign against "rootless cosmopolitans" and the start of the Doctors' Plot case.*

POLSKY: I applied for graduate school. You can imagine how *they* looked at me. I wasn't asked why I had applied or what I wanted. I was asked, "Who advised you to apply to graduate school?" I was the best student in my year—I had a diploma with distinction and before that a medal in school.

KOSHAROVSKY: *And what happened to you after that?*

POLSKY: I was directed to the Physics Institute. My fellow students were welcomed with open arms, but I was rejected. I went to clarify matters but it was useless. Then I was sent to the Eighty-Eighth Scientific Research Institute. I was booted out of there even faster because the Doctors' Plot had already started. Then it was decided deceptively to send me to Norilsk [in the far north]. I was told, "Here is a good enterprise not far from Moscow." I was young and trusting. I signed and then when I found out what they had in mind, I said, "I won't go." *They* brought a suit against me. The trial was scheduled for March 26, 1953, but the "mustachioed man" [Stalin] died on March 5, and I was included in the first amnesty.

Like other Jews of our group, I received a "free" diploma and had to find work on my own.[4] When I would phone, I was told, "Yes, yes, come, we need specialists like that." When I arrived, however, I would always hear the same conclusion: "Yes, you have the right specialty, but your profile is wrong." That was our Jewish lot until there was some easing of the regime.

Finally I was accepted at the design office of the Electric Lamp factory. The head of the factory was an intelligent Russian fellow, Tsvetkov, a Hero of Socialist Labor. He assembled an excellent design team that included a large number of Jews. They worked well and he received Stalin prizes. He thus kept his Jews and later hired even more when there was a relaxation in such discriminatory practices.

Dozens of Jews who worked in the design office found each other and began to discuss Jewish issues. In 1957 the Sixth World Festival of Youth and Students took place in Moscow and we chased after the Israeli delegation. That was the year of my marriage, and a year later my daughter Marina was born. People began to return from the camps and we gained new acquaintances. Our Jewish consciousness began to develop.

KOSHAROVSKY: *You had not yet come across Svechinsky or Khavkin?*

POLSKY: Not yet. However, we received literature from the Baltics. Lea Slovin would come to us. David Drabkin had a channel. We—that is, Drabkin, Libkovsky, and I—translated, copied, bound, and disseminated the novel *Exodus*. This book transformed my mother from a woman who had been intimidated by relentless persecution into a Zionist. For me, this was incontestable proof of the novel's power to exert a strong emotional effect. Previously mama not only did not support Zionist ideas but in fact opposed them.

In 1969 I received my first invitation from Israel. Around this time, people began to emigrate, and we also prepared to leave.

I wasn't able to apply for an exit visa before 1970, because my older brother was fatally ill with leukemia. He was an air force lieutenant colonel and he died in 1970. In the fall of 1970, I submitted documents for a visa. Then I participated in the famous demonstration in the reception room of the Supreme Soviet on February 28, 1971. We were promised there that our applications would be reviewed and, indeed, within a week, the first group, including Meir Gelfond, received permission. The next group was much larger. I think it left in October or November. Yuli Nudelman and other activists were in that group. Misha Zand left in the summer.

KOSHAROVSKY: *How was the issue of leadership decided then?*

POLSKY: It wasn't decided by a vote. People gained prominence in the course of events. Those who had more ideas, showed greater initiative, helped others more, composed collective letters and appeals came into leadership roles.

KOSHAROVSKY: *When did you feel that you had become a leader?*

POLSKY: It's hard to say. Perhaps in 1971, or 1972.

KOSHAROVSKY: *That is, after the group of former leaders left?*

POLSKY: Yes. Then the initiative moved to me and I handled financial activity as well.

KOSHAROVSKY: *Did you have links with Nativ?*[5]

POLSKY: Nativ was not in contact with me in particular.

KOSHAROVSKY: *How did you solve the problem of aiding refuseniks who lacked means?*

POLSKY: Misha Zand handled the public funds; when he emigrated, he left everything with me. Other people who wanted to leave money also came to me, as did those who were seeking funds in order to cover the expenses of leaving. Volodia Zaretsky, who left the Soviet Union in the fall of 1971, provided me with a direct link to Israel. As our guardian in matters of the Lishka, he accomplished great things and he deserves due credit.

KOSHAROVSKY: *I recall that many people would gather during your weekly telephone conversation with Zaretsky. This was a very important channel of communication.*

POLSKY: Yes. I received information from the Baltics, Georgia, Siberia, and Sverdlovsk. I considered it my duty to carry out all requests quickly and reliably.

KOSHAROVSKY: *Who became the leader after the departure of Gelfond and Svechinsky?*

POLSKY: I think that Misha Zand became the leader but more a spiritual than operative one. After his departure, this place was empty, and I filled it without a vote or elections.

Nativ—Lishkat hakesher—Halishka

The Nativ (Hebrew for Path) agency, also known as Lishkat hakesher (The Liaison Bureau) or simply the Lishka (Halishka, The Bureau), was founded in 1952 by Shaul Avigur as a mostly clandestine operation dedicated to investigating the problems faced by Jews in Eastern Europe and finding ways to bring them to Israel. Nativ worked behind the scenes to mobilize and coordinate international support through informational campaigns, conferences, and personal contacts. They supported research on Jews in Eastern Europe and the Soviet Union and helped establish and maintain communications with Soviet Jewish activists.

Some activists considered Viktor Polsky to be the leader, while others looked to Vladimir Slepak. An open, friendly, accessible person lacking elitist airs, he immediately won people over. At his open home in the very center of Moscow, he hosted an endless stream of Muscovite and out-of-town activists and Jews from all over the Soviet Union who sought his advice. Foreign visitors usually gathered there and Western journalists trusted Volodia implicitly. People would sit at the Slepaks' home until way past midnight, sometimes remaining overnight in the two-room communal apartment. The unceasing human conveyor belt sometimes had its effect on Vladimir, who could be half dozing without taking his open gaze from his interlocutor. However, his mind always remained completely lucid.

Polsky and Slepak were two different personality types. Whereas Viktor was drawn to politics, discipline, and the establishment, Volodia had an independent and warm nature and was always ready to help.

From a conversation with Slepak:[6]

KOSHAROVSKY: *Where did you study?*

SLEPAK: At the Moscow Aviation Institute. I graduated in 1950, specializing in the field of radio electronics. I received a work assignment to Novosibirsk. According to the rules at that time, I had to do my diploma work there.[7] But because this was at the height of the anti-cosmopolitan campaign, I received a refusal: after all, I was a Jew and had been abroad—even though that was during my childhood.

KOSHAROVSKY: *How did Zionism enter your life?*

SLEPAK: Via Drabkin or, more accurately, via his wife, Noia, who was educated in Riga in a Jewish academic high school and grew up in a Jewish environment. We lacked this in Russia and therefore we became cosmopolitans. My first moment of lucidity occurred during the period of the Doctors' Plot. I then understood that something was not right in the

Soviet kingdom. It was a sick society. But I understood nothing more than that. I was twenty-five and I was still a zealous Komsomol member.[8]

KOSHAROVSKY: *And then there was the Sinai Campaign in 1956.*

SLEPAK: I took an interest in it but nothing more. Israel was somewhere far away in a fog.

KOSHAROVSKY: *And then there was the Six-Day War.*

SLEPAK: Yes, indeed! Then I understood that I had to go there. In my situation, however, nothing might come of it—it could remain a dream for my entire life. After all, since 1962 I had been working as the director of a laboratory and the chief designer of an anti-aircraft defense system for command points. Not bad, huh?

KOSHAROVSKY: *And when did you decide that you had to leave?*

SLEPAK: We decided to apply when we learned that Jews were leaving from Riga. Until then, I didn't know how it was done. And suddenly someone asked, "Do you want to meet with people from Riga who are immigrating to Israel?"

Of course I did. I thus met Mark Blum [Mordecai Lapid],[9] to whom my wife, Masha, and I gave our pertinent personal information.[10] It was November or December 1968. Then I informed my father, who raised a big fuss.

KOSHAROVSKY: *And [he] refused to sign a statement with his opinion about your departure?*

SLEPAK: He wasn't even close. I said to him, "Write that you are against." He said, "I won't sign anything!" and that was it. He promised to do everything in his power to prevent us from leaving. Later, however, our documents were accepted without his opinion on the matter.

He severed all relations with us. I found out how he was doing via my cousin, his nephew. My brother said that my father ostensibly did not want to hear about us, but our neighbor admitted that occasionally my father would come and ask permission to sit near the door and listen to his grandchildren's voices. He was already seventy-five years old.

I was arrested eight years after we applied to leave. My father's second wife said that when he learned this, he went and sat on the couch in the corner and began to rock back and forth and to mutter something in an unintelligible language. She was Russian and didn't know this language.

He didn't eat, only drank, and three days later, he died of a heart attack. For the entire three days, he sat on the couch.

KOSHAROVSKY: *Volodia, how long did you work at the rank of chief designer?*

SLEPAK: Until I left work in 1969.

KOSHAROVSKY: *And in 1970, you already applied for an exit visa?*

SLEPAK: Impudent, wasn't I?

KOSHAROVSKY: *Some kind of daredevil. You probably had zero access?*

SLEPAK: On the contrary, I had first-level access.[11] I was a member of a state commission for selecting the country's anti-aircraft and anti-missile defense systems. The commission was headed by Col. General Tsyganov, the head of the country's anti-aircraft defense headquarters. That's the level it was. And I was the only non-Party person among them.

KOSHAROVSKY: *You applied before Polsky, Prestin, and Abramovich?*

SLEPAK: A little earlier. Vilia Svechinsky, David Khavkin, and Tina Brodetsky applied before me.

KOSHAROVSKY: *You decided and right away went for broke?*

SLEPAK: Not exactly. We got together and discussed matters. I even copied Hebrew textbooks with David Khavkin.

KOSHAROVSKY: *When?*

SLEPAK: In 1968 and 1969 by photographic copying. We rented a one-room apartment for the purpose. Not only textbooks. In Riga, *Iton* was published, and we also copied it.

KOSHAROVSKY: *Polsky and Prestin dealt with* Exodus?

SLEPAK: Yes, they worked on a typewriter. Later we got to know many Zionists. Once Izia Shmerler phoned from Novosibirsk—in Israel he became Izia Shamir—and said, "I made the acquaintance here of a girl at the KOGIZA warehouse." Do you remember, Yuli, it's that organization that distributes books among the stores? "Well, they got stuck with sixty copies of Shapiro's dictionary. Do you need them?" asked Izia. "In a hurry," I said. "You'll get them, but where can we get the money?" "How much is needed?" He named a sum. We announced a collection and sent him a money transfer.

For a long time, OVIR would not accept my application for an exit visa. It was useless to try to get a reference from work and my father wouldn't sign any paper. With the help of Volodia Prestin, I found a job at the Geophysics Trust near Moscow. It consisted of transferring data from a seismogram into a computer-compatible form. Prestin and I worked on this. He, it's true, mainly taught Hebrew.

KOSHAROVSKY: *Why did your house become the most frequented?*

SLEPAK: First of all, because of geography. We lived near the hotels where the foreigners stayed. They would arrive at night, drop their suitcases in their rooms, and come directly to me—even at three or four o'clock in the morning.

KOSHAROVSKY: *And within the movement?*

SLEPAK: Perhaps because of my brazenness and also because I knew some English. I would contact the correspondents.

KOSHAROVSKY: *Did you maintain relations with the general [democratic] dissidents?*

SLEPAK: Vilia Svechinsky introduced me to them.

KOSHAROVSKY: *Did you sympathize with them?*

SLEPAK: Of course.

KOSHAROVSKY: *Were you yourself prepared to participate in their affairs?*

SLEPAK: Yes, but with the intention of leaving.

KOSHAROVSKY: *Did it not seem contradictory to you that you were fighting for the reformation of a country from which you intended to emigrate?*

SLEPAK: I wanted to reform it in any case, at least regarding the issue of emigration.

KOSHAROVSKY: *But the dissidents had a much broader view: democracy, human rights.*

SLEPAK: I wasn't opposed to democracy or human rights. Now, too, I am not against that, and then it didn't repel me.

KOSHAROVSKY: *That is, even before the Jew in you awoke, the dissident already existed?*

SLEPAK: We understood that we were in our own closed circle and had to find a way out, to connect to Israel, but there was no Israeli embassy.

KOSHAROVSKY: *You did this with the help of the dissidents?*

SLEPAK: At first I gave them information to transmit to the foreign correspondents, who would dispatch it to the West. Then Volodia Bukovsky came to me and said, "I am being tailed so closely, I feel that I'll be taken any day." He brought with him correspondents from UPI and

Reuters, saying, "Work directly with them. We wasted about three hours and were able to come without the tails." Volodia, indeed, was taken two days later, and I was picked up on the day after our meeting, directly at the gateway of our building, after a meeting with a foreign correspondent. But, unlike Bukovsky, I received only fifteen days. That was in March 1971.

KOSHAROVSKY: *In March I also received my first fifteen-day sentence in Sverdlovsk. Was any reason given for your arrest?*

SLEPAK: "Refusal to obey police orders"—petty hooliganism. Sania [Slepak's older son] went to tell Bukovsky that I had been taken. Do you remember, in those days there were "magic slates," a children's toy: you write on the plastic part and then you lift it up off the bottom and all that was written disappears. Of course, there were listening devices all over Bukovsky's place so Sania wrote on such a plastic pad. Suddenly the door burst open and the KGB workers flew in. And the first thing they did was head for that writing pad, but Sania managed to erase it. He was detained and taken to the police station, where he was held for some time and then released, but Bukovsky was arrested.

KOSHAROVSKY: *In 1971 activists began collective marches to the supreme organs of power, demonstrations, and public hunger strikes. From your point of view at that time was there a leader or leadership group that stood out?*

SLEPAK: Formally, there was no leadership. Moreover, we had an agreed principle among ourselves that we didn't and would not have leaders or a formal organization. We could consult, help each other, and exchange information but we would not have an organization—we learned this from the Riga and Leningrad trials.

KOSHAROVSKY: *Many Jewish activists distanced themselves from general dissident activity. Lishkat hakesher objected to cooperation with the dissidents and even exerted pressure on some people.*

SLEPAK: And how!

KOSHAROVSKY: *Did they pressure you?*

SLEPAK: The guys from the establishment National Conference on Soviet Jewry told me secretly that Nehemiah Levanon said about me, "His arrival in Israel is undesirable."[12]

KOSHAROVSKY: *Because of your dissidence?*

SLEPAK: Not entirely. The Jackson-Vanik Amendment tried their patience. The Israelis kept drumming into us that we should behave quietly.

KOSHAROVSKY: *When did the pressure begin?*

SLEPAK: It continued all the time. I remember when Congressman Vanik, the initiator of the amendment in Congress, came to visit us and begged us to write that we were against it. Jackson stood firm but Vanik was broken. We were constantly pressured from Israel. When I was told that Levanon himself thought it was necessary to act quietly, and we would be brought out of the USSR by means of quiet diplomacy, I couldn't contain myself and said on the phone to Israel that if Levanon adheres to such an ideology, he should be driven from the leadership of the organization. At the time, I didn't even know what kind of organization.

KOSHAROVSKY: *What? They were against the Jackson-Vanik Amendment?*

SLEPAK: They were for it, but they thought one shouldn't actively advocate it.

Another of the leaders to emerge in the early years of Moscow's ascendancy in the national movement, Vladimir Prestin, was tall, wiry, and elegant looking. He had the reputation of being an exceptionally honest and principled person. People nicknamed him "the count." The basis for this was not only his noble bearing but also his origins: his father came from a line of Russian nobility and on the maternal side his grandfather was the noted compiler of the Hebrew-Russian dictionary, Feliks Lvovich Shapiro.

Prestin shared details about his remarkable family:[13]

KOSHAROVSKY: *The aristocratic line comes from your father?*

PRESTIN: Yes, with regards to aristocracy, I don't know, but they were noblemen. The counts, however, are Drabkin's invention. At first, I was teased as the count and then it somehow stuck. In my case, everything started with the grandfathers—from the Russian and Jewish sides. From the Jewish side, it was Shapiro, who wrote the famous dictionary. He was, of course, a completely unusual and very talented person.

KOSHAROVSKY: *Did you know him personally?*

PRESTIN: Yes. We lived in the same room for thirteen years.

KOSHAROVSKY: *Was your father persecuted because of his origins?*

PRESTIN: Yes.

KOSHAROVSKY: *In what year was he born?*

PRESTIN: Like my mother, in 1913.

KOSHAROVSKY: *That is, he was only four at the time of the revolution and grew up under the Soviet regime.*

PRESTIN: Yes, and they were such Komsomol members, mama especially. Father, in fact, restrained her in some matters. The Soviet regime carefully kept an eye on anyone in whom it took an interest. My father had to endure more than my Jewish stepfather, who was my father's friend. My mother married him after my father's death.

KOSHAROVSKY: *Did you know your father's parents?*

PRESTIN: His mother survived the blockade of Leningrad and died at the age of ninety. She studied at an institute for girls from the nobility and then in a conservatory. She used to sing at concerts. His father was one of the first radio operators in the Soviet Union. He was exiled. *They* eradicated the Russian part of my family. My grandfather married a second time—with Princess Khovansky. They were both exiled. And that was it. I don't know anything more about them.

KOSHAROVSKY: *There isn't even a grave?*

PRESTIN: Nothing.

KOSHAROVSKY: *What about your father?*

PRESTIN: When the war started, he volunteered for the army. During the war he taught radio technology at a tank school in Moscow. He died in 1942 and was buried in the Novodevichy cemetery.

I thus lost my father rather early and even before then, I didn't really know him well. After the war, we moved to Moscow, to the four-room apartment of my Jewish grandparents, which my grandfather had built at one time for himself and his three daughters. I was placed in a room with my grandfather.

KOSHAROVSKY: *Was there anything special about this room?*

PRESTIN: This room was different from all the other ones in the apartment. It was full of Jewish books and there wasn't one Russian book in it. Tall shelves extended from the floor to the ceiling, filled with Jewish books mainly in Yiddish and Hebrew.

KOSHAROVSKY: *Where did so many books in Hebrew come from?*

PRESTIN: Before the revolution, many works were translated into Hebrew: Russian classics, and the works of Jewish writers were published. You can't imagine what kind of a life there was in Hebrew, and my grandfather lived in this milieu! He taught Hebrew from the start of his residence in Petersburg. In the Jewish school he attended in Baku, studies were conducted in Hebrew. That was his world and he preserved it in his room. He had only three books in Russian: *Great Jews*, Dubnov's three-volume history, and the *Jewish Encyclopedia* in Russian.

KOSHAROVSKY: *Did this influence your development?*

PRESTIN: In some way, yes, but it's rather difficult to formulate. I related positively to my grandfather's activities, but I can't say that I took a particular interest in them at the time. However, from the age of ten, my grandfather saw to my upbringing. From 1945 to 1958, when I lived in that room, I was surrounded by Hebrew letters.

KOSHAROVSKY: *Did he try to teach you?*

PRESTIN: Never. Partly because of that, his daughters didn't know either Hebrew or Yiddish. My mother's husband was Russian. Her older sister was married to a Russian. That's how it was then. He didn't try to exert influence in any direction.

KOSHAROVSKY: *And when did you yourself begin to take an interest?*

PRESTIN: It was a long process that found expression in the idea that I didn't want to be ashamed of my Jewish mother.

KOSHAROVSKY: *That is, you sensed that there was something shameful about belonging to the Jewish people?*

PRESTIN: In a Russian milieu, I was considered Russian and heard and saw many anti-Semitic manifestations. They weren't directed at me, but I saw everything and that was nightmarish and shameful. In our courtyard, I was Shapiro. People knew the entire family very well. This was normal, however, and I didn't have any problems there. I was able to defend myself. Indeed, anti-Semitism gradually became stronger and some tough kid began to tease me. I dragged him along the asphalt in one case.

KOSHAROVSKY: *Was there any turning point in your life after which you felt yourself a Zionist and decided to get involved in practical activity?*

PRESTIN: After graduating from the institute in 1958, Lena [Vladimir Prestin's wife] was assigned to the Electric Lamp factory at which Polsky, Slepak, Drabkin, and Libkovsky worked. Lena fell in with this company and then also introduced me to it. I now think that she consciously shielded me from various Russian groupings. In fact, they never made sense to me.

KOSHAROVSKY: *Did you ever feel any duality? Both of your formative sides were mighty powerful.*

PRESTIN: No I didn't. After the war, I lived in a Jewish family and Jewish milieu, which was natural for me. There was no duality. Our group didn't understand that. The question that existed was whether it was necessary to leave. Yet it was natural that I, registered as a Russian, was in essence a Jew and the question didn't exist for me. I immediately married a Jewish woman and I chose her because of that.

KOSHAROVSKY: *When did you hold your first Zionist discussions?*

PRESTIN: Real, serious ones took place rather late, when I was thirty years old. Don't forget, it was 1964. Our son Mishka was born. We had already traveled for several years on tourist trips inside the Soviet Union. At the time, domestic tourism was a way of getting away from the existing regime into a forest or wherever so as not to see or hear anything. Those trips with like-minded friends also afforded an opportunity to discuss Jewish and Zionist topics.

KOSHAROVSKY: *Did you first have a dissident attitude toward the regime?*

PRESTIN: I can't even say that there was such an attitude or that Drabkin, Polsky, and Libkovsky were great "democrats." Dissidence as a group concept didn't yet exist and they were not yet Jewish nationalists. Yet there was something, perhaps not very rational, that they all understood. For example, they understood the reason why they landed at that factory and were received in a certain way. They were four or five years older than I and thus more mature during the last years of Stalinism, and they better understood the nature of the regime.

Through Drabkin's wife, who was from Riga, we had a connection with that city. Drabkin himself is a very intelligent person. In the Baltic republics, people's Jewish consciousness was aroused already after the Sinai Campaign in 1956, whereas with us, it started only after 1967. Yet by

1964 I already knew that I would go to Israel. That's hard to imagine, isn't it? We moved forward very quickly. We already had printed material and journals. After a few trips to the Baltics, Drabkin couldn't talk about any other topic than the Jewish question.

KOSHAROVSKY: *When did you apply for an exit visa?*

PRESTIN: In 1970. We all continued to travel together and celebrated Jewish holidays together. We didn't celebrate any other holidays. This was even before the Six-Day War. People started to receive exit visas in 1968, after the Soviets invaded Czechoslovakia. Whereas before the Six-Day War, people were allowed to leave only on the basis of an invitation from first-degree relatives such as parents and siblings, now it was permitted to go to aunts and uncles. After this, I didn't have any doubts that things would work out. Everyone immediately requested invitations from Israel.

KOSHAROVSKY: *Who was the leader in your group?*

PRESTIN: Drabkin and Libkovsky on Jewish matters. They left rather quickly. I remember Libkovsky agonizing about whether to leave or not. He seriously considered remaining in order to struggle for everyone else. We were very ardent then.

In addition to new leaders such as Polsky, Slepak, and Prestin, the movement was enriched around late 1971–early 1972 by the additions to its ranks of prominent academics and scientists. Among those who became active around this time were Alexander Lerner, Alexander Voronel, Veniamin Levich, Vitaly Rubin, and Mark Azbel. Their involvement significantly enhanced the movement's authority and expanded its international links and support, a development that the Soviet leadership had to take into account. Scientific seminars surfaced in Moscow and other cities and new samizdat appeared. Scientists opened their front in the struggle for aliya and for survival during the period of refusal.

Personal Recollections: From Sverdlovsk to Moscow

KOSHAROVSKY: In Sverdlovsk at the end of May 1971, the investigation into Valery Kukui's case had been completed and we tensely awaited the trial.[14] Everyone who had been dismissed from his job but had not received an exit visa needed to find work or else he or she faced the threat of arrest on a charge of parasitism. I found myself in a difficult situation. It was hard enough with a blacklisted identity card to find even simple work without the extra burden of being a Jew, an engineer, and the subject of pejorative comments in the press.

Ilia Voitovetsky rescued me: "[Vladimir] Markman said that the director at the freight rail station is a Jew and they need loaders," he said. "There they won't start poking into our work booklets. Let's try. I also left work before applying for an exit visa."

We were accepted. The work was not easy. All day one had to transport various loads from the freight cars to the warehouse and from the warehouse to the cars: refrigerators, consumer goods, semifinished products. We worked in a team of twelve men. As they paid by the brigade, one had to work in coordination with the others. Our muscles ached for the first weeks but, gradually, we became accustomed to it. The loaders, some of whom were good professionals, usually drank a hundred grams of vodka in the afternoon in order to reduce the tightening of the muscles. We tried it, too, and things became jollier.

In the evenings, we continued to meet with friends, discuss the situation, and stay in contact with Moscow. After Valery Kukui's trial, we sent petitions to various officials and wrote letters of protest.

In August two men in civvies picked me up from work and brought me to the KGB. Again I saw Lt. Colonel Pozdniakov. Again he presented me with a warning to curtail my activity. And then, unexpectedly, he said, "Money transfers arrived here from abroad in your name. We presume that as a Soviet citizen you renounce them."

"Is that a question or a demand?"

"For now, it's a question."

"If it's illegal, send it back and write to the senders, 'It is against Soviet law.' If it's legal . . ." I began.

"Then what?"

"Do you really think that I shall insult them by rejecting it?" I asked. "After all, they know that you ruined my life, refused me an exit visa, and had me fired from work and arrested."

"Now, now, Yuli Mikhailovich, go easy. You ruined your life on your own," said Pozdniakov.

A week later, I received three transfers, each of 150 foreign currency rubles, which was a large sum at that time. We were immediately dismissed from work. The Jewish director didn't need visits from the security services.

A few weeks later, we were already working at a new place, a factory manufacturing electric cables—again as loaders. The work was easier and the pay was the same so there were no regrets about the previous place. Here we more often worked as a twosome, which made it possible to talk to our hearts' content.

At one of our meetings, Volodia Aks drew me aside and asked, "Iliusha didn't tell you anything?" Volodia told me a strange story about Iliusha's formal agreement to cooperate with the KGB. Ilia immediately informed Markman, Aks, and (Boris) Rabinovich about this, saying he wasn't a coward or a traitor but decided that insofar as they wouldn't let him go anyway because he had a high level of security clearance, at least he could be of some use to us.

As Ilia later explained it, "I was young. It seemed interesting. Both a game and sacrifice—I was willing to pass through fire and water for my friends. I was quite sincere. After that, I became very active and wrote collective letters in defense of Kukui and others."[15] There was no doubt about the sincerity of Ilia's intentions; he radiated a desire to help. But he was playing a dangerous game. Even telling him that I knew about it meant that, to some degree, I, too, became an accomplice. That was all I needed!

On the other hand, how many informers about whom we knew nothing were circulating? Of course, from the very beginning, we understood that the KGB would not let us live without its own eyes and ears, and whenever it was truly necessary, we always took this into account. Ilia and I did not go into the details. I personally preferred not to know too much. Ilia merely added that if I wanted to, I could "leak" information via him in the form that I preferred or ascertain what activities of mine were of particular interest to the security services. I was not particularly enthusiastic. My intuition told me to keep as far away from the KGB as possible; otherwise, one could be inadvertently crushed. After all, in essence, we were not their clients. We did not represent any threat to state security: we wanted to leave and nothing more. With this stance, one could struggle to leave without being especially apprehensive about informers. The KGB's goal was clear: to destroy the movement, suppress individual initiative, and keep people fearful. The KGB had already demonstrated some of its possibilities so that I had no illusions about them. Once they started to break a person, their talk about the motherland, honor, and dignity was immediately replaced by bared fangs.

Ilia did not make any mistakes: he did not betray anyone or cause anyone to be arrested. At the end of 1971, he miraculously received an exit visa, arrived in Israel, and related everything to the appropriate people. In addition, he published several articles about the KGB's methods. We remained on good terms.

The security services tried to make trouble for my younger brother Leonid, who was working as an engineer at a defense factory. He was successfully pursuing a career, and he was not yet planning to go to Israel. He was summoned to the first department, where two men in neat black suits immediately explained that they had nothing against Leonid personally.[16] They knew that he was a Soviet man, not involved in anything, and a good worker. Leonid proved unwilling to work with them.

They tried to make trouble for my wife. We were formally divorced because otherwise they would not have accepted my documents for an exit visa.[17] This time, they received a categorical reply: "I will not spy on my own husband!"

The security services kept a close watch on me as before. Sometimes I was detained and threatened. Over time, I developed an instinctive reaction to them: I could feel their presence with my back. . . . And I began to sense danger like an animal.

There were few new people but occasionally some appeared and they would seek to meet me under the impression of the newspaper articles. Among them was an attractive couple, Mark and Anna Levin.

We continued to prepare for the court hearing of Valery Kukui's appeal, sending letter after letter to various officials. We felt that our letter to KGB chairman Yuri Andropov produced a strong impression. We ended it like the group letter of the Georgian Jews with the words "Israel or death."

I was detained on the street and brought to the police station, where two KGB officers were waiting for me. They said, "Our patience is at an end. We have more than enough material on you. You'll rot in prison. This is our last warning: we will not talk to you again!" Then in a more peaceful tone: "It seems like you do not know how to draw the necessary conclusions. We would be happy to toss you out of the country but your missile institute categorically objects. You will not receive a visa in the coming years. Do not even try. With such behavior, only prison lies in your future." This time it was serious: I felt it. I consulted with Aks, who was supposed to leave in a few days.

"Look," Aks told me,[18] "this whole region is full of security-related enterprises,[19] the KGB is fierce, and it goes overboard in protecting itself. Perhaps it is worth trying for a visa from another place. Indeed, at the beginning, we thought of applying from someplace in the Baltics or from Georgia, where there are no security enterprises and the atmosphere is different. Finkelshtein moved to Vilnius precisely for this purpose." Volodia Markman had a different opinion: "They'll get you wherever you are. Here, at least, you have friends and relatives. You have to try to break through from here."

When I shared Aks's idea with the family, mama immediately seized upon it. To my surprise, my wife also did not object. I decided to try in Georgia. We discovered a distant relative living near Tbilisi who was ready to host me in the beginning. After parting with Aks a week later, I took the train toward Georgia. My route took me to Moscow, where I knew only three names: Slepak, Polsky, and Prestin, the new leaders of the Moscow refuseniks. I had not met them personally and I was happy for the opportunity to get acquainted.

Polsky was very businesslike: he inquired about matters in Sverdlovsk and asked me to drop in before my departure—perhaps he would transmit something to Kiev or Tbilisi. Slepak received me in a warm, friendly way. People were flocking to his apartment, coming and going all the time. Someone was whispering in the kitchen and partially filled tea mugs and an unfinished cake were in evidence on the table. Volodia asked about our Sverdlovsk affairs and immediately introduced me to someone. He reacted unexpectedly to the idea of getting out via Georgia: "You have no secrets from them. You will stand out there like a sore thumb. It might become even worse. Stay in Moscow. We have plenty of people like you here. Together things will go more quickly and reliably."

He told me about his first level of security clearance and gave some other examples. I asked, "Who will give me a residence permit for Moscow? The city is closed to ordinary people, and with my record . . . !" Volodia smiled. "You underestimate us. Go and stroll around until the evening and then we will see."

When I returned, he already had an alternative. He found a girl for a fictitious marriage so that I could register in Moscow. She also planned to emigrate. The following evening I was introduced to a charming girl named Nora, who did not nix the idea. We applied at ZAGS [the marriage registration office] and the marriage was registered in a month. A month later, we applied for an exit visa and were rejected. Thus began my Moscow refusenik life, which continued for a long seventeen years. In a year and a half, Nora received a visa. The marriage of convenience ended, and she left.[20]

Despite the absence of relatives and the lack of a normal living arrangement, life in Moscow turned out to be easier and more pleasant than in Sverdlovsk. People were open, sociable, and friendly. On the Sabbath, a kind of "refusenik club" gathered on the hillock near the central Moscow synagogue. There one could learn the latest news, meet people, arrange to go to farewell gatherings for those who were leaving, order invitations from Israel, find Hebrew teachers, and meet with tourists and foreign correspondents. On this hillock I made my first Moscow acquaintances.

Valera Korenblit, who knew everything that was going on among refuseniks, generously invited me to live in his one-room apartment for a few days. He lived in that room with his wife and daughter and in the little kitchen was a trestle bed, just for me. Valera acquainted me with Zhenia Epshtein, a weight lifting trainer of the "Trud" sport organization. Although educated as a chemical technician, Zhenia loved sport, completed the training, and changed profession. A week after we met, Zhenia received the keys to a cooperative apartment. He did not plan to move there right away. "If you want, go live there," he offered. "Only keep in mind that it is empty and lacks a telephone." The offer was generous. I didn't have any personal belongings—only a briefcase that served as a pillow. My coat served as bedding or a blanket. After a few weeks, I bought a cot and felt completely comfortable.

Later, Boria Tsitlenok took me in. His relatives obtained exit visas and left, but he received a refusal and remained alone in a two-room apartment. A most kind fellow, he selflessly participated in all the demonstrations. Nora then acquainted me with a friend who, like Zhenia Epshtein, had received the keys to a cooperative apartment but was in no hurry to move, and I settled down there. It did not occur to me to try to find a more or less fixed residence. The ranks of the departing constantly grew, many veteran activists received exit visas, and refusenik life seethed in expectation of a breakthrough.

About the time of my arrival in Moscow, the change in leadership of the movement was completed. The founding fathers—Khavkin, Svechinsky, Gelfond, and also Drabkin and the members of the All-Union Coordinating Committee

(VKK) from other cities who were still at liberty—left the Soviet Union by around March 1971. Misha Zand left in the summer. At the end of 1971, Vladimir Rosenblum, Pavel Goldshtein, Mikhail Margulis, and Vladimir Zaretsky emigrated.

The new leaders were not newcomers to the movement, having shown their colors during the wave of trials in the early 1970s, with communications to the Brussels Conference, and to summits in Moscow and Canada. They were experienced in organizing successful actions, such as the numerous collective protests at the Central Telegraph Agency building or in the reception rooms of highly placed officials, protests which frequently ended with fines or fifteen-day arrests. They were involved in the composition of numerous personal and collective letters, petitions, and appeals, which were signed openly on Saturdays near the synagogue—sometimes several letters a day.

Later, I often heard that the aliya struggle was conducted by a small group of selfless refuseniks, but this assertion is not true. The movement had a broad social base that included hundreds of thousands of people who listened at night to Kol Yisrael and the broadcasts of other "Voices," tens of thousands who sought an opportunity to leave, and many thousands involved in the process of applying for exit visas. They comprised the breeding ground for the movement. The refuseniks simply stood on the front line of the struggle.[21]

The movement that I saw in Moscow in 1972 appeared mature, with a ramified network of domestic and foreign links, mutual help, and a group of representative leaders. Although there was no formal leadership or external signs of an organization, some people stood out in terms of their activity, knowledge, and authority. In addition to their work in organizing life in refusal, the activists supported an effective link with the Jewish world abroad, receiving foreign politicians and public figures. It was a special environment, struggling for the right to leave and for survival.

Détente and the Jackson-Vanik Amendment

The Jewish movement in the 1970s developed in the context of détente. In the summer of 1971, it was announced that Richard Nixon and Leonid Brezhnev would meet at a summit in May 1972.

The start of détente raised a question for the forces struggling for the free emigration of Soviet Jews: in what way could the process of détente reflect on human rights practices and on the prospects for Jewish emigration?

Both the United States and the Soviet Union attributed great significance to Nixon's visit to the USSR. As a first confidence-building measure, an agreement worth several hundred million dollars was signed in November 1971 concerning the sale of American grain and drilling equipment to the Soviet Union. Such ties would become important in the struggle to influence the Soviet Union to observe human rights. Activists on both sides of the Iron Curtain used the visit as a pretext for raising the volume on the issue of Jewish emigration. Prisoners of Zion and activists sent greetings and telegrams to the Twenty-Eighth Zionist Congress, held in Jerusalem in January 1972. "Brethren!" wrote Arkady Voloshin, Lassal Kaminsky, Lev Korenblit, Yosif Meshener, Leib Khnokh, and Arkady Shpilberg, "Even here, behind the barbed wire, amidst the howling of guard dogs and in the sight of machine guns on the watch towers, we are with you in striving toward our common goal." Moscow activists wrote to the Zionist Congress: "We are numbered among those Jews who are not invited to press conferences. We are among those . . . for whom participation in the building of a free, independent, and democratic Israel is a vital need and a national duty."[22]

Trying to minimize the effect of Jewish emigration issues in preparation for the Moscow summit, the authorities introduced a corrective to their emigration policy. The results proved to be ambivalent. On the one hand, for some time (from October 1971 until the end of May 1972), the regime did not conduct anti-Zionist trials, which invariably attracted considerable attention from the Western press. On the other hand, the arrests of individual activists (Ilia Gleizer in Moscow, Yuli Brind in Kharkov, Vladimir Markman in Sverdlovsk, and others) continued. At the same time, while sharply increasing the number of exit visas issued (from 999 people in 1970 to 12,897 in 1971 and up to 31,903 in 1972),[23] the regime significantly restricted the departure of youth and certain categories of specialists.

Just before the summit, the authorities isolated the most active Zionists, utilizing administrative arrests and army reserve call-ups. There was an intensification of anti-Zionist propaganda and extrajudicial harassment in the form of dismissals from work with consequent warnings about punishment for a so-called "parasitic way of life." Despite the relative outward calm, the time was full of inner drama. In January, searches were carried out in the homes of the Kharkov activists Solomon Grinberg and Konstantin Skoblinsky.[24] On January 21, 1972, Mikhail Rozik was beaten while attempting to enter the Dutch embassy. On January 27, Yuli Aronovich, conductor of the All-Union radio and television orchestra, suffered serious injuries from an attack of "hooligans" near his home. After submitting documents for an exit visa to Israel, he had been fired from his position. On February 7, a young Moscow biologist, Ilia Gleizer, was arrested; a month earlier, he had applied for an exit visa to Israel.[25]

Vladimir Slepak was warned about the possibility of a criminal charge "for leading a parasitic way of life." Other activists were also threatened with arrest for "parasitism," including Vladimir Makhlis, Boris Orlov, and Sergei Gurvits in Moscow; Solomon Rozen in Leningrad; and Ernst Levin in Minsk.[26]

As the date of the summit drew closer, the authorities expanded and intensified their pressure. Five Jews were summoned to the Moscow KGB on March 27: Gabriel Shapiro, Viktor Iakhot, Boris Orlov, Yosif Begun, and Sergei Gurvits. They were warned not to conduct any celebrations near the synagogue on the approaching Passover holiday. On the eve of Passover, on March 29, police units began to disperse the crowd, but the youth gathered in another place, on Nogin Square, and continued to sing and dance. Soon the police appeared again, this time accompanied by anti-Semitic thugs. The Jews were knocked off their feet, trampled upon, and dragged to police vans by their feet and hair. About thirty people were detained. They were released after three hours but some had to go to the hospital rather than to work the next day.[27]

A month before Nixon's visit, additional pressure was exerted through orders to appear for army service, which were received by Moscow activists, including Viktor Iakhot, Gabriel Shapiro, Sergei Gurvits, Dan Roginsky, Misha Kliachkin, David Markish, Pavel Abramovich, Boris Ainbinder, Mark Nashpits, and Leonid Ioffe. These men were primarily Hebrew teachers, capable of quickly mobilizing a large number of people via their students. Two—Ainbinder and Roginsky—were in constant telephone contact with Israel and London activist Michael Sherbourne. Three activists—Kliachkin, Iakhot, and Slepak—requested permission from the Moscow city council to conduct a protest demonstration during the US president's visit.

It was clear that the regime was trying to purge Moscow of Jewish activists during Nixon's visit. The majority of the activists, incidentally, did not obey the army notices for fear that the army service could be used in the future as the basis for a visa refusal on the grounds of secrecy.

On May 21, 1972, a day before Nixon's arrival, KGB officers went to the apartments of leading Moscow activists Vladimir Slepak, Viktor Polsky, Roman Rutman, Lev Libov, and Boris Orlov and arrested them. They were kept in prison until the end of the visit. Yosif Begun and Valentin Prusakov were also arrested on the same day in Moscow. On the next day, Vladimir Prestin disappeared on his way to work. He was picked up near the Kursk metro station, accused of harassing a woman, and held fifteen days for "hooliganism." It must have been amusing for the KGB to accuse the aristocratic Prestin of an unseemly act using witnesses Prestin had never seen before.

On May 24, 1972, Leonid Tsypin and Alexander Slepak (the son of Vladimir), who had planned to carry out a protest demonstration during the visit, were arrested. A day before Nixon's planned one-day visit to Kiev, on May 25, Alexander Feldman, Lazar Slutsky, and Zinovy Melamed were arrested for ten days. In Sverdlovsk Leonid Zabelyshensky was arrested for ten days and in Leningrad the famous ballet dancer and refusenik Valery Panov was imprisoned for ten days. Many Jews in other cities were sent to army call-ups or provoked and arrested for ten to fifteen days.

The regime welcomed Nixon and his delegation hospitably. The business part of the meeting was successful. A treaty on the limitation of strategic arms was signed (START-1). A joint Committee on Trade was created, and a Declaration on Principles of Mutual Relations was signed. Most attractive for the Soviet Union, the USSR obtained most-favored-nation status in trade and advantageous credits from the American Export-Import Bank for obtaining American goods.

Officially, the Nixon administration, despite expressing sympathy for the struggle of Soviet Jewry, refused to raise the issue.[28] In an unofficial manner, however, the Jewish issue was raised at the summit, as it was important to Nixon and Secretary of State Henry Kissinger to curry favor with the American Jewish community. Brezhnev reportedly assured the Americans he would raise quotas for Jews receiving exit visas, although it seemed unlikely that even such concessions, if implemented, would answer the demand among Soviet Jews.[29] The summit did not lead to free Jewish emigration although the numbers increased. All the former obstacles and difficulties connected to the gathering and submission of documents for an exit visa, the long waiting period, and the completely arbitrary granting of visas remained. The life of refuseniks did not become easier or more secure.

The euphoria from the successful summit played an evil trick on the Soviet leadership. Calculating that the considerations impelling the United States toward détente were much weightier than the issue of Jewish emigration, the KGB considered that the time was ripe for placing another, practically insurmountable obstacle on the path to emigration: an education tax. The upper ranks in the Kremlin evidently decided that it would be difficult to object to this as education in the West was paid for privately. Once again, however, the Soviet strategists were undone by their lack of a sense of proportion: the scale of the tax was monstrous, in effect, prohibitive. American legislators reacted indignantly to the education tax, introducing an exceptionally strong and significant countermeasure, the Jackson-Vanik Amendment, which established a legislative link between freedom of emigration from the Soviet Union and economic relations between the two superpowers. From being a specific, humanitarian issue, the question of Jewish emigration moved to the plane of strategic relations between the United States and the USSR.[30]

The Jackson-Vanik Amendment

The Jackson-Vanik Amendment, sponsored by Congressman Charles Vanik and Senator Henry Jackson, linked economic benefits for nonmarket economies, including most-favored-nation status in trade deals, to free emigration. The amendment was formally introduced on March 15, 1973, and President Gerald Ford signed the amendment into law on

January 3, 1975, making it the first human rights legislation to be passed in the United States. The amendment helped pave the way for the final Helsinki Act provisions later that year, which likewise addressed human rights within the framework of international treaties and obligations. The "education tax" imposed beginning in August 1972 by Soviet authorities on those with higher education seeking to leave the USSR served as a trigger for the campaign to pass the amendment, which had been controversial: President Nixon viewed it as a hindrance to his policy of détente, while the Soviet Union objected to foreign interference in its internal affairs.

Refuseniks understood that the goal of the tax was to make it impossible for the educated stratum of Soviet Jewry to leave the country. If the Jews had been able to pay this tax (the Levich family, for example, would have had to pay more than 100,000 rubles, which equaled about seventy annual engineer's salaries), the authorities would have introduced additional payments or restrictions. The tax also put Jewish youth in a lose-lose situation: they could study and then be unable to leave because of the high tax, or not study and become easy prey for army recruitment with the consequent secrecy restrictions and impossibility of leaving.

The tax was part of a general Soviet offensive against the Zionist movement. In response, the Soviet Union received the Jackson-Vanik Amendment, which linked privileges in trade agreements to free emigration. Soviet citizens who supported this idea put themselves at no small risk because, in the regime's eyes, they became advocates of economic sabotage against the Soviet Union. Only desperate conditions could impel the leaders of the Jewish movement in the Soviet Union to embark on such an initiative.

A struggle began that lasted more than two years. The Nixon administration's interests in speedy ratification of the trade law clashed with the adamant position of a group of senators and representatives who were not prepared to grant most-favored-nation status to a country with a nonmarket economy that did not observe human rights and had just introduced a barbaric decree legalizing a form of what was effectively a twentieth-century intellectual slave trade.

Despite persecution and arrests, the activists in the USSR continued to express support for the Jackson-Vanik Amendment. On September 19, 1972, the activists went to demonstrate at the reception room of the Supreme Soviet, which was in session at that time, in order to hand over a petition of protest against the education tax. Thirty-one people were detained during this action. Some of them were released but the remainder received sentences ranging from a fine to fifteen days of imprisonment.[31] On the same day a group of Jews attempted to hold a hunger strike protest at the Central Telegraph Agency building. Two participants, Vladimir Slepak and Efim Manevich, were sentenced to fifteen days.[32] On March 8, 1973, 309 refuseniks from six cities (Moscow, Leningrad, Kiev, Kharkov, Novosibirsk, and Vilnius) sent a letter to Senators Wilbur Mills and Henry Jackson supporting the amendment. On March 16, 1973, Senator Jackson officially presented that letter to the Senate on behalf of seventy-seven senators.

Wanting to dampen the Americans' enthusiasm and, as if hinting that it would be better to reach an agreement quietly behind the scenes, Soviet authorities twice released six hundred people without requiring payment of the education tax. But Senator Jackson was implacable, favoring only a legislative act. He did not want to leave the issue to the discretion of the Soviet leadership.

A discussion in the Politburo in March 1973 focused on the problem.[33] On the day after the meeting, March 21, 1973, the education tax was de facto abolished and the practice of requiring payment for education was not renewed. The tax continued to exist de jure, however, and the regime occasionally spread rumors that it was planning to re-implement it. From Senator Jackson's point of view, the abrogation of the tax represented only a partial concession by the Soviets because the amendment spoke about freedom of emigration as a whole. The senator continued his struggle. Patent opponents of the amendment included the presidential administration and American economic circles interested in expanding trade with the Soviet Union and countries of Eastern Europe.[34] It also included, of course, the Soviet government, operating via diplomatic channels and also trying to influence US public opinion. Supporters of the amendment included Zionist activists and the rights activists in the Soviet Union, whose opinions were widely publicized in the West. Supporters included leaders of American Jewry; various ethnic groups in the United States whose peoples were under the Soviet yoke (the Baltic peoples, Germans, and Ukrainians); American trade unions; and public opinion, which was very sensitive to freedom of emigration.

From the start of 1974, various circles exerted ever stronger pressure on the House and Senate to drop the amendment. The administration's pressure and, perhaps, the diplomatic art of Georgy Arbatov, director of the Moscow Institute of the USA and Canada, caused even the cosponsor Representative Charles Vanik to waver. The Israeli Nativ bureau found itself in a delicate position trying to balance the interests that would best lead to full-scale Soviet Jewish emigration.[35] Vanik visited refuseniks in Moscow to try to convince them not to support the amendment.[36] He did not succeed. The refuseniks remained steadfast in support of the amendment, despite the risk of harsh reprisals from the regime. Eighty-three Jews from Moscow, Leningrad, and other cities sent a letter in support of the amendment on September 1, 1974.[37]

Although President Ford signed the Jackson-Vanik Amendment into law as part of the Trade Bill on January 3, 1975, its effect was dampened significantly by the Stevenson Amendment, which received a favorable Senate vote in December 1974, and which threatened to undo the understanding reached in the framework of Jackson-Vanik.[38] In response to the Stevenson Amendment, the Soviet Union refused to sign the trade agreement and made the conditions for emigration tougher.

Life in Refusal

Refuseniks did not limit their concerns to the struggle for aliya. They had to make a living somehow, after having, in most cases, lost their jobs. They had to maintain their families and raise and educate their children while trying to protect them from the harassment their parents endured. They also had to prepare for life in Israel, which meant among other things studying Hebrew and trying to maintain their professional level. Dealing with these issues became more stressful when it became clear that life in refusal could last many years. The refusenik community was formed gradually in response to the need to find solutions to these problems.

Those who wound up as refuseniks underwent amazing changes. Rejected by Soviet society, they ceased to be guided by its false social norms, threw off the stifling totalitarian chains, and became inwardly free. Indeed, one facet of refusenik life was the constant persecution and defamation, but another facet was the struggle for the right—even in refusal—to live a Jewish life. Life in refusal became a fruitful basis for the development of various Jewish educational institutions, mutual help societies, and a samizdat press. Refusenik scientists established scientific, engineering, legal, and linguistic seminars and cultural and historical societies. Groups offering support to Prisoners of Zion and their families arose. Kindergartens, Sunday schools, and amateur Jewish theater activity were organized. A religious renaissance blossomed. In every sphere of refusenik life, leaders emerged who acquired the necessary experience and connections and attained prominence. Western Jews provided social, political, and material support for the nationalist initiatives, thus enabling the refusenik community to hold out in the struggle.

Hebrew ulpans helped prepare refuseniks linguistically and practically for the process of emigration and life in Israel.[39] Teaching Hebrew was officially discouraged in various ways.[40] In 1971 the refuseniks Vladimir Prestin, Sergei Gurvits, Viktor Polsky, and Pavel Abramovich succeeded in obtaining an official permit to teach Hebrew and pay state taxes. In February 1972, however, Abramovich received a notice from the district tax office that he should cease teaching because "[i]n the Soviet Union, Hebrew is not a recognized language and is not taught in any institution of higher learning." In 1976 Abramovich tried via the Moscow Information Bureau to announce officially that he was teaching Hebrew. After the bureau refused to accept his notice, he sued them in court and won: the court obligated the office to publish his notice. Abramovich's apartment was subsequently subject to a search during which all his material in Hebrew was confiscated. The KGB operatives demanded that he completely halt instruction in Hebrew.[41]

Many Hebrew teachers who combined teaching with Zionist activity were subjected to similar pressure. They were threatened with serious punishment. However, the regime did not dare try them for language instruction, preferring to convict them for "parasitism," "slander," "hooliganism," or "possession of drugs." The authorities' inability to fight openly against language instruction enabled a large number of ulpans to exist on a semilegal basis. In Moscow alone in 1972, several hundred people were studying Hebrew.[42]

One of the most persistent and stubborn fighters for the de facto legalization of Hebrew and of Jewish culture was Yosif Begun. By November 1972 he had written his third letter to *Pravda* about the problem, in which he pointed out the contradictions between official Party policy on the national question and the obstacles to Hebrew language instruction.[43] A man of great personal courage, he decided if he could not gain official permission, he would assert his legitimacy by not contesting the matter. Smiling with his kind, fearless eyes (three prison terms did not leave noticeable traces in them), Begun explained his approach in the following way: "I became a conscious 'parasite.' I decided that their arresting me would prove in and of itself that they did not recognize Hebrew teaching as a legal occupation. They didn't touch me for two years. Every two to three months, I would be called in and a protocol on parasitism would be drawn up, but they didn't take me."[44] The regime showed its true colors in 1977. Begun was arrested on March 1. The regime did not hesitate to convict Begun, a PhD with twenty-five years of work experience, of parasitism.

Letters advocating the legalization of Hebrew were sent to Soviet ruling bodies, to the media, and to foreign organizations. In March 1972 forty-six Minsk Jews protested to the Central Committee of the CPSU and also to that of the Communist Party of Belarus against the refusal of the financial authorities to register them as private Hebrew teachers, terming it a violation of the Soviet Constitution in the form of national discrimination.[45]

In addition to those who combined teaching activity with the struggle for aliya and for legalizing the language, a group of teachers who regarded Hebrew teaching as their basic calling began to form in Moscow. The leader of this group, Moshe Palhan, had developed a very successful method of instruction.[46] He founded a school that produced the most prominent Hebrew teachers. "Those teachers constituted a rather interesting group," Mikhail Chlenov recalled.[47] "At the time [Moshe Palhan began teaching in 1968—see below], many of them did not plan to leave; it wasn't considered obligatory then. They taught the activists, who viewed them as some kind of esoteric group possessing some secret knowledge and reading a special literature." Understanding their significance for the movement, the members of this group tried to avoid irritating the authorities through blatant participation in other forms of refusenik activity and the latter pretended not to notice their activity.

Zeev Shakhnovsky, who later became one of the most popular teachers, recalled Palhan's infectious enthusiasm: "Moshe Palhan was crazy about the language, and this simply inspired others. Moshe looked at us and spoke in such a way that we understood: this was the best language in the world! And our tongues were loosened and we wanted to converse. He knew how to convey this feeling, this linguistic rapture."[48] Moshe Palhan's students—Leonid Ioffe, Zeev Shakhnovsky, Israel Palhan (Moshe's younger brother), Aleksei Levin, Benia Deborin, and Mikhail Goldblat—became the best teachers of the aliya group. Ioffe's students included Dan Roginsky, Boris Ainbinder, and Zeev Zolotarevsky. Fima Kraitman and Lev Gorodetsky studied with Zeev Shakhnovsky. Mikhail Chlenov worked with Israel Palhan. Leonid Volvovsky and Yuli Kosharovsky studied with Mikhail Goldblat. Many teachers departed but the chain reaction continued until the gates opened wide in 1990.

Israel Palhan described his brother Moshe, who had finished technical school and served in the army, as a nonprofessional linguist with a passion for languages. "Moshe managed to accomplish a great deal. A circle of people in Moscow who spoke Hebrew arose only after his activity," Israel said.[49]

Moshe Palhan explained his interest in Hebrew:[50]

KOSHAROVSKY: *How did your interest in Hebrew arise?*

PALHAN: It was before my army call-up. My mother was one of the first tourists to visit Israel, having received permission in 1956 to visit her mother there.[51] She returned and said that we ought to leave. I was then studying in school and recall objecting, "What! You want to bring us to that imperialist puppet state?" She then gave up on the idea, but she brought back a couple of records from Israel that interested me. The

Hebrew music made a strong impression: I heard proud and free people singing. After all, we were living on the outskirts of Moscow, an anti-Semitic place where I was always fighting with the local boys, who would attack in a mob when we returned from school. Jewish music helped me understand that the world was not as I perceived it. That is, early on I felt that something wasn't right. In school, there was one world—that of goodness, beauty, and logic—and the other was on the street, in my village. Only after the army, something clicked. At first, it seemed to me that the world abroad was an insane asylum. At some moment, I understood that I was looking at the world beyond the Soviet border from inside an insane asylum.

KOSHAROVSKY: *I understand that you began to teach after you received a refusal.*

PALHAN: Yes, I was in refusal from 1966. In this connection, there were many hassles: my brother was expelled from the institute, my wife was condemned at a workers' meeting, my father lost his job, and so did I. We had to organize our life anew, and this wasn't easy in our situation. My mother continued to try to obtain an exit visa, making the rounds of all the government offices, but she received one refusal after another. The last was in May 1967, when it was hinted that never in her life would she see her relatives again. She came home in tears. Then there was the Six-Day War and the entire upheaval.

KOSHAROVSKY: *Where did you get your conversational experience?*

PALHAN: I would listen to the radio, sometimes I would meet Israelis, and I made the acquaintance of Professor Mikhail Zand, who spoke Hebrew excellently.

KOSHAROVSKY: *Where did Zand learn his Hebrew?*

PALHAN: Independently. He is a scholar, an Orientalist, and he met many Israeli Arabs; he was connected to the Institute of Asia and Africa.

Moshe Palhan left for Israel in March 1971. Although he taught for a relatively short period, he succeeded in instilling such a love of Hebrew in his students that it sufficed for several generations of his followers.

After the departure of Moshe Palhan and Leonid Ioffe, Zeev (Vladimir) Shakhnovsky became the central teacher. A native Muscovite and graduate of the Moscow State University Department of Mechanical Mathematics, he grew up in a family of scientific workers who had also graduated from Moscow University. At first he taught according to Moshe Palhan's method and then began to introduce his own elements: a selection of radio broadcasts from Israel and Israeli songs, excerpts from the Torah and Rashi's commentaries. Together with Beniamin Deborin, he organized the first Moscow *dibbur* (Hebrew for "conversation," referring to meetings where the conversation was only in Hebrew) for their students. His open and friendly nature attracted people to him. For some time the Sabbath meetings of the best teachers took place at Shakhnovsky's apartment. As Vladimir gradually became more interested in Judaism and began to observe the commandments, he inclined more and more toward Torah teaching. For some time Alexander Ostronov and Kosharovsky perfected their Hebrew with Shakhnovsky. Shakhnovsky, who at first was affectionately called Vovulia and then Zeev, taught in Moscow for eighteen years, from 1971 to 1989, and he continued teaching in Israel.

Shakhnovsky talked about the first ulpans in Moscow:[52]

SHAKHNOVSKY: The first groups arose even before Palhan, but they basically were not part of future developments. Palhan was lucky and we with him. He assembled a group that consisted of strong fellows. In 1969 Lyonia Ioffe and Misha Goldblat began to study with him and they soon began to teach on their own.

KOSHAROVSKY: *How many people were in your group?*

SHAKHNOVSKY: Five.

KOSHAROVSKY: *How long did Palhan teach you?*

SHAKHNOVSKY: Not long at all. He wrote a booklet, "Thirteen Hebrew Lessons." That's about us. We had thirteen lessons but it was a very strong group.

KOSHAROVSKY: *When did you begin to teach?*

SHAKHNOVSKY: In August 1971. That summer Volodia Prestin came to me and said, "They say that you learned Hebrew well." "Nothing special," I answered. "I am reading and developing." "What's the point of reading? I'll send you five people and you'll have a group." Thus my first group was formed in August 1971, which included, incidentally, my best student, Fima Kraitman.

KOSHAROVSKY: *How did you deal with the lack of textbooks and teaching material?*

SHAKHNOVSKY: Volodia Prestin handled that. He dropped in on the Lenin Library where he found the textbook *Elef Milim*—both parts—and ordered a copy. We made copies of this in our apartments. Misha Zand left us part of his library that had made its way to him after the closing of the Israeli embassy. It included several years of the newspaper for beginners, *Shaar lemathil*. I distributed it to many teachers and they actively used it in their lessons.

KOSHAROVSKY: *Did each teacher take care of his own supply or was there some coordination of efforts?*

SHAKHNOVSKY: I received excellent-quality film from Volodia Prestin and used it to make textbooks. Other teachers had the same film. Each took care of his pupils.

KOSHAROVSKY: *Ainbinder and Roginsky had telephone channels to Israel. It seems to me that you had one, too, at one time.*

SHAKHNOVSKY: People would leave and the links would pass from one person to another. Sara Frenkel,[53] a journalist for a popular Israeli newspaper, used to call me in 1973, particularly during the Yom Kippur War. We would exchange information. At that time, the regime began to jam shortwave broadcasts that we had been able to hear. She would carefully read out the news in Hebrew. I would record it on a tape recorder and then go over it with my students. This continued until the beginning of 1974, when my telephone was disconnected.

Do you remember the English parliamentarian Greville Janner?[54] He also called several times. Once the KGB started to jam us during a conversation. He recorded this jamming and then played this in Parliament, raising a commotion about it. After that, my telephone was disconnected. And I'm telling you, I heaved a sigh of relief because people had started to call us from schools and kindergartens at inconvenient hours.

KOSHAROVSKY: *I understand you well; I went through the same thing. Did they ever reconnect the phone?*

SHAKHNOVSKY: No.

KOSHAROVSKY: *Zeev, did foreigners visit you?*

SHAKHNOVSKY: Yes, a variety of them, from Europe and America.

KOSHAROVSKY: *What kind of help or support did you request?*

SHAKHNOVSKY: In matters related to Hebrew.

KOSHAROVSKY: *Did the organization Haivrim from Israel help you?*[55]

SHAKHNOVSKY: They sent us books in the mail. In 1973–74 I received around two hundred books just from them.

KOSHAROVSKY: *How did Lena [Shaknovsky's wife] relate to your activity?*

SHAKHNOVSKY: In a businesslike manner, just as I did. After all, she, too, was a teacher. Our pupils and the pupils of our pupils include five Knesset deputies. Marina Solodkin studied with Lena and (Natan) Sharansky with me. (Yuli) Edelstein studied with my student (Lev) Gorodetsky. He called me grandfather. Yuri Shtern sometimes would come to lessons but I can't consider him my pupil although he recalled my lessons with gratitude.

Those who handled the Hebrew-language telephone channels to convey information about the movement to supporters in Israel and other countries needed a high level of Hebrew and the ability to translate texts quickly. They also had to possess considerable knowledge about events among refuseniks in order to inform people abroad. Those who had such channels did not always participate directly in public protest actions. Their basic task was to follow the course of events and, if necessary, quickly and accurately convey information abroad. Boris Ainbinder was one of those who handled such communications.

Boris talked about his activity and how he got involved:[56]

AINBINDER: I applied for an exit visa in November 1971, and from that time on, I began to sign group letters. In December 1972, on the first anniversary of the Leningrad Trial, a protest hunger strike was held in several apartments. Polsky, Roginsky, Prestin, Abramovich, and I were at Prestin's home. We fasted for three days. Hunger strikes were also conducted at Slepak's apartment and elsewhere. That's how it started.

KOSHAROVSKY: *What channels of communication did you have and in what languages?*

AINBINDER: I constantly received phone calls from Israel from Sara Frenkel. Michael Sherbourne called from England.[57] I communicated in English and Hebrew.

KOSHAROVSKY: *Who else had channels?*

AINBINDER: Polsky had a regular channel. Then, in 1972, the KGB began to disconnect telephones.

KOSHAROVSKY: *How long did your channel last?*

AINBINDER: Until my departure.

KOSHAROVSKY: *You were never disconnected?*

AINBINDER: I was for a short time.

KOSHAROVSKY: *Did you have to convey requests for invitations from Israel or information?*

AINBINDER: Yes. Polsky would convey the most detailed information and protest letters. I conveyed brief information in Hebrew.

KOSHAROVSKY: *Were your meetings held regularly?*

AINBINDER: The most regular meetings were conversations at Polsky's place. We would gather there once a week. In addition, there was the synagogue once a week, holidays, and birthdays.

KOSHAROVSKY: *Some activists were oriented toward the Western Jewish establishment organizations and the Liaison Bureau while others were oriented toward nonestablishment movements in various countries. How do you explain this?*

AINBINDER: This is very natural, just as it is in Israel. After all, even if the goal is the same, the methods can vary.

KOSHAROVSKY: *Did foreigners visit you?*

AINBINDER: Yes, and handling such visits was one of my main functions. I dealt often with those contacts.

KOSHAROVSKY: *What was the reason for your arrest?*

AINBINDER: It was December 1972. I think there was a jubilee session of the Supreme Soviet. Many people were detained.

KOSHAROVSKY: *How long were you detained?*

AINBINDER: Two weeks, in Volokolamsk prison.

KOSHAROVSKY: *Did the KGB bother you on any other pretext?*

AINBINDER: In connection with Nixon's visit in May 1972. Then there was a whole story about call-ups for military reserve service.

One of the leading Hebrew instructors, Dan Roginsky, talked about his path to teaching:[58]

KOSHAROVSKY: *Dan, did you become a teacher even before you started to study with Lyonia Ioffe?*

ROGINSKY: Yes, but I became a genuine teacher after him. Ioffe's Hebrew was fluently conversational and he was a worthy example to follow. Later on we conversed entirely in Hebrew, which was very inspiring and helpful. One of the elements in the teaching was that at the first lesson, all the pupils had to choose Hebrew names and try to speak in Hebrew. As experience showed, this was a very effective method. Paradoxically, here in Israel we began to converse again in Russian.

KOSHAROVSKY: *What memories do you have of life as a refusenik?*

ROGINSKY: I had the good fortune to live at the time of Soviet Jewry's awakening and to participate in its victory.

KOSHAROVSKY: *In Israel, did you participate in the group of teachers that helped Moscow teachers?*

ROGINSKY: Yes, of course. Israel Palhan arrived in Israel in 1972 and set up an *amuta* (nonprofit organization) called Haivrim. He was the first to understand that one could overcome the postal barrier and make another breach in the Iron Curtain. He used to send books in Hebrew by ordinary mail. Not all arrived but he was persistent. This continued for years and the teachers in the Soviet Union received many books.

In the refusenik community, Hebrew teachers often became a focal point of refusenik activity. Their students (and others) would come to them with their problems and questions and they would often be invited to family celebrations. The friendly relations that formed in the ulpans created an atmosphere of trust and mutual support. Those who met in ulpans often celebrated Jewish holidays together. People who were just preparing to apply for exit visas also were in contact with the ulpans, which thus served as a bridge between the refuseniks and the remaining Jewish population. The ulpans spread the creative energy of the movement that liberated the Jews from the bonds of fear and ignorance, isolation and solitude, humiliation and despair. The ulpans and circles of Hebrew teachers contributed much to the fight for aliya and the rebirth of Jewish national life. Moscow became the center of the Hebrew renaissance. Through the joint efforts of local and Israeli teachers, more effective teaching methods were gradually implemented and disseminated throughout the country.

Seminars

Under the prevailing Soviet policy on emigration, academics with advanced degrees were unable to obtain exit visas and lost their jobs and the opportunity to engage in scientific activity. The stream of academics enhanced the prestige of the movement. Scientists needed their own niche, however, in which to maintain their scientific level and remain in contact with colleagues and to utilize their collective potential for the aliya struggle. For these purposes, the scientists established a network of refusenik scientific seminars. Professors Alexander Voronel and Alexander Lerner were among the founders of this system.

The KGB reacted nervously to any form of refusenik activity, especially one in which the best and most educated minds of that community gathered together. Thus one had to appraise possibilities carefully before undertaking something new. Voronel was the first to tread on this thin ice with his seminar titled Collective Phenomena, which began to operate in April 1972. Because of the role of physicists in this seminar, in refusenik circles it was informally referred to as the Physics Seminar. A few months later, in the summer of 1972, as Lerner wrote, "It became obvious that the authorities had no intention of freeing refuseniks soon, especially those highly skilled in professions. We would have to prepare for a new way of life, for a long siege."[59] Lerner's seminar devoted to control systems and the application of mathematical methods to medicine and biology opened at that time, and refuseniks called it the Cybernetics Seminar. In the fall of 1972, Vitaly Rubin's Humanities Seminar began to operate. A year later, I organized the Engineering Seminar. In time, other cities and refusenik groups (Hebrew teachers, historians, and religious groups) seized upon this initiative and opened seminars elsewhere as well.

Voronel's penchant for independent thought manifested itself at an early age, leading to his arrest and incarceration in a work camp for youth when he was fourteen. He spoke about that difficult period and the beginning of his Jewish struggle:[60]

VORONEL: My mother went from Leningrad, where I was born, to Kharkov, where she began studying in the history department of the university. During the war we lived in evacuation in Cheliabinsk. In 1945–46 the situation there was terrible. People were dying from hunger and war invalids were begging on the streets. At the same time, if one had a lot of money, it was possible to buy everything at the commercial stores.

I did well in my studies and was friendly with boys from elite families, for example, the son of a factory director. When we would go to his home for birthday parties, they would serve soda! And we thought that only the state could sell and serve soda. Or they would show a movie! We viewed this as the corruption of the Soviet leadership. The picture of inhuman suffering against the background of abundance for the wealthy ignited the fire of the class struggle in my youthful heart.

I used to discuss this ardently with a group of boys. The father of one of them had been repressed in 1937. He had a rich library with books that were printed before the Communists learned to excise the problematic spots. There we would read Lenin in a 1929 edition in which he expounded on Marxist science. It was accompanied, however, by [the Menshevik] Pavel Axelrod's remark that this was a mediocre philosophy and, in fact, things were much more complex. Or else Lenin would roundly criticize the workers' opposition and the notes would append the programs of the workers' opposition, which were naïve but truly Communist programs. We acquired a revolutionary spirit from these books and understood that the revolution had taken the wrong path. We decided to disseminate this knowledge in the workers' settlement of the Cheliabinsk tractor factory. We pasted up leaflets several times calling on the workers to fight against the bureaucracy and injustice.

KOSHAROVSKY: *And you were caught.*

VORONEL: Our group consisted of seven youths, all Jews. The KGB treated us rather humanely; they released all of us except for two. As I was a fourteen-year-old minor, I received three years in a youth colony.

KOSHAROVSKY: *And did you get the full treatment in the colony?*

VORONEL: The colony consisted mainly of boys aged fourteen to sixteen from the PTU (Polytechnical School). They were arrested for leaving work and running back home. That was considered sabotage, for which sentences from one to three years were handed out. They were immature, weak boys, easily dominated by hooligans, which the administration supported.

I might not have survived until the end of my term, but I was released early, after half a year. This was the result of a new decision by the Supreme Court according to which minors could receive a suspended sentence, and my future stepfather, a frontline soldier, interceded on my behalf.

After my release, my relatives categorically declared that in the future I would study only physics, mathematics, or something similar. My father, Vladimir Poliakov, perished at the front. My stepfather adopted me and my name became Voronel.

KOSHAROVSKY: *How did the "tremor of Judaic anxieties" awaken in you?*[61]

VORONEL: I was so attracted to science that I forgot about my humanitarian pursuits. Then, after the Six-Day War, the Poles demanded that the Jews swear loyalty to Poland or leave. And I began to think that in Russia, too, we have to decide this issue for ourselves: either we are Russians or we are Jews. Until then, the question hadn't occurred to me. And then the Leningrad Trial came up. I decided that, ultimately, I was a Jew. I became spiritually liberated and I began to read relevant literature.

KOSHAROVSKY: *When did you decide to leave?*

VORONEL: In March 1971 a small group of Moscow refuseniks received exit visas—activists with whom I was friendly such as Meir Gelfond and his circle. I asked him to send me an invitation from Israel. He sent it five times but I didn't receive it. A year later, in January 1972, Viktor Iakhot went into the Dutch embassy, requested and obtained a state invitation [entry visa] for me. After that, I received the invitations—all five of them.

KOSHAROVSKY: *How did the idea for the seminar arise?*

VORONEL: I gave a lot of thought to the fate of scientists. I saw how my colleagues suffered from the systematic refusal to let them leave. Some said that what they feared most of all was losing touch with their discipline and with scientific colleagues. The scientists came from different fields, but I was always inclined toward interdisciplinary thinking and thought it would be a good idea if each person acquainted the others with his or her work in terms that would be comprehensible to all academics even if they were not specialists in that field.

KOSHAROVSKY: *What was your assessment of the degree of danger in this initiative? After all, you intended to bring together refusenik social outcasts, Zionists, ideological enemies of the regime.*

VORONEL: I thought about it and consulted with [Valery] Chalidze. Poring over the criminal codes of the Russian Soviet Federated Socialist Republic (RSFSR) together, we found that no scientific activity could be prohibited in the Soviet Union.

KOSHAROVSKY: *After Chalidze you went to Lerner?*

VORONEL: To Lerner and [Veniamin] Levich.

KOSHAROVSKY: *Veniamin Levich had already applied for a visa?*

VORONEL: No, but I heard via third parties that he was considering it. I knew him as an outstanding physicist. We even shared some interests. Levich questioned me in detail: "Sasha, were you ever dragged into the KGB?" "Yes," I said. "They don't beat one, do they?" he asked. He was afraid. But Lerner didn't ask about that—he was more informed than I was.

KOSHAROVSKY: *Was he more informed about aliya?*

VORONEL: He was more informed about everything. He said, "I have been abroad twenty-six times. I know they won't just leave me alone. I know I must prepare for a long period of refusal, but I am confident it is worth the risk. In another decade or so everything here will collapse." He said that in September 1971! "And who will be blamed? We will be blamed, of course."

KOSHAROVSKY: *Despite its usefulness for scientists, the idea of a seminar at that time did not seem so convincing.*

VORONEL: Yes, I argued about it with Polsky. He said, "Our cause is Zionism: we should leave and that's all." Later on, however, he saw that it was successful and joined it. Incidentally, at first he also didn't approve of samizdat. He said that it reminded him of the democrats' struggle for human rights. I objected, "No, we must first identify ourselves as a separate group, let's say ethnic or social, and declare that these are the normal conditions for our life as a group. If these conditions don't suit the Soviet authorities, that's their problem, and ultimately they'll have to realize that their case is hopeless." This was, of course, an optimistic statement but it worked to a certain degree because within this logic they couldn't offer any arguments.

KOSHAROVSKY: *You initiated the seminar and let them use your apartment. In parallel, you founded a practically open samizdat journal [Jews in the USSR* (Evrei v SSSR)*] with the names of the editors and contributors on the cover. After a youth like yours, wasn't that reckless?*

VORONEL: Probably, but I myself didn't feel it. Essentially, we had to lead our life in a way that would antagonize the authorities as little as possible but at the same time was completely unacceptable to them. We had to behave in such a way that the Soviet regime would want to get rid of us. That entailed a certain risk. As you know, the regime violated laws when it considered it necessary. I was publishing samizdat, I was being dragged to interrogations at the KGB, where they would say something and threaten me but not once was I charged with anti-Soviet behavior. Yet, when it suited them, they accused Brailovsky of anti-Soviet behavior for doing the same thing.

KOSHAROVSKY: *Brailovsky was arrested in 1980 when the political circumstances had changed.*

VORONEL: I understood that it was a dangerous balancing act, but I thought it was the only option.

KOSHAROVSKY: *As far as I know, at first people did not rush to take part in the work of the seminar or journal.*

VORONEL: Yes, but afterwards everybody wanted their name on the cover.

KOSHAROVSKY: *Well, that was after the initial risk was already behind us and powerful international support materialized: participation could serve as a trampoline for aliya.*

VORONEL: At first, I didn't even dream of the grandiose support that we received, although I had hoped, of course, for some kind of backing. Before applying for an exit visa, Azbel and I met at an official international symposium in Leningrad with two Western scientists. Each of them promised support in his own way. They represented two opposing approaches that always coexisted in the Jewish support community.

Pierre Hochenberg immediately grasped the matter and said he would go anywhere and speak with whomever was necessary. He talked to Yuval Neeman, who spoke with Nehemiah Levanon. The other scientist believed in the value of secret diplomacy. He said that he would speak with Kissinger and someone else but all this led nowhere. He wanted to act individually, without the Committee of Concerned Scientists.[62] At first, we hoped that Jews would support us, perhaps some scientists also, but it turned into such a powerful and fashionable form of solidarity that people simply flocked to us. People from India, France, and so forth arrived.

KOSHAROVSKY: *Attending your seminar guaranteed them broad publicity.*

VORONEL: That was a possibility, for which we must thank Nehemiah Levanon. He, and of course Yuval Neeman, backed us with their authority.

KOSHAROVSKY: *Were you in contact with the Liaison Bureau?*

VORONEL: No. I met Levanon only in Israel.

KOSHAROVSKY: *Nehemiah loved you.*

VORONEL: Yes, and I also loved him. I saw, of course, that he was a gangster, but I liked that kind of gangster. It seems to me that one needs to be a gangster in that type of underground politics.

KOSHAROVSKY: *The arrival of important scientists was probably more than a matter of solidarity. What was the scientific level of the seminar?*

VORONEL: The main task was not to impress professionals with the achievements in one's narrow field but to try to make one's field and ideas accessible to a broader scientific circle. In most cases, this was accomplished successfully and I am proud of it.

KOSHAROVSKY: *You and Mark Azbel were old friends from Kharkov. Did he lead the seminar while you were still there?*

VORONEL: He conducted the seminar after my departure. I always led them myself. Among scientists, as among writers, there are many ambitious people who eagerly put each other down. Sometimes I had to restrain them and correct matters. Several times Mark told me later over the phone that it was a very difficult school of social behavior for him.

At first, eight people took part in the work of the seminar at Voronel's apartment: Voronel himself, Mark Azbel, Irina and Viktor Brailovsky, Dan Roginsky, Viktor Mandeltsveig, Moshe Giterman, and Veniamin Fain. In time the composition of the group expanded considerably and numbered more than twenty people. After Voronel's departure in December 1974, Mark Azbel headed the seminar.

I asked Azbel about how the seminar was run:[63]

KOSHAROVSKY: *How did you manage for so many years to stick to purely scientific topics with people who were focused on leaving the country?*

AZBEL: I had my convictions: I knew exactly what I was doing and why. Before each session, I categorically declared that during the seminar nothing other than scientific matters would be discussed. From start to finish, questions such as the following were not permitted: Who are we? Where are we? How are we doing? The start and conclusion of a seminar were always announced. It's true that I didn't interfere if people conversed quietly among themselves in the room.

Yes, we worked in various fields of physics but the discussion of ideas did not require going into complex details and didn't lower the level of discussion. We wanted to know about everything of interest in any scientific field. The program of our colloquium most frequently touched on some area of physics but there were also reports on biology and economics. We discussed current and future aspects of science.

KOSHAROVSKY: *Did foreign scientists visit you?*

AZBEL: At first, guests came just to support us in our troubles, but they left very favorably impressed by the seminar, especially because no one complained about his or her problems. People responded only to direct questions. They were astonished that we were conducting a purely scientific seminar. The results were fantastic. Nobel Prize winners were our guests!

KOSHAROVSKY: *Were your guests only Jewish scientists?*

AZBEL: There were certainly non-Jewish scientists too. It's also true that the majority were Jews. We never asked. Usually the guests were on a very high level, people who were invited everywhere but usually accepted only one invitation out of ten or twenty. The word got out about us.

KOSHAROVSKY: *Were refusenik matters discussed after the session?*

AZBEL: Usually after the end of the official part, some people left—after all, we weren't all refuseniks—and some stayed. Those who remained were free to talk about any topic. I merely warned them, "Speak freely, but keep in mind that we have a KGB presence in the room recording everything on tape." We therefore frequently used children's "magic slates." Do you remember them? You wrote on the plastic and when you lifted it up from the waxed board, the writing disappeared.

On June 10, 1973, the scientists went on a hunger strike, timed to coincide with Brezhnev's visit to the United States and designed to make sure he would be confronted with uncomfortable questions about Soviet Jewish emigration.[64] Azbel declared for the world press, "We don't want to die. We want to live and work in Israel. But we prefer to die than live here as slaves."[65] Azbel, Voronel, Giterman, Lunts, Brailovsky, Roginsky, and Anatoly Libgober participated in the strike. Hundreds of telephone calls expressing support and concern came in from all over the world. Libgober received an exit visa during the hunger strike. The KGB, caught off guard by the strike, took several days to disconnect the line, and they reconnected it after just a few hours, after indignant international protests. Three months after the hunger strike, Roginsky received an exit visa.[66]

The seminar's next large project was the holding of an international scientific symposium, scheduled for July 1–5, 1974.[67] The symposium was to be strictly scientific, devoted to questions concerning the application of physics and math to other branches of science. According to Azbel, the coincidence of the dates of the seminar with the scheduled arrival of Nixon for a visit to the USSR was unintentional, although it made the seminar seem politically provocative.[68] The planned international seminar of 1974 did not take place: Soviet authorities refused to issue entry visas to foreigners arriving for the event, and they arrested and held members of the organizing committee until the end of Nixon's visit. Not until three years later would the refusenik scientists successfully run an international seminar, in April 1977.

It was a heady time, with challenges, frustrations, and successes. Viktor Brailovsky recalled the situation in those years:[69]

BRAILOVSKY: There was a time that if a Western scientist came to Moscow and didn't visit our seminar, he would encounter dissatisfaction after he returned home. At our seminars, I became acquainted with and heard lectures by six or seven Nobel laureates—an unbelievable number. Andrei Sakharov attended the seminar. Ernst Neizvestnyi [the famous sculptor] gave a report, and there were rabbis from the various denominations who visited. One seminar a month was devoted to cultural issues. The regime was afraid of closing the seminar because it could have a serious effect on the country's scientific and technological contacts.

The American scientist Arno Penzias received the Nobel Prize for his discovery of cosmic microwave background radiation. He received it in 1978 and came to Moscow from Stockholm, visited our seminar, delivered a report that repeated his Nobel lecture, refused to visit the official Academy of Sciences institutions, and went home. This was a very powerful act and it contributed to uniting the scientific world on behalf of aliya. This segment of society had many opportunities to influence the higher ranks of the regime and this opportunity for them to show solidarity with Soviet Jews was an important part of what the seminar made possible.

Alexander Lerner, another prominent scientist internationally known as a cyberneticist, ran a seminar in his home and became an authoritative member of the movement's political leadership although he never strove to be at its head. The Weizmann Institute's department of medical cybernetics took Lerner's seminar under its wing. Eventually the seminar's activities began to include reports and discussions on the problems of Jewish life in the Soviet Union and Jewish history and culture. Anatoly Sharansky, Eitan Finkelshtein, Viktor Brailovsky, Alexander Ioffe, Alexander Lunts, Yosif and Dina Beilin, Vladimir Slepak, Yuli Kosharovsky, and many others participated. Important foreign scientists frequently visited the seminar. Lerner, a broadly educated person with a shrewd grasp of the functioning of the state apparatus, quickly attained international recognition. Practically all the distinguished guests who visited the Soviet Union tried to meet him.

Lerner spoke about his attitude to his activity:[70]

KOSHAROVSKY: *You belong to a generation that lived through the Stalin terror. Many Jews of that generation developed an insuperable fear of anything national.*

LERNER: Yes, but I wasn't intimidated.

KOSHAROVSKY: *How did that happen?*

LERNER: Starting in 1960, I was permitted to travel abroad. My expertise was in a field that was very timely: the theory of optimal control. Essentially, I initiated this direction and thus received many invitations. I was allowed to accept one out of ten. I was in France, Italy, the United States, Japan. Abroad, I understood that freedom was worth any risk.

KOSHAROVSKY: *The KGB, no doubt, tried to recruit you for their tasks?*

LERNER: It tried, but I made it very clear that I wasn't suited for that and they desisted.

KOSHAROVSKY: *You weren't attracted to the dissident movement?*

LERNER: No. Soon after I applied for an exit visa, I met with Andrei Sakharov. We agreed to cooperate with regard to aid to prisoners and we agreed that people from our movement would deal only with issues of emigration and that they would help us only in this matter.

KOSHAROVSKY: *When did you make the acquaintance of the leaders of the Jewish movement such as Polsky, Slepak, and Prestin?*

LERNER: In 1971, with my daughter Sonia's help, I met Slepak, and he introduced me to the circle of activists.

KOSHAROVSKY: *Did you work with Vitaly Rubin's humanities seminar?*

LERNER: No, but I worked with Rubin personally; he delivered lectures at my seminar.

Vitaly Rubin's humanities seminar began in Moscow in the fall of 1972.[71] Voronel played a large role in its organization. The organizing committee also included Mikhail Chlenov, Viktor Mandeltsveig, and Dmitry Segal. Reports touched on Jewish culture, language, history, tradition, and religion. There were, for example, interesting reports on Jewish mysticism, the history of Russian Jewry, Hebrew language, and anti-Semitism, and there were book reports. Some physicists, including Voronel, enjoyed attending this seminar. Refuseniks showed great interest in the seminar; at times, fifty to seventy people piled into Rubin's apartment.[72] Rubin was, undoubtedly, a charismatic personality. He quickly became known in the West and many people fought actively for his freedom. His excellent linguistic ability enabled him to establish good relations with foreign correspondents, with Western activists, and with people in the American embassy. He developed many friendships in those circles. Vitaly left for Israel in 1976.

Personal Recollections: The Engineering Seminar

Kosharovsky: At the end of 1973, I moved to the apartment vacated after Nora Kornblum's departure and acquired friends among my new neighbors. Soon I was receiving a stream of visitors who wished to consult about visa issues related to emigration, Israel, and refusenik life. One of my new acquaintances, a charming dissident, Igor Abramovich, introduced me to Lev Karp, who possessed an advanced degree in technical sciences and was interested in emigrating. Karp and I agreed that it would be good to have our own seminar. Lev Karp and Igor Abramovich were immediately invited to deliver several lectures and I decided to check whether the idea was feasible. I talked with Slepak, Polsky, Prestin, Abramovich, Begun, and Volvovsky, who all had an interest in radio electronics. They liked the idea and most expressed a desire to participate. I spoke with several more refuseniks and got together about ten people.

At that time, about thirty thousand people were emigrating annually and we were sure that we, too, would succeed in getting out in a year or two. It was perfectly natural to wish to maintain our professional level before our departure. Aside from our professional interests in the seminar, as active members of the Jewish movement we found it useful to associate in a close circle and exchange opinions on the numerous pressing problems we faced. I was responsible for arranging the seminar's meeting place and other organizational matters. We used to meet once a week for about three hours, after which several people remained to discuss current issues.

The engineering seminar operated for about two years. Under its influence, a similar seminar was set up in Leningrad that met in the apartment of Aba Taratuta.

Demonstrations

Several young refuseniks who wanted more action—genuine demonstrations on the streets and squares of Moscow with posters and slogans—coalesced into a group. They were not anti-Soviet; they simply wanted to go to Israel, and the sooner the better. They personally could not rely on quiet diplomacy or the Western establishment because Western social and political figures appealed directly to the Soviet leadership only in the cases of major scientists and well-known refuseniks. As they did not fit into those categories, they decided to escalate the struggle.

It was a risky game. Not everyone supported it, because many considered such methods could provoke the regime to carry out punitive measures against the entire refusenik community. There was a measure of truth to those assertions but, in essence, all our actions and even the very desire to leave the Soviet Union were provocations in the authorities' eyes. This group with its militant temperament and uncompromising nature was nicknamed the "Hong Wei Bing."[73] They were also called "Herutniki" after the Israeli right-wing party Herut although there was no special connection with this party. Led by its founder, Mikhail Babel, the group staged its first demonstration on May 3, 1973, in Pushkin Square. Demonstrators included Valery Krizhak, Boris Tsitlenok, Lev Kogan, Leonid Tsypin, and Babel. The demonstration coincided with the visit to Moscow of US Secretary of State Henry Kissinger, who arrived to coordinate Brezhnev's upcoming visit to the United States. As the summit meeting was planned for the middle of the following month, the Western press carefully followed everything that occurred in the Soviet Union at that time.

Babel's group also demonstrated in the next two months outside the prosecutor's office, near the Kremlin Wall and near OVIR. In less than two months, the group held five demonstrations.

Mikhail Babel spoke about this activity:[74]

KOSHAROVSKY: *Misha, they call you the founder of the group. What impelled you to take such a risky step?*

BABEL: The founder? No, not exactly. There were other fine fellows—Valera Krizhak and Boria Tsitlenok—who constituted the hard core, and then the rest joined one by one. We concluded that the old methods were not working, and we very much wanted to go to Israel.

KOSHAROVSKY: *You yourself wanted to leave for Israel or you thought you were helping everyone?*

BABEL: No, I didn't intend to struggle for everyone. I simply understood that we could go on writing letters for dozens of years, but that wouldn't get us out. I was strongly influenced by Rabbi Meir Kahane, who, I could see, blazed the trail for us.

I saw, Yuli, that I was alone, and I didn't want to remain a refusenik for years. After a while, I perceived that Krizhak felt the same. Then we noticed that Tsitlenok, Zakhar Tesker, and Lev Kogan were like-minded. We checked them out, considering such verification was important. There was also, of course, the provocateur Tsypin.[75] Such people couldn't be avoided in those matters. The most important thing, however, was that we weren't operating secretly; there was nothing anti-Soviet in it. At the start, I consulted with Andrei Tverdokhlebov.[76]

KOSHAROVSKY: *Did you support close ties with the democrats?*

BABEL: No. I wasn't interested in democracy [in the USSR] because I felt that it wasn't my country and I didn't need to bother with it. I had one goal and I asked his advice with regard to demonstrations. He replied, "Look, you want to jump across a puddle; why must you announce this to anyone or to ask permission for that?" I very much liked his approach—he was a marvelous person. I understood that, in general, there was no violation of the law. Later, the KGB officers also explained that the Constitution does not prohibit demonstrations.

KOSHAROVSKY: *With which aliya leaders were you in contact?*

BABEL: Not with anyone in particular. They all condemned us.

KOSHAROVSKY: *Did Polsky condemn you?*

BABEL: Yes. Via his wife, he told me, "You are kicking up your heels in vain. It's better to sit quietly."

KOSHAROVSKY: *Did Slepak condemn you?*

BABEL: I didn't hear that he did.

KOSHAROVSKY: *No doubt Lunts supported you.*

BABEL: He supported us in words, not deeds. None of them supported us in deeds as they considered it too risky. Several years later, Ida [Nudel] and Volodia [Slepak] hung up big signs on the balconies of their apartments, after which they were arrested.[77]

KOSHAROVSKY: *But before you, too, there were demonstrations—at the Central Committee office, in the OVIR reception room, and the Central Telegraph Agency. There were also hunger strikes but not posters.*

BABEL: I participated in all of that but I understood later that it was all idle dreams.

The group's last demonstration with Babel took place on June 28, 1973, on the Mayakovsky metro station platform. Babel then received an exit visa and two weeks later, on July 19, he left for Israel.

Valery Krizhak talked about the group's activity and its continuation after Babel emigrated:[78]

KOSHAROVSKY: *Who led the group after Misha Babel's departure?*

KRIZHAK: It's hard to say. It's clear that Misha was the locomotive. Afterwards, things continued by inertia.

KOSHAROVSKY: *What attracted you to this group?*

KRIZHAK: Look, I signed letters but it didn't seem to produce results. The letters turned the protest into something that didn't bother anyone. I was feeling down and then Misha appeared. As you know, the granting or denying of exit visas was completely arbitrary. Misha said, "All these letters are a waste of time. We should make sure that the dust doesn't settle on our files."

KOSHAROVSKY: *Misha says that many aliya leaders were dissatisfied with you. They said that you endangered aliya.*

KRIZHAK: Possibly, but I used to meet also those kind of quiet Jews who said to us, "We don't know whether your actions helped you, but they definitely helped us."

KOSHAROVSKY: *What happened after Babel's departure?*

KRIZHAK: A lot of demonstrations.

Natan Sharansky also participated in these demonstrations:[79]

KOSHAROVSKY: *How did you wind up in this group of cocky demonstrators?*

SHARANSKY: It's more a story of how I became part of the refusenik community. Near the synagogue, I made the acquaintance of Lev Kogan, who explained the structure of the refusenik world as follows: "Look, over here are the big shots, all kinds of Slepaks, Luntses, Prestins, and Abramoviches who run everything and consider that they know everything. They call our group 'Hong Wei Bing' and we call them 'big shots.' We go out to demonstrations and don't obey anyone." Anarchist types!

Kogan said that at every occasion, the big shots ask Israel what to do and what not to do. "Israel has its political considerations. We don't ask permission from anyone. We are struggling for our right to depart and we hold demonstrations. Join us." He was the first person I met and I liked his freedom-loving approach. While still in the process of applying, I began to meet with this group regularly.

KOSHAROVSKY: *Once I also went out with them and sat out my fifteen days. That demonstration took place on October 2, with ten participants but you weren't there.*

SHARANSKY: I remember that demonstration very well. That day played a very important role in my life—my link with Avital began on that day. You stood near the TASS building and served time during the Yom Kippur War. Why wasn't I there? I was not yet a refusenik as I had applied for an exit visa in the summer and had not yet received an answer. The Hong Wei Bing decided that the end of September was a good time for political demonstrations. No one knew the war would break out then. On the one hand, many people advised me that it didn't pay to demonstrate before receiving a refusal: "How can you demand that you be given an exit visa when you are not yet a refusenik?" On the other hand, Lev Kogan encouraged me, saying, "Let's go."

Thinking that the important thing was not that I hadn't received a refusal but that I did not yet have a visa, I decided to participate in the next demonstration. I liked their spirit of freedom and the romance of struggle. The first demonstration was at the end of September. Lev Kogan explained, "The first time we don't say when and where. Come to me, make yourself a poster: 'Visas instead of prison,' 'I want to go to Israel,' or whatever you want, better if it's in English." We arranged to meet an hour before the demonstration. One of the few that were photographed, it took place near the Interior Ministry building. In the photograph, I am shielded by a policeman. We arrived and held up our posters. What happened? We were taken to the eighth Moscow detox station. Subsequently, I was at that detox station eight times, but that was the first. Several people received fifteen days. Kogan and I were fined. The following day, the Sabbath, a tall young man named Misha Shtiglits appeared near the synagogue. He said that he heard about the demonstration over the radio and he wanted to join us. He spoke openly even though the KGB was all around and looking at him.

Bella Ramm sent him to me, saying "Look, that fellow was at the demonstration. He could probably help you." Misha was over six feet tall. As you know, I'm a bit shorter. In order to hear each other, we had to speak loudly. "You know," I said, "the KGB men are all around. Let's change places." He went out into the street and I stood on the sidewalk but with the difference in our height, it didn't help that much. I said, "If you want to participate in a demonstration, I can help you. We have already planned the next one." I brought him to my home and explained, already feeling very important: "I don't have the right to tell you where and when but let's meet at such and such a time at Pushkin Square. Bring a placard and I'll take you to the place."

We arranged to meet, but at that time, I unexpectedly received a message that the director of OVIR wanted to see me urgently. The demonstration was scheduled for 10:00 a.m., and he wanted to see me at 8:30. The head of OVIR wants to talk to me! This was the authorities' first reaction of any kind to my application. I dressed warmly in preparation for the demonstration, put the poster over my stomach, and went to OVIR. Zolotukhin, the head of the Moscow OVIR, said that my case was going to receive an affirmative response. "In a few days you will receive an official reply." "Why did you summon me today if you don't have an official answer?" "Well, so that you take it into consideration." That meant that they knew something (of course, they knew everything because Tsypin was involved), and I was in an absurd situation. On the one hand, if I am going to receive the visa in a few days, it's stupid to go to a demonstration. On the other hand, it was too late to warn anyone about my ambivalent situation.

With those thoughts, I went to Pushkin Square, met Misha, and told him frankly—even though we hardly knew each other and had met only two or three times—about my dilemma. He said, "What kind of monkey business is this! Our goal, after all, is to leave, and they are telling you that you shall leave. If they deceive you, we'll have a lot more demonstrations. Now explain what I should do." I told him, "In fifteen minutes go to the TASS building. You'll see other people there and you'll raise your placard with them." That was the very demonstration in which you participated.

KOSHAROVSKY: *By deceiving you so roundly they reinforced your motivation for the future.*

SHARANSKY: After that, it became clear to me that one must never react to what they say. That's one of their tactics.

I'll tell you why that demonstration played such an important role in my life. Natasha Shtiglits,[80] who had no idea that her brother was planning to go to a demonstration, was by chance riding in a trolley past the TASS building when she saw the demonstration. Catching sight of her brother, who is hard to miss, you'll agree, she yelled to the driver, "Stop, stop!" But he drove on to the trolley stop, which is somewhere near Pushkin Square. By the time Natasha ran back, there was no one there. She began to rush about hysterically. After that she came to the synagogue to clarify what had happened to her brother. Lyova Liberman sent her to me. As you recall, at that time, the Yom Kippur War broke out. Naturally, we were all preoccupied with the war, writing letters to the Red Cross and demanding the opportunity to donate blood for Israeli soldiers. I was collecting signatures for this near the synagogue. After the demonstration, I had acquired KGB tails for the first time in my life. I approached the tails and suggested that they sign too. And at that moment Natasha, who had landed in this fantastic world, approached.

KOSHAROVSKY: *Did she have any relationship to the movement?*

SHARANSKY: None at all. I started to reassure her that it was nothing terrible; he received fifteen days. The KGB men observed us sullenly. In short, it was love at first sight. And that's how our romance began.

Although the TASS demonstration was quickly dispersed, it was part of a cascading demonstration; that is, every few days new people went out to demonstrate and each time in a different spot in Moscow. Authorities regularly jailed participants, but some also received exit visas relatively quickly: Valery Krizhak received an exit visa at the beginning of June 1974 and went to Israel. In September 1974 Lev Kogan received an exit visa. After Kogan's departure, there were a few more demonstrations. On Purim, February 24, 1974, a demonstration was held near the Lenin

Library that lasted half a minute. Consequences for a few of the participants were more severe this time: while Tsypin and Sharansky were released and the rest were arrested for fifteen days, Mark Nashpits and Boris Tsitlenok were brought to trial and sentenced to five years of exile. Sharansky recalled, "Two people were sent into exile for five years after an ordinary demonstration near the library. That caused people to think twice before going to a demonstration, knowing it might result in being sent to prison. Other forms of activity got under way at that time but that was the last purely Hong Wei Bing demonstration."[81] Street demonstrations ceased for awhile but hunger strikes and demonstrations in government institutions continued.

Religious Revival

The Jewish religious renaissance followed the Zionist renaissance, which stimulated a search for roots, a return to national values, and the study of Hebrew. At first, for the great majority, attending synagogue, wearing a yarmulke (*kippah*), and celebrating religious holidays were perceived more as elements of national identification rather than of faith. Gradually, however, a group of people evolved for whom the study and teaching of religious knowledge became primary, and they formed the religious core of the refusenik community.

Mikhail Grinberg, later a well-known Israeli publisher of Russian-language works, shared his recollections:[82]

GRINBERG: I remember being invited to a succah for the first time in 1969, when I was eighteen years old. About ten old men and eighty young men and women were sitting inside. That was in Saltykov near Moscow. Srolik Pinsky, then the Chabad treasurer, brought me there from Malakhovka in great secrecy.

KOSHAROVSKY: *Did you play any active role in Russia?*

GRINBERG: In the 1980s I did. I lived on the outskirts of Moscow in my own home. We loved to organize Chabad gatherings, which are a central part of Hasidic life, with celebration, study, and discussions. In addition, I performed some tasks, delivered lectures, and then I was asked to head the Malakhovka community. I repaired the synagogue there and renewed Torah lessons. There was a lot to do. Zeev Shakhnovsky was also there. Grigory Rozenshtein and Reb Geich Vilensky were in charge. I was in contact with Geich. I was then instructed to restore the graves of *tsadikim* [revered righteous men]. I visited twenty-five places and restored many things. Thus, when I arrived in Israel, I became a hero of the Hasidic population.

KOSHAROVSKY: *Were you also in contact with Zionists?*

GRINBERG: I didn't engage in politics and tried not to associate with Zionists, only with Yuli Edelstein, whom I inherited, as I was friendly with his father. Sometimes Yuli would drag me to some place.

KOSHAROVSKY: *I remember that. I was at your house several times.*

GRINBERG: Yes, and Edelstein's wedding was at my house. He was arrested a few months after the wedding, in 1984.

By the beginning of the 1970s, a popular Hebrew teacher, Zeev Shakhnovsky, also turned to teaching Torah. Many Hebrew teachers included excerpts from the Bible in their lessons. This material made it possible to become familiar with the most ancient sources of the language and to hear the voice of one's distant ancestors. Shakhnovsky's Torah studies became his primary preoccupation. He mastered the special Rashi script and included Rashi's commentaries in his lessons.

Shakhnovsky discussed his experience as a religious refusenik:[83]

KOSHAROVSKY: *How did you wind up in the Chabad camp?*

SHAKHNOVSKY: Pinsky had a role in that.

KOSHAROVSKY: *You not only delved deeper into the Torah but also began to teach Torah.*

SHAKHNOVSKY: All the initial Hebrew teachers, even without becoming religious, introduced the Torah into their lessons, considering that one ought to read from it.

KOSHAROVSKY: *Yes, they did it because of an interest in the language, but in your case, it became a way of life.*

SHAKHNOVSKY: Correct. Then it was, at least, part of everybody's culture, but now it's not that way. At the time, many wanted to read the Torah.

KOSHAROVSKY: *We proceeded from total ignorance, exploring our national "I," trying everything. It fit some people and not others.*

SHAKHNOVSKY: Yes, and it's hard to say why it fit. I have been observing this phenomenon for many years but have not found a clear-cut answer. Apparently, some people have a predisposition toward this.

KOSHAROVSKY: *How did the Chabad circle begin to form?*

SHAKHNOVSKY: For some reason, it is characteristic of Chabad to be active in approaching others. If you travel to Nepal, you can be 90 percent sure that you will meet a chabadnik there. Take, for example, 1970–72, when all religious people in Russia were very intimidated. I knew only one of our chabadniks who had not been in prison. Do you remember Reb Motel Lifshits the mohel? He was imprisoned for fourteen years because he performed circumcisions. They were all very intimidated.

According to a legend, the Lubavicher Rebbe said that Jews should stop being afraid and reach out to people, and chabadniks were the first to do that. In our time, when a rabbi would arrive from abroad, there was no particular private home to direct him to, but it was already possible to visit a chabadnik at his apartment. A few—Minsky and Geich—were not afraid to invite even young people. I remember, for instance, sitting in Geich's home on some holiday with Lev Gorodetsky. When I married Lena in 1975 in a religious marriage ceremony, I was permitted to invite to the huppah only Misha Goldblat in addition to the old men.

KOSHAROVSKY: *Inna and I had our huppah in September 1975. An American rabbi, Haskel Lookstein from New York, conducted the ceremony and there were a lot of people.*

SHAKHNOVSKY: Yes, because already in August 1975, a huppah ceremony was held directly in the synagogue in Marina Roshcha and there were about sixty people attending. In 1975 Grisha Rozenshtein became heavily involved. He turned to religion and quietly studied Hebrew. I don't like administrative work whereas he organized everything, including meetings with foreign guests. He left his mark in these matters; he was a strong organizer.

At approximately the same time, Ilia Essas became active. He has a good head and is a good organizer.

KOSHAROVSKY: *Indeed, Essas began as an activist: he signed letters and was part of the central circle of activists.*

SHAKHNOVSKY: But Essas didn't go to the barricades. He arranged to study Talmud and Torah with an old man, one on one. He went there quietly and studied. They set it up for him from Riga. He studied with a man who served time for ten years because of that activity.

Chabad, Aguda, and the Religious Zionist Movement

Chabad (Lubavich), Aguda (Agudath Yisrael), and the Religious Zionist movements were the three religious trends represented among Soviet Jews in the late Soviet period. Chabad is a specific Hasidic sect known for its active outreach to Jews. The Chabad Rebbe Yosef Yitzchak Schneerson was active in the Soviet Union until his arrest in 1927, before being allowed to leave. Aguda (Agudat Yisrael, or the Israelite Union) is a traditional Orthodox group spanning Hasidic and Lithuanian (Litvak or Mitnagdim) communities with branches in many countries. The best-known leader of Religious Zionism (also called Mizrachi) was Rav Abraham Isaac Kook.

Chabad activity in Moscow centered around Zeev Shakhnovsky, Mikhail Shneider, and Grigory Rozenshtein and in Leningrad around Yitzhak Kogan. The Aguda activity in Moscow was concentrated around Mikhail Nudler and Ilia (Eliyahu) Essas and in Leningrad around Grigory Vasserman. The religious Zionist leaders in Moscow were Vlad Dashevsky, Mikhail Kara-Ivanov, Pinhas Polonsky, and Alexander Kholmyansky.

Ilia Essas explained his work and position among the religious refuseniks:[84]

KOSHAROVSKY: *I recall that you had many groups.*

ESSAS: In 1977 I had fifteen students. In 1980 there were fifty students, and when I left in 1986, those who studied with me in one way or another numbered around two hundred.

KOSHAROVSKY: *How did you supply them with textbooks?*

ESSAS: One of my students made photocopies. As you know, I respected the criminal code and therefore did not make Xerox copies. We copied excerpts from the siddur [prayer book] and Chumash [five books of Moses]. Then, gradually, I got to know the old men who had books.

Some were the descendants of religious Jews; they either gave or sold us those books. They no longer needed them but were embarrassed to burn or discard them.

KOSHAROVSKY: *When you were in refusal, you were defined as the leader of Aguda, Dashevsky as the leader of Mizrachi, and Rozenshtein as the leader of Chabad. How accurate is it to define you as a person adhering to the Aguda Party's worldview?*

ESSAS: Not one of the above-mentioned organizations can say that I am an adherent of their political ideas, so that is simply untrue. If you consider the rabbis who came to give lessons to my group, I would say that four out of five were associated with Aguda and one of five with Mizrachi. You understand, however, that I didn't invite those foreign guests. They were people sent by the Liaison Bureau or friends from England or America.

KOSHAROVSKY: *Ilia, you were, after all, a serious activist in the aliya struggle and a Zionist. Eretz Yisrael is very serious for you.*

ESSAS: Yes, more serious, I think, than for many others.

KOSHAROVSKY: *But Aguda, as far as I understand, still does not accept the State of Israel. Help me resolve this contradiction. The way I remember you and the way you are defined seem incompatible to me.*

ESSAS: Jewish life is complex, Yulik. I consider that Jews ought to live in Israel, and through my own life I show this. I respect rabbis and teachers of the Torah without any connection to politics. Aguda people were living in Israel long before we came here. They were part of the government and the Knesset before we applied for exit visas.

Vladimir Dashevsky was a leader of the religious Zionist group in refusal:[85]

KOSHAROVSKY: *Who was your Hebrew teacher?*

DASHEVSKY: I am embarrassed to say that I never had a teacher. I studied Hebrew on my own; therefore, there were many gaps. My first textbook was that of Shlomo Kodesh and my first 200–300 words came from there.

KOSHAROVSKY: *How did you study Torah? Didn't you need a solid knowledge of Hebrew?*

DASHEVSKY: Not only of Hebrew. When we began to study Talmud, we also needed to know Aramaic, but the question was how to learn it. I remember that it took me a week to read the first page of Gemara [the Talmud] and I wept copious tears. I couldn't understand what was written. But when you really have to. . . .

KOSHAROVSKY: *You began in 1979–80?*

DASHEVSKY: In 1979 we just started, and in 1980 the structure was completely formed. Ten of us would meet once a week for about five hours and teach each other. During the week, each had his circle of Torah study that met once or twice a week. I decided to teach Talmud for the first time in 1984, when I myself was on a fairly low level. It is worth emphasizing that starting from a clear, nationally motivated decision to leave for Israel, we moved in the direction of religion, but there were groups that moved in the opposite direction. All the people I knew in our group started with a focus on Israel and moved toward religion. None went the other way.

KOSHAROVSKY: *Did your group have a name?*

DASHEVSKY: It had the underground name "the firm." We were all unemployed and earned some money tutoring graduate students.

KOSHAROVSKY: *Did you have some principled disagreements with Ilia Essas's group?*

DASHEVSKY: Look, we didn't develop in a vacuum. America and Israel exerted a strong influence, and a significant part of the organizational structures were imported. Three trends thus developed rather quickly in the refuseniks' milieu: Chabad, the Lithuanian direction, and religious Zionism.

KOSHAROVSKY: *Were you involved with the organization of a kindergarten or school?*

DASHEVSKY: Yes. Slavik Uspensky, Ania Chernobylsky, and others studied with us. In the summer we organized a kindergarten at a dacha in Povarovo, then for several years in Ukhtomka. It was a religious school. In addition, we worked with the school of Elazar [Liusik] Iusefovich and supplied him with teachers. We established kindergartens up to 1990–91.

KOSHAROVSKY: *How would you estimate the scale of religious activity in refusal and its influence on the aliya struggle?*

DASHEVSKY: Of course, the majority were far removed from religion, but I can hardly recall any refuseniks in our day who were anti-religious.

KOSHAROVSKY: *Yes, it was a time of searching for national identification.*

DASHEVSKY: For people of our generation of refuseniks—both religious and nonreligious—the feeling that religion is a part of self-identification remains an important fact even today. I hope that I shall never lose it. The presence of a religious sector in refusal was absolutely necessary because without it, we would have been in some way like the dissidents, who, after the fall of the Soviet regime, had nothing left to do.

The Jewish religious renaissance was made possible by the numerous links with foreign religious communities and the help that they extended to refuseniks by supplying religious literature, religious objects, and kosher food. At the same time, the help came with corresponding ideological influences on the newly religious (*baalei tshuva* in Hebrew).

Unofficial Publications: Samizdat

Uncensored, informal production and circulation of texts, known as samizdat, helped fill in the gaps created by Soviet censorship. Among the refuseniks, such unofficial publications helped to educate people, through books on Jewish history, religion, and culture and Hebrew textbooks. It provided Soviet Jews with information, in the form of newspapers, journals, informational bulletins, and chronicles of the struggle. Samizdat was an instrument of the struggle, inasmuch as people used it to circulate letters and appeals to Soviet and foreign bodies. It also allowed for the self-expression of the community. Samizdat served as a means of communicating with the Jewish world and the West, facilitating mutual understanding.

The Jewish national movement did not aim at reforming the Soviet social or political order. The content of Jewish samizdat reflected the emigration struggle and the national revival, and its editors and authors tried to keep their published material within that framework. Neither of these themes was in conflict with the Soviet Constitution; therefore, as the rules of the game became more or less defined around the beginning of 1972, Jewish samizdat began to acquire a practically open character.

Initially, unofficial Jewish literature circulating as samizdat included literary works on Jewish themes by well-known literary authors, such as Joseph Brodsky, Vladislav Khodasevich, Ilia Erenburg, and others. One could also find new works by Nina Voronel, Alexander Radkovsky, Yuri Kolker, Boris Khazanov, and many others whose works first circulated there. Historical research was also published in samizdat.[86] Original and translated religious literature circulated too: for example, *Chabad* by Grigory Rozenshtein and *Commentaries on the Bible* by Ilia Essas. Textbooks for the study of Hebrew written by the refuseniks Ida and Aba Taratuta, a Hebrew grammar by Leonid Zeliger, and other pedagogical materials enjoyed wide distribution among refusenik networks.

As contacts with the West expanded, refuseniks resorted increasingly to *tamizdat*, works published abroad. Because the growing demand for books with cultural, historical, and religious content could not be met by books brought in from the West, some of those books were translated and reproduced in the Soviet Union, thus also turning into samizdat. Popular works in this genre included Leon Uris's *Exodus*, Cecil Roth's *A Short History of the Jewish People*, excerpts from Simon Dubnov's *History*, and articles by Vladimir (Zeev) Jabotinsky, Joseph Trumpeldor, and others. After access was arranged for supplying to the USSR books from the Russian-language series Biblioteka Aliya produced in Israel, many of them were also reproduced and distributed in samizdat.[87] Other popular items in refusenik circles were cassettes with recorded songs in Hebrew and audio material for studying Hebrew.

Periodicals appeared only at the stage of an open struggle for aliya in 1969–70. At that time, the democratic movement already had its periodical editions, including the poetic collections *Syntax* (1959–60), the literary and publicistic journal *Phoenix* (1961, 1966), and the important human rights bulletin *Chronicle of Current Events* (1968).[88] The decision to publish the first periodical, *Iton*, was taken by the All-Union Coordinating Committee. The editorial board, which included representatives from Moscow, Leningrad, and Riga, produced two issues of *Iton*—*Iton Alef* and *Iton Bet*—in 1970. The third issue of the journal was confiscated and the editor, publishers, and distributors were arrested and convicted. Some of them were tried at the Leningrad Trial.

A few weeks after the appearance of *Iton,* the journal *Iskhod* (Exodus) was published in Moscow. Vitaly Svechinsky and Viktor Fedoseev worked on *Iskhod,* a Jewish counterpart to the *Chronicle of Current Events.*[89] At first, Jewish samizdat reflected the influence of the democratic samizdat on the more assimilated Moscow Jewish intelligentsia. Considerably less influence was exerted on the Riga Jewish samizdat as the manifestation of old Zionist traditions was stronger there. In time, Jewish samizdat journals freed themselves from external influences and began to develop independently.[90] The development of a refusenik community coincided with the appearance of the next journal, *Evrei v SSSR* (Jews in the USSR), according to Svechinsky.[91]

The longest lasting and most influential Jewish samizdat publication, the literary-publicistic journal *Evrei v SSSR,* first appeared in October 1972. In accordance with its subtitle—"a collection of material on history, culture, and the problems of Jews in the USSR"—the journal published material on emigration and assimilation; Jewish culture, history, and religion; and short stories and poetry. The authors of the articles in the journal were expected to be competent in the topics they undertook to write about and the material was not to be political in nature or contain slanderous information. Activists Alexander Voronel and Viktor Iakhot were founders of the journal.

Voronel talked about the concept of the journal *Evrei v SSSR:*[92]

VORONEL: I thought that Jews should express themselves in their own words. Thanks to Nelli [Voronel's wife, Nina, a writer], I often associated with writers, and almost all of them were Jews. I was astonished at the degree to which none of them felt free to express himself as a Jew. There were tragicomic meetings in this sense, for example, with Alexander Moiseevich Volodin, a very successful playwright in Russia. We were close acquaintances and I would often visit him when we were in Leningrad. When I was already in refusal, I once dropped in with my samizdat and gave him something to read. He grabbed it, read it avidly, and said, "This was so nice! For the first time, I read the printed word 'Jew' without a blush of shame. Indeed, every time that I pronounced this word, I would look around and somehow feel awkward." His real name was Lifshits, and, as a Russian writer, he was not only simply afraid, he was somewhat ashamed of being a Jew.

KOSHAROVSKY: *Were you pressured because of the journal?*

VORONEL: I was often dragged to the KGB, especially before the international seminar in 1974, when it happened almost daily. They tried to intimidate me on account of both the seminar and samizdat. The KGB officer would say about the journal, for example, "Of course this is not Article 70, but it approaches 190." I would reply, "No, because Article 190 is about slander, that is, a patent untruth. But I think that everything that we publish is the truth." He: "That's what you think, but I am telling you that it's slander!" "And who are you?" I ask. "Who can determine what is true and what is falsehood?" He says, "What do you mean? The KGB is telling you that it's untrue!" I say, "That's the first time that I heard truth defined that way. After all, I am a scientist." And he said, "Keep in mind, if you persist, sooner or later, it will end in Article 190."

Article 190

Soviet authorities introduced Article 190 into the Criminal Code of the Russian Republic of the USSR in 1966. Article 190-1, commonly used for cases involving samizdat, covered "knowingly false fabrications that defame the Soviet state." Article 190-3 dealt with public meetings that disturb the peace. The article was part of a new infrastructure put in place at the KGB in the late 1960s to deal with dissidence. The Fifth Directorate of the KGB was established in 1967 to focus on dissidence and complement the work of the Second Directorate, tasked with maintaining internal political control. Article 190 represented a finer tool for handling activists than preceding articles. Article 58.10 had been widely employed under Stalin against supposed counterrevolutionary agitation and ideological diversion. Article 70 replaced Article 58.10 in 1958 to cover anti-Soviet agitation and propaganda. Article 190 omitted the "anti-Soviet" charge and because it carried lesser penalties, it was less likely to provoke the vigorous international protests that began occurring in the late 1960s. Analogous articles with different numbers were added to the criminal codes of other Soviet republics.

The last editor of the journal was Viktor Brailovsky. The human rights situation in the USSR deteriorated sharply after the Soviet invasion into Afghanistan in 1979. The rules of the game changed. What had been acceptable during the period of détente became cause for indictment under the new conditions.

Brailovsky spoke about *Evrei v SSSR* toward the end of its run:[93]

KOSHAROVSKY: *Viktor, what was the concept of the journal in your day?*

BRAILOVSKY: It was very simple: to acquaint people with the foundations of Jewish philosophy, with the viewpoints of noted Jews in Russia, and with what others think about us. We translated a lot of material. There were rather interesting interviews with Father Men and with Andrei Sakharov.[94] We also published belletristic works, philosophy, and even religious literature.

KOSHAROVSKY: *The authors' names were in the open, but the printing and dissemination were secret.*

BRAILOVSKY: Far from all of the authors' names were open. Many published under pseudonyms.

KOSHAROVSKY: *Were you dragged in [to the KGB] because of journalistic matters?*

BRAILOVSKY: All the time. In the end, I was separated from the common case and charged specifically.

KOSHAROVSKY: *Who else was dragged in besides you?*

BRAILOVSKY: I think they brought in [Ilia] Rubin, [Emma] Sotnikov, [Mark] Azbel,[95] and [Vladimir] Lazaris.

KOSHAROVSKY: *It was a case about slander?*

BRAILOVSKY: Yes, Article 190-1.

KOSHAROVSKY: *After you were taken, the journal stopped appearing?*

BRAILOVSKY: Yes, and it did not start up again. The last issue, no. 21, appeared in August 1979.

After the Soviet invasion of Afghanistan, the tense international and domestic situation affected the functioning of the refusenik community. The regime persecuted all forms of organized activity, including the publication of periodicals. In 1982, when the regime had almost crushed Jewish samizdat in Moscow, the *Leningradskii evreiskii almanakh* began to appear, forced like the earliest journals to keep its editors' names secret. It published literary works and articles on literary criticism, religion, and history. Among the participants were Eduard Erlikh, Grigory Vasserman, Semyon Frumkin, and Mikhail Beizer.

The regime began to ease up at the start of perestroika. Refusenik publications of this era included the *Evreiskii ezhegodnik* (Jewish Annual) (nos. 1–3, 1986–88, Moscow), with Vladimir Mushinsky, Grigory Levitsky, and Zeev Geizel serving as the editorial board. Beginning in 1987, issues of the *Evreiskii istoricheskii almanakh* (Jewish Historical Almanac) (nos. 1–3, 1987–89) were published by the Jewish Historical Society, founded by Valery Engel. The editorial board of the *Informatsionnyi biulleten' po problemam repatriatsii i evreiskoi kul'tury* (Information Bulletin on Issues of Repatriation and Jewish Culture) (1987–90, Moscow) included Alexander Feldman, Alexander Smukler, and others. From 1988 to 1989, the legal seminar journal *Problemy otkaza* (Problems of Refusal) appeared.

The independent publication of textbooks was a particular aspect of samizdat activity. The demand for such material continually increased, and in Moscow alone each month saw the preparation of hundreds of copies of the textbooks *Elef milim* and *Mori*, verb tables, dictionaries, reading texts in easy Hebrew, and other pedagogical materials. Textbooks were generally prepared by photographic copying, whereas belletristic and nonfiction samizdat works were more likely to be produced on the typewriter. Textbooks (like journals) circulated from hand to hand and were read until they were worn out. Some people copied over dictionaries and textbooks by hand for their personal use. The demand for textbooks increased sharply from the start of the 1980s, when Moscow instructors helped develop Hebrew teaching in provincial cities. Several groups worked simultaneously to prepare and distribute samizdat, but they worked in isolation from each other so that if one was exposed, the others would not suffer.

Vladimir Mushinsky, for example, assembled a production line for samizdat. He worked with Prestin, Kosharovsky, Fulmakht, and Geizel. Gradually, a large publishing "syndicate" arose under his wing. Mushinsky became involved in the movement in 1976. His longtime friend, the Kiev activist Lev Elbert, introduced him to Prestin. Good-natured and sociable, Mushinsky knew how to get along with everyone. His keen understanding of human nature and rich personal experience enabled him to utilize the services of people who either were not connected to the movement at all or outwardly did not manifest any link, including a considerable number of non-Jews.

Samizdat helped Jews survive in refusal. It brought a breath of fresh air into the stagnant, poisoned atmosphere of the Soviet Union. For many, it became a window to the larger world extending beyond the borders of the Iron Curtain. For friends and supporters abroad, samizdat sent out of the USSR became the voice of the Jewish movement, facilitating their understanding of what we were fighting for and the conditions of our struggle.

The Hill and Ovrazhki

The Moscow refusenik community adopted two outdoor meeting places or "clubs." One, the "Hill" (hillock, *gorka*), was located near the central synagogue on the sloping Arkhipov Street (now called Bolshoi Spasoglinishchevsky Lane). Refuseniks would come to the "Hill" every Sabbath to sign letters, exchange opinions, and meet with out-of-towners and foreigners. If a visitor to Moscow had no acquaintances, he or she could go to the "Hill," meet activists, and find out where to study Hebrew or find lodging. It was the refuseniks' club in the center of Moscow.

Many foreign tourists and high-ranking guests in the capital considered it their duty to visit the "Hill" on the Sabbath and see this remarkable phenomenon with their own eyes. The spot was also of interest to foreign correspondents, who were frequent guests there. Refuseniks observed proper rules of conduct. They did not hold demonstrations or meetings near the religious site or disturb the public order. The regime tried to pressure the synagogue leadership, holding it responsible for the "correct" implementation of religious practice, but insofar as the Zionists gathered on the street were concerned, the leadership possessed few persuasive arguments. In an effort to stem the tide of people, the KGB officers would demonstratively photograph people from the crowd. Sometimes the authorities would cordon off the street with buses or trucks and place police barricades. Nothing helped. The Jews still went to the "Hill," ignoring the ubiquitous surveillance.

In 1973 Alexander Lerner, whose apartment had long ceased to contain all those who wished to celebrate the Jewish holidays together, suggested going to the forest for Israel Independence Day. After a time, these meetings in the forest moved to Ovrazhki, where there was a pine forest and wonderful air. The first meeting at Ovrazhki was on May 9, 1976.

A variety of activities took place at Ovrazhki. Leonid Volvovsky, who helped organize lectures, talked about how they were run:[96]

KOSHAROVSKY: *How was the program of the meetings decided?*

VOLVOVSKY: Generally, it was divided into two parts. The first part included a short lecture on history, culture, tradition, or a story about an approaching holiday or something about Israel, and the second part was Jewish songs. I myself would speak, or I would ask someone else. Misha Nudler was a big help. Either Essas or someone else would speak. Then came the singing. There was already a good group that sang at farewell parties or holidays: Zhenia Finkelberg, Igor Gurvich, and Lyova Kanevsky.

In addition, there was a sports section such as soccer, volleyball, or so forth. I used to listen all the time to song contests on Israeli radio stations and saw that we had a rather large number of people who sang. I thought that we, too, could do something similar. Then Misha Nudler, Zhenia Liberman, and I decided to organize a Jewish song contest. I chose to do it on Succot, when many people would come. The first contest took place in 1977, and a contest was subsequently held each year.

KOSHAROVSKY: *As far as I recall, the song contest was conducted four times.*

VOLVOVSKY: The last time was in 1980. I missed it because in January 1980 I was exiled to the city of Gorky.

Leonid Volvovsky was expelled from Moscow in January 1980. The climate by 1980 had become more repressive, and Leonid was too active, noticeable, and bold. In that year the authorities were "cleaning up" Moscow for the Olympics. Nevertheless, about two thousand people gathered for the final song contest at Ovrazhki.

Mutual Aid

Mutual help and support constituted the backbone of the refusenik community. Concern for one's neighbor and aid to the needy brought to life the most ancient and blessed traditions of the Jewish people. In the Soviet Union, unfortunately, most Jews were not inculcated with those values, but our genetic memory and Western help enabled us to overcome that deficiency.

On the whole, the refuseniks did not go hungry. They were more or less adequately supplied with clothes and shoes, and in cases of need they even received Western medicines. For the most part, Prisoners of Zion and their families also received the necessary support. Whenever someone faced danger, everything possible was done to protect him or her from the regime's retribution. The authorities, however, contrived in every way to make the refuseniks' life more bitter and unhappy, letting them serve as an example of the fate that would befall anyone who dared to oppose them. Official propaganda constantly asserted that the activists were paid agents of international Zionism, imperialism, or even of Western intelligence services.

While our mutual aid overcame the Soviet citizens' complete defenselessness vis-à-vis the regime, it nevertheless remained a very complex and dangerous matter that was organized informally. There were many forms of aid, each of which was independent of the other. First, there were a number of well-to-do people among the Jews of the Caucasus, Western Ukraine, the Baltic republics, and even Kiev and Moscow. When they left the country, several of them allotted considerable sums for refuseniks they knew personally or about whom they had heard on the radio. Second, local Jews who emigrated were often unable to take with them part of their furniture, personal goods, or everyday items. These were distributed to acquaintances or needy people whom they knew about via ulpans or from the groups around the synagogue. When the mass departure began, at times there were more things to distribute than people who wished to utilize them. Third, we all received considerable support from Western Jews. Tourists would bring the refuseniks jeans, cameras, electronic goods, and so forth. Refuseniks who spoke Hebrew, English, or French received the most visitors and they would help the others. Many tourists visited ulpans and seminars.

There were always several refuseniks who gathered information about people in need of emergency help. Eventually, lists were compiled of refuseniks around the country. On the basis of those lists, the aid became more organized. A system of personal "guardianship," known as the "Adopt-a-Family" program, became popular in which an American family, for instance, would take on the care of a refusenik family, corresponding with the family and often providing material support. In pairing families, an effort was made to link those that had common professional or family interests. The Americans had considerable experience in such matters.

Another effective method involved sending refuseniks checks or monetary transfers that they could exchange at Vneshtorgbank for so-called "certificates,"[97] legal foreign currency that could be used to acquire scarce commodities in special "Berezka" stores or exchanged profitably for Soviet rubles. Unfortunately, this system became obsolete after the Soviets introduced a 30 percent tax on monetary transfers. Even with all the varieties of help, life in refusal was complex and difficult. The regime controlled the overseas aid and could halt it at any moment or it could intimidate the recipient and force him or her to reject it. The situation was even more complicated in the provinces, to which foreigners did not always have access. In those areas, gifts from abroad frequently were the sole form of help.

The most difficult task was aiding Prisoners of Zion. The main burden, of course, fell on their families, who themselves often needed support—and not only material support. One of the most famous activists who was devoted to the cause of aiding prisoners was Ida Nudel, a woman with a very strong character. Many lovingly called her the mother of the Prisoners of Zion.

Ida Nudel talked about her activity helping prisoners:[98]

KOSHAROVSKY: *When did you begin to deal with prisoners?*

NUDEL: In 1972. Some of the prisoners' relatives began to leave the country and the connections with the outside were broken.

KOSHAROVSKY: *You mean that you got involved because the wives and relatives of some prisoners began to receive exit visas and left?*

NUDEL: No, that's not it. I would say rather that it's my nature. I began to take an interest in the matter and decided I had to do it.

KOSHAROVSKY: *Dealing with Prisoners of Zion was a difficult matter involving correspondence with the authorities and with the prisoners themselves. One needed to know how to maintain relations with the families and to prepare and send packages to the camps.*

NUDEL: I dealt with everything, but I did not have the right to send packages. I would give everything to the relatives. I was living in Moscow. The relatives stopped by my place on their way to the camps or prisons and received whatever I had been able to collect.

KOSHAROVSKY: *Did you have a connection with any Western organization?*

NUDEL: I had a link to a French group.

KOSHAROVSKY: *What about Michael Sherbourne in England? After all, he knows Russian.*

NUDEL: While I had a telephone, there was a link. I myself led a semi-underground way of life and hardly associated with anyone because I knew that the Jewish circles were very talkative. It was necessary to be very cautious in dealing with information: people took a risk. People who were released from camps would come and bring information, which sometimes they had concealed in their anal passage.

KOSHAROVSKY: *Did you have helpers?*

NUDEL: Yes, Arik Yakov Rakhlenko and Boris Tsitlenok. They would travel to the places of incarceration, accompany relatives to meetings, and so forth.

All information about prisoners was sent to me. Moreover, every prisoner knew my address. I would write to them, send birthday greetings, collect signatures in their defense near the synagogue, and go to the Interior Ministry in connection with their cases. When I came to the head of the division in the ministry, he would get up and shake my hand. I used to explain to him frankly my relationship to those people and why I was concerned. Once, even the head doctor of the Gulag decided to make my acquaintance. He then taught me how letters should be written and whom to intimidate and how. He was not a Jew—he was simply a human being.

KOSHAROVSKY: *How did you explain things to them?*

NUDEL: I didn't hide anything or lie to anyone. I explained everything openly and frankly. I always had the Constitution of the USSR in my bag and I spoke only in terms of the articles of the Constitution. They had difficulty arguing with me. Then I would tell the activists how I managed to get people out of the penalty isolation cell or to provide a doctor for a sick person and then persuaded him not to send the sick prisoner to hard labor. I sat and worked day and night. Thanks to that, I survived in refusal. I am simply the kind of person who needs something to keep herself busy. In addition, I worked because the KGB continually threatened to arrest me as a parasite.

KOSHAROVSKY: *How did you locate prisoners and their relatives?*

NUDEL: My sister Elana (Fridman) sent me addresses from Israel. The newspapers published the addresses and names. She would write them down and send them to me. Arik [Yakov] Rakhlenko went to the Interior Ministry and clarified where people were serving time, in which republic. Most frequently, I used to go to the synagogue and question people. I had extensive ties with other cities until my telephone was disconnected. Do you remember [Vladimir] Markman?

KOSHAROVSKY: *Yes, he was my friend from Sverdlovsk. He was arrested in 1972.*

NUDEL: I knew his wife, Greta, very well. She lived at my place.

KOSHAROVSKY: *Did you manage that case?*

NUDEL: I went with Greta to the Supreme Soviet. I remember that five people from Kishinev and Volodia Slepak were with us. I was in close contact with the Zalmansons' father, and in touch with the democratic dissidents, in particular with Nina Ivanovna Bukovsky. They didn't give up and stuck to their business.

KOSHAROVSKY: *There were problems?*

NUDEL: And how. This was a society deep in pain and suffering. There were women who were afraid to associate with me, women who were afraid that I wanted to take their husbands away. There were all kinds. There were some who didn't want help, but I didn't know that. They concealed the fact that they were Jews and were leaving. There even were mothers who had their own children arrested so that they wouldn't leave, but they regretted it later. When the KGB began to conscript seventeen- to eighteen-year-olds into the army, there arose a kind of protest movement. Those boys hid in my place.

KOSHAROVSKY: *You had a one-room apartment. Where could anyone hide there?*

NUDEL: I had one room and a kitchen. There was a little sofa in the kitchen on which everyone slept—the prisoners who were released from camps, the army lads, everyone.

KOSHAROVSKY: *To my knowledge, Dina Beilin dealt with some prisoners and took care of some people until the trial.*

NUDEL: I don't know whom she helped. When I got into this, Volodia Prestin explained to me that I must regard each person as a potential codefendant because we probably all would be arrested. "You see," he told me, "this is a dangerous matter." And I followed that advice. Dina didn't tell me anything about her life and I didn't tell her anything about mine because our lives were not normal.

KOSHAROVSKY: *In 1977 you organized a women's group and you initiated a series of demonstrations.*

NUDEL: I chose six women who had a chance of not landing in prison and who agreed not to tell anyone what we would do: Natasha Khasin, Galia Nizhnikov, and others.

KOSHAROVSKY: *How did you know that they wouldn't be arrested?*

NUDEL: Khasin had a small child and the others also had certain extenuating circumstances. In my case, the chance was fifty-fifty, but at that time, I had already become well known.

KOSHAROVSKY: *How many demonstrations did you manage to hold before you were arrested?*

NUDEL: Six.

KOSHAROVSKY: *When you were in exile, did you correspond with other prisoners or was that impossible?*

NUDEL: I was busy with my own survival there. I wrote letters, but it wasn't the same thing. Correspondence among prisoners was prohibited, which made it very difficult. I received a few letters from Tolia Altman and something from Zalmanson. I worked and therefore I had considerably less time and energy.

KOSHAROVSKY: *What work did you do?*

NUDEL: I was a guard. I had a dog and we worked together.

KOSHAROVSKY: *Without a weapon?*

NUDEL: Yes. Prisoners are not allowed to have arms.

KOSHAROVSKY: *Were you helped by people at liberty?*

NUDEL: Of course. People came endlessly. Lvovsky came, Tsirlin, and others.

KOSHAROVSKY: *I heard that it was hard for you in exile.*

NUDEL: It was very hard. A person who has spent all her life in Moscow winds up in a Siberian village. The temperature was minus 40 to 50 degrees centigrade. I needed wood for the stove. There were no food products. In the summer I had to raise everything myself. There was no water in the hut and it was very hard to carry the water bucket. I would have to drag it back and forth all day. If you are a man, you can arrange something, but if you are a woman, everyone is afraid of you and no one will help.

I organized a protest because of the rats in the house. As an exception, I was permitted to purchase a little house. In principle, an exile can rent lodging, but no one agreed to rent to me. I bought a small one-room house that had a stove but I didn't know how to use it. No one showed me how and I almost died there a few times. Finally the police chief showed me. When he found out who I was, he would summon me, lock the room, and we would converse for hours. If he forgot to lock the door and some policeman entered, he would say to him, "Leave, I'm busy now." He was a person with a strong legal education; he was forced into the deep backwoods.

KOSHAROVSKY: *When you finished your exile, you weren't given a residence permit for Moscow?*

NUDEL: No one was given that.

KOSHAROVSKY: *After you settled down in Bendery, did you continue to correspond with prisoners?*

NUDEL: Of course I did. People got out and left the country. Life continued. The Royaks and Libermans were refuseniks there. They received me very nicely. But the police simply threw me off the bus whenever I would try to leave town. They grabbed me by the arms and legs and tossed me off.

It was another five long years after her release before Ida Nudel received an exit visa. In March 1987 she was flown out on the private plane of the well-known businessman Armand Hammer. Five thousand people gathered at Ben Gurion airport to welcome Ida upon her arrival.

Along with Ida Nudel, Dina Beilin did much to help refuseniks and Prisoners of Zion. An active person with clear leadership abilities, she dealt with many issues. For several years she was the academic secretary of Alexander Lerner's seminar. She took part in the preparation of analytic surveys of the situation of refuseniks for Israel. She participated in meetings with important Western public and political figures. She also maintained contacts with aliya activists from many cities. For several years Dina was in charge of preparing and compiling lists of refuseniks, including those lists that later figured as part of the espionage charge against Sharansky.

Ida Nudel dealt with those who had already been imprisoned. Beilin got involved when an activist was threatened by arrest or a file was opened against him or her. She often had to prepare material to send to the West about legal trials.

Dina Beilin remembered interesting details about her work and that time:[99]

KOSHAROVSKY: *What cases did you deal with?*

BEILIN: Lev Roitburd, one of the well-known Odessa activists, tried to travel to Moscow to meet with some American senators in June 1975. The local KGB warned Lyova that he would have to pay for it if he tried to leave Odessa. Not long before that, a threatening article featuring Roitburd appeared in the local paper *Vechernaia Odessa* (Evening Odessa). Despite the threats, Lyova decided to go. He was arrested at the airport for allegedly resisting the police. Misha Liberman and I flew down for the trial. We managed to record the testimony of the witnesses, including the chief navigator of the local steamship company, an important person by Odessa standards. He stated directly that he saw how Lyova was pinned down and taken away without any cause or explanations and that Lyova didn't raise a hand against anyone. To this day, I don't understand how this person was allowed to appear at the trial!

We immediately transmitted the lawyer's speech and the witnesses' testimony by telephone to the West. We needed to show our friends that this was a provocation. In those years the regime usually portrayed the arrests of activists as part of the struggle against criminals. After all, in the West, too, people attack police. The case, however, was concocted very clumsily. Evidently the local KGB did not expect our intervention or such a speedy reaction. It was on the eve of the signing of the Final Act in Helsinki,[100] and at a preparatory meeting, the Soviet delegates were asked how the protection of human rights in the USSR was in keeping with the arrest of Lyova Roitburd for his desire to immigrate to Israel. Lyova was threatened with up to five years in prison. Without an explanation, the sentencing was put off for a week. Lyova received two years, which in those conditions represented a victory.

KOSHAROVSKY: *Were there other such victories?*

BEILIN: The most impressive in that sense was the [1976] case of Boria Chernobylsky and Yosif Ahss.[101] They were both released before the trial although they had faced the threat of a serious charge.

KOSHAROVSKY: *Do you remember who was in the delegation to see Shchelokov, minister of the interior?*

BEILIN: According to the notes that I made soon after those events, the three were Slepak, Chernobylsky, and Sharansky. A total of fifty-two people with yellow stars on their clothing went to the Interior Ministry. Shchelokov declared that he was not responsible for the security of the refuseniks. At the end of the day, the demonstrators were transported to the forest, but they were not beaten. Four of them—including Boris Chernobylsky—were separated from the others and detained.

On October 22, 1976, the refuseniks returned to the Supreme Soviet, after which more than forty people with yellow stars on their chests, encircled by the police, moved toward the Central Committee reception hall. Yosif Ahss, Yosif Beilin, Vladimir Slepak, and Anatoly Sharansky were received by Albert Ivanov, the director of the Central Committee's Department of Administrative Services.

On October 25, thirty-eight people again set out for the Central Committee. Seventeen were arrested on their way, including Yosif Beilin, Vladimir Slepak, Yuli Kosharovsky, Vladimir Shakhnovsky, Anatoly

Sharansky, and Leonid Volvovsky. Feliks Kandel was arrested near his home. They all were sentenced to fifteen days.

Six women were fined twenty-five rubles each and released. Yosif Ahss was arrested at home and placed in the Butyrka prison. He and Chernobylsky were charged with hooliganism. You, if I recall, were sent to Serpukhov, a branch of Butyrka, and your wife and I went to see you.

When it became clear that Chernobylsky and Ahss could be sentenced to lengthy terms, I turned to Sofia Kalistratov and we had the idea of forming an "assistance group to the investigation."[102]

KOSHAROVSKY: *Dina, how did this group operate?*

BEILIN: Sofia Vasilevna [Kalistratov] was the chairperson of the group and also played the role of judge. We summoned witnesses; not everyone had been sentenced to fifteen days. I was the secretary and wrote a genuine protocol. The jurors were Professors [Naum] Meiman, Brailovsky, Lerner, and some other professors and refuseniks who were well known in the West. Sofia Vasilevna posed questions to each witness. It soon became clear that Chernobylsky and Ahss had not struck the policemen; rather, the police had beaten them.

KOSHAROVSKY: *Yes, we were transported a distance of about fifty kilometers, dropped in a forest, and the policemen began to push us away from the cars in order to leave, but we demanded that they bring us back to where they had picked us up. It was already rather cold. One of us lay down under the wheels. The policemen acted roughly, beat us, and cursed. They broke Tesker's nose.*

BEILIN: We brought the document, which we called "The account of the assistance group to the investigation," to the prosecutor's office and also transmitted it to the West. Near the synagogue, we handed out two pictures to all the foreign tourists: one of Ahss's wife with his two small daughters and the other of Chernobylsky's wife with his two little girls. The photographs were extremely touching. Boria and Yosif sat in prison for less than a month but it was the real thing—they even shaved their heads! They were released before the trial under the formulation that they "do not constitute a danger to society."

Chernobylsky appeared at my place at night immediately after his release, finding it hard to believe that he had been freed. After all, the case fell under the article "resisting the authorities," for which one could receive three years or even more. As far as I know, that was the sole such case in the Soviet Union.

KOSHAROVSKY: *What can you add about the material aid to the refuseniks and Prisoners of Zion?*

BEILIN: In addition to the Georgian millionaires who helped us, we were also left money by people from Lvov, Kiev, and Moscow. They left rubles, and that was entirely "kosher" [i.e., legal]. Israel helped with money to pay for visas. That aid arrived via the Dutch embassy. We also helped the relatives of Prisoners of Zion with money for lawyers, trips, and food parcels. There were many expenses. We were not acquainted with the majority of the relatives. It was dangerous to be in touch with some of them.

KOSHAROVSKY: *Did you also help prisoners?*

BEILIN: Yes, I handled the cases that came to me. Ida dealt with those who had been imprisoned earlier. She carried on an extensive correspondence with people in prisons and labor camps, transmitted information to the West about the condition of prisoners, and supported their families. I had my contacts in various cities, and people also came to me.

KOSHAROVSKY: *Did anyone help you?*

BEILIN: Various people helped, depending on what needed to be done. No one refused. Arik Rakhlenko, Misha Kremen, Gena Khasin, Boria Chernobylsky, and others. Sharansky was continually dealing with those matters. Press conferences were held at Lerner's or Slepak's place. I was helped by lawyers, most often by Kalistratov.

KOSHAROVSKY: *Did she act out of altruism?*

BEILIN: Amazingly so. She called herself "the Russian national minority among the Jews."

KOSHAROVSKY: *From time to time women's mutual help groups were formed, for example, that of Ira Gildengorn.*

BEILIN: Women's groups became active after Sharansky's imprisonment. I asked them not to go out to demonstrate before his trial, thinking that it was preferable not to divert attention from the trial, but others thought differently. My attitude toward the women's groups, therefore, was ambiguous.

KOSHAROVSKY: *How did you manage with medicines?*

BEILIN: Foreigners brought them at our request. If something could be obtained in the Soviet Union, it was taken care of locally. In this matter, we were aided by sympathetic doctors who had not applied for visas. We also received help in obtaining food parcels and delivering them to prisoners. There were sympathetic store managers.

Mutual aid in refusal, despite the tragic nature of many situations, played an enormous role in providing a moral uplift and consolidating the movement. Activists, especially in small towns, knew that if misfortune befell them, they and their relatives would not be abandoned.

17. Refuseniks celebrating Simhat Torah, Moscow, October 17, 1976. Left to right: Vladimir Slepak, Anatoly Sharansky, Yosif Beilin. Collection of Enid Wurtman.

18. Professor Alexander Lerner, former Prisoner of Zion Yuri Berkovsky from Novisibirsk, and Anatoly Sharansky in Moscow, October 1976. Collection of Enid Wurtman.

19. Inna and Yuli Kosharovsky (waving, bottom right and center) celebrate Simhat Torah with a crowd of fellow Soviet Jews near the Choral Synagogue in Moscow, October 17, 1976. Collection of Inna and Yuli Kosharovsky.

20. Left to right: Enid Wurtman, Leonid (Ari) Volvovsky, and Veniamin Fain discuss the planned international cultural symposium, Moscow, October 1976. Collection of Enid Wurtman.

21. Press conference prior to planned international symposium on Jewish culture. Moscow, November 17, 1976. Center: Anatoly Sharansky. Standing on the left: Yosef Begun, unknown, Arkady Mai, Vladimir Prestin. Standing in the doorway: Pavel Abramovich. Sitting on the right: Viktor Brailovsky, and in profile Veniamin Fain. Inna and Igor Uspensky collection, Association "Remember and Save."

22. International symposium of refusenik scientists, Moscow, April 7, 1977. Included in the photo are Irina and Viktor Brailovsky, Mark Azbel, Eduard Trifonov, Rimma Iakir, Lev Ulanovsky. Collection of Enid Wurtman.

23. Refuseniks celebrate Hanukah, Moscow, 1977. Left side, seated, left to right: Gennady Khasin, Dina Beilin, Ida Nudel, Rita Beilin, unknown, Evgeny Iakir. Standing on the side: Rimma Tesker, Lena Khasin, Maria Slepak, Vladimir Slepak, Steve Stadlin (foreign guest), Zakhar Tesker holding child. Right side, left to right: Boris Chernobylsky, unknown, foreign guest, foreign guest, Maxine Stadlin (foreign guest), Vinia Belkin, Arik Rakhlenko. Collection of Miryam Maxine Elkins, Yuli Kosharovsky archives.

24. Leningrad activists Aba and Ida Taratuta, late 1970s. Aba Taratuta collection, Association "Remember and Save."

25. Left to right: Leonid (Ari), Kira, and Mila Volvovsky. Moscow, 1978. Collection of Alan Molod.

26. Refusenik children celebrate Purim in the Jewish kindergarten in Natasha and Gennady Khasin's home. Moscow, 1978. Lea Chernobylsky collection, Association "Remember and Save."

27. Refuseniks celebrate a Pesach Seder at the home of Lea and Boris Chernobylsky, Moscow, 1979. From left, seated: A foreign visitor, Mikhail Kremen, Olga and Leonid Shabashov, Svetlana Ainbinder, Sergei Rozenstein. Standing: Lea Chernobylsky, Igor Gudz, a foreign visitor, Boris Chernobylsky, Yuri and Lena Shtern, Arik Rakhlenko, Gennady Khasin, Galina Kremen. Lea Chernobylsky collection, Association "Remember and Save."

28. Refuseniks and rights activists (including Elena Bonner, second from left, top row) bid farewell to former Prisoners of Zion from the Leningrad hijacking trial, following their release and prior to their departure for Israel, Moscow, 1979. Sitting, left to right: Arye Khnokh, Vulf Zalmanson, Boris Penson, Anatoly Altman, Hillel Butman. Association "Remember and Save."

29. Second Jewish Song Festival for refuseniks in Ovrazhki during Succot, 1979. Collection of Enid Wurtman.

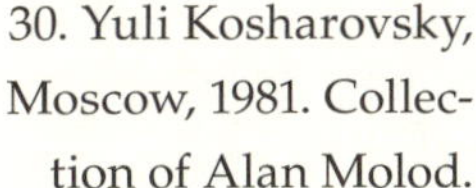

30. Yuli Kosharovsky, Moscow, 1981. Collection of Alan Molod.

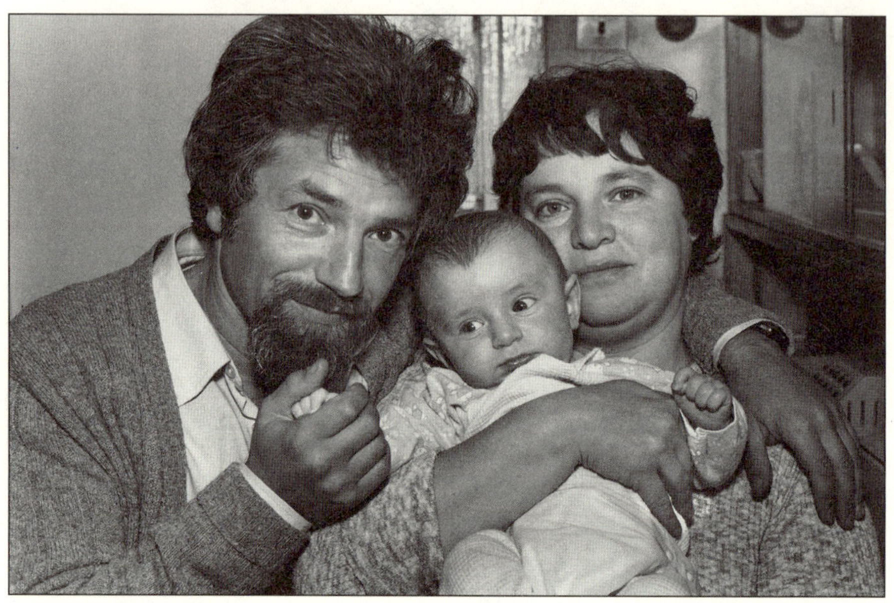

31. Inna and Yuli Kosharovsky with son Moty, Moscow, 1981. Collection of Bill Aron.

32. Evgeny Lein next to a sign for the museum commemorating V. I. Lenin's Siberian exile in Shushenskoe, 1982. Evgeny Lein collection, Association "Remember and Save."

4

Developments and Divisions

A POWERFUL ERUPTION OF CONSOLIDATING ENERGY accompanied the process of transforming Jewish national identification into a positive attribute. Indeed, the difficult conditions under which Jewish activists worked created a need for unity. There were, however, causes for disagreements. These derived partly from the nature of a social movement (which faced issues of tactics and strategy, differing modes of activity, leadership struggles, personal clashes, and so forth) and partly from the complex situation of refusal. The KGB made arbitrary decisions regarding refuseniks, trapping certain categories of citizens and specific individuals inside the Iron Curtain and slowing down emigration as a whole. It seemed that by making the refuseniks' life as bitter as possible, the KGB hoped to intimidate others who were contemplating emigration.

As we have already seen, refuseniks adopted a variety of approaches to strategic and ideological issues. For example, the issue of cooperation with (democratic) rights activists evoked many disputes in Jewish activist circles. The majority of Jewish activists considered that the Jews had already spilled enough of their blood on alien fields and altars in return for which they had received stark ingratitude and renewed anti-Semitism. This generation of Jewish activists regarded the revival of national independence after two millennia of dispersion as a divine gift. Refuseniks perceived a genuine opportunity finally to break the chain of endless persecutions and to take Jewish fate in our own hands. The struggle for aliya to Israel, Hebrew instruction, the study of the Jewish nation's history and culture, a Zionist education, and a link with Jewry in Israel and the West facilitated the realization of this noble goal. While aware of the limited forces of the movement, Jewish activists felt that only Zionists could carry out these tasks. At the same time, the ranks of the democratic rights activists seemed to be much greater than those of Zionists and included a significant number of Jews.

The desire of participants in the Jewish movement to focus on specific problems did not exclude contacts with the democrats and mutual aid on certain issues. It is worth noting that the authorities treated the general rights activists more harshly than they treated the activists in the Jewish movement. They were particularly nervous about members of the Jewish movement who established coordination between the two movements or took part in both, as the arrest of Anatoly (Natan) Sharansky and other events showed.

The *Politiki* and the *Kulturniki*

Another disagreement within the movement emerged into the open at the time of an official visit by US senators, headed by former vice president Hubert Humphrey in June 1975. The group that arrived in Moscow included also Jacob Javits, Patrick Leahy, Abe Ribicoff, and Charles Percy. The senators expressed a desire to meet refuseniks, and Natan Sharansky arranged the meeting. Whereas one group, consisting of Alexander Lerner, Vladimir Slepak, Vitaly Rubin, Alexander Lunts, Ida Nudel, Dina Beilin, Lev Ovsishcher, and Veniamin Levich, intended to talk to the senators about emigration, another group of refuseniks, including Vladimir Prestin, Pavel Abramovich, and Ilia Essas, demanded a separate meeting to speak about the situation of Jewish culture in the USSR. The rivalry between the activist groups led to a near diplomatic scandal that Sharansky managed to avert. From that time, however, Prestin's group acquired the label *kulturniki* (the cultural wing of the Jewish movement), and the Lerner-Lunts group members were the *politiki* (the political wing of the Jewish movement).[1]

In fact, the division of activists into kulturniki and politiki was arbitrary. Both groups actively participated in the struggle to emigrate and in the attempt to revive Jewish culture. Nevertheless, the terms stuck. They possessed a certain validity that found expression both in the emphasis of the activity and in the ideological tendencies of these two influential groups.

Professor Alexander Lerner, Dr. Alexander Lunts, and Vladimir Slepak, who headed the politiki, asserted that the basis of the Zionist movement in the USSR was the struggle to emigrate. Lerner recalled, "I headed the segment of the movement that considered one must first escape from the Soviet Union to Israel and one could master Jewish culture there. Each would absorb as much of it as he or she could."[2] The politiki did not think it was possible to achieve significant results in disseminating Jewish culture in conditions of a hostile totalitarian environment. Moreover, in their opinion, cultural activity would divert forces from the struggle for aliya and would enable the regime to offer insignificant concessions in that area at the expense of emigration.

The group of politiki was formed and consolidated in the struggle for the Jackson-Vanik Amendment (1972–74), in the analytic monitoring of the emigration situation throughout the country (1974–75), in the writing of letters of protest, and in meetings with influential public and political figures from the West.

At the same time, many of the politiki studied Hebrew, read and disseminated samizdat, and utilized the recently opened channels of communication with the West to obtain and distribute Jewish literature. They displayed notable activism and independence and utilized all accessible—and occasionally extremely dangerous—levers of pressure on the regime. Sharansky, Vitaly Rubin, and Slepak cooperated closely with the democratic rights activists. However, they also actively engaged in various cultural activities.

The meetings with Western public and political leaders were particularly significant, as the Kremlin listened to their opinion. New York congressman James Scheuer was the first to ask to meet refuseniks in Moscow. He went to Alexander Lerner's apartment on December 16, 1971, to meet with Lerner, Polsky, Slepak, and other leaders of the movement. The KGB interrupted the meeting and tried to detain the congressman, but the activists managed to convey information about the incident to contacts in the West almost immediately, and a scandal erupted in the international media. Scheuer was released and returned to Lerner's place. After the Scheuer incident, every US congressman and senator who visited Moscow tried to meet with refuseniks. These meetings took place in Lerner's apartment.[3]

Usually three or four people prepared for the meetings with visiting politicians: Professor Lerner himself, Viktor Polsky, and Alexander Lunts. Sometimes the noted physicist Veniamin Levich joined them. Lerner would invite ten to fifteen people to a meeting. The latter realized that the guests, who were trying to gain a deeper understanding of the refuseniks' problems, would subsequently meet with the leadership of their country.

The cultural direction developed in the course of the struggle to legalize Hebrew, through ardent disputes at Vitaly Rubin's humanitarian seminar, and via the publication of various samizdat journals. The revival of national culture was always one of the main components of the Zionist movement's program. In addition to satisfying the thirst for Jewish knowledge, it enhanced the activists' motivation. Cultural activities helped create a normal national milieu, and they facilitated a return by Soviet Jews to common roots with Israel and with Western Jewry, enabling them to reach beyond the bounds of the Iron Curtain. The campaign for Jewish culture served also as an effective tool in the struggle for aliya because the regime, reacting nervously to any dissemination of information that was not under its control, strove to get rid of the initiators of this enterprise. Editors of journals, prominent Hebrew teachers, and seminar leaders frequently emigrated more quickly than others. Just as in the direct struggle for emigration, however, it was a form of Russian roulette in which it was impossible to predict in advance whether activism would lead to an exit visa or to many years in the Gulag.

People active in the cultural trend also participated in the struggle for passage of the Jackson-Vanik Amendment, in meetings with foreign leaders, in demonstrations, and in sending letters of protest. Among the outstanding Jewish cultural leaders were Vladimir Prestin, Pavel Abramovich, Yosif Begun, Veniamin Fain, Mikhail Chlenov, Viktor Brailovsky, Felix Kandel, Eliyahu Essas, and Leonid Volvovsky.

Vladimir Prestin reflected on the beliefs that prevailed in the period up to 1974:[4]

PRESTIN: We thought it was sufficient to open the door and millions would pour out, i.e., that the problem was opening the door. That was an illusion, not reality, because the door, in fact, was practically open but there were no millions.

KOSHAROVSKY: *Volodia! The regime had dozens of levers by which they regulated the process (of applying to leave): they issued thousands of refusals; they made the process of submitting documents unpredictable and complex; there were related dangers of losing one's job and ostracism; there was the general anti-Israeli hysteria, the education tax, and judicial and nonjudicial harassment. The door was only slightly open.*

PRESTIN: I have a completely different view about this. The door was open practically all the way toward the end of 1973. What happened in 1974 is clear proof of that.

KOSHAROVSKY: *The decline in the number of applications was also a result of the Yom Kippur War and the stream of negative letters from Israel.*

PRESTIN: There were enclaves where Jewish communal life was preserved: the Baltics, Georgia, Central Asia, and Bessarabia. Although the regime set up obstacles on the path to aliya such as letters of reference one had to obtain from one's place of employment, meetings of condemnation, and so forth, in those enclaves people overcame them.

KOSHAROVSKY: *And in Moscow, they also overcame them.*

PRESTIN: Yes, the Zionists who were born in a certain period, such as you and I, went through the process, but their number was very limited. Toward the end of 1974, I said simple things: the reservoir is empty and the door is open. I said that because the number of refuseniks did not increase. I'm not speaking of five to ten new ones—that doesn't count. Those who were prepared to leave—left.

KOSHAROVSKY: *And those who remained needed to be prepared?*

PRESTIN: Correct. Toward the end of 1974, there was a colossal breakthrough. We were obsessed with the desire just to open the door. We pushed it, opened it a little, and it seemed like we were almost there. The Jackson Amendment hung over all of us. You remember the basic points in the negotiations: fifty thousand exit visas a year; no one should be delayed for more than five years; and the release of everyone who had been in refusal longer.

Polsky's trial was in the fall. He ran over a woman pedestrian who testified that he was not guilty, although she later changed her testimony. Western correspondents and Sakharov attended the trial. Polsky was sentenced to a fine of one hundred rubles. That's because it was hoped that the negotiations would be successful. Two months later, the trial of Mikhail Stern, an endocrinologist from Vinnitsa, took place. He received eight years for speculating in medicines and taking bribes. Here's the difference: Polsky, an active participant in the aliya struggle, was fined one hundred rubles and Stern—for the contrived "bribes" in Vinnitsa—eight years. During those two months, the talks broke down. In the recesses between court sessions in Polsky's trial, the correspondents would call their offices to find out about the course of the negotiations. Polsky left and [Alexander] Voronel left. They were leaders of the movement. The rector of Tel Aviv University, Yoram Dinstein, came to Moscow. I gave him an earful: the reserve is depleted, no one is prepared to leave, and the approach must be changed. This analysis was rather obvious. The number of refuseniks did not grow at all!

KOSHAROVSKY: *Jewish culture was supposed to serve the Jews' exodus?*

PRESTIN: I never said such a thing. I never said the word "Zionism." My language was entirely different, and in my head was Jewish enlightenment—that's a tradition. I didn't understand why we had to curtail that tradition at the Soviets' dictate.

KOSHAROVSKY: *What did you mean by Jewish enlightenment?*

PRESTIN: Everything! History, literature, religion—everything that is part of Jewish culture. The tradition should be continued: that's natural.

KOSHAROVSKY: *In your head, you thought that the door was open and there was no one who wanted to leave?*

PRESTIN: That's part of it. We thought that even if we didn't motivate people to leave but only imparted some knowledge to them, that also would be worthwhile. I am speaking seriously. That is, it was broader than aliya. Look at how much is invested today in Jewish education in the West and the former Soviet Union! Are all of them leaving? Why did we start with the little journal *Tarbut* (Culture)? Because it was "kosher" (legal and safe): the word *Zionism* was absent. At first, we didn't go beyond the little journal. And the whole publication was ours.

Neshira

The term *neshira* (Hebrew for "dropping out") refers to the phenomenon of Soviet Jews who left the USSR with an exit visa to Israel but settled in North America or Europe. In the early years of Jewish emigration in the 1960s to the early 1970s, there were practically no "dropouts," but by the mid-1970s, the percentage of dropouts became significant. Opinions among Western and Israeli organizations supporting the movement were divided on issues of the émigrés' right to choose, the impact of neshira, and what to do about it.

Professor Veniamin Fain was particularly concerned with the problem of "dropouts" (*neshira*),[5] those "stiff-necked" people who did not go to Israel when they left:[6]

KOSHAROVSKY: *How did you hope to influence the stiff-necked people?*

FAIN: Recalling that Einstein wrote several articles about Zionism, I located them, and [Grigory] Rozenshtein and I translated about fifteen articles into Russian. I then went to the printing press near the main telegraph agency and asked them to bind twenty copies. I also purchased a photograph of Mikhoels and Einstein, which I placed on the title page. After I paid for the bound copies, the binder said to me, "Don't come here again." He was a Jew and when he read it all, he became frightened. I then began to make copies of the collection without a binding. Around that time, I made the acquaintance of Yosif Begun, who dealt with the distribution of the collections.

Gradually I elaborated the viewpoint that our movement was lacking an important, indeed essential, aspect: the spiritual and cultural. I concluded that we needed to work systemically in that direction.

At the end of 1974, I made the acquaintance of Volodia Prestin, who supported those views. Later, we did everything together.

The multifaceted activity of those involved with the cultural trend helped create a supportive social milieu and facilitated a national revival in the difficult conditions of living as social outcasts in a totalitarian country. At the same time, the kulturniki viewed their efforts as part of the struggle for aliya.

The Schism: Origins of the Split

Formally, the schism was provoked by the visit to the KGB of Alexander Lunts, one of the movement's leaders. Lunts initiated the idea of contacting the KGB. He received the consent of other leaders of the movement's "political wing" (Lerner, Slepak, and Voronel), and implemented the idea himself. The break occurred toward the end of 1974, when the "secret" contacts came out in the open. In the eyes of the refuseniks, the KGB was branded by former and recent crimes: it embodied universal evil. That institution issued refusals with no explanation or time limit, it instigated harassment at workplaces, and it conducted anti-Zionist trials against people whose sole desire was to immigrate to Israel. In addition, it persecuted refuseniks' families; fired, trailed, bugged, intimidated, and turned people against each other; broke them and then recruited them. Yet, at the same time, the KGB regulated and controlled emigration from the Soviet Union, analyzed the situation, and proposed decisions to the political leadership. Although refuseniks understood that the security services held the real power in issues of emigration, they addressed protests, requests, and complaints, including those against the KGB, to the Party and open governmental institutions. Lunts decided to try a different strategy.

Lunts recalled his thinking on the subject:[7]

KOSHAROVSKY: *Your contacts with the KGB evoked a serious split in the refusenik community.*

LUNTS: Perhaps, but it was more a pretext than the cause for the split. Post factum, however, I concluded that it was a mistake and I shouldn't have tried it. At the time, however, I thought that we must obtain a meeting with the KGB at a sufficiently high level and explain certain circumstances to them. I discussed it with three colleagues in the movement: Slepak, Lerner, and Voronel.

KOSHAROVSKY: *When did it take place?*

LUNTS: At the beginning of 1974. I assumed that if the meeting was on a sufficiently high level, they would have to report it to the appropriate superior in the hierarchy. All three agreed that it could facilitate a change in policy.

KOSHAROVSKY: *Did you all understand how dangerous it was?*

LUNTS: Oh, Voronel reacted immediately: "I also had that idea but I think it's dangerous." Voronel, by the way, was not a coward.

I wrote a text and typed it up.

KOSHAROVSKY: *Did you coordinate the text with the others?*

LUNTS: I don't remember now, but we did agree on the idea. The text said that the Jackson Amendment was proposed because of the harsh restrictions imposed on the emigration of Soviet Jews and that, as result, the ties that the Americans were trying to establish with the Socialist camp would not be established with the Soviet Union but with China, which would receive all the benefits.

KOSHAROVSKY: *That is, you tried to play power politics with the KGB?*

LUNTS: Yes. In the first discussion, I conversed with an intelligent person, seemingly, someone with a high rank. I declared that I represent only myself; however, if there were positive results, I could convince people close to me. At the next meeting, I conversed with the head of the entire Jewish division. Even now, I don't know his last name. He was called Viktor Ivanovich.[8] There were in total four conversations.

KOSHAROVSKY: *How did it start? You transmitted a letter to someone with a request for a meeting?*

LUNTS: No, I didn't send a letter to anyone. I simply dropped in at their reception room, waited in line for five minutes, and was received by some man. I declared that I wanted to meet with a high-ranking representative. Subsequently, they contacted me. At the third meeting, Viktor Ivanovich began to yell at some point but, already having been tempered by my time in refusal, I simply listened and when he finished, I said that I could change my opinion in one of two cases: if I received some kind of positive information or was intimidated. The positive information was not forthcoming and I had not been intimidated. In reply was silence.

KOSHAROVSKY: *What did he yell about?*

LUNTS: About the harm, the danger, that it was treason—those kind of things. At the end of the fourth meeting, I said that I would not continue these meetings. And at that it ended. Subsequently, when Pasha

Abramovich was at Mark Nashpits's apartment, KGB men arrived, and one of them said to Pasha, "You'd do better to come and speak with us too."

When Polsky heard about it, he called a meeting at Lerner's home. Lerner, Slepak, Polsky, Prestin, and someone else were there. Polsky and Prestin went on the attack, but Lerner spoke confidently in defense of the plan, saying there was no harm in it, some attempt had been tried. That's how the schism began.

KOSHAROVSKY: *There were far-reaching consequences. The activists split into opposing groups not only in Moscow but also in many cities in the Soviet Union. Prestin considers that he was considerably at fault in this regard. He took charge when Polsky left.*

LUNTS: Yes, he was in the group that had been active practically since 1968. Prestin and I, in fact, were not in contact. When Volodia [Prestin] arrived in Israel after many years, however, and we first met, I remember that he entered the room and we simultaneously said almost the same thing: that we regretted all the arguments.

KOSHAROVSKY: *What was your reaction at the height of the schism when young fellows began actively to oppose you? Or did you simply not pay any attention to it?*

LUNTS: I paid attention, and how! I thought, however, that any active struggle would harm them and us. I considered that the best thing was not to respond, in the hope that everything would calm down, although that did not occur.

Hebrew teacher Mikhail Chlenov recalled having a similar idea about talking to the KGB for the benefit of the movement. For him, too, the schism thus did not necessarily depend on the decision to try to talk with the KGB. As Chlenov explained it, the more significant split was that between the political trend (politiki) and the cultural activists (kulturniki):[9]

CHLENOV: Faced with the question of how to deal with those who were not leaving, I thought that we should try to negotiate with the Soviet regime rather than fight against it. I think that I was the first in that milieu who formulated such an approach. It coincided with a very dubious episode in my life that caused me some discomfort. The fact is that Lunts was not the only one who tried to reach an agreement with the KGB—I was almost involved in a similar story. A colleague in my Institute of Ethnography, Stanislav Korolev, was a former KGB officer, something that he did not conceal. Once, at a drinking session, he approached me and said, "I know that you teach Hebrew and so forth. That interests us, and we would like to talk. We would like to arrange some contact with you, perhaps with your friends, with circles."

"The KGB," I said, "is not the organization that we dreamed of contacting. We include Prisoners of Zion, refuseniks. Contact with the Central Committee, however, would be another matter and of some interest." "Our chief, Andropov," he said, "is a member of the Politburo of the Central Committee. Think about it and let's organize a meeting between Andropov and those whom you name."

KOSHAROVSKY: *He was a person at such a high level?*

CHLENOV: He was lying, of course. I therefore said that it was awkward. I asked, "What would we actually speak about?" He replied, "We would like to know more about your movement, its goals." I decided to assemble a small group.

KOSHAROVSKY: *Polsky, Slepak?*

CHLENOV: No, they weren't involved. Almost no one is aware of what I am going to tell you now. I invited several people with whom I was very close: Eliyahu Essas, Sasha Voronel, Mikhail Agursky, and a few others. I didn't invite [Vitaly] Rubin although that would have been natural because I feared that he would drive me away as soon as he heard the words "KGB" and "Andropov." Rubin was considerably older than me—by fifteen or sixteen years—and he had endured German captivity and Soviet labor camps.

I told those guys that there was an opportunity, and I knew a person who wanted to act as an intermediary for us. And I also said that it seemed to me that it was even more important to put together some kind of platform than to meet with Andropov: "Let's sit down and try to understand what our movement represents, and what, in fact, we want." We agreed that it was a matter limited to our group—no one else should know. We began to meet.

KOSHAROVSKY: *Did anyone fault you for this later?*

CHLENOV: No, it remained a forgotten and unknown episode, but to my mind it was important.

KOSHAROVSKY: *Was there a meeting?*

CHLENOV: No. I asked Stas (Korolev) about it a couple of times. He said, "Yes, yes," and then I stopped asking him.

KOSHAROVSKY: *Did you give him a document?*

CHLENOV: No. We didn't work out a final version but I kept some drafts.

KOSHAROVSKY: *What was the document's basic idea?*

CHLENOV: The basic idea was that our movement, which had unexpectedly formed in the Soviet Union, was a Jewish national movement whose goal was to assure both the freedom of repatriation to Israel and the development of cultural activity and normal Jewish existence as a national group in the Soviet Union.

The rivalry between the two groups drew in more and more activists, spread to other cities, and sometimes manifested itself in unpleasant ways.

Vladimir Prestin remembered that time:[10]

KOSHAROVSKY: *Polsky left and anointed you to lead the movement and the big split occurred. I remember that one of the main topics at our meetings was the harsh opposition to Lunts and his supporters. The attempt to negotiate secretly with the KGB in those conditions was, possibly, naïve and even objectionable, but was it worth it to break apart the movement because of it?*

PRESTIN: To this day, I don't understand it. What he did should not have provoked such a scandal. Our mistake was not our negative attitude toward his deed but, rather, the form in which it was expressed. If I had known then what I understood two years later, we never would have let things reach a schism.

KOSHAROVSKY: *Did you know that Lerner supported Lunts?*

PRESTIN: Of course, I knew. I was not sufficiently experienced. I thought that we would speak with Lunts and Lerner and explain to them. Let them go their way, we wouldn't bother them, but Lunts had to stop being in charge of things.

KOSHAROVSKY: *In other words, it was an ordinary power struggle? Lunts, who appeared much later than most of us, rises like a meteor, takes the initiative in his hands, and locks up all the connections inside the country and abroad. Then he commits an act that, from the point of view of those opposed, was morally unacceptable.*

PRESTIN: Not at all true. There was no power struggle. Polsky not only anointed me, but he also supplied me with what was needed. I was completely independent. You understand, I got started in these matters earlier. For those who entered the movement later, the KGB represented not so much the tough operative in harsh situations as merely the polite soldier who saluted at the departure gate at Sheremetevo airport. A lot had changed during that time. It's impossible to imagine that someone would have gone to speak with the KGB five years earlier, in 1970.

KOSHAROVSKY: *Did you restore relations with Lerner and Slepak?*

PRESTIN: Yes, I was forty-one years old and it seemed that my evaluations of social relations were more or less correct. I trusted them based on previous experience.

The conflict had gone so far that it began to seem idiotic. It was truly idiotic when we didn't want to meet in the same room with the senators. We had to find a way out and I felt some responsibility. At some point, a conflict arose with Dina Beilin over what someone said. Volodia Albrekht said, "Write her a letter," and he explained the basic approach and how to write it.

KOSHAROVSKY: *Why did this particular conflict upset you?*

PRESTIN: I was upset by the never-ending nonsense with which I had to learn to cope. Albrekht's idea seemed logical, and I wrote her a letter, which I gave her the following Saturday. A week passed and she told me, "You know, Volodia, if this incident is closed, I'm ready to forget about it." I felt that his advice was working: I wrote and she responded calmly. I was also calm with her although, by nature, as you know, I am a temperamental person.

Encouraged by the results, I wrote a letter to Lunts about our relations but he didn't reply and he left the country. Pasha Abramovich later had a problem with someone and he asked me what to do. I said to him, "Look, write a letter." He came to me again because he was having trouble writing the letter. It was in 1975, when I was working as an elevator operator in a residential building. There was a reception room there. It was marvelous work. Fantastic! I had free time. I worked for twenty-four hours every four days, studied psychology, and read in English. There were interesting books. I began to explain to Pasha why this method of conflict resolution worked and gradually convinced him. When Pasha understood it, I already had prepared a theory for dealing with situations of conflict. Subsequently, I spoke often on that topic. I traveled to Leningrad, where there was a serious conflict between four activists; there I spoke in Aba Taratuta's group, then in another place, and afterwards, I traveled to Riga.

KOSHAROVSKY: *All the time on the topic of the split?*

PRESTIN: Not specifically on our split but on behavior theory in situations of conflict. Indeed, there were groupings in all the cities. In Moscow I delivered this lecture at Azbel's seminar and then at Lerner's seminar. Ultimately, I succeeded in changing the situation throughout the USSR. People stopped speaking about a split. It was as if I expiated my guilt.

Context of Détente

The Helsinki process created new hope. The signing of the Final Act in Helsinki afforded new opportunities to refuseniks.[11]

> **Helsinki Accords**
>
> The Helsinki Accords—comprising the Final Act of the Conference on Security and Cooperation in Europe (CSCE)—were signed on August 1, 1975, and ratified by the Soviet Union on September 18 of that year, changing the context for dissidence and activism in the Soviet Union. The articles of agreement were divided into four "baskets." The third basket contained humanitarian provisions and triggered much new independent public activity, including the formation of unofficial Helsinki monitoring groups. Subsequent review meetings for representatives of signatory states were held in Belgrade in 1977–78, Madrid in 1980–83, and Vienna in 1986–89, offering opportunities to exert further international pressure on the Soviet Union in the context of its Helsinki obligations.

The different approaches of the kulturniki and the politiki were even more evident in this context. The cultural activists sharply expanded samizdat activity and began producing periodicals with cultural themes, *Tarbut* (Culture), *Nash ivrit* (Our Hebrew), and others. An international symposium on culture was planned and partially implemented.[12] A week devoted to the Hebrew language took place. There were festivals of Hebrew song, Purimspiels,[13] and other cultural events. The scale of the movement's cultural activity, including the international attention it garnered, seriously concerned the regime, as they showed when they disrupted the symposium on culture. The KGB opened a case against the journal *Evrei v SSSR* (Jews in the USSR), conducting searches and detaining several activists in the cultural wing. At the end of 1976, there was a feeling that the regime was planning a major trial against the cultural activists.

The political activists continued to increase pressure on the Soviet leadership by collecting information on emigration and the situation of refuseniks and Prisoners of Zion, organizing aid to those who needed assistance, initiating marches to Soviet institutions, organizing demonstrations, and preparing analytic reports for the West. In the first half of 1976, two members of this group, Vitaly Rubin and Anatoly Sharansky, took part in the formation of the Helsinki groups that took upon themselves the monitoring of human rights observance in the Soviet Union. Of course, as mentioned earlier, a clear boundary between the groups of cultural and political activists did not exist and in the case of some activists, it was hard to assign them to a particular group.

Prestin explained how they came to understand and respond to the new conditions:[14]

PRESTIN: Based on numerous replies that I received from refuseniks in various cities, I drew up a table in which one column indicated a person's place of work, another his profession, and a third how much time he had spent in refusal. I showed the table to just a few people. This was the first time such a thing had been done, and it revealed a very interesting picture. Up until the end of 1974, we had assumed that months separated us from our departure; therefore, it was not worth undertaking major initiatives. In November 1974 it became clear that the Jackson-Vanik Amendment would not help us in the immediate future, and, apparently, we faced many years of refusal to come. We thus had to consider how to proceed further in this completely different situation. Second, up until the Jackson-Vanik Amendment, we kept trying to open the door. In 1974 I concluded that the door was practically open. Third, there was the Helsinki process in August 1975. Until then the Soviet Union had talked about security and economics and managed to avoid such a "petty matter" as human rights. Now, it was the Helsinki process and human rights! That opened up new possibilities. We thus opted for the cultural symposium.

The Jewish community consisted of Prisoners of Zion, refuseniks, and the rest. Only we refuseniks were free: the former were imprisoned and the rest were not yet ready. We had to prepare a program for each group. For the two million (Jews in the Soviet Union) we began to publish the journal *Tarbut*. This was a fantasy, of course, with the (limited) number of copies produced.

It was important for me to do something for the prisoners, particularly because there were many new refuseniks who did not know the "Leningrad hijackers" or any of those who had been imprisoned earlier. On December 24, 1975, the anniversary of the verdict in the Leningrad Trial, we therefore organized an evening of solidarity with the Prisoners of Zion at the apartment of Feliks Dektor. This tradition went on for several years. Our desire to inform people about the prisoners turned out not to be so simple a task because not everyone was willing to share information. An information sheet, however, served the purpose well. It indicated where a prisoner was currently located, where he had been earlier, and the formal charge against him or her. We distributed many of these sheets. We set up a room and hung photographs. Feliks Dektor showed strength of character and courage—his building was surrounded by the KGB. That first evening, which later became known as Solidarity Day with Prisoners of Zion, had great moral significance.

With the help of refuseniks, legal seminars were organized throughout the country. We switched from demonstrating with our feet to intellectual work, utilizing the democratic dissidents' experience for our goals. A legal group or seminar appeared in almost every city. The seminar leaders were replaced every few months as they received exit visas.

KOSHAROVSKY: *Many perceived this as a trampoline.*

PRESTIN: It turned out that the majority of the leaders went to America but that's unimportant.

KOSHAROVSKY: *What was your attitude toward neshira?*

PRESTIN: I didn't fight with them, and not because I was for neshira. I was, of course, actively opposed, but I thought that at first something had to be changed in Russia if possible.

KOSHAROVSKY: *Did you already have great hopes then for culture?*

PRESTIN: Well, yes, should we send people by force to Israel? The journal *Tarbut*, after all, was a symbolic matter. How much could we do there? We needed to do something that would be noticed. Thus we arrived at the idea of a symposium.

Second Brussels Conference

The Second World Conference in Support of Soviet Jewry was held in Brussels, February 17–19, 1976. The passage of the Helsinki Accords in summer 1975 had created new opportunities for international pressure on the Soviet Union for human rights violations. However, additional challenges had arisen with UN Resolution 3379, which passed on November 10, 1975, thanks in large part to Soviet advocacy, and which defined Zionism as a form of racism. With approximately 1,200 delegates from thirty-two countries, the well-attended conference helped consolidate international support for Soviet Jewish emigration in the changed circumstances. While "Let my people go," the slogan of the First Brussels Conference, continued to resound, two additional slogans were adopted reflecting the emphasis on Jewish culture as well as emigration rights: "Let my people know" and "Let them live or let them leave."

The politiki and the kulturniki sent separate messages to the Second Brussels Conference. The kulturniki wrote about culture and the depressing situation in which any attempts by refuseniks to revive elements of spiritual life, to teach Hebrew, and to produce independent journals were suppressed by the regime. They appealed to the conference participants to strive to obtain permission for Hebrew teaching and for the publication of books on the history, culture, and religion of the Jewish people.

At the same time, it was stressed that the development of Jewish culture was in no way regarded as a substitute for aliya to Israel. The signatories included Vladimir Prestin, Veniamin Fain, Pavel Abramovich, Viktor Brailovsky, Mark Azbel, Yosif Begun, Vladimir Kislik, Yuli Kosharovsky, and others.

The politiki prepared an impressive analytical report in which they called for the continuation of an uncompromising struggle for emigration. It was signed by Alexander Lerner, Alexander Lunts, Vladimir Slepak, Dina Beilin, Natan Sharansky, Ida Nudel, Vitaly Rubin, and Eitan Finkelshtein. The American grassroots group Union of Councils published it on February 2, 1976, and presented it at the conference (the politiki had complex relations with the establishment and therefore chose to do it that way). The report raised the issues of unjustified refusals, the use of army service to pressure activists, legal and extra-legal harassment, and anti-Zionist propaganda. The section on Prisoners of Zion presented new details obtained from places of imprisonment about harsh measures against specific prisoners. The case against the journal *Evrei v SSSR* (Jews in the USSR) was considered separately: no one had been charged but almost everyone who was interrogated was threatened that at any moment he or she could switch from being a witness to being a defendant. The authors of the report asserted that the material presented therein explained the real reason for the decline in the level of Jewish emigration.

Symposium on Jewish Culture

After the Brussels Conference, the tension between the kulturniki and politiki escalated. Both, however, decided to test the Soviet Union's willingness to observe the human rights obligations of the Helsinki Accords. The linkage between the three baskets seemed like a provocative and serious possibility. These baskets included recognition of the postwar borders in Europe and détente between East and West, scientific-technological and trade exchanges, and human rights. The kulturniki began preparing a major international undertaking entitled "A Symposium—Jewish Culture in the USSR: Its Current State and Prospects." The politiki worked to set up global mechanisms for public monitoring of the Soviet regime's compliance with the Helsinki Accords in the field of human rights. These were the so-called Helsinki groups, committees, and associations.

Veniamin Fain described the impetus for the symposium:[15]

KOSHAROVSKY: *Why did you decide that the cultural trend was so important for the Zionist movement?*

FAIN: The first stimulus came at the end of 1973, when I had not yet applied for an exit visa. The large-scale neshira began and something had to be done about it.

At the end of 1974, I made the acquaintance of Vladimir Prestin. After discussing the issue, we came to the conclusion—and this is an important point—that Jewish education has significance for Jews independent of Zionism and emigration. Jews have a right to their own culture, just as they have a right to emigration. One does not contradict the other because when a person acquires a normal national consciousness, then he begins to think about what to do with it. For us, this conclusion was not directly linked to whether or not education would help emigration. That is a separate topic.

KOSHAROVSKY: *You were people with a technical education and without the appropriate cultural base. Why did you decide that precisely you should, and—most importantly—could, do this?*

FAIN: If the Jewish cultural figures had not been shot and if they had been prepared to take this upon themselves, I would have been only too happy to support them with all my heart and not play any visible role. But they were shot.[16] We thus planned the symposium, speaking loudly about the current situation of Jewish culture and what we intended to do about it.

KOSHAROVSKY: *How did you plan to reach the Jewish masses? Clearly, 150–200 copies of* Tarbut *(Culture) were insufficient for this.*

FAIN: We did what we could. The symposium was designed to put the topic on the international agenda.

KOSHAROVSKY: *That's how you tried to bring the issue to the attention of the Soviet regime?*

FAIN: Them too, but primarily to the attention of the West, which considered that emigration was proceeding, neshira was occurring, and that's how it should be.

Preparations for the symposium lasted several months. During that time, there were intensive discussions about the strategy and means for developing Jewish culture. The organizers succeeded in involving more than one hundred activists from various cities in the Soviet Union and a large number of Jewish scientists and humanities scholars in the West in the work of the symposium. Seventy-seven reports on various aspects of the current state and development of Jewish culture in the USSR were prepared.

Chlenov, an ethnographer, brought his expertise to preparing materials for the symposium:[17]

CHLENOV: We conducted a poll with questionnaires among acquaintances and relatives, interviewing people in the summer at the beaches, dachas, and rest homes. As a result, we obtained a respectable quantity of 1,200 respondents throughout the USSR. It's true that it was not a random sample but the results were close to the results of later polls that we conducted professionally in the post-Soviet period.

The poll showed a demand for Jewish culture. In response to the question, for example, "Would you buy a book on Jewish history if it was sold in a Soviet store?" 98 percent answered, "Yes, of course." There were questions about schools: "If there was a Jewish school, what kind of school should it be?" There were also questions about the attitude toward emigration and about how they envisaged the future of Soviet Jewry.

KOSHAROVSKY: *What ideas about the development of Jewish culture were elaborated in the process of preparing the symposium?*

CHLENOV: Four programmatic reports were presented: the main one was signed by [Vladimir] Prestin, [Pavel] Abramovich, Tsilia Roitburd, [Semyon] Kushner, and [Veniamin] Fain. There was also my report, which, in essence, was the one I delivered at [Felix] Kandel's seminar, and there were reports by Ilia Essas and Grisha Rozenshtein.

KOSHAROVSKY: *What did the central report with the five signatories propose?*

CHLENOV: Basically, Jewish culture in the USSR ought to serve aliya and be oriented toward Israel and the West.

KOSHAROVSKY: *What did you propose?*

CHLENOV: Culture as an independent direction based on a dialogue with the regime.

KOSHAROVSKY: *What was Essas's approach?*

CHLENOV: The movement must strive—and in this he saw the future of Soviet Jewry—to create minyanim of a new kind.[18]

KOSHAROVSKY: *What about Rozenshtein?*

CHLENOV: Grisha Rozenshtein wrote that the future of Jewish culture depends directly on the presence of *tsadikim* (righteous people) in the Jewish milieu. Those were the four basic reports. There were some interesting things here and there. For example, Lerner, who was head of the politiki, explained why the Jews in the Soviet Union must not get involved with culture: it's not only harmful but also illegitimate because no one authorized us to act in the name of the Jewish people. He considered the movement for the right to emigrate was the fundamental stimulus for the revival of Jewish consciousness in the USSR and that there were no grounds for a discussion of Jewish culture in the Jewish national movement. Judeo-Christians [a sect that proposes Christianity as the meaningful continuation of Judaism, rather than its replacement] also applied to the symposium, offering a report about Christianity as a contemporary form of Zionism in the Soviet Union. Essas objected and did not permit the organizing committee to accept this report.

The organizing committee for the symposium on Jewish culture consisted of many activists of the cultural movement: Veniamin Fain (chairman), Leonid Volvovsky (deputy chairman), Vladimir Prestin, Pavel Abramovich, Ilia Essas, Mark Azbel, Viktor Brailovsky, Vladimir Lazaris, Arkady Mai, Felix Kandel, Yosif Begun, and others, including activists from Moscow, Leningrad, Riga, Vilnius, Odessa, and Baku. The activists' broad spectrum of views on the revival of Jewish culture in the USSR could be divided into three basic categories: secular Zionist (the reports of Fain, Prestin, Abramovich, Semyon Kushner, and Lev Roitburd), religious Zionist (Essas and Rozenshtein), and legalist (Chlenov).[19]

Vladimir Prestin explained what distinguished his secular Zionist approach from Chlenov's legalist approach:[20]

PRESTIN: We assumed that we could organize educational-cultural activity on our own with the support of Israeli and Western Jewish organizations. An indispensable condition for this was the regime's noninterference.

KOSHAROVSKY: *What made you think that the authorities of a totalitarian state would agree to farm out such an important part of its brainwashing activity?*

PRESTIN: They wouldn't do so voluntarily. We had to fight for it with the support of our Western friends. You see, we were not so naïve as it might seem at first glance. For the first time in the Soviet period, the question of human rights had become a political issue. I mean the Jackson-Vanik Amendment, not Helsinki. The country realized that it would have to pay dearly for violating certain of its citizens' rights. Second, of course, was the Helsinki process. Did we really want so much? We were trying to revive the culture that had been crushed and destroyed by the Soviets. Mika (Chlenov) asserted that one couldn't get around the Soviet regime and that one had to cooperate with it on cultural issues; otherwise, nothing would come of it. The totalitarian Soviet regime, however, couldn't become democratic overnight and start to cooperate with us even if Chlenov wanted it to do so. In reality, only after the fall of the USSR did the new regime recognize the Jews' right to national education.

Chlenov's approach seemed too revolutionary and fantastic for its time. His viewpoint was unacceptable to the majority of activists. No one, of course, would object to the free development of Jewish culture in the Soviet Union, but on the whole Jewish activists did not believe that the anti-Semitic and anti-Zionist tyrannical state would ever cooperate in the development of truly normal Jewish culture. Many activists thought that the Jews did not have a future in the Soviet Union and that anyone who wanted to remain a Jew should go to Israel and live a normal national life there. Without denying its value, these activists considered that culture ought to serve aliya and prepare people to return to their people and for life in Israel.

What, in essence, was Chlenov saying? That aliya was a very important, but not the sole, element in the solution to the "Jewish question." He maintained that Jewish activists ought to remember those who remained in the Soviet Union, that they could be reached only by legalized Jewish culture, and that it was necessary to exert pressure on the regime and try to reach an agreement with them to permit such culture. He saw the future of those Jews who would remain in the USSR in the revival of a national culture that would not intimidate or repel them.

This sounded, at the very least, untimely in the mid-1970s. However, the years passed, the Soviet regime weakened and disappeared, and Chlenov succeeded in realizing his program. Those Jews who remained in the territory of the former Soviet Union received the freedom to develop a legal, autonomous Jewish culture that he had dreamed about in the mid-1970s.

The organizers carried out extensive preparations for the symposium. Moreover, they did everything completely openly, in full accordance with the Helsinki Accords.[21] The committee solicited participants from within the country and abroad, describing the approximate range of topics for the reports and indicating that they would be accepted until November 15, 1976.

Dozens of invitations were sent to representatives of the regime, highly placed officials in the Ministry of Culture, local and foreign journalists, scientists, and prominent rabbis abroad. According to Fain, the announcement of the forthcoming symposium was broadcast by the Voice of America, the BBC, and other Western radio stations. Although it was initially scheduled for December 19–21, the organizers decided to delay it by two days. December 19 was Brezhnev's birthday, and they did not want to give the authorities a pretext to declare the symposium a "provocation."[22]

Veniamin Fain spoke about the strategy he and other kulturniki pursued:[23]

KOSHAROVSKY: *How did you envisage the revival of Jewish culture?*

FAIN: Unlike Chlenov, we said to the authorities, "Let us do things on our own." We foresaw, however, a gradual process that would entail, for example, a journal under UNESCO's aegis devoted to Jewish culture that would be accessible in Russia, something similar to the journal *America*. This would be a struggle for the legalization of Hebrew. That is, we intended to begin with small steps, gradually expanding our sphere of activity.

KOSHAROVSKY: *Did you want to legalize culture with the help of the West, utilizing the tools of the Helsinki process?*

FAIN: Yes, we wanted open access to culture in the West but we didn't want the regime to create a Jewish culture that was national in form and Socialist in content [which was the formulation that the Soviet Union tried to impose on all minority cultures]. We wanted genuine culture.

KOSHAROVSKY: *What was your attitude toward the political activists' contention that attempts at a broad revival of Jewish culture would deflect significant forces from the aliya struggle?*

FAIN: Nonsense. Would you think that a person would have reduced motivation to leave for Israel if he feels himself to be a Jew?

Invitations to participate in the symposium were sent to forty prominent Jewish cultural figures in the West, including Elie Wiesel, Salo Baron, Gershom Scholem, and others.

The program included seventy-seven reports divided into six sections:[24] the state of Jewish culture in the USSR; the role of religion; new breeding grounds for the shoots of Jewish culture in the USSR; Jewish culture in Israel and the West; a characterization of Jewry; and prospects for the future. Among noted Western figures sending reports were Salo Baron; Nahum Goldmann, chairman of the World Jewish Congress; and Rabbi Adin Steinsaltz.

Leonid (Ari) Volvovsky, deputy chairman of the organizing committee, spoke about the organizational work of preparing the symposium:[25]

VOLVOVSKY: Many of us had organized dozens of symposiums in our lives, but in those cases we understood what we were organizing. This time, however, we wanted to organize a symposium on a topic about which we understood nothing. The main task of the symposium consisted of stimulating public opinion around the world and drawing attention to the fact that Jewish culture was suppressed in the Soviet Union.

KOSHAROVSKY: *I don't understand. Did you intend to develop Jewish culture or to raise a worldwide hullabaloo—to arouse a wave of protest so that the authorities would feel the heat and let you go?*

VOLVOVSKY: It was understood that none of those present could really advance culture. We only taught Hebrew. Venia Fain edited a journal.

Volodia Prestin wrote some articles and Pasha Abramovich edited something—that was the entire culture. For us, however, it wasn't a matter of hopping a ride on this enterprise and leaving the country. We hoped that under pressure, the regime would allow some center of Jewish culture to develop. We pondered for a long time and drew up a plan. Then we compiled a list of names from newspapers and personal acquaintances and prepared letters. Although we understood that we would get nowhere with Soviet figures, we had to observe the niceties and send invitations to Soviet organizations. We also sent invitations abroad, thinking that one or two answers would arrive, but then they began to stream in. We asked people to send the basic theses of their talks and these began to arrive in a large quantity. Not through the mail; people would bring them in. From the Soviet official side a sepulchral silence reigned. We also began to prepare materials. Our basic task was to organize a sociological survey.

KOSHAROVSKY: *That's what Chlenov did?*

VOLVOVSKY: He prepared the questionnaire. Everyone took part. I took on responsibility for gathering all the data that needed to be processed. It turned out that conducting a poll in the Soviet Union was a terrible criminal act. The first signals from the authorities came in November: we received an invitation from the Yiddish newspaper *Sovetish heymland.* Pasha [Abramovich], Volodia [Prestin], Venia [Fain], a fellow who knew Yiddish, and I went. Vergelis [the editor in chief] came to meet us and began to speak in Yiddish. We stood there. As soon as he finished, we all began to speak in Hebrew. It was their turn to be silent. Then one of us said, "Well, the performance is over; now let's speak in the language that we all know." In truth, they did not want to speak with us about anything. They kept directing the conversation to our supposed plan for an anti-Soviet action that could harm everyone. We kept on evading that topic and asking about the development of Jewish culture in their milieu, about the number of young people who were involved, and how they spent the holidays. "What holidays do you observe?" I asked. Vergelis got up and replied, "We Soviet Jews have only one holiday: the day of the Great October Revolution."

A half hour after the meeting, this sentence appeared in all the Western media. It was a blow for them. After that, we were prepared for anything—we had bags ready with an assortment of underwear and necessities in case of arrest.

After this meeting the authorities began to tail the organizers assiduously. Searches were conducted at their homes. They looked particularly for sociological questionnaires. Kosharovsky was questioned several times, and particular pressure was put on Abramovich, Fain, Prestin, and Chlenov. Chlenov's unwillingness to be a member of the organizing committee did not mean he could avoid this pressure in the end.[26] Only one of the foreigners invited to the symposium managed to make it to Moscow: Rabbi Rabinovich from Maaleh Adumim in Israel, who, at the time, was teaching in Jews' College in London. However, the symposium did not take place. On the day of its scheduled opening, the organizers and participants were detained. The audience arrived at Grigory Rozenshtein's apartment, where the symposium was supposed to take place. The organizers, anticipating possible arrest, had prepared a letter, which was hidden in the handle of a mop. It was read aloud to the audience when it became clear the participants would not arrive.

Vladimir Prestin disputed some possible conclusions from the aborted attempt:[27]

KOSHAROVSKY: *Volodia, they disrupted the symposium and confiscated the material. Several people were dragged in for interrogations and they were afraid that things would not end well for them. Some participants in those events assumed that the regime was planning two trials, against both the cultural and political wings. In the end, they selected the politiki and in 1977, heads began to fly.*

PRESTIN: You know my attitude toward that terminology. There were no kulturniki. We participated in all activities on behalf of everyone.

KOSHAROVSKY: *Understandably, it's an arbitrary division.*

PRESTIN: I can't speak about the regime's intentions. However, I do not agree with the evaluation that the symposium was completely disrupted. During the searches, part of the material was confiscated, but we managed to preserve all the reports and we published them in samizdat. It's true that the regime did not allow foreign participants to come to Moscow or permit us to conduct a normal session of the symposium. By their behavior, however, they only highlighted their own policy of suppressing Jewish culture in the USSR. The disruption of the symposium was widely publicized on the first pages of many newspapers in the democratic world. The materials comprised a broad program for us and for our supporters in the West. Reviving Jewish culture became an essential component in our life.

In general, I presumed that, given the lack of freedom, undertakings that were limited in time were more viable than any kind of ongoing committees or working groups, which is why a symposium was chosen. And the symposium, which was as you said "disrupted," nevertheless provided a powerful spiritual charge for the Jewish national revival.

Chlenov also positively evaluated developments in Jewish cultural life in the wake of the symposium:[28]

KOSHAROVSKY: *In your view, how did the cultural process develop subsequently?*

CHLENOV: I would call the years 1977–80 the period in which the Jewish cultural movement in Moscow flourished—and not only then. In the summer of 1977, we got together and tried to figure out what to do next, the more so because the crushing of the political movement occurred at that time. In the summer, suddenly Jewish youth began to appear because of this very symposium. These young people went on to initiate song festivals, Purimspiels, and many other things that had not existed previously.

Helsinki Groups and the Sharansky Trial

The Zionist movement elaborated an effective system for monitoring developments in the USSR and transmitting information to the West. This multilevel system evolved gradually. The different levels did not always work well together, but with time, they managed to coordinate activity and exchange information. The Liaison Bureau (Nativ, or Lishka) organized the first and most effective channels. These included regular telephone conversations from Israel and other countries with key aliya activists, a stream of foreign tourists to various Soviet cities, and of course, debriefing new immigrants in Vienna and in Israel.

The information collected by the Bureau was analyzed and processed with the help of the Centre for Research and Documentation of East European Jewry of the Hebrew University of Jerusalem and dispatched to various Soviet Jewry support organizations around the world or published in the press. In addition to those establishment channels, independently minded organizations that were critical of the establishment and its methods cultivated their own sources. The Bureau did not share information with such grassroots groups as the Union of Councils for Soviet Jews, Student Struggle, the "35s," and other large international organizations that began to set up their own monitoring systems and willingly exchanged information with each other. The latter groups' methods of collecting information were the same as those of establishment bodies, particularly after neshira acquired serious proportions, but their methods of utilizing it differed. As a rule, they immediately transmitted information to colleagues around the world and went to the press in appropriate public and political instances. The independent organizations conducted an open struggle.

Many Jewish activists tried not to go beyond the bounds of Jewish affairs. Nevertheless, Jewish circles respected highly the courageous activity of Academician Andrei Sakharov and his colleagues that was aimed at democratizing the Soviet order, and some individuals in those Jewish circles were prepared to participate directly in that struggle. The Liaison Bureau anxiously followed our disputes and did everything possible not to burden the Jewish aliya struggle with what it regarded as extraneous, dangerous tasks. It followed the same line with regard to Jewish activists in the West.

The Bureau's efforts were not completely successful. Two prominent activists in the Jewish national movement, Vitaly Rubin and Anatoly (Natan) Sharansky, were among the founders of the Moscow Helsinki group. The initiative aimed at establishing special nongovernmental groups that would gather information on human rights violations in various countries and report that information to the governments of countries that signed the Accords. The formation of the group was announced at a press conference at the Moscow apartment of Academician Sakharov on May 12, 1976. Similar groups were formed in Ukraine, Georgia, Armenia, and Lithuania during 1976–77. The Helsinki groups in the Soviet Union became the main centers that had the infrastructure to monitor human rights violations there.

Helsinki Groups

Initiated by physicist Yuri Orlov, the Moscow Helsinki group, including Andrei Sakharov; Sakharov's wife, Elena Bonner; Lyudmila Alexeyeva; Alexander Ginzburg; Malva Landa; Vitaly Rubin; Anatoly Sharansky; and others, was founded on May 12, 1976, to monitor Soviet compliance with the human rights provisions of the Helsinki Accords. A number of other activists, including Vladimir Slepak, joined later. Despite repressive measures by Soviet security services, until 1981 the group managed to document, publicize, and protest rights abuses. Associated initiatives included the Working Group to Investigate the Use of Psychiatry for Political Purposes and Helsinki groups in Ukraine, Lithuania, Georgia, and Armenia.

One of the founders of the Moscow Helsinki group, Vitaly Rubin, received an exit visa two weeks after the group's formation. His place was taken by Vladimir Slepak, who, according to his own testimony, signed only those documents that touched on issues of freedom of emigration or anti-Semitism. Anatoly Sharansky, who did not divide the work into "kosher" and "treif" (nonkosher), helped initiate the group. Along with Slepak, he represented primarily the interests of the Zionist movement, but as the press secretary of the group, he also dealt with other issues.

Sharansky talked about his involvement with the Helsinki group:[29]

KOSHAROVSKY: *Were you in constant contact with Sakharov even before the founding of the Helsinki Committee?*

SHARANSKY: Yes, ever since Alik Goldfarb left at the beginning of 1975. You see, I became a member of the Helsinki group precisely because I had been very active and had already been friendly with Yuri Orlov for a year. I taught English to Orlov, Andrei Amalrik, and Liudmila Alekseev. Everyone earned additional money through lessons and I did too. The idea for the Helsinki group arose in the course of discussions between Orlov, Amalrik, and me.

KOSHAROVSKY: *In your book, you write that you suggested the idea to Orlov.*

SHARANSKY: Very true. I proposed a much more modest idea, however, which I formulated at the beginning of 1976, when, if you remember, there was a congress of the international Communist parties, which took place once every few years. In that context, I proposed writing a letter to the Communist Party leaders of Italy and France. Those parties operated under the conditions of European democracy. They were influenced by the pressure of Western public opinion and first began to express their disagreement with the Soviet Union over a number of human rights issues. "Let's propose that they meet with refuseniks to discuss the situation of Soviet Jews. That falls within the framework of the Helsinki Accords, and we want to hear their opinion on this matter," I suggested. Rubin liked the idea a lot. He drafted a text and said, "Let's immediately sign up me, Lerner, Sharansky, Slepak, and Lunts." After that, I went to give the letter to the journalists from *l'Humanité* and *l'Unità* [organs of the French and Italian Communist parties]. You should have seen how frightened they became! One said that this was a propagandistic letter and he would not transmit it. Another said that he would do so but . . . Naturally, I also went to other Western journalists in the non-Communist press, in particular *Le Monde* and *La Stampa,* and told them the story. This caused a big stir.

I said to Orlov and Amalrik, "We wrote a letter to the Communists about one specific issue and proposed that they monitor whether the Soviet Union is complying with the Helsinki Accords. Look at how frightened and excited they got. What would happen if a large group of various kinds of dissidents, disturbed by the Soviet Union's noncompliance with its obligations, turned not to the Communists but to the broader public of various countries and suggested that people in those countries begin collecting and exchanging information about compliance with the Accords? As we have seen, it is much easier to reach an understanding about the meaning of these Accords with representatives of independent public opinion than with governments." Amalrik was very pleased with the idea and immediately began compiling a list that comprised sixty or seventy activists who would be prepared to sign such a letter. My idea thus was only to write a letter and to propose initiating a discussion about creating a network of such groups in all the Helsinki Accord countries.

KOSHAROVSKY: *To check on the observance of the Accords in the Soviet Union?*

SHARANSKY: No, each group in its own country. Orlov and I agreed to meet after some time and discuss the situation. He arrived and said, "You know, I decided that there was no point in writing letters; we should simply declare that we established a group and anyone who wants to should do the same. Otherwise, it will be just chatter. Unlike your proposal, for which they won't necessarily arrest us, for this, in the end, they will arrest people. It will thus force the West to pay serious attention to the issue of compliance with the Helsinki Accords." My proposal was good for a one-time action. Orlov's proposal was much more serious and it was an act of great civil courage.

KOSHAROVSKY: *Orlov understood that he was crossing a dangerous line.*

SHARANSKY: He said that we would probably be arrested. "In that case," he said and repeated it many times, "under Article 64, for treason." "No, you are exaggerating," I said. "I think they will arrest us under Article 70, for slander, but I agree—they'll surely arrest us. If you take this step, I'm with you." The irony of fate is that in the course of a year they arrested everyone, but he was arrested under Article 70 and I was arrested under Article 64.

KOSHAROVSKY: *You had some additions to your charge.*

SHARANSKY: My Article 64 was for Zionist activity but the Helsinki group was Article 70.

At the end of 1976, the basic initiatives that had arisen in the Soviet Union after the signing of the Helsinki Accords encountered problems. At first, there was the feeling that the regime intended to take reprisals against the kulturniki. In the end, however, the KGB decided to strike at the politiki, the democrats, and members of Helsinki groups. The blows were harsh, indicating a patent desire to intimidate and crush both the political wing of the Zionist movement and the Helsinki movement among the democratic rights activists and other dissidents.

On January 7, 1977, the Helsinki group reported repressive measures against the Moscow branch, including searches at the apartments of Yuri Orlov, Alexander Ginzburg, and Liudmila Alekseev. Fourteen activists of the Jewish movement, including Lerner, Slepak, Finkelshtein, Prestin, Azbel, and Sharansky, protested to the West and to the US Congress that the Soviet authorities were "trying to get rid of this source that is revealing violations of agreements made at Helsinki."[30] This was followed by several phone conversations with members of the US Congress.

On January 20 an appeal that was signed by 163 Jewish activists from Moscow, Leningrad, Minsk, Riga, and other cities was sent to the heads of states that had signed the Helsinki Accords. Sharansky took an active part in preparing and dispatching this letter, which described the Soviet Union's gross violation of the spirit and letter of the Accords with regard to emigration. It mentioned that, despite the stipulation in the Helsinki Accords that the authorities could issue refusals only on a legal basis, they were giving oral refusals that were unmotivated and unlimited in time.

In response, Soviet propaganda unleashed a round of heavy artillery. The central television station broadcast a sixty-five-minute documentary film entitled *Traders of Souls* on January 22, 1977. Following the classic canons of Soviet anti-Zionist propaganda, the Zionist activists were portrayed as the "traders of souls" and their victims were all those who wished to leave the Soviet Union. One of the supposed tourists shown in the film said in front of the camera that he did not rule out the possibility that the Zionists were working in close contact with American intelligence and carrying out its missions, and that the refuseniks engaged directly in brainwashing, working as hired hands and soldiers of Zionism and of those with whom the Zionists cooperated. The camera panned over lists of refuseniks and then showed in close-up the faces of several Jewish activists: Slepak, Begun, Kosharovsky, and Sharansky. The behind-the-scenes narrator reported that all these people were "soldiers of Zionism," engaged in subversive activity against the USSR.[31] Shown on prime time, the film was seen by millions of viewers.

Following the film, an article appeared in the government newspaper *Izvestiia* on January 23, 1977, that asserted the invitations sent from Israel were falsified. On January 29 the popular weekly *Ogonek* published an article, "The Spying Ways of Zionism," contending that on the eve of and during World War II, Zionists cooperated closely with Nazi Germany. The article implied that the only reason for capturing and hanging Eichmann was to avert publication of that information.

The weekly *Literaturnaia gazeta* (Literary Gazette) published an article on February 2, 1977, under the signature of Alexander Petrov-Agatov, entitled "Liars and Pharisees." It presented at length the views of a dissident who "saw the light" about the human rights movement in the USSR in general and individual participants Alexander Ginzburg and Yuri Orlov in particular. Ginzburg was arrested on the following day and Orlov a week later.

Deciding to fight the campaign of slander and incitement, the four activists whose names and photographs appeared in the film *Traders of Souls* went to the Dzerzhinsky district court with a petition to defend their honor and dignity against the slander in the film. No one was willing to accept the petition, nor was anyone willing to give a written reply concerning the refusal to accept the document. After several hours of waiting and delays, the petitioners were received by the on-duty judge. The representative of justice declared that the activists were undertaking another anti-Soviet provocation and therefore he did not intend to take any action on the case nor did he plan to give a written reply explaining the refusal. An enraged Yosif Begun angrily retorted to the judge, "What kind of judge are you? You're just a fascist!"[32]

Yosif Begun was arrested on March 1, 1977. The formal charge against this prominent scientist who had worked more than twenty years was "malicious parasitism." Sharansky returned to Moscow that same day and moved into the apartment of a friendly acquaintance, Alexander Lipavsky. On March 4 the Soviet newspaper *Izvestiia* published an article under Lipavsky's signature that shook up the refusenik community. Entitled "An Open Letter," it was addressed to the Presidium of the Supreme Soviet of the USSR, the US Congress, and the UN. It was accompanied by extensive commentary and photographs of a spying instrument prepared from a piece of cable and supposed instructions from American intelligence—a genuine spy thriller. The authorities initiated searches in the apartments of seven Moscow activists: Lerner, Slepak, Sharansky, Nudel, Chernobylsky, Dina Beilin, and Mikhail Kremen.[33]

Sharansky talked about that tense time:[34]

KOSHAROVSKY: *The arrests of members of the Helsinki groups made extra work for you.*

SHARANSKY: Yes, especially after the arrests of Orlov and Ginzburg. I remained practically the sole "voice." At the same time, there was tension on the Jewish front as searches were under way. People kept telling me that the noose around me was likely to tighten.

KOSHAROVSKY: *In fact, many refuseniks thought that they were planning to strike at Lerner.*

SHARANSKY: Completely true. At Lerner and perhaps at Dina Beilin because she was in charge of the lists. I was pressured, however, from two sides. I had enormous "tails" [KGB agents following their subject's movements] around the clock, probably because of the Helsinki group. Suddenly Lipavsky disappeared.

KOSHAROVSKY: *Did you live with him?*

SHARANSKY: That's interesting. About two months earlier, I said that I had to live in Moscow and I was beginning to look for a place, but Lipavsky said that he, too, was thinking about that. He rented a room and suggested that we could rent together. I moved to that room, and he suddenly disappeared. Several days after his disappearance, on Purim, the article appeared and searches were conducted in various apartments.

KOSHAROVSKY: *The article appeared on March 4, 1977.*

SHARANSKY: Yes, that evening we went to celebrate Purim at Arik Rakhlenko's home and read the newspaper on the way.

KOSHAROVSKY: *Your feeling?*

SHARANSKY: That they were planning to make arrests.

KOSHAROVSKY: *It mentioned four names.*

SHARANSKY: Lerner, Slepak, Sharansky, and Azbel. I was the only one, however, who, several hours before that, suddenly acquired eight "tails." That had not happened before and they accompanied me constantly up to the arrest.

KOSHAROVSKY: *You remained very active up to the last moment.*

SHARANSKY: I went to the embassies, to journalists, and was on the telephone incessantly.

Sharansky was arrested on March 15, 1977. A powerful campaign in support of Sharansky got under way within the Soviet Union and abroad in the first weeks after his arrest. Everyone understood that this was no ordinary refusenik case but an attempt at another blood libel that could be followed by the crushing of the Jewish emigration movement.

Sakharov appealed to US president Jimmy Carter to intervene on Sharansky's behalf. The Knesset held an emergency session and appealed to other parliaments to help avert the reprisals against Sharansky and Soviet Jews. More than one hundred American congressmen and senators sent letters and telegrams to Carter and Brezhnev. Three hundred French intellectuals published a petition against his arrest. By March 17 student groups in support of Soviet Jewry organized demonstrations in New York, Ottawa, and London. A demonstration of ten thousand people was held in Israel on March 21, with the participation of Golda Meir, Israeli Chief Rabbi Shlomo Goren, and Knesset deputies. Demonstrations also took place in Los Angeles, Baltimore, San Francisco, Washington, Paris, and Montreal.[35]

After Sharansky's arrest, the basic burden of working with the Western media fell upon the shoulders of Lev Ulanovsky, who already had been helping Sharansky in organizing press conferences and meeting with foreign visitors. Ulanovsky described his role:[36]

ULANOVSKY: I had to do the work of the two of us with the press, work that was even more intensive because of the universal interest in Tolik's case. The Soviet regime tried to manipulate this interest, minimizing Tolik's Jewish activity and presenting him as a political opponent of the Soviet regime and even as a spy. The world understood the absurdity of the espionage charge immediately, but the regime, evidently, had a more cunning idea. They wanted to deprive Tolik of the support of Israeli and Western Jewish organizations. An unspoken warning hovered in the air: "If you Jews take on this case, then you, too, will land in this dangerous category." Worried by this threat, Israeli and Western advocates of secret diplomacy bombarded us with questions: "Is it true that things will become worse for refuseniks if the world supports Sharansky?" I replied, "On the contrary, such support will only help us." Unlike Tolik, I was a Hebrew teacher and activist for the revival of Jewish culture. My opinion, therefore, carried some weight in those Western circles in which the Soviets tried to sow doubts.

In the first months, Sharansky knew nothing about what was happening outside the prison walls, and no one outside knew anything about Sharansky himself—what was happening to him in his highly isolated stone cell. No one knew what charges had been brought, what measures were being used against him, and how he was withstanding his ordeal. Having publicized the terrible accusations against him, the authorities would do everything in their power to break him, and if they succeeded, they would conduct a big show trial, as they knew so well how to do.

Sharansky recalled the personal and legal challenges he faced:[37]

KOSHAROVSKY: *You weren't expecting a charge of treason, which carries the death sentence. How did you handle this during the sixteen months of the investigation?*

SHARANSKY: For the first two or three weeks, the most difficult thing was somehow getting used to this thought.

KOSHAROVSKY: *You were very strong ideologically, it seems to me.*

SHARANSKY: That was *their* big mistake. They thought that I was young, relatively unknown, and had a pretty wife whom no one knew, and we wanted to be together. They made a big mistake with regard to Avital.[38]

KOSHAROVSKY: *When the cell door slammed after you and you were charged with an article that carried capital punishment, didn't you have some doubts about whether you had chosen the right path?*

SHARANSKY: There were moments of fear and weeks of lonely solitude, but I never doubted the correctness of my chosen path. Having become a Zionist and dissident, I turned into a free person, and this feeling of freedom was stronger than the fear of death.

KOSHAROVSKY: *The Lishka said that several lists compiled by Jewish activists indicated the workplace of people who received refusals on the grounds of access to classified material and gave addresses and the names of institute directors.[39] This information in and of itself was classified and when you collect a whole list, there is an element of collecting secret information. I was told that if someone tried to gather such information in Israel, he, too, would be arrested.*

SHARANSKY: I myself didn't deal with compiling lists. Sasha Lunts and then Dina Beilin did that. Moreover, I never kept the lists at my place. I was responsible only for dispatching the lists via journalists, diplomats, or some other way. Precisely because of my familiarity with the process, I understood that the lists should not include any secret information. After all, the refuseniks themselves brought the information and they wouldn't compromise themselves. One of the questions that we asked was, "Are you willing to give the reason for the refusal?" If the refusal was "on grounds of secrecy" and the person worked, for example, in an agricultural academy, then he himself would decide whether it was worth giving such information. The rest was basic information: name, birth date, members of the family, address, and whether there were relatives in Israel.

KOSHAROVSKY: *Many people who were working in open institutes in the Soviet Union nevertheless received refusals on the grounds of secrecy. That applied to academics who published abroad and who would have wanted to travel to conferences. They had no access to classified information but received a refusal on the grounds of secrecy. They themselves wanted to show the West the true state of affairs: look, you see that I worked in an open institute; my bosses calmly travel abroad but I am refused an exit visa. They gave information in order to pressure the leadership of those institutes.*

SHARANSKY: Not everyone traveled abroad. Sometimes international conferences were held inside these institutes. Dina Beilin, Sasha Lunts, Lerner, Levich, I, and several others wanted that information to be known in the West.

KOSHAROVSKY: *Everyone who received a refusal on grounds of secrecy and worked in an open institute was prepared to write that.*

SHARANSKY: You're right. I think it began with Levich. I remember that the journalists discussed it. The situation became absurd. For example, a person was working in the Academy of Sciences on a certain project. His colleagues on the project traveled to international forums where they discussed his ideas, while at the same time he himself was not only forbidden to discuss these ideas with foreigners but also he was refused an exit visa because of them. In 1975–76 there was much talk of the Soviet Union's effort to expand contacts with the West. After the signing of the Helsinki Accords, it was assumed that scientific exchanges would increase. The idea arose from discussions among refuseniks that if you work in a specific institute and you never had access to classified material, the proof of that was the fact that your institute invites people from America and lets them into the laboratory in which you work. The journalists began to take an interest in such things. Now we are coming to the critical part of this whole story.

Hoping to help those who had received refusals on grounds of secrecy when, in fact, such secrecy didn't exist, Robert Toth thought that there would be interest in an article about that matter at a time when expanding scientific contacts was under consideration. I think Toth asked Dina to give some blatant examples. The idea was to show that secrecy was used as a pretext for refusal. That's how I understood the article and, honestly speaking, it truly was about that. If you read it over today, the only problem is in the headline, which the editor, not Toth, chose: "Russia Indirectly Reveals 'State Secrets.'"[40]

KOSHAROVSKY: *The headline assumes that people in open institutes really engaged in secret work.*

SHARANSKY: Look, the journalist wrote, you see, the Russians invite the Western scientists to cooperate with a certain institute. They declare that it is an open institute that does not engage in classified work but at the same time, they refuse exit visas to Messrs. A, B, and C on grounds of secrecy. In other words, Russia is obliquely revealing that the authorities were lying to us in declaring that these institutes were secret.

KOSHAROVSKY: *In some cases that was really so.*

SHARANSKY: I, for example, asserted that I never had access to any kind of secrets in the Moscow Institute of Physics and Technology and that three students in my faculty received visas while I was refused on secrecy grounds. I dealt with computer programs for chess games. I used that argumentation and they published it. That headline implied: here is indirect information about secret research. A terrible thing. I met Robert Toth and said, "You don't understand what you are doing." "But the Soviets affirm," replied Toth, "that all these people possess secrets."

KOSHAROVSKY: *He gave the names of activists?*

SHARANSKY: Yes, he gave some list, of course. Ida Nudel, my name, [Naum] Meiman, and so forth. All these people wanted their names to be mentioned.

KOSHAROVSKY: *But there were people who truly worked in classified places. I, for example, participated in the development of a missile guidance system, and I never mentioned my place of work.*

SHARANSKY: Sakharov never mentioned his place of work. Those who truly had access to secret projects never gave such information because they would immediately be charged. During the investigation, hundreds of people were interrogated in an effort to find someone who would say that his name appeared on a list without his consent. Some witnesses said that they didn't remember whether or not they gave such information but they immediately added that there was nothing secret about their work. That was the most that the investigators could obtain and I utilized this point in my speech at the trial.[41]

Dina Beilin spoke similarly about the refusenik lists, which were a basic element in the espionage charge:[42]

KOSHAROVSKY: *Dina, was there a line in the questionnaire that activists asked people to fill out near the OVIR office about the address of one's enterprise and the name of the general director?*

BEILIN: No. I coordinated the format of the lists with senior lawyer Sofia Kalistratov, a member of the Helsinki group. She said, "Look, this is absolutely open information but insofar as there will be a lot of it, be prepared for possible unpleasantness because someone could insert a provocation into the list." I said that I would try to filter it.

KOSHAROVSKY: *Did the KGB know that you, not Sharansky, compiled the lists and gathered information?*

BEILIN: They knew.

KOSHAROVSKY: *How did your interrogations go?*

BEILIN: They didn't speak about the lists at all. I have a copy of my interrogation. They spoke about Sharansky, about communism, about whatever, but not about the lists.

Sharansky's trial began on Monday, July 10, 1978, and lasted five days. He was charged with two articles: 64 (treason) and 70-1 (slander with the intent to subvert the Soviet social order). The compiling and transmission of lists of 1,300 refuseniks with the addresses of two hundred enterprises in various cities of the USSR was characterized as espionage. His Helsinki group activity was qualified as slander.[43] Sharansky conducted himself with courage and dignity during the proceedings. Instead of refuting each element in the charge, he presented a general picture of his activity, which was directed at assuring freedom of emigration and Soviet compliance with its international obligations and own laws. In his concluding speech, Sharansky declared, "I am happy that I lived them [the past five years] honestly and at peace with my conscience."[44]

Other activists in the political wing before, during, and after Sharansky's trial were hurried out of the USSR or put on trial. Lunts, as noted, received an exit visa on the eve of the Second Brussels Conference on behalf of Soviet Jewry. Dina Beilin and her husband were deported from the USSR in March 1978. Dina was very active in all aspects of the campaign in Sharansky's defense. Vladimir and Maria Slepak and also Ida Nudel were charged with "hooliganism" on June 1, 1978, after demonstrations with placards hanging from the balconies of their apartments. The trial was quick and unjust. On June 21, Vladimir Slepak was sentenced to five years of exile and Ida Nudel to four years of exile; Masha Slepak received a suspended sentence. Alexander Lerner, who was expecting arrest at any moment, was forced to reduce his level of activity somewhat. He was over sixty-five and had heart trouble, and his wife had high blood pressure. He displayed great courage, remaining accessible to other activists, and continuing to meet with foreigners and conduct his seminar. Nevertheless, one can say that the political wing of the movement ceased to exist after Sharansky's trial.

The Jewish movement activists were not intimidated by the harsh punishments. They continued to fight for emigration, compiled lists of refuseniks, wrote protest letters, demonstrated, published journals, and taught Hebrew. Repressions only encouraged many of them to apply for exit visas. Emigration from the Soviet Union continued to grow, reaching 51,331 in 1979.[45]

Cultural Activity after Helsinki, 1975–79

In parallel with the rise in emigration figures after the signing of the Helsinki Final Act (August 1, 1975), the quality of samizdat publications improved and the quantity increased. In addition to the journal *Evrei v SSSR* (Jews in the USSR, 1972–79), other journals that appeared in Moscow included *Tarbut* (Culture, 1975–80), *Nash ivrit* (Our Hebrew, 1978–80), *Evrei v sovremennom mire* (Jews in the Contemporary World, 1978–81), and *Vyezd v Izrail* (Departure to Israel, 1979–80). Riga Jews produced the journals *Din umetsiut* (Law and Reality, 1979–80) and *Haim* (Life, 1979–86). In this period the activity of the refusenik seminars intensified, new ones were added, and they were established in additional regions. Legal, humanitarian, scientific, and teaching seminars arose in various cities. The network of ulpans for Hebrew study expanded considerably and the quality of instruction improved. Moscow teachers extended their activity to other cities. In Moscow the number of so-called *dibburim*—organized groups of teachers and advanced students in which lectures and discussions were conducted in Hebrew—continued to increase. A seminar for Hebrew teachers began operating in 1977.

The basic goal of the *dibbur* (from the Hebrew word for speech) was to create the conditions for conversational language practice. One could arrange a friendly meal at a dibbur as Benia Deborin and Vladimir Shakhnovsky used to do in 1972, speak about various topics over a cup of tea as was the practice at the dibburim of Mikhail Goldblat in 1973–74, or listen to interesting reports and sip tea with pies as was customary at Lev Ulanovsky's place from 1975 to 1979.

Not limiting his teaching activity to Moscow, Lev Ulanovsky also made the rounds of other cities. His pupils include many prominent figures such as Alexander (Ephraim) Kholmyansky, Yuli Edelstein, and Alexander Iakir.

Ulanovsky recalled his start teaching Hebrew:[46]

KOSHAROVSKY: *When did you begin to teach Hebrew?*

ULANOVSKY: Even before applying for a visa. Having already studied several languages, I understood the importance of conversational practice. With the help of Lena and Zeev Shakhnovsky, I organized a weekly dibbur at my place, a kind of salon in which only Hebrew was spoken.

KOSHAROVSKY: *Were there many participants?*

ULANOVSKY: Hebrew study turned into a mass phenomenon in Moscow and our dibbur became popular. As word about it spread abroad, Hebrew-speaking tourists began to show up regularly. We and our guests would deliver lectures in Hebrew.

KOSHAROVSKY: *What topics were treated?*

ULANOVSKY: Various topics such as Jewish history, Judaism, Hebrew grammar, contemporary Israel, literature, ethics, and so forth. After the lecture, we would drink tea and eat pies. It was noisy and cheerful. Everything was done openly, without secrets or conspiracies. Anyone, even a stranger, could come as long as he spoke Hebrew.

KOSHAROVSKY: *The KGB didn't interfere?*

ULANOVSKY: Everyone understood that the KGB would send its agents to us. We didn't object, considering that the KGB should also study Hebrew. Earlier dibburim had been closed ones to which only acquaintances were invited. The novelty of my dibbur was its complete openness. The walls of the apartment were covered with Israeli postcards, leaving no free space. People would come to see the pictures of Israel. Maps were added to the wall and books to the shelves. I opened a mini-library, assuming that the more the books were in people's hands, the less the chance of their being confiscated in a search. My apartment started to resemble a small museum of Israel. Soon dibburim like mine sprang up in other homes. We tried to divide them into levels for advanced students and beginners. For the youth who visited us from America and Europe, it was a school of Zionism, a reflection of the Ben Yehuda period but transposed to Moscow of the 1970s. It made a strong impression on them. They often said that we helped them no less than they helped us. Professors would come from America, Europe, and Israel to deliver one or a series of lectures on topics ranging from Israel's archaeology or fauna to computer simulation of Hebrew grammar. Rabbis, politicians, and journalists arrived singly or in groups. Isi Leibler brought Bob Hawke, who soon became the prime minister of Australia. Not all of the guests knew Hebrew and I would have to translate.

KOSHAROVSKY: *Lev, I was told that you conducted other activities, too.*

ULANOVSKY: Yes, we held daily readings of the Torah at my house, also in Hebrew, under the direction of Zeev Shakhnovksy, who had an unusual talent for this. For the majority of Muscovites, who were unfamiliar with the Torah, it opened a new world. A small but rapidly growing circle of young Jews who were discovering religion appeared.

KOSHAROVSKY: *Under the influence of Chabad?*

ULANOVSKY: I don't know about Chabad. Shakhnovsky and I studied and discussed Torah and Gemara [the Talmud] only in Hebrew. Incidentally, we used the Steinsaltz edition of the Gemara. As far as I know, Essas's style of study was different. He conducted lessons in Russian and the primary focus was on attracting the students to religion. We, by contrast, studied the texts themselves.

KOSHAROVSKY: *You were one of the first who extended teaching activity beyond the Moscow city limits.*

ULANOVSKY: It happened naturally. Hebrew teachers would come to the dibburim from other cities such as Leningrad, Vilnius, Minsk, Dushanbe, Riga, and Frunze (now Bishkek). I then began to travel to them. I used to go to Leningrad, Vilnius, Minsk, and Dushanbe. Now it's hard to remember all of the places. We tried as much as possible to operate openly and not to create an "organization." I also tried unsuccessfully to register officially as a Hebrew teacher and pay taxes as such. With rare exceptions, the level of Hebrew was much lower outside of Moscow.

Do you recall, Yuli, you and I organized the first summer camp for Hebrew teachers from various cities at Koktebel [in Crimea]? Around ten people came. It was great: songs, jokes, fun, skipping rocks in the sea, the nearby mountain peak of Siuriu-Kaia, and Hebrew, Hebrew, and more Hebrew. A year later, in 1980, I was already in Israel and heard that the participants in that camp increased tenfold. They were in heaven and you were jailed for fifteen days.

KOSHAROVSKY: *The KGB reacted sharply to the teaching for out-of-towners.*

ULANOVSKY: Yes, when I heard that you were arrested, I was already in Israel. I felt guilty that I was no longer with you. I traveled around the world, telling people your story, but the guilty feeling remained. I remember once in Stockholm just after a phone conversation with

Moscow with the families of those who had been detained, I was placed in front of a microphone. I was in tears and felt ashamed in front of the audience.

In 1977 Kosharovsky organized a seminar of Hebrew teachers that differed from previous humanitarian seminars primarily in that all sessions were conducted only in Hebrew. In that sense, it became the successor of the dibburim. At the seminar, teachers discussed, studied, and elaborated ideas for Hebrew pedagogy that seemed effective to them: the topic was inexhaustible and of necessity very creative under Soviet conditions.[47] Participants also heard lectures and reports on topics of common interest. The main seminar participants were Hebrew teachers from Moscow and other cities and advanced students, many of whom would soon become teachers. The seminar thus turned into a creative laboratory in which the most effective Hebrew teaching methods, the best textbooks, and auxiliary material were selected and approved.

Aside from those differences, the teachers' seminar resembled all the others. Each session consisted of one or two lectures, followed by a discussion. The reports were prepared by the best Moscow Hebrew teachers or by guests from abroad. Among the Moscow teachers and lecturers were Mikhail Chlenov, Lev Gorodetsky, Yuli Edelstein, Alexander and Mikhail Kholmyansky, Lev Ulanovsky, Ilia Essas, Evgeny Grechanovsky, and Alexander Ostronov. Of course participants also had reports on Jewish holidays, various aspects of life in Israel, and religious topics. While still on the level of a dibbur, the seminar very quickly became a popular meeting place for those who wanted to make progress in Hebrew, were interested in spreading knowledge of the language around the country, and wanted to study contemporary Jewish culture in its original language.

For several years, the seminar was held at the hospitable apartment of Irina Nekrasov, whose son Mikhail was a successful student of Kosharovsky's and also a teacher. Usually about twenty to thirty people, primarily Hebrew teachers, attended a session. Up to fifty or more people would crowd in to listen to the reports on history and culture. The seminar gradually produced a group of well-informed, highly motivated, and Zionist-oriented people.

Israel began to take part in Moscow's biennial international book fairs beginning in 1977. Two Israeli participants arrived for the first one, but the delegation grew each time and numbered seven people in 1985. The delegation's two-week stay in Moscow provided an opportunity to gain familiarity with Israelis, Israeli culture, and Israeli books. Activists in the Soviet Jewish movement prepared carefully for each fair, informing people in Moscow and other cities, and arranging meetings with members of the Israeli delegation. The Israeli pavilion was always the most popular at the fair; the long line for it wound around the aisles between other pavilions. The Israelis were generous, willingly sharing books from the exhibition, Israeli souvenirs, and lapel pins.

The number of well-trained Hebrew teachers in Moscow began to increase rapidly. Activist leaders estimated that by the end of the 1970s there were more than one hundred teachers and more than a thousand people studying in Moscow ulpans.[48]

Mikhail Nudler organized and conducted a seminar on Jewish culture in 1977. A graduate of MGU (Moscow State University), he was still quite young, loved to play ball at out-of-town gatherings at Ovrazhki, and led a cultural program there together with Volvovsky. He was actively involved in samizdat work, appeared in Purimspiel ensembles where he invariably played the role of King Ahashverosh, and, in general, engaged in a multitude of activities.

Mikhail Nudler recalled the seminar:[49]

KOSHAROVSKY: *You added a seminar to all your other activities?*

NUDLER: At the time, there were no seminars for youth. Moreover, as far as I recall, all the other seminars were oriented primarily toward refuseniks. Non-refuseniks, especially the young and vulnerable, were advised not to attend them. I was involved in various matters but I was not a refusenik and had not yet applied for an exit visa. There were many like me. I felt that there was a need for a seminar serving that circle of people. At the first session, which took place at the end of October 1977, there were six people in all, but the number rose sharply with the second session. People would come directly from the synagogue. From forty to fifty people would crowd into my one-room apartment.

KOSHAROVSKY: *Who gave the reports?*

NUDLER: Deciding that we would not be both organizers and lecturers, we invited speakers. Misha Pontilias gave a report on Hanukah, Volodia Prestin on ways to resolve conflict situations, Mika Chlenov on the coexistence of the Russian and Hebrew languages over the centuries, and Vladimir Albrekht on his book *How to Be a Witness at an Interrogation,*[50] and many others. The cultural program moved to Ovrazhki in the summer.

Leningrad suffered the most from the wave of legal repressions in 1970–71. Many activists were charged in the first and second Leningrad trials; three Leningraders were included in the Kishinev Trial; hundreds were summoned to interrogations; and many searches were carried out. As a result, the development of social and cultural activity in Leningrad at the beginning of the 1970s was significantly slowed down. People continued to apply for exit visas, and activists, generally not linked to the sixties generation, renewed the preparation and distribution of samizdat and Hebrew instruction. Many people would gather near the synagogue on holidays, a refusenik mutual help system began to function, and seminars developed.[51]

Feliks Aronovich ran the first seminar on Jewish culture in Leningrad from 1975 to 1977. In addition, an engineering-technological seminar operated in Leningrad from 1976 to 1981, initiated on the model of Kosharovsky's engineering seminar in Moscow and run by Aba Taratuta and Boris Granovsky. That seminar, designed to help refuseniks keep up their professional level, was taken over by Abram Kagan after Granovsky emigrated in 1979. There was also a legal seminar held in Taratuta's apartment beginning in 1977. It was run by Valery Segal and functioned until 1979, providing a place where people could learn about their legal rights, restrictions on the actions of the KGB, and how to handle encounters with them. Grigory Kanovich's humanitarian seminar ran on a semimonthly basis from 1979 to 1981. Kanovich presented on history, and Taratuta, Abram Kagan, and Lev Furman helped present on literature in English. Grigory Vasserman talked about religious topics. Lev Utevsky got involved and proved to be an extremely popular lecturer.[52] Kanovich's seminar helped develop a new generation of activists. Evgeny Lein was arrested at the seminar on May 17, 1981, and his trial provided an opportunity for the community to show its solidarity openly.[53]

Subsequent seminars, Leonid Kelbert's refusenik theater, and the samizdat journal *Leningradskii evreiskii almanakh* (Leningrad Jewish Almanac, LEA) followed. Mikhail Beizer's historical seminar represented one significant facet of this cultural activity. Beizer began by conducting excursions around Leningrad in 1982–83 to show people sites of importance for Jewish history in the city.[54] In 1982 Beizer also began leading a small historical seminar, with about fifteen people. Participants were expected to prepare presentations based on their research, and several of those later appeared in the *Leningradskii evreiskii almanakh,* which Beizer edited until his departure in 1987.[55]

Humanitarian seminars opened also in Kharkov, Riga, and Kishinev. The seminar groups were in contact with each other and lecturers traveled from seminar to seminar. The regime's attitude toward their activity varied. Years of relative tolerance were replaced by periods of harassment and arrests, but the seminars survived and for many years served as centers for a revival of Jewish cultural and scientific activity and as breeding grounds of a collective Zionist struggle.

Purimspiels became an act of defiance against the refuseniks' fate. Merry comedies about the marvelous salvation of the Jewish people in ancient Persia resonated in an astonishing way with the harsh everyday refusenik life. Amateur performances were extremely popular, particularly in the gloomy 1980s. The heroes were contemporary and recognizable, and refusal, Israel, and the aliya struggle constituted the basic content. The first Purimspiel of this type in Moscow was supposed to take place at Yosif Begun's apartment on March 1, 1977. In the morning, a group of refuseniks was practicing yoga at Yosif's apartment and we finished around one o'clock. Our hospitable host reminded us that the Purimspiel would begin at seven in the evening and those who wanted could remain. A special delivery messenger arrived at that time and handed Yosif a notice to appear at the district police station. "Don't go away, I'll be back soon," he said. "If you have to, close the door and put the key under the rug." Yosif returned a year and a half later—that was his first arrest.

Toward evening, we realized that Yosif would not be let out by the beginning of the performance. The performers and audience then went to celebrate at the apartment of Mikhail Nudler. The Purim show was cheerful and interesting.[56] Nudler was the first performer in the role of Ahashverosh, and he continued to play him until his departure in 1980.

Nudler recalled preparing the Purimspiels:[57]

KOSHAROVSKY: *Misha, how did you land such an important role in the Purimspiel?*

NUDLER: Before the Purimspiel, I once went to hear an ensemble. Zhenia Finkelberg, Lyova Kanevsky, and Misha Tigai all sang well. The director was Misha Gorbatov, a professional musician; Lyova Kanevsky was the star of the group: a veteran performer of Hebrew songs, he knew about three hundred songs and was the best at playing the guitar.

When Hanukah was approaching in 1976, Lyova Kanevsky came to me and said, "Hanukah falls almost at the same time as the symposium on culture. It is highly probable that we shall wind up in police detention because of the symposium. Let's therefore do the following: you will prepare a Hanukah program and keep away from the symposium." I agreed and that became my first cultural activity.

At Hanukah time, I invited everyone to my place. About one hundred people came to my two-room apartment in Orekhovo-Borisov. They came and went. Lyova told about Hanukah, we lit the first candle, and we then sang. Three months after that, my first Purimspiel took place.

In fact, the proposal to organize the performance came from Andriusha Okunev. He read in some book that performances used to take place on Purim. I was fired up by the idea and decided to stage a performance using Racine's seventeenth-century play *Esther* (1689). I went to the library and copied down the entire night scene in which Haman is exposed. There were three roles in that scene: I gave Haman to Volvovsky and Esther to my sister.

That was, however, only the first half of the Purimspiel. The second part was a *kapustnik* [a "roast" or revue-sketch comedy]. Fifteen people took part in the revue, which was composed mainly of songs.

Around Purim time the next year, I was busy and didn't have a head for that. Two or three weeks before Purim, Volvovsky phoned and asked, "What about the Purimspiel?" "You know," I said, "something isn't jelling for me this year." He began to yell at me: "What's the matter with you? All of Moscow is waiting and something isn't jelling! Do something so that it jells." In 1978 we put together a performance at the last moment and it was rather weak. We performed it once at the Rozenshteins' place. Between those two Purimspiels, I started the seminar on culture that lasted until the summer of 1978.

The theatrical group included a couple: Evgeny and Roza Finkelberg. Evgeny sang and played the violin and guitar, and Roza wrote the Purimspiel texts. The composition of the troupe changed as people left the country, but the Finkelbergs spent ten creative years in it.

Roza Finkelberg, a principal scriptwriter for the Purimspiels, started writing all the scenarios for her group in 1981. She recalled working on the Purimspiels:[58]

KOSHAROVSKY: *How long did it take to prepare a performance?*

FINKELBERG: Not so long; we started preparations about a month to a month and a half in advance. I wanted to write not merely a comic sketch but something that resembled a play with a subject line.

KOSHAROVSKY: *We really liked the texts of the Purimspiels. They were so humorous! Whence this talent?*

FINKELBERG: I don't know. From God, from my mama—she wrote stories—and from a sense of duty. I didn't want the Purimspiels to fade away. After each performance, we were invited to do the next. In the first week there were several performances a day; then until Pesach there were several per week. In light of this success, other Purimspiels began to appear: the children's Purimspiel of Mila Kaganov and the one of Vladimir Geizel. Purimspiels were staged at kindergartens. That, indeed, was a gloomy period of refusal. Where, however, does real humor flourish? In a totalitarian state, because so much is forbidden there. It was funny because associations arose, everyone understood the subtext and laughed from the heart.

KOSHAROVSKY: *What happened to the ensemble?*

FINKELBERG: First of all, it became the foundation for a permanent Purimspiel cast: Sasha and Klara Landsman, Ira Razgon, Zhenia (Evgeny) Finkelberg, Igor Gurvich, with Alla Dubrovsky playing the violin. Sasha Mezheborsky appeared in later years. Second, the ensemble functioned all year round, traveling to other cities with several programs. Twice the group went to Leningrad and Riga. I generally did not perform, only substituting if someone became ill.

KOSHAROVSKY: *Do you know anything about Purimspiels in other cities?*

FINKELBERG: Purimspiels appeared in Leningrad even before ours in Moscow. There, too, several groups were formed. We also had a pair of professional actors who put on plays. Our Purimspiel, however, was unique because it sparked the development of the Purimspiel as a phenomenon. We even acquired a tradition: the first Purimspiel was always performed in the southwest of the city at the home of Inna Moiseevna Badanov. It was the most dangerous performance because we didn't know how the authorities would react to it. Even though they wouldn't disperse it, during the first performance the police were always on the street below and there would be spats with the neighbors.

Once we performed a Purimspiel at the Litvaks' apartment. In the course of the action, there was a scene in which Haman knocks on the door, Mordecai says, "Come in," Haman knocks again, Mordecai repeats, "Come in," and Haman: "Open, or else I'll break open the door." The Purimspiel would start and end with that same scene. Lo and behold, it's the first scene, the second scene, and then the doorbell rings. Everyone laughs. Zhanka Litvak opens the door—and it's the police. Everyone thinks that the police are part of the performance and they laugh like crazy. But it really is the police, who have been summoned by the neighbors, who said, "they are bothering us, making noise." However, to put it briefly, we got away with it. I should add that the "actors" used to come to the performances with a change of underwear and a toothbrush, just in case. My authorship was carefully concealed until 1986, and in that year Mika Chlenov came on stage and announced it festively.

KOSHAROVSKY: *Different times, Roza.*

FINKELBERG: But we were not yet aware that times were different. Starting in 1984 I had a coauthor: Gena Melikh. We tried to collaborate with professionals but it never worked out. How can a professional work with a group when the entire show is performed on a door removed from its hinge, there is no possibility of moving around, and, on top of that, the actors are amateurs?

On the tenth anniversary of the Purimspiels, in 1986, we put on a jubilee performance that was a collection of the best of the Purimspiels. That was in March, and in May we were summoned and told to reapply for an exit visa. They seemed to be saying that the issue was resolved. It was completely unexpected. No one had received exit visas yet. It was after Chernobyl. We arrived in Israel in July 1986.

The second group that performed a Purimspiel in 1977 consisted of Aron Gurevich, Polina Ainbinder, Boris Chernobylsky, and others. When reading Ahashverosh's decree, Mordecai (Gurevich) held the newspaper *Izvestiia* in his hands and read the decree from it. Literally, the day before, Lipavsky's article had appeared in that newspaper, and the entire audience understood the subtext. The group gave only one performance and did not continue. Aron Gurevich became an organizer of children's Purimspiels. A year before the first Purimspiel, he also organized a choir in which Ainbinder's sisters played an active role.

In the refusenik community, Purimspiels were merry and popular activities that were most in tune with the Jewish tradition of rejoicing, abandon, and abundant libations on this holiday. Thanks to the skill of the scriptwriters and actors, in the Purimspiels our own fate became intertwined with ancient history in a marvelous way: the Jews emerged victorious against a powerful and cunning enemy. The celebration of Purim, like that of other Jewish holidays, spread to many cities and became part of the expression of identity for the refusenik community.

Pavel Abramovich, the founder and editor in chief of the journal *Nash ivrit* (Our Hebrew), initiated the "Week of Hebrew" in Moscow, which took place March 5–11, 1979. The timing was not accidental. In 1879 in Paris, Eliezer Ben-Yehuda published an article, "A Burning Question," that set the stage for the revival of modern Hebrew. Hebrew Week thus marked the centennial celebration of the revival of the language. In addition, 1979 represented one hundred years since the birth of Feliks Shapiro, the compiler of the official Hebrew-Russian dictionary.

It was decided to conduct Hebrew Week at the time of Purim. Reports, concerts, and Purimspiels were prepared. Abramovich was universally liked, and it was impossible to refuse him anything.

Abramovich talked about the idea for a "Week of Hebrew":[59]

KOSHAROVSKY: *How did the idea arise?*

ABRAMOVICH: In the newspaper, I read about a Week of Kazakh Culture, then I glanced at a notice about another such Culture Week, and I started to think: why shouldn't we have a "Week of Hebrew Culture"? I went to discuss the idea with Chlenov, who said it was a brilliant idea.

KOSHAROVSKY: *As I recall, it was a large undertaking. Other people helped?*

ABRAMOVICH: Of course, there was a lot of work to do: addresses, apartments, lecturers, notices. Volodia Prestin, Mika Chlenov, and Lyonia Volvovsky got involved in the project.

KOSHAROVSKY: *How many apartments did you use?*

ABRAMOVICH: About twenty.

KOSHAROVSKY: *How did it work?*

ABRAMOVICH: Lectures were delivered, there were evenings of Hebrew song and theatrical performances. On March 6 there was a Purimspiel. Improvised concerts frequently took place after the reports. In one apartment, the reports were given only in Hebrew. Do you remember? That was for you and Ulanovsky.

KOSHAROVSKY: *Yes, indeed. Ulanovsky gave a talk on grammar and I spoke about the history of the language.*

ABRAMOVICH: In the second issue of the (samizdat) journal *Our Hebrew*, 40 out of 140 pages dealt with Hebrew Week.

Sergei Lugovsky delivered a report about Hebrew's place among the languages of the world, and he also spoke about the modern revival of conversational Hebrew. A separate report, prepared and read by Ruth Okunev, touched on Eliezer Ben-Yehuda's activity. She livened up her speech with photographs and melodies of that time. Lia Prestin-Shapiro gave an outstanding report about her father, Feliks Shapiro.[60] Alexander Bolshoi devoted his report to contemporary Israeli prose. Mark Lvovsky recited excerpts from his own work "Biblical History," a transposition of the Bible into verse. There was considerable interest in Chlenov's report on "Hebrew and Russian, a Millennium of Contiguity" and in an evening on Jerusalem prepared by Leonid Volvovsky. About a thousand people participated in Hebrew Week.

Renewed Repressions

On December 25, 1979, a Soviet army column crossed the Soviet-Afghan border on a pontoon bridge over the Amu Darya River. Two days later a KGB Alpha unit stormed the presidential palace and carried out a bloody coup in Afghanistan. Afghan president Hafizullah Amin, his son, and all two hundred presidential bodyguards were killed. Thus began the unexpected Soviet invasion of Afghanistan.

Several months before the invasion, in June 1979, Leonid Brezhnev and Jimmy Carter made a major breakthrough in reducing international tension by signing in Vienna SALT-2, the Strategic Arms Limitation Treaty. The surprise Soviet invasion caused genuine shock in the West. The achievements in détente of the past few years were wiped out in a moment and the Iron Curtain again descended on the borders of the Soviet bloc.

The voices of those defending Jewish movement activists—liberals, human rights, and Jewish organizations—were drowned out in the powerful chorus of opposition to the Soviet invasion. In the first months after the invasion, however, another important event weakened the effect of the sharp cooling of the international atmosphere: the summer Olympic Games were scheduled to take place in Moscow in 1980. The games offered the USSR a chance to show itself in a better light, but punitive operations against refuseniks and dissidents would not further that goal. The KGB, therefore, limited itself to administrative arrests, conversations, warnings, and threats, and only in rare instances resorted to stricter measures. For example, the authorities banished Andrei Sakharov, who voiced sharp criticism of the Soviet invasion into Afghanistan, and expelled the Jewish activist Leonid Volvovsky from Moscow. Several people were detained for fifteen days, including Vladimir Kislik in Kiev on July 4 (after fifteen days he was transferred to a psychiatric hospital and held there until the end of the Olympic Games), Grigory Geishis in Leningrad on July 14, and Dmitri Shtiglik in Moscow on July 16. Anatoly Khazanov and Mikhail Chlenov were sent on forced work trips by the Institute of Ethnography of the Soviet Academy of Sciences and certain rights activists had similar experiences.

Moscow Olympics

Sixty-five countries did not participate in the 1980 Summer Olympics in Moscow. Many, like the United States, announced they were boycotting the games to protest the Soviet invasion of Afghanistan. The Soviet invasion marked a sudden end to détente, and the boycott of the Olympics demonstrated the new state of affairs. Although repressions against refuseniks at the time of the games were not severe, the new post-détente era would see renewed repressions against all types of dissident activity, in addition to the dramatic drop in Jewish emigration from the USSR.

Although Jewish emigration was not halted completely, it declined from 51,331 in 1979, to 2,692 in 1982 (by a factor of twenty), and to 896 in 1984.[61] It could have been stopped completely but, following the same reasoning as that of Andropov and Gromyko at the start of emigration, the regime considered a minimum of emigration necessary in order to get rid of "nationalistically inclined individuals and religious fanatics" who had a harmful influence on their milieu, and it enabled the KGB to continue using this channel for operative goals.[62]

Jewish activist circles initially formed the impression that the regime started winding down emigration at the beginning of 1980 in connection with the new round of the Cold War. In fact, it abruptly put a brake on the emigration process several months earlier, at the peak of détente.

Yakov Kedmi talked about the timing of the drop in emigration:[63]

KEDMI: The regime made the decision at the beginning of 1979 and began implementing it in April. The leadership decided that emigration was getting out of control and if they did not do anything, the numbers would significantly exceed the level that was acceptable to them. The potential for emigration was enormous and it was snowballing.

KOSHAROVSKY: *Yasha, how did they manage to do this without the Jewish human rights organizations or us refuseniks or even Lishkat hakesher reacting to it?*

KEDMI: Western human rights groups and Jewish organizations were concentrating their efforts more and more on specific refuseniks and dissidents. In response, the Soviet Union in 1979 gradually changed the rules, declaring that only those with direct relatives would be permitted to emigrate. Thus they did not need to issue a refusal; they simply did not accept the applications. The new practice started in Odessa and then, over the course of a year, it spread throughout the country. Those whose relatives immigrated to America could not apply at all because invitations were accepted only from Israel. This broke the chain that enabled a relative to send a genuine invitation. The quantity of invitations thus began to decline, as did the number of applicants, and the number of documents that were accepted for review was reduced even further.

International conferences were conducted, demonstrations held, streams of letters were exchanged, and, from time to time, some refusenik was released, and a festival started. Everything was in order. And even the Soviet regime was satisfied. Do you know why?

KOSHAROVSKY: *Why?*

KEDMI: There was no emigration.

In connection with the spread of rumors that year that emigration would be stopped and that a high emigration level would last at best until the end of the Olympics, many who possessed an invitation began to fear that they "would miss the train." "In the second half of 1979," recalls the Leningrad activist-refusenik Mikhail Beizer, "the lines at OVIR became awful. People would stand all through the night, write down numbers, and hold places in line, as if buying rugs. I probably stood in line for a month. There was a terrible panic."[64]

The well-known activist from Kiev Vladimir Kislik tells a similar story: "In 1979, emigration was practically halted entirely, and thousands of people in Kiev suddenly wound up in refusal. They dashed about without housing or money, not knowing what to do. They had left work, sold their apartments in anticipation of departure—it was awful what happened. Many also had a terrible fear of the system and all this together produced complete despair."[65] A similar situation developed in other cities as well. The number of refusenik families increased considerably in 1979–80.

There are no official statistics about the number of refuseniks at the beginning of the 1980s. The circumstances suggest, however, that the reduction in the number of exit visas in 1980 occurred primarily because of new refusals. This does not take into account those who went through a significant part of the application procedure but were unable to complete it because of the stricter process of accepting applications in some places. On the one hand, the greater number of refusals and the new punitive measures were extremely dispiriting, but, on the other hand, many energetic people thirsting for action filled the refusenik ranks.

Personal Recollections: The Intercity Hebrew Seminar and New Repressions

KOSHAROVSKY: I had forged good ties with teachers from the provinces who, when they visited Moscow, would try to attend the Hebrew seminar.[66] If out-of-towners arrived for two to three weeks or more, I would organize a course of intensive lessons for them with one of my students and supply textbooks and technical support.

The level of instruction in the provinces was considerably lower than in the capital at that time. I thought more and more about how to help them, discussing some ideas with Israelis and Moscow Hebrew teachers. In talking with Lev Ulanovsky, who had some experience in teaching in other cities, we developed a concrete proposal to combine vacation time with intensive training of out-of-town teachers at Koktebel on the Crimean shore. We implemented our plan in the fall of 1979. Nine teachers arrived from Moscow, Minsk, and Leningrad, studying for six hours a day: three in the morning and three in the evening. The rest of the time was taken up with hiking and swimming. I familiarized them with my teaching ideas, with audio and audiovisual courses, and with textbooks. A month of studies flew by, no one hindered us, and we decided to operate the same course the following fall.

The next year, fifty-six Hebrew teachers from Moscow, Leningrad, Odessa, Minsk, Chernovtsy, Tashkent, Kiev, Tiblisi, and Sverdlovsk attended. We divided them into eight groups and began intensive studies. In 1980, however, relations between the USSR and the West cooled sharply in connection with the Soviet invasion of Afghanistan. We could feel this already in Koktebel.

At that time, I was teaching Hebrew, conducting a seminar for Hebrew teachers, and preparing to hold the second intercity seminar for Hebrew teachers in Koktebel. In advance of the seminar, it was necessary to prepare considerable study material, select teachers capable of working according to the new methods, and to rent places to stay.

Holding an intercity seminar of that level was a serious challenge to the regime. As it was, they hardly tolerated Hebrew teaching and would send one teacher or another to jail from time to time and now, to top it off, there was Afghanistan, the Olympics, and a boycott.

It was not possible to hold an underground seminar, as there were too many participants. Naturally, we took the necessary precautions with regard to sending technical items and samizdat and tamizdat material, and we tried not to "stick out" or speak out too much. To all outward appearances, it was a vacation among a circle of friends.

The seminar was scheduled for August–September and the Olympics for the second half of July. Many activists left Moscow earlier, however, knowing from experience that in Moscow they could be subject to preventive arrest for several weeks.

In the context of the approaching Olympics, we met more frequently with foreigners, who discussed issues of a boycott of the games and the regime's possible reaction. We also began to receive guests who were officially accredited to handle preparations for their Olympic teams' arrivals and accommodations. Israel [Isi] Leibler, for example, an Australian businessman and public figure and old friend of the refuseniks, was in charge of the arrival and housing of his country's team. In that capacity, he visited the USSR several times on the eve of the games and met with Soviet officials, but each time he would also arrange to meet refuseniks.

The KGB surveillance was intense. A car with four plainclothes agents was on constant watch near my house, as was customary on the eve of major holidays or important foreign visits. The agents' conduct, however, changed. They did not conceal their surveillance and at times even demonstratively flaunted it. I remember thinking to myself: how many agents must they have in order to use them so wastefully on people who simply want to leave the country?

Less than two months remained before the Olympics when the head of the group approached me and started speaking: "Have no doubts, Yuli Mikhailovich, we know that you are gathering together teachers in Koktebel. Go ahead and travel. You can stay in Moscow during the Olympics. It doesn't bother us. If you want, I can even get you tickets to the opening and to the competitions; just say so!" I was astonished. He could not say such things on his own initiative. It was, undoubtedly, a premeditated step, but what was the meaning of this message? Perhaps they were trying to use us to transmit a message abroad that the situation inside the country would be calm and no serious harassment of Jewish or human rights activists was contemplated? I, naturally, refused, but the anonymous officer's proposal calmed me down—and to no good purpose.

Four days before the opening of the games, I was taken to the 119th police station. Three KGB officers for Moscow and the Moscow region—Yuri Solovev, Valery Gromov, and Petr Petrov (I refused to talk until they presented their credentials)—conducted a prophylactic conversation of several hours with me. Their threats included the possibility of expulsion from Moscow, a trial similar to Sharansky's, or fabrication of material implicating me in sexual crimes or malicious hooliganism. They were well acquainted with my case. For them, I was already a person who had been there.

This time the conversation was conducted in a businesslike and cynical manner. They demanded that I stop teaching Hebrew and running the teachers' seminar in Moscow. Afterwards, I wrote down the highlights of the conversation from memory and transmitted them to the West: it had been rather intimidating.

The games took place without incident. Our departure to Koktebel proceeded smoothly. At the beginning of the study sessions, the small resort of Koktebel, located on the southern end of Crimea on the Black Sea shore, was filled "to the gills" with Jews. It had always been a popular vacation spot for our brethren, and that summer around three hundred people arrived with the teachers: family members, friends, and students. Twice-a-day study sessions were held on the beach. Groups were located at a distance of forty to fifty meters from each other, the majority of those vacationing were Jews, and externally nothing attracted particular attention. People were sunbathing in groups, conversing quietly, or reading. Excellent teachers accompanied me: Misha Kholmyansky, Yuli Edelstein, Zhenia Grechanovsky, Misha Nekrasov, Lev Gorodetsky, and others. In the evening people noisily enjoyed themselves: there were several good guitarists, we sang Hebrew songs, built campfires, and strolled in the neighboring hills. The atmosphere was marvelous. Many young people later told me that their path to Jewishness began with that summer in Koktebel.

On the third day a new, important element was added to this pastoral Koktebel scene. About eight to ten people appeared on the beach wearing neat black suits, ironed white shirts, and black ties. This continued for about ten days. The morning study session lasted from nine o'clock to noon. I used to rise early, and at six I would jog with one of the seminar participants. On the evening of September 14, however, we were out until late and members of our group slept soundly that night. Thinking it most likely that the agents were also sleeping after their late watch, I went jogging alone. The agents were not sleeping. They appeared ready to act on the warning they had given me at the police station on July 15: "Yuli Mikhailovich, you have two months. If you don't halt your nationalist activity during that time, we shall take measures."

Not far from the spot where I was warming up stood a man with a package in his hand. When I started to run, he turned slightly and moved in my direction. I managed to outdistance him but he staggered and contrived to extend his hand with the package in my direction in order to brush against me and immediately drop the package. A bottle with wine wrapped in a newspaper fell with a clunk on the rocks and broke. The "drunk" noisily and angrily started yelling and immediately two civil militiamen with armbands appeared—this at around six in the morning! The "producers" did not even bother to make the staging seem realistic. Fortunately, a member of our group had seen this "drunk" circling around the place where I was sleeping for half an hour and then waiting patiently while I warmed up. If they cooked up something serious, I had a witness.

We were taken to the local police station, from which, a few hours later, we were dispatched to the nearby city of Sudak. A quick trial on administrative violations was held there. We were both given thirteen days, after which the suddenly sober stranger disappeared somewhere and I was sent to sit out my term in a preliminary detention cell at the local police station. This was already the seventh administrative arrest with a 10- to 15-day conviction during my time as a refusenik. I was sure that they did not consider this a sufficiently serious warning and waited for the sequel.

When I left, six friends were waiting for me as well as my wife, who had flown in from Moscow. The seminar ended successfully before I got out. We spent another two days in Koktebel and returned to Moscow.

A little more than a month had passed since my departure for Koktebel but the atmosphere in Moscow had changed completely: systematic pressure started against the seminars, samizdat, Hebrew teaching, and other organized refusenik activity. It was even worse in other cities. I sent a complaint to KGB chairman Yuri Andropov about the provocation that his workers organized against me and sent a copy to the West. I did not plan to stop either teaching or running the seminar. Perhaps the complaint would play a small role in protecting me against further provocations, which proved to be not long in coming.

On October 15, 1981, the KGB conducted searches in the homes of several Moscow activists involved in the teaching and dissemination of the Hebrew language. Among them were Pavel Abramovich, Natalia and Gennady Khasin, Leonid Tesmenitsky, and myself. Printed material, books, typewriters, tape recorders and tapes, textbooks, and everything in foreign languages were mercilessly confiscated. We all were warned to stop teaching. On the following day, other Moscow teachers including Boris Terlitsky, Yuli Edelstein, Viktor Fulmakht, and Vladimir Kuravsky received similar warnings.[67] After a twelve-hour search, a KGB officer took me away, declaring to my wife, who was holding our infant son, "Say good-bye, your husband will not be returning." Apparently that was an "innocent joke," because I was released in the middle of the following day. I found my pale and weeping wife at home. The KGB "joke" had dried up her milk and she could not nurse the baby.

At first I thought that this was another campaign: a few months would pass and the KGB workers would calm down. They did in fact back away from some teachers. They continued, however, to apply increasing pressure on me, annoyed at the fact that I did not curtail my activity. I continued to conduct the seminar for Hebrew teachers, received many out-of-town and foreign guests, and actively taught Hebrew. I also had a telephone channel to Israel and people from other countries frequently called me.

A year and a half later, they finally did succeed in forcing me to stop conducting the seminar and teaching, but that is another story.

A Wave of Repressions, 1980–1983

In August 1980, for the first time in seven years, the USSR began jamming Russian-language broadcasts of the Voice of America, BBC, and Deutsche Welle. On January 6, 1981, it was reported that Soviet authorities were returning packages sent to refuseniks from Israel and other countries.[68]

The ideological struggle against Zionism was intensified: anti-Zionist and anti-Semitic articles were published regularly in newspapers, books, and brochures around the country. Vladimir Mushinsky, whose duty in the Jewish movement involved monitoring anti-Zionist printed material in the USSR for fifteen years (from 1976 to 1991), calculated that, taking into account the provincial press, on average throughout the country anti-Zionist and anti-Semitic articles appeared twenty-four times a day, one article per hour.[69]

The authorities also began to persecute forms of Jewish activity to which they had earlier turned a blind eye. Seminar leaders and Hebrew teachers were subject to harsh pressure. In the period from 1981 to 1982, there was considerable pressure on teachers and pupils.[70] Moreover, not all harassment was publicized abroad or reported in Jewish chronicles.[71] Professor Alexander Lerner was forced to close his cybernetics seminar: at the hour that the seminar was scheduled to meet, policemen were placed in front of the entrance and prevented the participants from entering. The authorities subsequently demanded that Lerner and many other Moscow refuseniks stop meeting visitors from abroad.[72]

Viktor Brailovsky, coordinator of the physics seminar and the final editor of *Evrei v SSSR* (Jews in the USSR), was arrested. Between August and September 1981, about ten key lecturers of semi-official Jewish seminars, including Irina Brailovsky, Alexander Lerner, Alexander Ioffe, Yakov Alpert, and Yuli Kosharovsky, were warned that they would be expelled from Moscow if they continued to give lectures.

The regime would go after Hebrew teachers in earnest in 1984, when an underground network of Hebrew instruction set up by Moscow teachers in various cities would be partially uncovered. Developments indicated that the KGB had received much greater latitude to suppress any opposition to the regime. Arrests and prison terms became significantly more frequent. In the second half of the 1970s, authorities sentenced twenty-one Jewish activists to long prison terms. In the first half of the 1980s the number reached forty.[73]

The regime struck at the democratic rights activists first. Without an investigation or trial (although he had demanded a trial), Andrei Sakharov was exiled to Gorky. In 1980 thirty-three members of the Helsinki groups were arrested. Toward the end of the year, only three members of the Moscow Helsinki group were at liberty: Sakharov's wife, Elena Bonner; the mathematician Naum Meiman; and the lawyer and defender of human rights Sofia Kalistratov. They held on for another two years. However, by September 1982, Elena Bonner declared that thanks to the arrest of most of the Helsinki group members, further work had become impossible. She announced the dissolution of the Moscow Helsinki group.[74] From the fall of 1979 until the summer of 1980, 150 dissidents representing a broad spectrum of nationalists and religious activists were arrested and tried. Any independent group with a civil or legal inclination became the target of harassments.[75]

The political wing of Jewish activists had been crushed in the course of the Sharansky trial from 1977 to 1978. Vladimir Slepak and Ida Nudel were exiled. Dina Beilin received an exit visa. The patriarch of the movement, Alexander Lerner, already weak from the constant stress and hedged in all around by the regime, was forced to close his seminar. It was made very clear to Lerner that he should have been in Sharansky's place and it would not be difficult to correct that in the future. Lerner's wife, Judith, died in January 1981 while in refusal, a tragic event that was mourned by all the refuseniks. She suffered from high blood pressure, and the stressful refusenik life no doubt shortened her life.

The regime conducted more significant trials with large international resonance after the Olympics. In Moscow, Viktor Brailovsky was the only one remaining from the group of scientists who had organized the first scientific seminar in 1972 and worked on the publication of the samizdat journal *Evrei v SSSR* (Jews in the USSR). Despite official pressure, he continued with his activities and became widely known in the West. At the time, Western scientists who were advocating a complete scientific boycott of the Soviet Union in protest against Sakharov's exile to Gorky constantly discussed that topic with refusenik scientists and members of the physics seminar. Because Gorky was a closed city and foreigners thus could not visit Sakharov, they maintained a link with him via the refusenik seminar. Even though the scientists in the seminar did not support a boycott, the situation was a sore point for the authorities.

Viktor Brailovsky explained the scientists' position:[76]

BRAILOVSKY: We thought that it would be more useful if foreign scientists came to our seminar and constantly raised the issue of Sakharov at meetings with the Soviet leadership. Moreover, in 1980 we started planning a fourth international seminar on collective phenomena that would take place in 1981. That work required considerable coordination, clarification, and meetings. We began preparing in earnest and we thought that important scientists, including Nobel laureates, would attend as they had in the past. I myself sensed that those preparations became yet another source of irritation to the regime. In other words, instead of an external boycott, we considered that a more effective path would be to stir things up domestically.

KOSHAROVSKY: *What happened to the journal [*Evrei v SSSR*]?*

BRAILOVSKY: Although we did not have a strict schedule, we usually tried to put out an issue every three months but that became impossible after the Afghan invasion. We still managed to produce a final issue in 1980. The situation then began to deteriorate rapidly.

KOSHAROVSKY: *Did you announce that you had halted publication of the journal?*

BRAILOVSKY: No. It simply became very difficult technically to support the entire process of work with authors, typists, and distributors. And it was too dangerous.

There were three searches at the Brailovskys' apartment in the year and a half before his arrest. The last one was three months before his arrest. As usual, the KGB turned everything topsy-turvy and confiscated all samizdat and foreign material, including the scientific reports of the previous international symposium. Viktor was arrested on November 13, 1980, and sent to Butyrka prison.

The regime understood very well that this arrest was a signal, and it chose the date deliberately. Two days earlier was the opening of the Madrid Conference on compliance with the statutes of the Helsinki Accords. The regime in this way made it clear that the refuseniks could not count on the West's protection and that no Helsinki Act would help them.

Brailovsky was charged with slandering the Soviet social and state order and disseminating the journal *Evrei v SSSR* (Jews in the USSR). The case against the journal had been dragging on for many years, since 1974. There were no accused, only witnesses in that "case." The impression was thus created that the case existed as a way of reining in the publishers and authors. When a convenient moment appeared, however, the KGB struck. Viktor declared to the investigation that this was a blatantly political trial, falsified from start to finish, and he therefore refused to answer any of their questions. The trial took place June 17–19, 1981, in the Moscow municipal court building.

On the Sunday following her husband's arrest, Irina, like her husband, Viktor, a brilliant scientist and editor of *Evrei v SSSR*, invited the seminar participants to a session, as usual, in her apartment. Glancing out the window, she saw that two policemen were sending back each person who had come to the session. When she went downstairs and approached the policemen, they said that they did not know why they had received an order not to allow the seminar to take place. Nevertheless, they would stand at that spot the following Sunday and every Sunday after that. "Today is the first time in eight years that we missed a seminar," Irina told Western correspondents.

Brailovsky's arrest demonstrated that under the new conditions, no one was safe. Even quiet nonpolitical activity such as leading seminars, teaching Hebrew, or dealing with Jewish culture provoked a sharp response from the authorities.

In Leningrad on November 6, 1982, Yosif Begun, the well-known veteran Moscow refusenik and fighter for the revival of Jewish culture, was arrested for the third time. He was sent on a transport from Leningrad to the city of Vladimir, where he was placed in the notorious Vladimir investigative prison. He was charged with "agitation and propaganda with the goal of subverting the Soviet regime under the guise of struggling for Jewish culture and the right to study Hebrew." For the first time, the regime demonstrated that it viewed Jewish culture and the struggle for it as anti-Soviet propaganda with the added goal of subverting the Soviet regime. The arrest of Begun was a symbolic move in the regime's battle to prevent the spread of Jewish culture, one that exposed him to the threat of severe punishment. Previously, the authorities had preferred to punish those fighting for Jewish culture with fabricated charges of hooliganism, resistance to the police, parasitism, or other petty crimes. Begun himself had been arrested and imprisoned for "parasitism" in 1977.[77] His second arrest, in 1978, was related to violation of residency rules. The 1982 arrest marked the first time that the real reason for the authorities' dissatisfaction with Begun—his dissemination of Jewish culture and fight for its legalization—was spelled out in the charge. On October 12, 1983, Begun was sentenced to seven years of imprisonment and five years of exile, the maximum term under Article 70.

Begun commented on the severity of the sentence:[78]

KOSHAROVSKY: *Wow! That was really harsh, Yosif.*

BEGUN: Honestly, I myself did not expect it. After so many years of activity, Brailovsky had been given five years of exile and in my case [the punishment was worse]. It's true that for me this was already the third round. The repressions against kulturniki reflected the regime's fear of Jewish culture. In its eyes, culture was the most dangerous thing of all: it represented subversion of the foundations. The Soviet Union, after all, was multinational. If the Jews were allowed to develop their culture, then others would demand the same. The regime needed a thunderous trial, to be followed by other trials, against Hebrew teachers and others. I think that national culture was more dangerous for them than Zionism because Zionism was diminished by emigration whereas culture was nurtured from within and had an all-encompassing nature, and the ideas could spread to other national minorities.

Begun's sentence was the harshest one given to a Jewish activist since Sharansky's trial. He did not, however, have to serve the entire term as he was released in 1987 along with other Jewish and democratic rights activists.

Over a period of a little more than two years, up until Yuri Andropov's formal accession to power in November 1982, seventeen anti-Zionist trials were conducted in the USSR. The KGB demonstrated that the rules of the game were changing: henceforth, they would arrest the rebellious ones rather than send them out of the country. Arrests were customarily accompanied by attacks in the media at all levels: local, regional, or countrywide. The refuseniks who received warnings were told that emigration would be halted in the near future and they would spend the rest of their lives in the USSR. There would be no more "rewards" for activism in the form of exit visas. Arrested activists would also not be allowed to leave after their release as had been customary in the past.

Ronald Reagan's victory in the 1980 US presidential elections led to a new phase in Soviet-American relations. Reagan initiated a tougher policy toward the Soviet Union. The Soviet invasion in December 1979 and the crackdown on Solidarity in Poland in 1981 helped shape Reagan's conviction that the USSR was, in his words, the "evil empire," and the extension of American power would mean the extension of the sphere of liberty against the tyranny and stagnation of Moscow's hegemony.[79] Reagan's determination to utilize human rights as an ideological weapon against the USSR meant that the activity of Jewish organizations and of Israel in the struggle for Soviet Jewry's rights was more in tune with the general course of the American administration. Thus Soviet intensification of repressions only stimulated a tougher reaction by Jewish organizations.

33. Refuseniks meet with British historian and Soviet Jewry advocate Martin Gilbert in Moscow in 1985. From left: Oksana Kholmyansky, Yuli Kosharovsky, Alexander Ioffe, Martin Gilbert. Front row: Mikhail Kholmyansky. Collection of Mikhail Kholmyansky.

34. Wives of Prisoners of Zion: Tatiana Edelstein (Yuli Edelstein), Dina Zisserman (Vladimir Brodsky), Mila Volvovsky (Leonid [Ari] Volvovsky). Moscow, 1986. Collection of Mila and Ari Volvovsky.

35. Refuseniks meet with American TV talk-show host Phil Donahue in Moscow, February 4, 1987. Collection of Mila and Ari Volvovsky.

36. JEWAR (Jewish Women against Refusal) in the home of Inna and Igor Uspensky, at the start of a three-day hunger strike that would involve dozens of refusenik women, coinciding with International Women's Day. Moscow, March 8, 1987. Photographed by Mikhail Kremen. Inna and Igor Uspensky collection, Association "Remember and Save."

37. JEWAR (Jewish Women against Refusal) in Kiev to honor the memory of Jews murdered in the ravine at Babii Yar, September 29, 1987. Front row, left to right: Lena Dubiansky, Roza Kholmyansky, Viktoria Lifshits, Inna Uspensky, Ada Lvovsky, Mara Abramovich, Roza Ioffe, Viktoria Khasin, Rimma Iakir. Second row: Lena Krichevsky. Back row: Aleksei Lorenson, Alexander Kholmyansky. Mara and Pasha Abramovich collection, Association "Remember and Save."

38. Refusenik symposium on denial of exit visas based on secrecy, held at apartments of the Menzheritzkys and the Kisliks. Moscow, November 1987. Photo by Vily Palanker. Association "Remember and Save."

39. Inna and Yuli Kosharovsky on a seventeen-day hunger strike in Moscow marking seventeen years of refusal, Moscow, March 1988. Photograph by Gerry Potik. Collection of Enid Wurtman.

40. Reunion of Yuli Kosharovsky and Yuli Edelstein, Moscow, January 1989. Collection of Inna and Yuli Kosharovsky.

41. Former Prisoner of Zion Vladimir Kislik and his wife, Bella Gulko, arrive in Israel on April 4, 1989. Collection of Enid Wurtman.

42. Zeev Dashevsky and Stuart Wurtman (foreign guest) in the Steinsaltz Yeshiva in Moscow, May 1989. Dashevsky was a leading religious Zionist and member of the group that founded Mahanaim, an underground network of Jewish learning. Collection of Enid and Stuart Wurtman.

43. Reunion of Martin Gilbert and Yuli Kosharovsky in Jerusalem in the summer of 1989, shortly after Yuli's aliya to Israel. Sir Gilbert had dedicated the sixth volume of his biography of Winston Churchill (*Finest Hour*, published 1983) to Yuli Kosharovsky and Aba Taratuta "in friendship, and in hope." Collection of Enid Wurtman.

44. Alexander Smukler and Inna and Igor Uspensky waiting to meet with Leon Uris, the author of the novel *Exodus*, a popular book among Soviet Jews. Leon Uris was brought to the Soviet Union by Dan Mariaschin and B'nai B'rith to meet refuseniks. Moscow, November 1989. Photo taken by Frank Brodsky. Collection of Enid Wurtman, Yuli Kosharovsky archives.

45. Alexander Smukler presents a samizdat copy of *Exodus* in Russian to author Leon Uris. Moscow, November 1989. Collection of Inna and Yuli Kosharovsky.

5

Legalization and Mass Aliya

ALTHOUGH THE KREMLIN'S HARSH REPRESSIVE POLICY in the first half of the 1980s, which it enforced by numerous threats, interrogations, searches, and arrests of activists, dealt a serious blow to refuseniks' activities, it did not succeed in crushing the Jewish movement. The powerful accomplishments of the late 1970s, the significant increase in the number of refuseniks, and the appearance of new activists in their midst, as well as Western support that remained steady and, indeed, grew even stronger helped the movement to withstand the hardships. The movement continued to pursue the basic goals of the struggle, seeking to attain the rights to free emigration, national culture and religion, Hebrew study, professional self-expression, and the right to educate Jewish children in the framework of national culture.

As was already stated, the number of those able to emigrate from the USSR began to drop in 1979. Having reached a peak in 1979 of 51,331, the number of those who left fell to 21,648 in 1980, and in the following year it went down to 9,448. To a considerable degree, the comparatively high figures in 1980 and 1981 were the result of applications that had been received earlier. After the Afghan invasion, the authorities made the procedure for accepting documents more complicated, dragged out the processing period to two years or more, and sharply increased the number of refusals. In November 1982 Yuri Andropov, a member of the Politburo who was also chief of the KGB from 1967 until May 1982, replaced Leonid Brezhnev as head of the CPSU and of the state. Under his leadership, the already fierce ideological struggle against Zionism became even harsher. Under such conditions, the number of people ready to apply for exit visas also declined. In 1982 the number of those who emigrated fell to 2,692; in 1983 to 1,314; and in 1984 to just 896 people.[1]

Emigration had been reduced by forceful measures. At the same time, the circles of refuseniks and those close to them had been expanded considerably by the addition of Jewish people who felt ready to emigrate. These people wanted to get together and to study Hebrew and Jewish history and tradition. Most important, however, they wanted a renewal of emigration, and they were prepared to fight for that goal.

Those Soviet Jews who had already spent seven to ten years in struggle and refusal presented a different picture. Some of them were serving time in prison or camps, others had just been released from imprisonment, and still others had such a weighty dossier at the KGB that the least addition could tip the balance to arrest; they no longer had the resources to continue their activity of the 1970s. Moreover, some of them were simply tired, burned out, and no longer wanted to take a risk. Others became involved in underground work.

Meanwhile, the open struggle in the style of action beloved by Western correspondents continued: demonstrations, collective visits to institutions of power, and so forth. Now, however, it was the youth who followed that path. For example, on December 11, 1980, a group of 150 Jewish activists held a demonstration in the reception room of the Supreme Soviet, demanding exit visas.[2] On December 21, 1981, the first day of Hanukah, fifty Moscow and sixty Odessa Jews held a sit-down demonstration near the Lenin Library in Moscow. In addition, every December 24 demonstrations were held in solidarity with the Prisoners of Zion. Hunger strikes in protest against the refusal of exit visas were held in many cities in those years.[3]

Seminars, Cultural Life, and Religion

The authorities did not manage to close all the seminars. As was noted, the Leningrad humanitarian seminar, led by Grigory Kanovich and others, had been dispersed in the summer of 1981, but Mikhail Beizer organized a cultural-historical seminar with a restricted number of participants and closed sessions. This smaller seminar operated successfully in the gloomy 1980s. In Moscow the Hebrew teachers' seminar was replaced by a dibbur set up in 1982 under the direction of Yuli Edelstein, which functioned up until his arrest in September 1984. Lev Gorodetsky ran another seminar on Hebrew teaching methods that operated until the beginning of the 1990s. Both the dibbur and the seminar retained the traditions of the previous seminar and allotted time to reports on historical, religious, and general cultural topics.

Despite Viktor Brailovsky's arrest in November 1980, the Moscow physics seminar, officially called the Seminar on Collective Phenomena, kept going. Alexander Ioffe, an active participant in the seminar, said that the number of people attending the seminar declined after the arrest to around two dozen attendees. Foreign guests continued to come, but they were prevented from entering.[4]

During the biannual Moscow International Book Fair, the Israeli delegation held many meetings with refuseniks. The group from Israel always included interesting figures: poets, musicians, singers, and academics. The popular singer Sarale Sharon, who came with the delegation in 1981 and 1983, sang together with refuseniks and activists, teaching them new songs. Each day the Israeli delegates would bring books to their rooms in the hotel. In parallel with the Israeli delegation, several pairs of tourists would come to Moscow whose sole task was to bring the books from the hotel to the refuseniks' apartments.

Even in the 1980s, the regime put less pressure on the religious channel than on other ones. Evidently it did not believe in the possibility of a serious religious revival in an atheistic country. The refuseniks treated religion more seriously. Even for the secular refuseniks, Judaism and its attributes were among the attractive and basic elements of national identification. Religious holidays were carefully marked, many adult activists underwent circumcision, and there was mass attendance at synagogues on Simhat Torah and Yom Kippur. A number of talented people observed religious precepts and immersed themselves with increasing intensity in religious practice. Among them were many activists who taught Hebrew (Shakhnovksy, Edelstein, Kholmyansky, and others), participated in publishing journals (Essas, Vasserman), organized seminars and other public measures (Nudler, Vasserman), put on Purimspiels (Geizel, Gurevich), and wrote and signed protest letters. The different streams in the religious revival, including Chabad and the Lithuanian (Mitnagdim) tradition, continued their activity in the 1980s. The religious Zionists got started and developed in this period.[5]

Pinhas Polonsky, an activist of the religious revival in the USSR, spoke about his activity:[6]

POLONSKY: We organized the study and teaching of Judaism in Moscow in the following manner. We had an internal lesson attended by ten to fifteen people at which we studied by ourselves the Talmud and commentaries. Every participant prepared, read an excerpt of the Talmud and the commentaries on it, and gave a report. Each of these people was involved in additional weekly lessons that we coordinated. One person, for example, conducted a lesson for beginners and another led a lesson for the more advanced. Each person was aware of the general picture and accordingly would send students to the others. There were about fifteen lessons a week in our system, and it functioned, one could say, like an underground yeshiva. About two hundred people in total studied in our system from 1984 to 1987. That was the first part of our work. The second part was cooperation with Hebrew teachers. We would go to them to study Hebrew and they would come to us to study Judaism. We sent our teachers to them on various holidays, and we also set up an underground publishing house as an aid in the preparation of Judaism instructors. Vitia Fulmakht, Grisha Levitsky, and Natan Brusovani dealt with preparing and distributing this literature, and I did the writing.

My editing and publishing activity began in 1980, when there was a demand before the Passover holiday for a guide to celebrating the festival. As there are two Seder nights in the Diaspora, on one night you go to a teacher and on the second, you conduct it yourself for relatives and friends. We conducted the Passover Seder with commentaries in Russian: we took an existing translation of the Haggadah and wrote commentaries to the translation based on Hebrew sources, typed it all up, and photocopied it. Our direction was set by modern Orthodoxy and religious Zionism. At the time, there were no conservative or reform Jews in Moscow. There was a strong Chabad group with whom we were friendly but we didn't belong to it.

KOSHAROVSKY: *Did the KGB harass you in Moscow?*

POLONSKY: We were young and crazy and didn't think much about dangers. We tolerated with a grain of humor the KGB visits to our apartments to disrupt lessons and other forms of pressure such as tailing and visiting workplaces. At some stage, they intensified the pressure. In the USSR, it was forbidden to teach religion to minors and they threatened to arrest me. We then decided on a protective move: I stopped teaching Judaism to children and began to write books at home. When we would be summoned to the KGB, we usually declared that we had no disputes with them. We simply wanted to leave the country.

KOSHAROVSKY: *How would you divide the stages in your group's development?*

POLONSKY: The first stage was when we were students and engaged in visiting the synagogue and celebrating Jewish holidays. That was up to 1980. Then we became a separate organization (Mahanaim) and began to conduct our own underground yeshiva and publishing house. In 1987 we established the legal Mahanaim organization in Israel.[7]

There were certain figures in the religious refusenik community who did not belong to any one of the three basic religious streams, including the charismatic Boris Berman.[8] Some activists penetrated deeply into the field of Jewish knowledge and practice. Mikhail Khanin, a graduate of the philosophy department of Moscow State University, defended his candidate's dissertation (roughly equivalent to a PhD in the West) on the sociology of reading in 1976. In parallel with his work in the sociology sector of the Lenin Library, he worked as a guard at the Moscow Kauchuk factory, where he met the Jewish movement activist Mikhail Nudler. He had no previous acquaintance with Jewish culture and he was ashamed of his Jewish origins. Khanin recalled realizing through that contact that the Soviet regime had robbed him of his roots, spiritually decapitated him, and distorted his notion of his own people.

Khanin spoke about his further path:[9]

KHANIN: After I had studied Hebrew for several months, Nudler brought me to Ilia Essas's seminar on the Torah. In the philosophy department at MGU, I had been taught to work with primary sources and therefore I wanted to read Jewish texts not in translation or a paraphrase but in the original, in Hebrew. I began to study with Essas and he directed me at first to Misha Schneider's Bible lessons and then to Volodia Shakhnovsky to study the Bible with Rashi's commentaries. I then used to go to Uri Kamyshov for several years to study the Talmud. I began to teach Hebrew in 1979, while remaining a senior worker at the Lenin Library for another two years.

Naturally, when I started going to the synagogue, studying Torah, learning Hebrew, and visiting groups of conversational Hebrew, a file was opened on me. I found a plausible excuse, however, explaining that as a sociologist, I was interested in Hebrew culture and was studying the language and Jewish tradition. Of course, my explanation didn't convince my boss, but I was not dismissed from work in exchange for the promise not to emigrate to anywhere or to submit an application. Toward the fall of 1980, after the second Koktebel seminar, I worked out a final version of the methodology that I had been cultivating for seven years while teaching Hebrew.

Starting in 1980, I tried organically to combine the teaching of conversational Hebrew with the study of the foundations of Judaism. Among those who studied with me were Yosif Begun, Valera Prokhorovsky, Boria Berman, David and Inna Kvartin, Boria Ginis and his wife, and Yuri Iurev, who became a Chabad leader on the level of Grisha Rozenshtein. I was fortunate that I was able to occupy an intermediary, neutral position between the original two and later more numerous groups of people who had turned to faith.

KOSHAROVSKY: *How many years did you teach?*

KHANIN: Seven years, and I was in refusal practically seven years, including the two years that I waited for an official invitation. I applied at the beginning of 1981 and left in 1985. In 1979 and 1980, I already had advanced groups after the two seminars in Koktebel.

There was a problem in reviving destroyed communities: in order to establish minyanim [the minimum groups of ten males required for public prayers] and set up all the traditional Jewish social institutions, one needed to overcome the shortage of qualified people necessary for the communities' existence such as a shohet, mohel, melamed, and *sofer stam* (scribe of holy writings on parchment). I started to study to be a sofer stam secretly in 1981–82 with two old men, the last scribes in Moscow—Reb Sholom Krimenets and Velvl Shakhnovetsky. Later I was joined by Mark Lisnevsky and my student Sasha Bark. Starting in the early 1980s, the Jewish community of England and the US Agudat Yisrael would regularly send to Moscow and Leningrad rabbis and professional religious emissaries who taught *baalei tshuva* (the newly religious) how to become a shohet or sofer. In 1983 Reb Sholom Krimenets suggested that I write religious bills of divorce (*gittim*) in the synagogue. For decades there had been no rabbinical court (Beit din) in the USSR. The Beit din that arose in the early 1980s at the Moscow Choral synagogue consisted of two men: Avrom Shaevich, who had studied at the Neolog yeshiva in Hungary, and Rav Yisroel Shvartsblat. I studied the religious divorce laws at the level of a rabbinical court and I consider my participation in the rabbinical court for a period of three years as a most important function. It was the only place in the USSR where Jews could divorce according to religious law and solve related problems. There were many requests from traditional communities—dozens and perhaps hundreds. I have in mind not only refusenik families but also communities in the Transcarpathian area, North Caucasus, Trans-Caucasus, and Central Asia. We gave not more than a dozen or a dozen and a half gittim in a month.

As the last accredited sofer in the USSR during the year and a half before my departure, in addition to writing gittim, I had to deal with checking and correcting *tefilin*, mezuzahs, and Torah scrolls. In 1985, in view of my activity, the KGB decided to get rid of me.

Hebrew Teaching—The Cities Project

Despite the intensified pressure by the authorities, people still attended the ulpanim. They would switch from teachers who were under KGB pressure to lesser-known instructors with whom it was less dangerous to study. Moscow was well supplied with Hebrew teachers thanks to the efforts of the previous years; indeed, there were enough teachers not only for local needs but also for helping other cities. Guests from other cities often visited Kosharovsky's teachers' seminar, where people were happy to give them an intensive Hebrew course if they were able to spend some time in Moscow for that purpose. Otherwise, teachers traveled from Moscow to the periphery if there was an interested group. In addition, the Moscow teachers supplied them with textbooks and technical means.

In December 1979 Alexander (Sasha) Kholmyansky, a young teacher and active participant in the teachers' seminar, came up with a proposal to designate Hebrew teaching in provincial cities as a separate project. He was critical of the open courses of intensive training for out-of-towners on the assumption that it could put the participants from the provinces in a vulnerable position. Circumstances had changed after the invasion of Afghanistan, and the times demanded stronger precautionary measures. Sasha proposed closing the project to outsiders and making it conspiratorial. This represented a change: in Hebrew teaching and other Jewish activity, it was important that everything appeared natural, without external signs of underground organization or conspiracy. Activists understood they were going against official ideology and practice, but they behaved as if they were engaged in legitimate activity. After all, they were not in fact breaking the law. Indeed, the authorities were the ones violating the law in harassing the teachers. There was enormous moral strength in such an outwardly naïve position.

Finding the golden mean with regard to an appropriate level of secrecy was, therefore, important. Obvious conspiracy would be more likely to attract attention to the project. Undoubtedly, such a countrywide project had to be covert at the upper echelons: the financing, the organizers, the group of teachers, the production of textbooks and other material, and lists of addresses and telephones. Dividing the project into autonomous sectors would protect it in case of individual blunders in one unit. It was about two years after Sasha had applied for an exit visa, and, in the meantime, he had not gotten into any serious trouble. He did, however, study Hebrew with the prominent teacher Lev Ulanovsky, one of the first serious proponents of spreading Hebrew beyond the bounds of Moscow. The stakes were high and there was much to consider.

Kholmyansky's proposal emphasized initiative on the part of those at the center: the Moscow activists would not wait until others approached them for help but would actively seek contacts in the cities to organize ulpanim, receive literature and textbooks for independent study, and carefully collect information about the situation in the cities and about people who sympathized with the Jewish movement. Out-of-towners who came to Moscow for help could always be provocateurs or simply weak individuals who would blurt out everything they knew at the first interrogation. In any case, the Moscow teachers needed to develop ties around the country in order to reinforce the movement.

The Moscow teachers formed a group of four people who would implement the project and decide principled questions in a collegial fashion. The group included Alexander Kholmyansky, his brother Mikhail Kholmyansky, Yuli Edelstein, and Yuli Kosharovsky. Alexander Kholmyansky assumed implementation of the project in Odessa and the southern part of Ukraine, Moldavia, and the Caucasus. Misha took responsibility for Leningrad and the Baltics. Yuli Edelstein took Kharkov, Minsk, and the rest of Belarus. Yuli Kosharovsky assumed responsibility for the financing, procurement of materials, and reporting on the project.

Alexander Kholmyansky reviewed the inception of the idea:[10]

KOSHAROVSKY: *When did you conclude that it was necessary to find a special person, not under police observation, who on the basis of fragmentary information received from diverse sources, would travel to the various cities, corroborate the reliability of the information, and try to establish reliable contacts for forming Hebrew groups?*

KHOLMYANSKY: Rather quickly. I was consumed by this project, thought about it constantly, and tried out different models in my mind.

KOSHAROVSKY: *When did you develop the final model?*

KHOLMYANSKY: It took me about a year. I had two groups of teachers in Moscow who were working entirely for the cities: a senior and middle group of my students, already quite advanced by that time in language study. Yulik Edelstein began to have all sorts of unpleasant problems: the authorities wanted to deprive him of his residency permit for Moscow and the threat of being recruited into the army hung over him. In the end we diminished his activity, and I began to operate in his regions. It became clear that I had to direct this project. Yulik retained the mobile camps, that is, seminars on boats, trips, and the like. He, for his part, posited only one condition, that the group include people suitable for complete immersion in Hebrew. That's how it was and, thank God, he didn't have any slip-ups.

KOSHAROVSKY: *You had other activists who traveled around the cities, for example, Dov Kontorer. In my opinion, he was the most effective. Highly motivated, a conspirator, like you, he didn't stick out.*

KHOLMYANSKY: He worked for a few years with me and several years after my arrest. He used to travel, meet people, and evaluate the situation.

KOSHAROVSKY: *Did you basically send your students to teach?*

KHOLMYANSKY: Yes. I weeded out some of them, choosing people who I knew were not too talkative and could do what was necessary.

KOSHAROVSKY: *How was the project structured with regard to the various functions?*

KHOLMYANSKY: The first task was reconnaissance trips. The second function was teaching in the localities and in Moscow for out-of-towners. Starting in 1981, we brought together in Moscow people from other cities who were willing to sacrifice their vacation for intensive study. They either lived for a few weeks with various teachers or we rented an apartment for them. A third function was to supply literature to the cities. I traveled a lot to the cities that no one had yet visited in order somehow to inspire the public there. In addition, there was the storage of materials. There were dozens of addresses for warehousing. It's impossible to describe it.

KOSHAROVSKY: *Kontorer also taught?*

KHOLMYANSKY: At first he had a problem with teaching. He was so good at mastering a language that he didn't understand how it should be taught. But he managed that. Moreover, Dov became the first religious person in my system, and he began to read the Bible with the students. I was also successful with that kind of activity. The second successful instructor who taught in Moscow apartments was Mark Zolotarevsky. We would bring individuals who had taken our courses and were of unquestionable reliability to summer camps. I did that with my brother Misha and Yuli Edelstein. I also was always looking for other people to do that.

KOSHAROVSKY: *Were you the only person who knew the schedule of study in the cities?*

KHOLMYANSKY: Yes, there was a problem with guarding information. I used several methods. There was a sheet of paper that was so thin it could be swallowed if necessary. I always kept it with me. The complete list was kept in a certain place with instructions: destroy in case of danger. And there was yet another list in another place. When I was arrested, only one list was supposed to be destroyed but by mistake, they destroyed both so that (Zeev) Geizel and Kontorer had to reconstruct all the information.

KOSHAROVSKY: *How did you decide on the places to which you could send teachers?*

KHOLMYANSKY: I sent a person if it was possible to form some kind of group. If there was just a single person at the location with high motivation, we could send him to study in another place.

KOSHAROVSKY: *Did you yourself conduct a summer camp every year?*

KHOLMYANSKY: Yes, and that created a certain problem. There is an ideal model and there is reality. According to the ideal model, I was not supposed to run the summer camps. It was wrong, because it could end badly for the cause and for me. Every year, I thought that I would find someone to replace me and that I shouldn't be trying to patch up all the holes myself. Nevertheless, there were years when I organized more than one summer camp.

KOSHAROVSKY: *Who handled the preparation of printed material?*

KHOLMYANSKY: That was an entirely separate system. I was friendly with Igor Gurvich and Vitia Fulmakht. Misha Danovich appeared fairly early. He was a first-rate physicist, and for many years he took care of supplying the cities with textbooks produced by photocopying. At the time, I didn't know that he was doing that.

KOSHAROVSKY: *I also supplied you with material all the time.*

KHOLMYANSKY: Yes, you did. But the main part came from an autonomous system. At first we began to produce teaching material using Fulmakht's negatives. We told him that it was for special purposes. He didn't show any undue curiosity.

KOSHAROVSKY: *In how many cities were you teaching?*

KHOLMYANSKY: We made attempts in approximately fifty cities, but it didn't work in about thirty of them.

KOSHAROVSKY: *I remember that around seventy cities were involved in this project.*

KHOLMYANSKY: Seventy cities received self-instruction manuals and literature that we brought. I am referring to organized activity, where there was a regularly operating group. There were twenty such places. I didn't include in my count the cities in which people studied individually.

KOSHAROVSKY: *Did the KGB discover you because of some bungling or did they perceive the rapidly rising level of activity?*

KHOLMYANSKY: There were no particular blunders but information about our activity gradually leaked out. Honestly speaking, I had hoped to keep the project going for three years at the maximum. I think that for around two years, they didn't understand what was going on. At some point, via various people, I started to get the impression that the authorities were on to what I was doing. In 1983 the term "Countrywide Ulpan" appeared in their questioning, as I saw via my students. From 1982 onward, more and more people were summoned for questioning.

KOSHAROVSKY: *Were you also summoned?*

KHOLMYANSKY: I was summoned on various pretexts: for example, to clarify where I was working.

KOSHAROVSKY: *What was your family's attitude toward your work?*

KHOLMYANSKY: My parents also participated actively in the project. They transported material and information. Mama was simply a very active person. My whole family was involved.

KOSHAROVSKY: *You started to tire?*

KHOLMYANSKY: No, I was like someone possessed. It was my most important project, the kind that you have only once in a lifetime. Despite everything, we operated it for four years in the most difficult period when all possible screws were being tightened. We reached some kind of peak in 1984. I could no longer stop it, but I tried to transform our activity into semiautonomous sectors, to divide it into smaller cells.

KOSHAROVSKY: *And you were arrested.*

KHOLMYANSKY: In the summer of 1984. I was with my group in Estonia. I chose it because there were few Jews there and no Jewish activity.

After Kholmyansky's arrest, his two colleagues and students, Dov Kontorer and Zeev Geizel, continued the project.

Zeev Geizel talked about his involvement:[11]

KOSHAROVSKY: *Sasha (Kholmyansky) was arrested a year after you joined the project. What happened with the cities?*

GEIZEL: At first we didn't understand that his jail term was lengthy. When we did, I said to Dov that we had to continue the project. I went to Misha Kholmyansky and said that I was willing to keep the project going and he went to you. You two invited me "onto the carpet" and at some point gave me the go-ahead. The main thing was to reestablish the addresses. Grisha Levitsky and Volodia Mushinsky restored the book production and then I began my own production.

KOSHAROVSKY: *What reading material did you supply to the cities?*

GEIZEL: Primarily, books published by Biblioteka Aliya in Israel.[12] Translations of *Exodus* and *The City of Safed*[13] were tremendously popular; others were Uri Dan's book on Entebbe and a book about the Six-Day War by the two Churchills [Randolph S. and Winston S.]. I had the samizdat book *Forged in Fury* [by Michael Elkins about the hunt for Nazi war criminals after the end of World War II].[14] I used to give my students books to read and that helped in selecting the best ones to send to other places.

KOSHAROVSKY: *Did you refresh the line of books?*

GEIZEL: Of course, everything changed constantly. I collected the books from storerooms at (Reuven) Degtiarev's and brought them to Kontorer. "Look how many books there are," I would say, "they will last a long time!" Dov snorted and said, "Yeah, sure, for a long time! Perhaps for around three weeks." Each week I would drag books to him in a rucksack.

KOSHAROVSKY: *Were you the only one in contact with Degtiarev?*

GEIZEL: We didn't have super secrecy as Sasha did. We treated everything more simply. Grisha Levitsky was initiated into the Cities Project. He didn't know, however, what specifically was happening in a given city, but he didn't need to. He was in contact with Degtiarev and, of course, Kontorer.

KOSHAROVSKY: *How long did you continue the project?*

GEIZEL: Until my departure in 1988.

For his part, Dov Kontorer was highly motivated. At the age of ten, he decided to make aliya to Israel. That was during the Yom Kippur War. He saw how his parents agonized and how his father did not sleep at night, listening to the radio, but when he asked questions, his parents feared to say a word to their son. Dov did not want to live that way, and the ten-year-old decided that he would go to Israel. In 1979 he made the acquaintance of religious Jews at the Marina Roshcha (Chabad) synagogue in Moscow, underwent circumcision, and decided that he would not enter any Soviet institution of higher learning—he did not want to pursue a career in that country. Starting in the spring of 1982, he traveled around the country at the request of Shimon Yantovsky, who was involved in documenting old synagogues and neglected Jewish cemeteries. In January 1983 Alexander Kholmyansky drew Dov into the Cities Project.

Dov Kontorer recalled his participation:[15]

KOSHAROVSKY: *How did you manage to operate for so many years without botching things?*

KONTORER: We rarely traveled on planes in order not to purchase tickets by name. Almost all our trips were by train. Nothing was said over the telephone. In order to transmit any information about the program, a person would travel to the city. No one spoke in apartments [because of bugging], only on the street. No unnecessary information was conveyed. Not only we ourselves but also the people whom we contacted were in a dangerous situation. It didn't take much to get arrested in the provinces. For that reason, our expenses were greater but the security was effective. The authorities had no idea of the scale of our operation. From 1982 to 1984 I traveled incessantly. Then the KGB began to sense something but it absolutely was unaware of the real scale. I think that they would have arrested Kholmyansky earlier if they had understood what was going on. A very narrow circle of people in Moscow knew what I was doing. My friends who were not involved in it did not know about it. I didn't present myself as a *homo soveticus.* I followed the lifestyle of a religious Jew with some Zionist views and a corresponding social circle. Those people didn't know about my activity. I didn't even tell my parents about where I was traveling. Lyova Fridlender generally was informed about my itinerary, and my parents knew that if I didn't appear at any time, they could contact him. He was in some sense the contact for my parents.

KOSHAROVSKY: *How were the financial issues resolved?*

KONTORER: I always worked. I tried not to wind up in a situation where I would be critically dependent on my Jewish activity. I was not given money for my trips. I received a sum for daily expenses, say, five rubles a day.

KOSHAROVSKY: *Did you frequently bring books with you?*

KONTORER: Yes, and my home thus turned into a kind of warehouse. It was convenient, because I was always traveling.

KOSHAROVSKY: *How many cities did you visit?*

KONTORER: About thirty.

KOSHAROVSKY: *What agreements did you reach?*

KONTORER: Sometimes, we agreed that a teacher would go there to teach or that we were prepared to receive two or three people in Moscow for an intensive course of instruction or that we were planning to hold a summer camp in such and such a place and needed to know who wanted to come. One place would need a tape recorder and cassettes, another books, and so forth.

KOSHAROVSKY: *Dov, did you clearly understand the risks of going around with a full backpack? After all, there were not only textbooks but also samizdat.*

KONTORER: I understood and tried not to take unnecessary risks. I followed all of Sasha's rules and could explain to people why and how one should keep them. It wasn't so simple. For example, when a person would travel to Moscow, there was a circle of people with whom he would openly associate: he would go to the synagogue and drop in on a dibbur. Why did he have to hide his acquaintance with me so carefully? That was not so obvious. I could not, after all, say to him that there are another twenty cities, some kind of centralized project. I therefore said, "All right, don't ask any superfluous questions, just follow the rules."

KOSHAROVSKY: *What happened after Sasha Kholmyansky's arrest?*

KONTORER: Geizel and I took over his functions. He took on the representative part. He contacted you and foreigners while I remained with the cities. We worked well together, each doing his thing. At the same time, it was understood that both of us would teach.

KOSHAROVSKY: *And you did this without interruption?*

KONTORER: Until I left in May 1988. Geizel left three weeks before me.

KOSHAROVSKY: *As far as I recall, the project continued even after your departure.*

KONTORER: Yes. Soon, however, this activity became more or less legal.

Unlike Dov Kontorer, Yuli Edelstein, another one of the young leaders of the Cities Project, had already been in refusal for a year. Yuli knew English very well. He strove for the same excellence in Hebrew. In 1980, when the Cities Project started, he was barely twenty-two years old, yet he took a leading role in the project.

Edelstein recalled those years:[16]

KOSHAROVSKY: *During the difficult 1980s, the most difficult year for Hebrew teachers was 1984.*

EDELSTEIN: The Soviet leaders were dying one after the other, and the KGB agents felt that they were the masters of the situation because the KGB was the only stable element. My arrest occurred during Chernenko's rule, a time of total decay and complete KGB control. The hatchet jobs by the security services were not haphazard but part of a plan. When you want to show someone who's in control, you don't beat him up out of sight—you beat him in full view of the crowd.

KOSHAROVSKY: *They went after the teachers because they felt that they were the most steadfast element among the activists.*

EDELSTEIN: Remember our dibbur from 1981 to 1982? In 1981 Sarale Sharon came to the book fair. Was there a notice about that in the newspapers? At the dibbur, among thirty teachers and semi-teachers, I declared that a concert of the Israeli singer would take place at such and such an apartment. In the course of a week, hundreds of refuseniks knew about it—without telephones or anything else. It was a pyramid that operated on a countrywide scale and it worked in various cities. It was a constantly operating network. The regime attached top priority to disrupting it. Another objective was to settle accounts with longtime activists.

KOSHAROVSKY: *Were you in charge of Kharkov and Minsk in the Cities Project?*

EDELSTEIN: Yes, I taught there in 1980 and 1981.

KOSHAROVSKY: *After that, you switched to organizing summer camps in the form of canoe trips?*

EDELSTEIN: We did that for three years.

The Cities Project was carried out by courageous, highly motivated people, who trained others like them in the provinces. A number of them paid for this with their health and with years of imprisonment, but their efforts were not in vain. When perestroika arrived in the USSR, one could find active and educated participants in the Jewish movement in seventy cities of the Soviet Union, people who already had the opportunity to become acquainted with their national culture, history, and religion; in twenty cities, at least one group was studying Hebrew. These people, who were willing to take risks in the dark 1980s, even more enthusiastically joined in the struggle for national life in the more favorable perestroika period. Just as the Moscow activists succeeded in creating a ripple effect that encompassed many cities, within the cities themselves knowledge, connections, and activity spread. By the second half of the 1980s, a wide network of activists who were striving to make aliya and bring about a revival of Jewish national life was operating in the USSR.

Context for Mashka

In the course of the 1970s, Moscow was the center of Zionist ferment. Much of the activity that developed in that city then spread to the rest of the country: teaching of Hebrew, history, and culture; religious activity; legal, scientific, and cultural seminars; samizdat; the establishment of international ties; and so forth. To a significant degree, Moscow coordinated mutual aid for refuseniks and aid to Prisoners of Zion. More than others, Moscow activists were in contact with high-level foreign guests and took part in discussions of international initiatives and protest actions such as the Jackson-Vanik Amendment, the Brussels and Helsinki conferences, and the boycott of the Moscow Olympics.

In the beginning of the 1980s, influenced by the harsher atmosphere involving the closure of the gates for aliya, increased threats, warnings, and arrests, some veteran refuseniks gradually stopped carrying out these functions. Consequently, a certain vacuum was created by the lack of activity and coordination in those areas. The situation, indeed, required just the opposite reaction because there was a sharp increase in the number of needy refuseniks and in the number of arrests and related problems. And supporters in the West needed a constant stream of information about what was happening in the movement, a serious analysis of the ongoing processes, recommendations, and initiatives that corresponded to the changed situation. In light of the new circumstances, however, everyone understood that a continuation of activity in those forms that had been elaborated in the second half of the 1970s was impossible in the 1980s. This was the context for the formation of Mashka.

Personal Recollections: Mashka

KOSHAROVSKY: My personal situation reflected the generally tougher climate for Jewish activists. From 1980 to 1981 I had felt pressure in connection with my work in running the teachers' seminar and teaching Hebrew, and this pressure continued to intensify. It took the form of numerous detentions on the way to a lesson or seminar accompanied by warnings and threats of arrest, and calls to my wife while I was on my way someplace ("We heard that some people are planning to break your husband's hands and feet; stop him before it's too late!" they might say). I also experienced the disruption of lessons, the confiscation of teaching materials, and threats to my students, extending to dismissal from work or exclusion from institutes of higher education. It became physically impossible to teach in such conditions, and I decided to transfer my students to teachers not under KGB scrutiny.

I assumed that my actions demonstrated sufficient flexibility and willingness to make concessions, and that arresting me would contradict the regime's educative-repressive policy. In other matters, I therefore continued to lead my normal refusenik life, giving lectures at the teachers' seminar—which now was at Gorodetsky's house—participating in meetings with foreigners and in the organization of meetings with members of the Israeli book fair delegations, writing petitions, and so forth. Other refuseniks who had also exhausted their resources followed more or less the same tactics. Our natural behavior led the authorities to be less suspicious than usual of the activities that we concealed from outsiders. Based on my experience in Sverdlovsk, I knew that the legends of the KGB's omniscience were greatly exaggerated: their own resources were limited and they were not able to place informers everywhere.

At the beginning of the 1980s, my covert activity continually expanded. Contacts with Nativ, which had been developing for several years, intensified. Solutions were needed for a wider circle of tasks. The Cities Project required serious financing and an expanded variety and quantity of samizdat material. Contacts with foreigners had to be maintained by people with a mastery of foreign languages and an understanding of the situation, including all aspects of our multifaceted activity. In addition, there was a need for reliable, effective—and at the same time sufficiently secret—channels for supporting and stimulating certain initiatives.

I gradually developed good working contacts with people handling various areas: Natasha Khasin (Prisoners of Zion and families in trouble); Ira and Igor Gurvich and Slava Shifrin (kindergartens); Yuli Edelstein, Alexander and Mikhail Kholmyansky, Lyova Gorodetsky (Hebrew); Mikhail Chlenov, Viktor Fulmakht, and Vladimir Mushinsky (samizdat, cultural activity); Alexander Ioffe and Boris Klots (physicists' seminar, refusenik scientists); Anatoly Khazanov, a prominent ethnographer; and Vladimir Kislik (the legal seminar, after he served his prison term and moved to Moscow). In addition, I retained trustworthy working contacts with veteran activists who had to reduce their activities considerably in order to retain their freedom: Lerner, Prestin, Abramovich, and Levich, and in other cities Aba Taratuta and Roald Zelichenok (Leningrad), Evgeny Koifman (Dnepropetrovsk), and others. Those people could have a practical influence on the situation and possessed the most reliable information in their regions.

After one of the meetings with foreigners at the apartment of Anatoly Khazanov, a neighbor in my district, I suggested to some of the local participants that they take part in regular meetings to discuss and coordinate our activities. The first group included Lev Gorodetsky, Yuli Edelstein, Alexander Ioffe, Mikhail Chlenov, Viktor Fulmakht, Anatoly Khazanov, and Boris Klots, eight people, together with me. I proposed to Prestin and Abramovich that they join the group, but they preferred to interact with me on a personal level, and I understood them fully: they had been worn out by the ongoing intense KGB surveillance.

We met weekly at reliable apartments not under the KGB's eye. At each meeting, we set out a festive table with drinks and snacks: in case of a sudden KGB visit, everyone knew what festive date or holiday we were supposed to be celebrating.

In this context, Lyova Gorodetsky suggested called our meetings "Mashka" from the Hebrew acronym for "Club for strong drink,"[17] which sounded similar to the Hebrew word for a beverage, mashkeh. The name caught on for internal use, especially because we sometimes did have a swig or two. The members were ambitious and energetic people. To avoid any clash of interests, Vitia Fulmakht suggested that meetings be held in "an atmosphere of complete amity," i.e., an absolutely friendly environment, which became an inviolable principle. If in the course of a discussion, the atmosphere began to heat up, the person in charge would appeal to everyone to observe the law of "complete amity."

Foreigners and activists who were not part of the group were never invited to Mashka. No one mentioned anything that we discussed there, as well as the very existence of Mashka, even among our closest circle of acquaintances. Each person individually carried out the decisions adopted there in his own sphere of activity. Everything but the Cities Project and sources of financing, which were my spheres of responsibility, was discussed at Mashka. The expenditures for other projects and directions of activity were discussed constantly. In time, Mashka turned into a powerful analytic and coordinating instrument that operated up until the collapse of the USSR. In those years, no one except for people in Nativ, the members themselves, and the owners of the apartments where the meetings took place knew about its existence, but its influence was felt in many areas of our activity.

We created a circle of people for meetings with foreigners in which a Mashka member would come to the meeting as part of his group or individually and present topics there for which he was responsible in Mashka. In that way, each person spoke about his own area but it organically meshed with the general picture that had been carefully discussed at Mashka. That set-up was particularly important when high-level guests arrived and we had to give them a survey of refusenik life and its problems in order to prepare them before their meetings with the Soviet leadership. After Gorbachev became the head of state, the number of visiting foreigners increased sharply.

Nativ emissaries always received accurate and balanced information about the situation. Mashka prepared letters and appeals to important international forums and political figures, saw to it that problematic spots of refusenik activity received support within the USSR and abroad, that there were no hitches with samizdat, that Prisoners of Zion and their families were taken care of, and so forth. We regularly prepared analytic reports about developments regarding emigration and refusenik activity. These reports, in which each person described his sector, were sent to Nativ.

The sole member of Mashka who was arrested and sentenced was Yuli Edelstein, but he was arrested for leading a dibbur and participating in major social undertakings under the KGB's eyes, not because of his membership in Mashka, about which the KGB was ignorant—the subject never came up during his interrogations. When mass emigration began, new people were brought in to replace those who had departed.

Anatoly Khazanov recalled his participation:[18]

KOSHAROVSKY: *When did you join Mashka?*

KHAZANOV: A group of Canadian parliamentarians arrived in Moscow at the end of 1983. Because of various considerations, you suggested receiving them at my place. After the meeting, we decided to relax a little. You, Vitia (Fulmakht), Alik (Ioffe), and Yuli Edelstein—I remember it well—and someone else. Then, you came up with this idea: "I am beginning to feel that the old refuseniks are victimized and tired and retiring from activity. Anarchy is beginning to set in. The time has come to establish a coordinating organ." That historic event occurred in my home. I shall never forget it. We began to discuss whom we should co-opt.

Naturally, we brought in Mika (Mikhail Chlenov) immediately, and it seems to me you suggested Gorodila (Lev Gorodetsky). Boria (Boris) Klots was suggested and everyone agreed, despite Alik's minor objection. And that's all.

KOSHAROVSKY: *What issues did you deal with?*

KHAZANOV: I took part in discussions of strategy and the preparation of analytic memoranda and protest letters. I also did final editing of analytic surveys. Together with Mika, I dealt with the Jewish Cultural Association.[19] And, of course, representative functions. I remember an analytic memorandum of 1984 and the scientists' letter.

KOSHAROVSKY: *You didn't seem to have any special unpleasantness.*

KHAZANOV: Well, yes I did—there were all kinds of interrogations!

Mikhail Chlenov, a veteran of the movement, a humanitarian to the marrow, with a very broad cultural horizon, possessed excellent mastery of Hebrew, English, German, Indonesian, and several other languages. An elite Hebrew teacher since 1972, he proved himself during the preparations for the symposium on Jewish culture in 1976. Chlenov formulated the ideas of the legalist direction in the development of Jewish culture, in which context he organized a historical-ethnographic commission in 1980 and brought together a group of academics who dealt with Judaica in the journal *Sovetish heymland*. He also continued his work in the Institute of Ethnography of the Academy of Sciences. While taking part actively in the spiritual life of the refusenik community, he himself did not apply to leave because of family circumstances.

Chlenov reflected on the gravity of the endeavor in which he participated:[20]

KOSHAROVSKY: *Membership in Mashka entailed serious risks. It combined all the attributes of an underground on an organizational level and rather intensive open activity for each person individually.*

CHLENOV: That's true in principle, but it was not a silly demonstrative underground composed of kids who had read brochures about the Bolshevik underground in 1917. We had mature people, although, of course, Mashka was complex and so were the times. But it was one of the most interesting things in my generally interesting life.

KOSHAROVSKY: *What did you see as your role in Mashka?*

CHLENOV: For me, it was a natural continuation of what I had been doing for thirteen years. I saw myself as one of its political leaders, a person who deals with strategic planning and analysis and takes part in decision-making. Mashka was an important school for me in light of what followed. To a large degree, I am obligated to Mashka for my becoming a political leader of Soviet Jewry at the end of the 1980s to the beginning of the 1990s. It was my first real school of leadership training. Before that, I had directed some scientific expeditions but that was something entirely different. Mashka was a colossal school, very successful, and I am grateful to you for inviting me into it. To my mind, you made the right decision. Moreover, after your departure, I took the structure that you had created and built the Vaad upon it.

When Sasha Kholmyansky was arrested, we brought his older brother Misha into the group, and after that, you brought in Kislik. Deep into perestroika, you introduced Smukler as editor in chief and publisher of the *Herald*.[21] After your departure, I headed Mashka. That was the second Mashka. Out of the second Mashka arose the Vaad,[22] the third Mashka.

Viktor Fulmakht was part of Mashka from the very beginning. He had already been participating for a long time in refusenik undertakings, dealt with samizdat, and was an editor of the Russian-language journals *Nash ivrit* (Our Hebrew), *Evrei v sovremennom mire* (Jews in the Contemporary World), and *Magid* (Hebrew for Storyteller). His exceptional communication skills helped him to contact various refusenik groups easily. Like Chlenov, he had not applied to leave and still possessed significant reserves of buoyancy. Fulmakht participated, as did a few others, in the preliminary discussion about Mashka.

Fulmakht recalled his ties to the group:[23]

KOSHAROVSKY: *Vitia, did you work with Sasha Kholmyansky?*

FULMAKHT: My task was to supply products for the channels that he developed. Later on, out-of-towners whom he drew in used to come directly to me and take what they needed. The "traffic" through my apartment became so intensive that I began to organize warehouses at other people's places.

KOSHAROVSKY: *You and I used to meet rather frequently.*

FULMAKHT: Yes, and the idea of transforming our gathering into something more organized occurred simultaneously to three people: you, Mika, and me. We began to discuss it together and concluded that it would be a good idea to meet more or less regularly: there was always something to discuss and matters to coordinate.

KOSHAROVSKY: *I discussed the idea with several other people. As you recall, there were eight people in the first Mashka. What did you see as its purpose?*

FULMAKHT: Thanks principally to you, Mashka played an important role as a representative group. Foreigners, of course, associated with whomever they wanted to associate. Nevertheless, our group produced the impression of an organization capable of discussing and comprehending serious matters, elaborating a collective opinion on important issues, composing documents, and organizing people. We dealt with politics, and Mashka turned into a political organ. Our dealings educated us and imparted confidence. Another virtue of our group was that it was linked to the Jewish "masses." We taught, disseminated material, were connected to the youth and out-of-towners, and were in the thick of events. It was a first-class solution for that period, when other variants of natural leaders that arose in various contexts were neutralized.

KOSHAROVSKY: *In the 1980s it was already impossible to do the things that Prestin and Abramovich did in the second half of the 1970s.*

FULMAKHT: It was the next stage of the movement: from individual charismatic leaders to a more compact group with connections and opportunities, capable of working together.

One of the most important functions of Mashka was the equitable distribution of funds and material resources among the various directions of activity. Natalia Khasin took care of aid to Prisoners of Zion and members of their families; a circle of people helped her in her work. Kosharovsky maintained a separate working channel of communication with her. This direction had priority for financing. The financing of samizdat was handled via Fulmakht and Mushinsky, who became a member of Mashka in 1988. Emergency help to refuseniks who experienced misfortune was extended via all members of Mashka. Igor Gurvich and Slava Shifrin dealt with aid to kindergartens.

The Cities Project was not discussed at Mashka nor was the group involved in its financing. The centralized mechanism for receiving financial means was also concealed from Mashka. Large sums generally came from underground Georgian or Bukharan millionaires who sympathized with the movement. In that way, some of them helped their relatives in Israel, who received the equivalent in shekels of the sums that had been transferred to the Mashka group. Because the members of Mashka were not personally acquainted with the underground millionaires and both sides wanted to avoid failure in such a sensitive sphere, the process was rather complex. Fortunately, these delicate missions usually—although not always—proceeded smoothly.

Mashka quickly became the most informed and influential group in the movement, maintaining this status until emigration became completely free. It was conspiratorial as a group but each participant was a relatively well-known and influential person in the movement. In the most difficult times, it succeeded in competently analyzing and representing the situation, and in coordinating refusenik activity. The steadfastness and courage of refuseniks and activists stimulated the activity of the overseas movement in support of Soviet Jewry. With the general liberalization in the Gorbachev period and the emigration of refuseniks, a second Mashka was formed under Mikhail Chlenov's leadership that was practically legal and then a third: the Vaad.

Perestroika and the Jewish National Movement

Konstantin Chernenko, the general secretary of the CPSU Central Committee and the last of the faceless Kremlin elders who ruled the USSR and the Socialist camp in its waning years, died on March 10, 1985, at the age of seventy-three. Soviet society welcomed the sight of the young, energetic Gorbachev, a person capable of walking normally and speaking without a prompt. At last, it seemed, the Soviet public need not be ashamed of its leader.

Yet, at the time of Gorbachev's accession, the country was already in a state of deep stagnation. The planned economy was on the skids, consumer goods were in scarce supply, and the store shelves were empty. When he came to power, Gorbachev did not intend to dismantle the Communist system. A party functionary from the agricultural Stavropol region, he himself had been nurtured by this system, into which it seemed he intended to breathe new life. Under Gorbachev, new terms entered the Communist lexicon: "speeding up," "new thinking," "restructuring" (perestroika), and "openness" (glasnost). These attractive slogans were at odds with the fossilized Party-government apparatus and its continued control over all facets of Soviet society. Gorbachev came to power after the most difficult and gloomy period of the Jewish national struggle. The refuseniks at first reacted skeptically to the perestroika rhetoric. They had already seen waves of détente followed by waves of repressions. Their skepticism was heightened by the lack of change in the situation as a whole during the first years of Gorbachev's rule: emigration remained at the minimal level, activists continued to sit in prisons and new ones were arrested, and the movement continued its campaign to leave the country. Concerned primarily with accelerating the country's economic development and halting the arms race, Gorbachev was not interested in Jewish issues and Jewish emigration. In 1986, 904 people emigrated; anti-Zionist and anti-Jewish material still appeared in the media; arrests of activists continued; and the Anti-Zionist Committee of the Soviet Public continued its activity.[24]

However, it seemed that Gorbachev thought that excessive political repressions were holding back popular initiatives. A handful of developments fostered the sense that deep stirrings in the Soviet system were beginning to affect the sphere of human rights: Sharansky's early release from prison on February 11, 1986, and attempts by the government to establish a direct dialogue with activists appeared to lend more weight to the rhetoric of perestroika. The release of Andrei Sakharov from exile in Gorky on December 16, 1986, seemed to signal a new trend. Gorbachev personally phoned Sakharov and informed him that he and his wife, Elena Bonner, were free to return to Moscow.[25] In December 1986, however, when Deputy Foreign Minister Anatoly Kovalev proposed holding a conference on humanitarian issues in Moscow,[26] the refuseniks gave it the cold shoulder. At the time, the Jewish activists did not believe in the seriousness of Gorbachev's proclamations and thought that it would be a blatant mockery of common sense to discuss human rights issues in Moscow. After all, hundreds of thousands of citizens were not allowed to emigrate, Hebrew teachers were sitting in prisons on trumped-up charges, and students who had been expelled from institutions of higher learning, scientists, and activists were struggling for the right to leave.

Starting in January 1987, the rising tide of perestroika activity began to affect refuseniks. On January 16 Yuri Kashlev, head of the department on humanitarian and cultural issues in the Foreign Ministry, declared that the USSR had begun an intensive review of the sentences of prisoners who had been arrested for anti-Soviet activity. He also spoke about the introduction of a more liberal definition of familial ties that would lead to a sharp increase in the number of visas issued in the framework of family reunification.[27] On February 10, 1987, Gennady Gerasimov, spokesperson for the Foreign Ministry, announced that 140 to 150 prisoners had been pardoned. The well-known human rights activist Yuri Shikhanovich had been released on February 6, 1987. On February 20 Yosif Begun, who was serving his third sentence, was released, followed by Vladimir Albrekht and Zakhar Zunshain (March 6), Yosif Berenshtein (March 16), Vladimir Lifshits (March 17), Valery Senderov (March 18), Yakov Levin and Mark Nepomniashchy (March 19), Leonid Volvovsky (March 20), Yuli Edelstein (May 5), and others. They were released early, and for activists and their supporters, the release of every Prisoner of Zion was a holiday. With their liberation, people in the Jewish national movement began to feel the atmosphere of perestroika. It was a turning point.

On February 12, 1987, the Moscow evening newspaper (*Vechernaia Moskva*) reported that OVIR had begun reviewing refusenik cases and everyone except for refuseniks with real security clearance—Vladimir Slepak, Alexander Lerner, Yuli Kosharovsky, Yulian Khasin, Natasha Khasin, Valery Soifer, Lev Sud, and Yakov Rakhlenko—would receive exit visas.

The Jewish national movement did not hesitate to take advantage of the signs of the unfolding thaw. New refusenik groups, seminars, and initiatives in the sphere of Jewish culture appeared. Contacts with Western public and political figures rose to a new level. The legalist wing of the movement acted more assertively.

Along with the upswing in perestroika processes, Gorbachev's popularity in the West kept rising. Jamming of Voice of America broadcasts in Russian ceased in May 1987.[28] Exchanges of opinion at various levels and reciprocal visits by delegations occurred more frequently as did the number of international meetings and summits.

In advance of state visits and summits, Jewish circles in the West provided Western leaders with up-to-date information about the situation of Soviet Jewry and specific requests about refuseniks. Acutely aware of the Western media's heightened interest in their problems, activists inside the Soviet Union also intensified their activity on the eve of and during those visits. British Prime Minister Margaret Thatcher and Foreign Secretary

Geoffrey Howe were scheduled to visit Moscow from March 27 to April 1, 1987. Hanna and Lev Elbert had begun a hunger strike on March 5. Lev had been released from prison about three years earlier but now his son Karmi was called up to the army. The Elberts conducted a hunger strike for forty-five days until the regime backed down.[29]

On March 19, 1987, the Moscow refusenik Leonid Iusefovich began a hunger strike in protest against the refusal to give his family an exit visa. He continued it for forty-two days, until he received a promise from the authorities to review his case.[30]

On March 23, 1987, eight Leningrad refuseniks held a demonstration across from the Party's municipal committee at Smolny. The participants, who held posters saying "Let my people go!" and "Let us go to Israel," were Roald Zelichenok, Ida and Aba Taratuta, Boris Lokshin, Mikhail Beizer, Lia Shapiro, Inna Rozansky-Lobovikov, and Elena Keis-Kuna. Before the demonstration, they sent a letter to Gorbachev. The effect of the new trends could be seen in the course of the demonstration: it lasted for about two hours, after which the demonstrators were invited to meet with a provincial party committee secretary, two men from the KGB, and an official from OVIR. Two days later, Beizer received permission to leave.[31]

On March 24 fifty Moscow refuseniks went to the Presidium of the Supreme Soviet with a petition signed by 120 activists and former Prisoners of Zion calling for a review of the cases of Aleksei Magarik and Yuli Edelstein.[32]

On the day of Thatcher's arrival, Vladimir and Maria Slepak, long-time refuseniks and former Prisoners of Zion, began a hunger strike to mark seventeen years of their refusal, while thirty Moscow refuseniks held a demonstration in the center of Moscow. The police did not interfere nor did they interfere when the demonstrators assembled again on the next day. On the last day of the visit, April 1, Thatcher and Howe invited the refuseniks Inna and Yosif Begun and the wife of Professor Alexander Ioffe, Roza Ioffe, to breakfast. An invitation was also sent to Ida Nudel but it "got stuck" in the mail and did not arrive.[33]

French Prime Minister Jacques Chirac arrived in Moscow on an official visit on May 16, 1987. In the course of governmental meetings, he handed Soviet authorities a list of refuseniks with a request to expedite their emigration. On the first day of his visit, Chirac held a meeting in the embassy with fifteen leading refuseniks, including Ida Nudel, Vladimir Slepak, Viktor Brailovsky, and Yuli Edelstein.[34]

On December 1, 1987, Australian Prime Minister Robert Hawke arrived in Moscow for an official visit. On the next day he met with a large group of refuseniks in the embassy building, informing them about his meetings with Gorbachev and Shevardnadze. The correspondents at the meeting interviewed the refuseniks. Thanks to the influence of the refuseniks' longtime friend Isi Leibler, the Australian embassy always welcomed the refuseniks warmly and respectfully.

Among other events staged prior to the visits of Western leaders, on March 7, 1987, the eve of International Women's Day, one hundred refusenik women from various Soviet cities, including Mara Balashinsky, Inna Uspensky, and Elena Dubiansky (from Moscow); Ida Taratuta and Galina Zelichenok (Leningrad); Karmela Rais (Vilnius); and Polina Paritsky (Kharkov) started a three-day hunger strike in order to draw attention to the situation of women refuseniks.[35] On March 8 another two hundred women from seven cities joined them.[36]

At the third Reagan-Gorbachev summit, scheduled to take place in Washington from December 7 to 10, 1987, a treaty on the reduction of medium- and short-range missiles was to be signed. As usual, the refuseniks intensified their activity in advance of and during the summit, conducting various protest acts, some of which met harsh responses from the police and the KGB.

An initiative group for conducting a series of demonstrations timed for the summit meeting held a press conference on November 4, 1987, at the apartment of Yulia Ratner. On November 23, in a letter to the CPSU Central Committee, one hundred individuals who had received refusals on grounds of secrecy described their vain attempts at dialogue with the Presidium of the Supreme Soviet and the CPSU Central Committee. The refuseniks declared their intention to start a hunger strike on December 6 and to continue it throughout the duration of the summit.[37] On December 6, thirteen Leningrad families demonstrated at the Palace Square. On the same day, a large number of refuseniks demonstrated in Moscow at Smolensk Square opposite the towering Foreign Ministry building. Some 120 refuseniks made it to the square. A few dozen were detained on the way, and many others were prevented from leaving their apartments. In order to obstruct that demonstration on the day before the summit, the regime filled Smolensk Square with an official demonstration for peace.

The refuseniks' activity received broad coverage in the Western press, and, of course, it was reported to Gorbachev on the eve of his visit to the United States. In an interview with NBC correspondent Tom Brokaw, Gorbachev spoke brusquely about emigration from the Soviet Union, terming it a "brain drain." He also declared that refuseniks who had access to state or military secrets could not leave the USSR.[38]

The following summit, which took place in Moscow from May 29 to June 2, 1988, made an even greater impression on the Soviet leadership and society. The summit was very effective. The treaty on the limitation of medium- and short-range missiles was signed. The withdrawal from Afghanistan, a timetable for which was agreed upon in late 1987, was well under way. The refuseniks, of course, utilized the visit to increase pressure on the regime. Those who regularly organized demonstrations every Thursday announced that during the summit they would demonstrate daily. Various groups carried out acts of protest near the Lenin Library, across from OVIR, at the Foreign Ministry, and even on Red Square. The posters read "KGB and OVIR—It's Time for Destalinization" and "Refusal is Sabotage Against Détente." The women carried out a long hunger strike under the slogan "For Peace without Refusals." Western correspondents followed events on the spot and were not hindered this time.

Personal Recollections: During the 1988 Summit

KOSHAROVSKY: A significant event during the summit, unthinkable in earlier times, was an official reception at the American ambassador's residence at Spaso House for Jewish activists, dissidents, and religious figures. Two weeks before the meeting, I was asked by the US embassy to speak on behalf of the Jewish national movement.

I can picture the surreal scene in my memory: The normally congested ring road circling Moscow was empty as Soviet buses transported us to the residence of the American ambassador under Soviet police escort. Large round tables seating ten people were set up in the roomy hall—a member of the American group and representatives of the refuseniks, democratic rights activists, and one of the Soviet Union's Christian confessions at each table. My wife and I sat at a table at which George Schultz presided. One side of the hall was given over to journalists with their photo and video cameras. First, Sergei Kovalev, one of the editors of the *Khronika tekushchikh sobytii* (Chronicle of Current Events), who had been imprisoned earlier for seven years, spoke on behalf of the democratic rights activists. He said that the prisons still contained many political prisoners who had had the courage to state openly a number of truths that had by this time been publicly acknowledged. He pointed out that the present society had inherited a ruined economy, that lies permeated official information, and that society lacked positive ideals. He disputed the wisdom of the idea that the very same structures that formerly carried out repressions were supposed to enact reforms. Noting that the course of change was unstable, Kovalev said that the amelioration of the situation could be reversed, which would be a tragic outcome.

I pointed out that the contemporary leadership willingly condemned former "deviations," but when the Jewish movement activists tried to revive valuable elements from the past that had been destroyed, they came up against resistance: "Thus, while condemning the evil deeds that had been committed earlier, the regime preserves its results," I said. I pointed out that under the guise of glasnost, large editions of anti-Semitic material were being published, that pogromist organizations were developing apace, that more Jews were let out during the Brezhnev period of stagnation than under Gorbachev's more liberal regime, and that more than 80 percent of those refused on grounds of secrecy had lost access to so-called secret information more than ten years ago. At the same time, in statements directed to the West, the regime contended that the maximum period of refusal for reasons of secrecy generally does not exceed five years. I said, "If Mr. Gorbachev wishes to demonstrate new political thinking by deeds and not only by words, he must not limit my people's freedom of movement or their cultural and religious development . . . Life on earth depends on the way the helmsman on the vessel follows holy providence. Your hand, Mr. President, is on the helm of the vessel, and we trust it will be firm."[39]

We were all in a state of euphoria from this surreal experience. As we left, the correspondents pounced on us. I do not remember how many interviews I gave that day, but I had the feeling that either we would receive permission to leave or I would sit in prison for a long time if perestroika was reversed.

In my memory, the fall of 1988 represents a time of transition to near-open activity. It was also a period of nonstop meetings. One delegation or another would arrive almost every day, and I was the person to call for practically all of them despite the fact that we had set up a rather broad group for briefing foreigners. At the same time, I also had to deal with movement matters, prepare new projects, and part with friends who were leaving. It was difficult and painful. More and more veteran refuseniks left, but I remained with no end in sight.

As perestroika gained momentum, all kinds of anti-Semitic activity began to surface. Sometimes it was independent activity that was rooted in the preceding decades of state and everyday anti-Semitism. More frequently, however, the anti-Semitic organizations were backed by opponents of perestroika in the power and Party organs that wanted to demonstrate to the supporters of liberalization what they could realistically expect to receive as a result of democratic reforms. Whereas up until perestroika, public anti-Semitism had existed under the guise of anti-Zionist publications, now recently formed nationalist groups took the lead. Among them was the Pamiat (Memory) society, which grew out of an organization formed at the end of the 1970s in order to protect and preserve historic Russian monuments. In the 1990s Pamiat turned into an organization that aspired to the role of chief ideologist of the renascent Russian nationalism. It blamed the Jews for all the misfortunes of Russia and the USSR. Similar organizations sprang up in various cities.

Pamiat

Preceding the Pamiat (or Pamyat, Memory) Society, which became active in 1987, a historical association called Vitiaz (Knight) formed in the late 1970s as an informal historical and cultural association. Groups in Moscow and other regions of the Soviet Union loosely connected with this association consolidated over the subsequent years into Pamiat. Pamiat's emphasis on traditional Russian values and Orthodox spirituality included pronounced antagonism toward Jews as the source of Russia's problems. Many Jewish activists believed that the KGB supported or even organized Pamiat's activity.

On May 6, 1987, about four hundred Pamiat members held their first unsanctioned demonstration in the center of Moscow "against the oppression of the Russian people." The oppressors, naturally, were the Jews. On May 20 Pamiat held another demonstration in Moscow.[40] The Zionist movement was understandably repulsed by such activity; ultimately, however, those who advocated aliya would always say that anti-Semitism was inherent in Russian Orthodoxy, the Russian nationalist idea, and the Russian state. It had been that way under the tsar and remained that way in the USSR. Pamiat's dyed-in-the-wool anti-Semitism not only stimulated a rise in pro-emigration feelings but also oriented those Jews toward Israel. The legalist wing of the Jewish movement, which was concerned about the fate of those Jews who did not plan to emigrate, regarded this activity differently. When the situation became threatening, the legalist wing and the Zionist wing worked together. On June 30, 1987, a group of leading Jewish activists turned to Mikhail Gorbachev with a complaint against Pamiat's anti-Semitic actions, but they received no response. The activists then planned a protest demonstration, which they tried to hold on September 14, 1987. The demonstration was dispersed, but in the planning process a group of activists unconnected with refusal was formed. It played an important role in the further development of the legalist direction.

Activation of the Movement

With all the complexity and ambiguity of the processes set in motion by glasnost and perestroika, beginning in 1987 the authorities showed signs of a more tolerant attitude toward Jewish matters as a whole, including Jewish culture, Judaism, and Soviet-Israeli relations.

In the course of perestroika and democratization, Soviet-Israeli relations began to thaw. In 1988, after exchanging diplomatic visits, the Soviets allowed the Israelis to reoccupy their former embassy building, which had been empty since June 1967. This was the next important event on the path to the full restoration of diplomatic relations. The move had great psychological significance for Soviet Jews, who formed long lines in front of the building to receive entry visas to Israel, hitherto received at the Dutch embassy.

The more liberal atmosphere reinvigorated already existing activist groups and stimulated the rise of new ones. Hebrew instruction expanded considerably in both Moscow and other cities. The Cities Project continued its work, and camps to train out-of-towners operated regularly outside of Moscow. The harassment of Hebrew teachers ceased but attempts to register officially as Hebrew teachers remained unsuccessful.

The Poor Relatives group renewed its protest against bogus refusals.[41] On September 19, 1987, twelve refuseniks from that group wrote to the CPSU Central Committee requesting that their relatives either declare their financial claims or sign a waiver of such claims. On October 14, on the eve of a televised broadcast connecting the USSR Supreme Soviet and the US Congress, about forty refuseniks held a meeting near the television center at Ostankino, demanding that the authorities accept other people's testimony about the lack of material claims on the part of those relatives who would remain behind. The police dispersed the demonstration.[42] In support of the same demands, Anna Kholmyansky, wife of the former Prisoner of Zion Alexander Kholmyansky, conducted a hunger strike from October 18 to November 10, 1987.[43] On November 7 about two hundred refuseniks conducted a hunger strike in support of similar demands.[44] An article in the newspaper *Sovetskaia Rossiia* on November 27 defamed the Poor Relatives.[45] Having failed to receive concessions from the authorities, the Poor Relatives began to hold protest demonstrations near the workplaces of their relatives who refused to give them documents certifying the absence of material claims.

Women's groups expanded their activity in this period. Already, at the beginning of 1984, on the basis of kindergartens and refusenik schools, a women's group under the leadership of Alla Praisman had formed. The Jewish activist women fought for the right to renounce Soviet citizenship, organized press conferences, and appealed to international women's organizations for help. The group included Roza Finkelberg, Katia Iusefovich, Olia Ioffe, Ira Gurvich, Zhanna Litvak, Marina Kontsevy, and Zoia Kopelman.

A second woman's group was organized in 1985, when Gorbachev was already in power. Initiated by Yulia Ratner, Ida Nudel, and Nelli Mai, it was called Jewish Women for Emigration and Survival in Refusal. The group fought for the right to emigrate, took care of the needy, compiled lists of refuseniks, and went en masse to the Central Committee and to OVIR with prepared appeals.

A third group, Jewish Women against Refusal (JEWAR), was formed in September 1986, consisting of a consolidated collective of about fifteen women by the end of the year. Additional women from Leningrad, Kharkov, and Vilnius joined the group. It consisted of wives of longtime refuseniks who had been through many trying times and were well acquainted with each other. They and their families were well known abroad. They called themselves a Zionist group and all their members immigrated to Israel.

The women's groups participated in demonstrations, traveled to commemorative sites of mass burials of Nazi victims, and organized seminars. Inna Uspensky recalled this activity:[46]

USPENSKY: We visited Babii Yar three times on the anniversary of the mass shootings there. I remember our placing a wreath there with the inscription "To the unfortunate generation from the generation of hope." We traveled to Minsk, where we were not allowed to conduct a memorial meeting, and to Riga. About a dozen of us used to meet in Moscow every week at one of our apartments for lectures on Jewish subjects and discussions. It was our spiritual refuge. We still remain close and enjoy getting together.

The women formed a group called The Second Generation, which initiated efforts to allow their grown children, who faced the threat of army conscription, to emigrate on their own. They thus tried to break the vicious circle of having their children's future ruined by their parents' status as refuseniks.

Another problem presented itself to the community. The majority of refuseniks lost their jobs and simultaneously the opportunity to receive medical care. In 1984 Leonid Goldfarb, a refusenik doctor, spoke to the Uspenskys about organizing medical aid for the refuseniks. He contacted Western Jewish organizations (the 35s in England and the Union of

Councils for Soviet Jews in America), which quietly began to send medicines, at first only to Moscow and then to Leningrad. In January 1986 Goldfarb emigrated and turned the enterprise over to the Uspenskys.

Igor Uspensky explained the organization of medical care:[47]

USPENSKY: We gradually organized a group of our own doctors, and some non-refuseniks voluntarily helped us. On the one hand, we thus created a database of medicines and sick people and a group of local doctors who were willing to give consultations and, on the other hand, doctors from abroad who were willing to see patients began to visit. They would bring with them the elementary medical equipment needed to carry out a basic examination, and we organized modest reception hours for patients.

In addition to the practical aid, such concern gave moral support to the refuseniks: people understood that others cared about them and were thinking of them. There were many cases in which ill people traveled abroad and upon their arrival were given the necessary medical care.

KOSHAROVSKY: *Did you treat only Muscovites?*

USPENSKY: Out-of-towners also turned to us. In addition, we helped Prisoners of Zion, particularly later ones such as Lyonia Volvovsky, Aleksei Magarik, and others. Their wives would contact us. We gave them vitamins in the guise of candies as it was forbidden to send them medicine.

The Uspenskys also helped democratic rights activists in health matters such as providing necessary medicines to labor camp returnees. In these matters, the Zionist movement did not restrict itself to its own circle.

A new periodical appeared in the movement: the *Informatsionnyi biulleten' po voprosam evreiskoi repatriatsii i kul'tury* (Information Bulletin on Issues of Jewish Repatriation and Culture). In addition to featuring publicistic articles, analytic pieces, and protest letters, the bulletin offered a brief description of events related to the Jewish movement, and it became popular. Presenting information in real time, this bulletin became a reliable source of knowledge about events.

In November 1987 Yosif Begun brought in Alexander Smukler, another young refusenik, to work on the bulletin. For seven years Smukler had been unable to apply for an exit visa because of his parents' refusal to give him the necessary documents. A chess expert, he ran a chess school in the Pioneers youth organization building, which afforded him time to take care of other matters.

Smukler recalled his work on the *Informatsionnyi biulleten'*:[48]

SMUKLER: I tried to maintain a telegraphic style of chronicling. Begun gave money for the bulletin and we printed it, at first by photocopying, but that was expensive and the bulletin was heavy. Later it was done in a centralized way via Mushinsky's Jewish Information Center. That was another service of Mashka. Volodia Mushinsky's work relieved us of a great amount of labor and concerns because everything operated like clockwork with him. At some point Begun found a person who began to produce it on a rotary press.

KOSHAROVSKY: *Were you the editor in chief?*

SMUKLER: Yes, I had already become the editor in chief.

KOSHAROVSKY: *In that position did you become acquainted with the central circle of activists?*

SMUKLER: Yes, but that wasn't my only role. For example, Alia Zonis from Poor Relatives would call to say that they were going to demonstrate, and she would ask whether we could send someone.

KOSHAROVSKY: *Directly over the telephone?*

SMUKLER: Yes. Sometimes they did it on purpose so that the police would detain them while they were on the way in order to draw more public attention to their cause. Later there were people who took the bulletin and began to distribute it in various places. Sometime around July 1987, you invited me to join Mashka and I wound up at the center of many events there.

KOSHAROVSKY: *Were out-of-towners also on the editorial board?*

SMUKLER: Yes. Yosif Iurovsky from Lvov was responsible for dissemination in Western Ukraine and Leonid Govzman from Ivano-Frankovsk helped with collecting information and distributing the bulletin. Yakov Tsukerman—a professional journalist and publisher—dealt with everything concerning Leningrad after Syoma Frumkin's departure. The Muscovite Igor Mirovich joined the editorial board but quickly departed. Once in Israel, he settled in Beersheva and began to send material about his life there. He wrote a column on absorption. Meir Kharev, a mathematician from Baku, distributed the bulletin in Azerbaijan and wrote many items from there. Naturally, Yosif Zisels had an important role in the bulletin. He published a similar bulletin in Ukraine, and we included his material in our bulletin. Then they included our bulletin in theirs and printed and distributed it. In Uzbekistan, Biniamin Biniaminov and his relative Rafik Nektalov set up a network of ulpans and distributed the bulletin. Moreover, several correspondents there wrote for us. Finally, there was Lyonia [Leonid] Raitsen on whom I relied the most in my work. He collected material daily and manned the telephones, which were always ringing. Raitsen had been a Jewish movement activist for many years. Do you remember a tall fellow with a youthful face and a gray head of hair? He remained active under Chlenov. His home telephone number was printed on the cover of the bulletin along with his address.

KOSHAROVSKY: *How many people were on the payroll?*

SMUKLER: Around twenty. The only one who didn't receive a salary was Valia Lidsky. He represented the religious element on the editorial board. He and Vlad Dashevsky provided me with people to verify everything connected with religious canons and traditions. In fact, there were a mass of people around us. Lena [Elena] Roitman was secretary of the editorial board. Valery Sherbaum, whom you introduced to me, was a member of the board. Mozus Truskinovsky replaced Sherbaum when he left. Edik Markov participated very actively on the bulletin; he was on the editorial board, and we gave his telephone number to people in Leningrad. In addition, there were people who dealt directly with organizing, receiving, storing, delivering, and distributing the bulletin. It was the most widely read samizdat publication. Lishkat hakesher actively supported it.

KOSHAROVSKY: *The bulletin ceased publication because you left?*

SMUKLER: Not only because I left but also because in 1991 it was possible to publish everything legally, including Jewish publications. Tankred Golenpolsky then began to publish his newspaper *Evreiskaia gazeta* (The Jewish Newspaper).

Soon after the Moscow Symposium on Secrecy Issues formed, a seminar on legal issues organized by Vladimir Kislik and his wife, Bella

[Gulko], began to operate in Moscow. A group of seven people formed the nucleus, including Evgeny Grechanovsky, Evgeny Liberman, Feliks Kochubievsky, and Gennady Reznikov. The seminar met every week and every two to three weeks held an open meeting, which attracted many people. The seminar was not limited to theoretical issues. The Kisliks were sharp and fearless. They organized consultations next to OVIR, brought legal suits against enterprises and ministries that refused to give written replies concerning the issue of secrecy classification, organized joint visits to official reception rooms, and so forth. The seminar, which met at their apartment, quickly became popular among refuseniks. Activists from other cities often came to the seminar sessions; visitors also included foreign guests and representatives of international human rights organizations. A few months after the start of the seminar, Kosharovsky invited Vladimir Kislik to participate in the work of Mashka.

Kislik recalled his activity:[49]

KOSHAROVSKY: *I recall that you demanded that enterprises give a written justification for the reason that people in their employ spent many years in refusal on grounds of secrecy.*

KISLIK: Completely true.

KOSHAROVSKY: *Bella managed to receive an official document stating that her ministry had no secrecy claims in her case; that is, the KGB was lying all the time.*

KISLIK: She not only received it, but she also organized a group of about thirty people from her Radio Industry Ministry. They went there and demanded papers from the ministry on the existence of a secrecy classification. She obtained the power of attorney from many people and undertook about thirty suits against that ministry and other ministries that refused to give them a written reply. Bella and her friends organized consultations near the Moscow OVIR. They set up a little table and chair near OVIR, where they sat and advised people. We submitted a personal suit for each person refused on secrecy grounds and sought a Western lawyer to represent that individual. Irwin Cotler from Canada was particularly helpful. We ultimately found Western lawyers for a large number of refuseniks. We immediately sent them information on Bella's suits and other documents and initiated a correspondence. That activity continued up until our departure in March 1989. Baptists, Jehovah's Witnesses, even a Ukrainian Catholic bishop came to us for advice.

The Society for Friendship and Cultural Ties with Israel held its founding meeting on July 10, 1988. About seventy people attended, including participants from Leningrad, Vilnius, Kiev, Baku, Derbent, Liubertsy (near Moscow), Tbilisi, and Moscow. As prescribed by law, the founding meeting adopted a charter and program and formed a council and a presidium, after which documents were sent for registration to the Council of Ministers and the USSR Supreme Soviet. The presidium included Vladimir Dashevsky, Viktor Koretsky, Yuli Kosharovsky, Eduard Markov, Vladimir Meshkov, Alexander Ostrovsky, Semyon Frumkin, Alexander Smukler, and Nelli Shpeizman. Koretsky served as secretary of the society.

The society issued a press release stating that it would work toward the reestablishment of full diplomatic relations between the two countries and familiarize the Soviet people with the language, history, culture, and life of the State of Israel and would also seek to facilitate an objective presentation of events in Israel on the part of the Soviet media.[50] After waiting the legally permitted time of two months, the society undertook to clarify the fate of its application to register. It learned that the application had been sent to the Union of Soviet Friendship Societies with Foreign Countries [known by its Russian acronym as SSOD]. When members of the society's governing board arrived there, they tried to convince us not to form a society independently, but to wait until the SSOD established it. We refused. Our interlocutor, Mr. Ivanov, then explained to us that the SSOD does not register societies but only creates them within the Union, reserving for itself all the legal and financial rights.

We, naturally, continued to operate even without the formal registration since circumstances were relatively favorable. Our Soviet-Israel Friendship Society began to issue a *Vestnik obshchestva* (Herald of the Society). On September 21, 1988, the society opened a library of more than five hundred books at the apartment of Viktor Koretsky. On October 11 a library of audio recordings was opened.[51] The two libraries enjoyed considerable popularity among Moscow Jews. Lectures and discussions were regularly held there. The society also organized concerts of performers from the United States and Israel.

On September 18, 1988, about sixty Hebrew teachers from Moscow, Leningrad, Kiev, Rostov, Baku, Chernovtsy, Zaporozhie, and Gorky announced the founding of a union of Hebrew teachers called Igud Hamorim (Hebrew for "Teachers' Union"). The participants elected three cochairmen: Lev Gorodetsky, Avigdor Levit, and Evgeny Voronov. Teachers from many cities were involved in its founding. The Union published *Vestnik "Igud morim"* (Herald of the Igud Hamorim). Subsequently, about thirty lectures were given on topics related to Hebrew instruction and to Jewish culture.

On August 1–2, 1989, thirty-five activists representing Jewish communities from fifteen cities held a founding meeting of the Irgun Tsioni (Zionist Organization). Lev Gorodetsky from Moscow and Mark Mishne from Baku were elected to the posts of president and vice-president, respectively. A year and a half earlier, it would have been impossible to imagine the founding of such an organization. The very word *Zionism* had negative connotations in the USSR, and it was impossible to mention it without attaching a string of derogatory epithets; publishing a printed organ of a Zionist organization was all the more impossible.

Lev Gorodetsky talked about the founding of the Irgun Tsioni:[52]

GORODETSKY: I formed it at my own initiative. We very much wanted to make contact with the WZO (World Zionist Organization) and to join it. I had already met Simcha Dinitz, the chairman of the WZO and head of the Jewish Agency, and contact with him was good. He phoned us directly at the conference and congratulated us on the founding. This contrasted greatly with the rejection that followed. At first, I was told that we needed a federation of Zionist organizations of the USSR in order to join the WZO. At the end of November 1990 we specially established such a federation in order to join the WZO but, presenting all kinds of objections, they still did not accept us. Incidentally, we were the first in the Soviet Union who tried to join the WZO.

KOSHAROVSKY: *The Vaad also tried.*

GORODETSKY: That was after us. Don't forget that the Vaad was a community organization whereas we were a Zionist one. Later, I was told it was personal because I was too far to the right for them. In May 1989 I had set up a branch of Beitar, which, as you know, is affiliated with the Likud Party. For Dinitz, a member of the left-center Labor Party, this was unacceptable.

KOSHAROVSKY: *Was membership in the Irgun Tsioni individual or collective?*

GORODETSKY: Individual. At one point, we had about eight hundred applications for membership.

KOSHAROVSKY: *As I recall, you had a publication.*

GORODETSKY: Yes. We called it *Kol Tsion* (The Voice of Zion).

In 1987 the number of exit visas issued climbed upward. Whereas 904 people left in all of 1986, in 1987 the number reached 8,155—eight times greater.[53] In that year the number of Prisoners of Zion and longtime refuseniks who were given exit permits also increased, among them Ida Nudel, Yuli Edelstein, Yosif Begun, Viktor Brailovsky, Vladimir Lifshits, Lev Elbert, and Vladimir and Maria Slepak, as well as Pavel Abramovich, Alexander Ioffe, and Yulia Ratner. The regime tried to expedite their departure in order to create an atmosphere of real progress for the Washington summit, which took place December 7–10, 1988. Immediately after the summit, Professor Alexander Lerner received a visa. The departure of longtime refuseniks only added fuel to the fire. Those who had been refused on grounds of secrecy began to demand written replies indicating what, in fact, was restraining them: their enterprise, the ministry, the KGB, or other power structures. If they managed to receive a reply, they tried by legal means to clarify whether the secrecy restrictions were justified. They also demanded that detention on secrecy grounds be restricted to a maximum length of five years. The Second Generation group, with their parents' support, worked to enable the independent emigration of children whose parents were refused on secrecy grounds or for other reasons. Activists demanded more simplified procedures for assembling and submitting documents for emigration and the adoption of procedures used in other countries that had signed the Helsinki Accords. They also criticized the law on emigration adopted by the Supreme Soviet.[54]

The year 1988 represented a watershed. Significant, if not decisive, progress was achieved in several parallel spheres. The liberalization of emigration policy created the feeling that by the end of the year, emigration would become practically free. At the same time, the so-called "drop-out" (neshira) rate, representing those who left the Soviet Union but chose destinations other than Israel, reached 90 percent. The majority of drop-outs went to the United States, causing a strain there.

The laws concerning the entry of Soviet Jews into the United States were changed at the legislative level. On October 1, 1989, Congress adopted the Lautenberg-Spector Amendment. It redefined the categories of Soviet citizens who had the right to immigrate to the United States with the status of a refugee (Jews, Evangelical Christians, and members of the Ukrainian Catholic and Ukrainian Autocephalous Orthodox Church) and determined new immigration rules. For entry into the United States, it was now necessary to complete a complicated process in the US embassy in Moscow. Only applications of those who had close relatives in the United States were considered. Those who possessed entry visas to Israel issued after that date were no longer considered refugees. The US Congress determined the entry quotas on an annual basis. In 1990 forty thousand Jewish refugees were allowed to enter the United States.[55] At the same time, thanks to changes in procedures for processing immigration to Israel, the number of departures on Israeli visas continued to climb in 1989 to reach more than seventy thousand for the year.[56]

At the end of 1989, emigration became practically free. Frightened by the rampage of blatant public anti-Semitism, the deteriorating living conditions, and the growth of social and interethnic tension, Jews streamed to OVIR. The United States limited the number of potential immigrants by quotas and rules. The number leaving for Israel was limited only by the work capacity of the Moscow customs and OVIR. The majority of Soviet Jews at that time would have preferred to go to the United States, but it was now necessary to have a first-degree relative there, and, even in that case, the waiting period could take years. Not willing to remain for that long a time in the chaotic USSR, where fear of pogroms was intensifying, people chose Israel as the most acceptable alternative. The collapse of the Soviet Union only reinforced this tendency. The basic Zionist goal of directing Soviet Jewry to Israel was thus met.

Legalizing Jewish Life in the Soviet Union and Organizing Mass Aliya

The overwhelming majority of veterans of the Jewish national revival movement left the USSR in those years, but the movement did not die out. New activists appeared: perestroika Jews who believed in Mikhail Gorbachev and the possibility of reforming the USSR. A significant number of Jews remained who were for various reasons unable or unwilling to leave, among them even some veterans of the movement, who assured the ideological continuity during the new stage. While continuing to deal with emigration, the movement began to exert greater effort to reinforce a Jewish national identity, to revive national culture and Jewish communal life, and to fight anti-Semitism in the USSR and post-Soviet Russia.

The revival of national culture was always an important component of the movement's program. With the start of the perestroika period, this activity acquired an additional powerful stimulus. Seminars more frequently featured lectures on national topics. Hebrew teachers, women's groups, Poor Relatives, and the Second Generation also began to organize lectures and discussions on historical and religious subjects. The "Ovrazhki" joint trips out of town, which had been prohibited since 1980, were revived. Samizdat activity intensified, new periodicals appeared, and a Jewish historical society and Jewish library began to operate. Commemoration of Jews murdered by the Nazis at places such as Minsk (Belarus), Paneriai (Lithuania), and Babii Yar outside of Kiev evolved on a massive scale. The police did not interfere in such activities. Educational activity also increased.

A legalist wing, whose goal was a cultural revival, began to form as an independent direction separate from the traditional movement activity, which strove primarily to stimulate and serve aliya to Israel. With the departure of almost all the longtime refuseniks in 1987–88, the composition of the movement began to change rapidly. Many new people appeared, inspired by the opportunities of perestroika and not worn down by lengthy opposition to the regime. New cultural institutions developed that were oriented not so much toward the refusenik community as toward those Jews who decided to remain in the USSR. Of course the movement's cultural programs were always designed to acquaint all interested persons with the language, history, culture, and traditions of the Jewish people. Earlier, however, all national-Jewish initiatives had been forbidden and provoked harassment, and only people who transgressed the official social directives—dissidents, Zionists, and prospective emigrants—dared to pursue them.

Already in the early 1970s, several Zionist movement activists (Vladimir Prestin, Pavel Abramovich, Yosif Begun, Veniamin Fain, Semyon Kushner, Tsilia Raitburd, Ilia Essas, and others) acknowledged the intrinsic value of acquainting people with the national culture and tradition independently of the aliya struggle. As mentioned earlier, some people even expressed an opinion that was very unpopular at the time that, in order to develop and disseminate national culture, it was necessary to cooperate with the regime or else nothing serious would come of it. The most prominent and consistent advocate of that direction was Mikhail Chlenov, who already considered himself a legalist-kulturnik in the period leading up to the 1976 symposium. Chlenov assumed that Soviet Jews could live in the USSR as a normal community, and he strove to make that happen.

The legalist direction's first real test of strength was the formation of the Historical-Ethnographic Commission in 1981 at the initiative of ethnographers Mikhail Chlenov and Igor Krupnik.

Mark Kupovetsky talked about the commission, of which he was an active member:[57]

KUPOVETSKY: Formally, the commission was established under the auspices of the Geographical Society of the Academy of Sciences. Igor Krupnik and Mikhail Chlenov were directing the Society's Ethnographic Commission and a circle of future participants of our Historical-Ethnographic Commission was formed within that commission. People who were interested in Jewish topics used to come to the lectures. Because Krupnik did not always manage to arrange for reports about Jews, they decided to follow Velvl Chernin's suggestion and go to Aron Vergelis, editor in chief of

Sovetish heymland, where Chernin was working. Vergelis promised them a room for meetings and lectures, and the possibility of publications. For three months he honestly honored his promise: we managed to hold three sessions there and attract an audience. More than a hundred people, including refuseniks, attended the third lecture. Evidently, Vergelis was called on the carpet by the higher-ups, and he canceled the lecture activity, although we were able to meet there in a small format a few times. We then continued our meetings in private apartments in the framework of an ordinary seminar. Normally, about ten people would get together, but the general number of participants was double that number.

KOSHAROVSKY: *What was the basic direction of the commission's activity?*

KUPOVETSKY: When a national movement arises, some group within it invariably tries to formulate national goals. Chlenov tried to formulate and promote his program of cultural autonomy.

The commission would meet two to three times a month at various apartments. Under the aegis of the Geographical Society, the commission organized sessions with reports and carried out expeditions. Others who took part in the commission's activity included the prominent ethnographer Professor Anatoly Khazanov, the journalist Alexander Razgon, and leading movement activist Viktor Fulmakht. The ethnographers Galina Starovoitov and Natalia Iukhnev along with Mikhail Beizer, who led a historical seminar, would arrive from Leningrad. Far from all participants shared Chlenov's autonomist views and, therefore, the meetings frequently aroused productive discussions. Interruptions in the commission's activity began in 1987, and in the summer it ceased to operate.

The establishment in Moscow of the semiofficial Jewish Historical Society was announced on November 4, 1987. Its founders were the historian Valery Engel and journalist Alexander Razgon, both of whom were linked to the Jewish movement. Razgon was a refusenik while Engel had been in contact with refuseniks for several years and had studied and taught Hebrew. From the beginning, the JHS was conceived of as a legal institution working in contact with the authorities. The Historical Society, in a certain sense, filled the niche left by the Historical-Ethnographic Commission.

The announcement about the establishment of the society spoke about the formation and future development of an academic school for the study of Jewish history and about spreading historical knowledge of the Jewish people. In light of the stepped-up activity of anti-Semitic nationalistic groups that were spreading monstrous disinformation about the Jews, the dissemination of accurate historical information was most urgent. Under the society's auspices, public lecture courses and courses for teachers on Jewish history and culture were organized. Society members would travel to other cities to aid local Jewish groups in organizing cultural life.

Mark Kupovetsky answered a question about the Jewish Historical Society:[58]

KOSHAROVSKY: *Was the Jewish Historical Society the inheritor of the Historical-Ethnographic Commission?*

KUPOVETSKY: No, other people were involved: Valery Engel, Evgeny Satanovsky, and Leonid Praisman. But they, so to speak, took the baton. At first I took a cautious view of the society. In April 1989, however, Engel proposed that I participate in their work. He said that it was possible officially to register the society and perhaps there were some positions available. He actually succeeded in registering it. In 1990 it was transformed into the Association of Judaica and Jewish Culture, and it already became an Israeli project. It had a unit called the Research Center, of which I was the director. Applications for grants were accepted. In 1991 [the Israeli historian] Shaul Stampfer came to me and proposed collaborating to create a research-based educational structure. I conceived of a "Hebrew University" in Moscow, under whose roof I brought everyone who remained, plus Alexander Militarev and Rashid Kaplanov, who had headed the Historical Society, which by that time was no longer functioning.

The Hebrew University was a project of [Rabbi Adin] Steinsaltz. I see the Historical-Ethnographic Commission's value primarily in its effort to elaborate a strategy for the national movement. It was not directly related to culture. It was a successful attempt of many years of intellectual brainstorming in search of ways to effect a national revival as such. The most varied people were involved in it—Yiddishists, autonomists, and so forth—but they failed to reach any agreement. Mika Chlenov was an excellent moderator. He told us about dialogues that he conducted with you, but we viewed you as a pure species of practical Zionism, and we were seeking variations. A lot was accomplished in the framework of these discussions. Mika polished his plans. We stated our objections and he reworked his ideas.

On September 13, 1987, the first independent Jewish library was opened in a private apartment. Yosif Begun, who had received an exit visa a few days before the opening, played a major role in the establishment of this library. An indefatigable warrior for the legalization of Jewish culture, Begun had long harbored the idea for a library. He started to realize it soon after his early release from his third imprisonment, in February 1987. Although refuseniks possessed a considerable number of useful books, which it was possible to collect, there was no location for them or a suitable person willing to take the risk of possible reprisals for his involvement in the project.

After several months of searching, Begun found Yuri Sokol, a recently retired army officer. As a member of the Communist Party, Sokol endured much unpleasantness for his role in the creation of the library, but he did not yield to the pressure. The library began to be built in Yuri and Liuba Sokol's apartment on the basis of donated books and furniture. Alexander Smukler and Abram Torpusman helped organize the library.[59] Smukler and Torpusman set up a library council, and Smukler served as its executive secretary until he left the Soviet Union in 1991. After Smukler's departure, Leonid Roitman took over operations, and the library continued to function until the mid-1990s.[60] The library hosted lectures, in particular about the Jews' participation in World War II and their role in the creation of the Red Army, and people gathered to celebrate Jewish holidays there.

In addition, on January 24, 1988, a Jewish museum was opened in the home of Irina Rozenberg in Moscow. On April 8 the municipal council offered the independent Jewish Museum a location in a cellar near the Polezhaevskaia metro station.[61] While the preparations were under way at the building, the museum operated at Irina Rozenberg's apartment and attracted visitors.

The Jewish Cultural Association (JCA) was conceived as a countrywide legal organization for facilitating the development of the national culture of Soviet Jews. The charter carefully recorded the goals and tasks, rights and obligations of members, its structure and governing board, registration and financing. The association's tasks included establishing clubs and museums; organizing conferences, exhibitions, festivals, lectures, and concerts; arranging for studying the national language and history; conducting academic research, and scientific and folklore expeditions; preserving and restoring monuments; preparing its own publication and facilitating other publications; setting up a library; and much more. In other words, the JCA was conceived on a broad scale.

The founding congress of the JCA was scheduled for May 15, 1988. The organizing group, which included Mikhail Chlenov, Roman Spektor, Evgeny Satanovsky, Velvl Chernin, and Mark Batunsky, first went to the Soviet Culture Fund and to the CPSU Central Committee, where, according to the group members, the establishment of the association was considered a timely and useful initiative. Press representatives, guests, and 217 founding members from various cities were invited to the founding meeting.

A few days before the designated date, however, the owner of the conference hall that had been rented and paid for by the initiators canceled the deal. The initiative group subsequently found three other places in which to hold the meeting, and in each of them, permission was followed by cancellation within a few hours.[62] A day after the management of the Yakuza Culture House agreed to rent its hall, anti-Semitic leaflets were plastered on the building.[63] The JCA's organizing committee issued a statement for the press condemning the discriminatory attitude toward the Jews.

A founding congress was next scheduled for September of the same year but it encountered similar arbitrary complications caused by the authorities. Finally, a place in Bauman Gardens was rented, five hundred people showed up for the JCA meeting, and it turned out that the rented café was closed for urgent repairs. Then seventy of the prospective association members went to a private apartment and held the founding assembly there—illegally.[64] Mikhail Chlenov was elected president of the organization; his deputy was Roman Spektor, and secretary of the organization was Evgeny Satanovsky. A board of sixteen people was selected, and a charter was reviewed and adopted. The board included prominent Jewish scientists, musicians, artists, and writers from Moscow, Leningrad, Kiev, Tallinn, and elsewhere. The JCA board had to fight for another year for the association's legalization until it was officially recognized and registered on December 10, 1989.

The first international project in the field of Jewish culture was also undertaken in 1988 at the initiative of the vice-president of the World Jewish Congress (WJC), Australian Isi Leibler, a loyal friend of the refuseniks, and Mikhail Gluz, the artistic director of the Jewish Chamber Music Theater (JCMT), established in 1977. During a trip to Moscow, Leibler met with Soviet bureaucrats and Jewish activists to discuss a planned agreement between the WJC and the Soviet Cultural Ministry that would include the introduction of movement activists Mikhail Chlenov, president of the JCA, and Velvl Chernin to the board of the Mikhoels Jewish Cultural Center, and the provision for holding lectures and exhibits there on a regular basis. There was also talk of establishing a library as part of the center. It was assumed that the center would be located in the building of the JCMT. On October 20, 1988, Leibler signed an agreement with Gluz about supplying equipment and musical instruments for the future center. An agreement with the USSR Ministry of Culture was signed on the following day: October 21, 1988, the day of the founding of the Solomon Mikhoels Cultural Center, a first in Soviet history. The formal opening of the center on February 12, 1989, in the JCMT building on Taganka Square was a festive international event. On February 14, an evening in memory of Solomon Mikhoels was organized by JCA Vice-President Roman Spektor in the theater building. More than 1,500 people attended. From February 12 to 22, festivals of Jewish culture were held in Moscow, Leningrad, and Tbilisi. American, Australian, Israeli, and Soviet performers gave joint concerts of Israeli and Jewish songs. More than three thousand people attended those concerts.

The signing of an agreement between the WJC and the Soviet Ministry of Culture about the establishment of the Solomon Mikhoels Jewish Cultural Center had curious consequences. A week after that, a founding meeting was convened for yet another cultural center, but this time for one that was initiated by the authorities. Apparently, in tandem with talks about founding the Mikhoels Center, active discussions took place about establishing a parallel organization with the same goals but under the control of the regime. The Mikhoels Center was harder for the regime to control because it operated on the basis of an agreement with the World Jewish Congress.

A similar approach was frequently adopted later in various places: as soon as some independent cultural association (a society, club, or group) arose in a city, the local Party or municipal authorities would immediately create a parallel group from among their own henchmen. The founding meeting in the building of the Moscow Shalom Jewish Theater was set for October 28, 1988, a week after the signing of the agreement for the establishment of the Mikhoels Center. One hundred of the secretly invited founders met at the Shalom Theater on the Warsaw Highway. Five representatives of the informal Jewish organizations, however, were also in the hall: Chlenov, Kosharovsky, Smukler, Spektor, and Ostrovsky. It was difficult to imagine how the stagnant Anti-Zionist Committee of the Soviet Public would be miraculously transformed into the progressive Shalom Jewish Cultural Society.

The founding meeting resembled a performance that did not follow the planned scenario. The five representatives of informal organizations and Vladimir Zhirinovsky facilitated that turn of events.[65] Zhirinovsky and Ostrovsky harshly criticized the proposed charter. Kosharovsky proposed inserting points into the charter envisaging the establishment in the context of the society of an anti-defamation group and a publication of the society, the *Vestnik* (Herald). He also sharply opposed adding sections in the charter about the struggle against Zionism, saying, "the cultural society should deal with culture and not with politics." Before the start of the voting for board candidates, Ostrovsky suggested that each candidate tell about his activity in the Anti-Zionist Committee—the proposed candidates, indeed, were all "state Jews." Someone proposed including Kosharovsky on the board as the leader of the Hebrew teachers' seminar and the initiator of The Society for Friendship and Cultural Ties with Israel; Roman Spektor, deputy president of the Jewish Cultural

Association; and Gennady Estraikh, a member of the JCA board and a Hebrew teacher. Someone even suggested including Zhirinovsky. After passionate speeches by Efim Gokhberg and Alexander Ostrovsky calling on all those present to vote responsibly, the organizers proposed expanding the composition of the board from twenty to thirty members in order to include all the proposed candidates. The proposal was accepted and thus all the earlier nominated candidates were elected board members of the society.[66]

After the founding of the two official Jewish culture societies, new initiatives in that field multiplied. Under the chairmanship of Yulian Khasin, a club of Jewish bibliophiles was established on October 13, 1988.[67] The official Center for the Study of Judaism, which opened on February 22, 1989, accepted about eighty students, including refuseniks. The center's opening was broadcast on Soviet television. On March 31, 1989, under the chairmanship of the literary critic Tankred Golenpolsky and the Russian writer Sergei Baruzdin, the Association of Activists and Friends of Soviet Jewish Culture was formed.[68] The first issue of that association's bimonthly *Vestnik sovetskoi evreiskoi kultury* (Herald of Soviet Jewish Culture) appeared on April 26. On October 11, 1989, the Mikhoels Center, the Association of Friends of Jewish Culture, and the Herald of Jewish Culture founded the Association of Soviet Jewish Culture on a federative basis. On December 10, the association was registered and received official status. Somewhat earlier, the Moscow Jewish Cultural-Educational Society, headed by Colonel Yuri Sokol, was also registered.[69] Cooperative cafés belonging to members of the movement opened in Moscow; meetings, lectures, and discussions were held, and Jewish holidays were celebrated there. The Jewish movement cafés in Moscow included Efim Podolsky's café Vltava and Arkady Kruzhkov's café Aist (The Stork). There was another Jewish café in Moscow called At Joseph's.

The attitude toward Jewish national initiatives was considerably more liberal in the Baltic republics than in Russia. In January 1988, in Lithuania, a group interested in advancing Jewish national culture met with Lithuanian public figures to discuss the fate of Jewish cultural monuments and cemeteries. They adopted a decision to appeal to the Lithuanian Academy of Sciences to provide several positions for carrying out research on Jewish national issues. At a meeting of the Lithuanian section of the National Cultural Fund in February, a special group was set up to study and preserve the cultural heritage of Lithuanian Jews.[70] The Jewish Cultural Association of Lithuania held a founding conference on March 5, 1989, in Vilnius. It adopted a charter and a program and selected thirty-five members of a council. Very few Jews remained in Estonia, but on March 20, 1988, a Jewish Cultural Association was officially registered in the capital, Tallinn. In December the association published the first issue of a Russian-language information bulletin *Hashachar* (Hebrew for "dawn").[71]

Jewish national initiatives were more far-reaching in Latvia. On January 6, 1988, a group of Riga Jews, who had turned to Mikhail Gorbachev in December 1987 with a request to establish an official Jewish cultural center, announced the founding of the Magen Society. It arose on the basis of an unofficial seminar, "Riga Jewish Lectures," that used to meet bimonthly starting in 1975.[72]

Shmuel Zilberg recalled the developments in Riga:[73]

ZILBERG: In 1988 a full-fledged movement for rebuilding Jewish life in Latvia arose. It was decided to convene a meeting to establish a Jewish Cultural Society, and a large number of people passed through my apartment. Some people sat there, registering candidates for the society. Each person brought a signed sheet with the names of fifty Jews who delegated him or her, and then he or she was registered as a delegate to the meeting. We received permission to hold the meeting in the building that formerly (before Soviet times) lodged the Jewish theater. Our first point was a request to have the building returned to the community, not to the synagogue but to the secular Jewish community of Riga. Our lawyers prepared documents for registering the society: a charter and various other things. They also dealt with such issues as the status of the legal body and the restitution of property. All this took place over the course of a year.

Several thousand people came to the meeting in Riga, and we had to bring loudspeakers outside. You can't imagine what it was like. It was quite a demonstration of strength! A large Israeli flag hung over the stage and the meeting began with the singing of "Hatikva" [the Israeli national anthem]. Some people from the Israeli consular delegation attended. Proposals included establishing a Jewish children's choir, an art studio, and so forth. This was in September 1988!

In parallel, a more radical and completely Zionist organization was formed, which was called the Latvian Society of Friendship with Israel, but nothing came of it. It was more realistic to establish the Latvian Jewish Cultural Society. I had the feeling that the Latvians supported the Jewish Cultural Society. I think that even the Soviets supported our initiatives in order to reduce the tension. The idea of a democratic empire was attractive, and they were prepared to make some concessions to the Jews in the Baltic republics.

The Jewish Cultural Society was thus founded in Riga in September 1988. On January 19, 1989, the cooperative Tarbut for studying contemporary Hebrew was registered in the city.[74] On February 1, 1989, the Association of National Cultural Societies of Latvia was organized, in which the Jewish Cultural Society became a full-fledged member.[75] The first Jewish school in fifty years, since the Soviet occupation of Latvia in 1940, was opened with official approval on September 1, 1989. The school's curriculum included Yiddish as a national language, Jewish history, music, and literature.[76]

In late 1988 and early 1989, under the influence of the broad liberalization of public life and the sharp rise in anti-Semitism, some Soviet Jews who had hitherto been rather passive began to participate more actively in Jewish matters. It was clear that anti-Semitism was the other side of the coin of liberalization: the more permissive atmosphere enabled the reemergence of racial, anti-Semitic, and other negative phenomena that had been suppressed by the Soviet regime at the popular level. The need for joint action in opposing this evil was clear. Against the backdrop of the surfacing as of 1987 of thousands of informal associations, Jewish cultural societies opened in Samarkand and Bukhara (Uzbekistan); Odessa,

Chernovtsy, and Kharkov (Ukraine); Kishinev, Bendery, and Tiraspol (Moldova); Almaty (Kazakhstan); Minsk (Belarus); Baku (Azerbaijan); Krasnoyarsk; and other cities.

Under the leadership of Yosif Zisels, the Chernovtsy Jewish Social-Cultural Fund was established in June 1988. It began to publish the first Jewish information bulletin in Ukraine, working in close cooperation with the Moscow bulletin.

Yosif Zisels recalled the conditions in which he was working then:[77]

ZISELS: In accordance with a decision circulated through Party channels at the end of 1989, the Party organs tried to control the establishment of independent Jewish organizations. The decision was implemented by the Cultural Fund, which began to set up Jewish cultural societies in various Ukrainian cities. This was done, naturally, to counter our initiatives. It was a big mess, and some of our structures merged with theirs, for example, in Chernovtsy. The forces were divided evenly. Nothing came of this control, although vestiges of that Party system exist to this day. In December 1989 the regime established the Jewish Cultural Association, which united dozens of societies in Ukraine.

In Minsk, similarly, the Jewish society Hope (Nadezhda) was formed in December 1987, under the chairmanship of Mark Kagan, whereas the Society of Friends of Jewish Culture opened there in October 1988, in the framework of the municipal division of the Soviet Cultural Fund.[78]

In November 1988 the Jewish Historical and Ethnographic Society was established on a legal basis in Leningrad. In December 1989 the Ukrainian Cultural Fund established the Jewish Cultural Society of the Ukrainian Republic to coordinate the activity of Jewish educational organizations that had appeared in the course of the year in twenty-five Ukrainian cities.[79] In December 1989 the Maccabi sports club was revived in Leningrad, and it reappeared in Vilnius in January 1990.

In 1987, parallel to the rise of the independent and regime-initiated Jewish organizations, contacts with international Jewish organizations began to develop in line with the reinforcement of perestroika. Attracted by the expanding opportunities, directors of these organizations visited the USSR at the head of representative delegations. By extending their influence to the third largest Jewish community in the world and helping it to regain its standing within the USSR, they hoped to strengthen the Diaspora as a whole.

In March 1988 Rabbi Richard Hirsch headed a high-ranking Reform Movement delegation to Moscow. In September 1988 a B'nai B'rith delegation led by its president Seymour Reich and executive vice-president Dan Mariaschin arrived in the USSR. The visit culminated in the establishment of a B'nai B'rith lodge in the USSR with branches in Moscow and Leningrad. The Jewish Agency (Sochnut) showed an interest in the Soviet Union. Baruch Gur, a Sovietologist, became the architect of the Jewish Agency's work in the USSR. He prepared a general work plan and headed a specially created division in the Sochnut to implement it. Yosef Traupiansky, who had emigrated from Vilnius several decades before, became the Jewish Agency's pioneer in the USSR. In March 1990, with the consent of Vilnius authorities, the Sochnut opened its first official office in the USSR. The next emissary was Georgian-speaking Yitzhak Moshe, who was sent to Tbilisi. He opened a Sochnut office in Tbilisi, started courses in Hebrew, and began to work with the local youth. In January 1990 the Sochnut sent a letter to two hundred local Jewish organizations in the USSR proposing help in Jewish education and cultural undertakings. The local organizations responded with a stream of letters asking primarily for help in Hebrew instruction, which the Sochnut provided. In November 1990 Shmuel Ben-Zvi went to Moscow to facilitate the opening of a Sochnut office there—it was officially recognized on February 18, 1991. In expanding its presence in the USSR, the Sochnut worked to implement the following programs: language instruction, study of the history and culture of the Jewish people, training local leaders, working with youth, developing a national press, and stimulating aliya.

The American Joint Distribution Committee (JDC) started operating during the Soviet perestroika in 1989. Mikhail Chlenov described their arrival:[80]

CHLENOV: At first, the Joint was apprehensive about contacting independent Jewish organizations, and it tried to operate via official bodies, in particular the Maimonides Academy, which was associated with the Chabad movement. The Joint tried somewhat unsuccessfully to establish a network of Jewish libraries in the country. Subsequently, it began to contact us because our goals coincided with theirs: we were both trying to build Jewish communities. In January 1990 the Joint allocated to us $200,000 for that work, which represented considerable support. Changes soon occurred, however, in the Joint's leadership, and it backed away from community building. Given the existing high level of emigration, the Joint thought that all the young, working Jews would emigrate, and that the majority of the remaining Jewish population would be the elderly, who needed social aid. To deal with that problem, they began to build so-called "Heseds," centers for food and aid to the elderly.

The Joint began to send packages at the end of 1992 and the beginning of 1993.[81] The "Heseds" and packages from abroad provided substantial aid to older people, and this project continued for many years. Then, in the mid-1990s, ORT (a Russian acronym referring to the Society for Skilled Trades),[82] specializing in professional education, entered the USSR through the Education Ministry rather than via Jewish organizations.

The newly formed Jewish organizations around the country needed to unite, organize, and try to comprehend the developing situation. Such an attempt was undertaken at a roundtable meeting in Riga on May 21–22, 1989, which was attended by Jews from twenty-seven different cities in the Soviet Union and many guests from abroad. Guests came from Israel representing the Zionist Forum and the WJC. Other Western Jewish organizations such as the Joint, ORT, the Union of Councils for Soviet Jews, and others all sent representatives. This meeting led to the creation of an organizing committee to establish the first countrywide umbrella organization of Soviet Jews—the Vaad (Confederation of Jewish Communities and Organizations of the Soviet Union)—and to elaborate a program. Significantly, the Vaad was intended to be not a Soviet organization but a confederation, a sort of Jewish Union. According to the founders' plan, the Vaad would hold regular meetings, establish contacts among member organizations, and pursue formalized relations with international structures.[83]

Members of the roundtable organizing committee included Mikhail Chlenov (Moscow), Roman Spektor (Moscow), Shmuel Zilberg (Riga), and representatives from other major cities around the Soviet Union. The final document of the meeting acknowledged positive advances in the emigration process but pointed to many remaining deficiencies: "There is no law on emigration and no legal guarantee of freedom of emigration from the country. The shameful institution of refusal still exists. Jews, who leave on Israeli visas, are arbitrarily deprived of Soviet citizenship, while elderly people lose the entitlement to a pension." While acknowledging that the emigration of Soviet Jews to the West could be regarded as the realization of one of the fundamental human rights to choose one's country of residence, the final document noted with concern the extremely weak national motivation for the process: "Only aliya is part of the Jewish national movement." The document also emphasized the common struggle against anti-Semitism and Fascist groups, the need to set up anti-defamation structures, and the importance of free contacts with Western Jewry, especially with Israel.[84] Chlenov recalled, "The meeting in Riga was very interesting and it was brilliantly organized. A decision was adopted there to convene the first congress of Jews in the USSR and an organizing committee was formed, which met monthly between May and December. We no longer met at my apartment but at the Shalom Theater in Moscow."[85]

Soon after the Riga roundtable, Yosif Zisels and Shmuel Zilberg organized another intercity meeting, successfully bringing together in Riga representatives of Ukrainian, Latvian, Lithuanian, Georgian, and Estonian national movements. Viacheslav Chornovil, the leader of Ukrainian nationalists and a leading rights activist, was one of the participants.[86] Some of the Georgian nationalists who arrived soon became ministers in the government of Georgian president Zviad Gamsakhurdia.[87]

Shmuel Zilberg responded to questions about that meeting:[88]

KOSHAROVSKY: *What was the idea behind that meeting? What did you want to accomplish?*

ZILBERG: We sensed that the situation differed in various places and we needed to understand it. The most important thing was that the

Soviets were trying to play the anti-Semitic card in various localities and to incite [popular sentiment] against the Jews. Chornovil said, "Look, in Ukraine there is no informal anti-Semitic organization but in Russia there is Pamiat. That's what they want to palm off on us." You can't imagine how important it was to the Ukrainians and Lithuanians themselves that there be no anti-Semitic excesses in their countries.

KOSHAROVSKY: *Do you think that Pamiat and informal anti-Semitism was directed from inside the secret services?*

ZILBERG: It was absolutely a KGB affair. I am sure that it was the result of a struggle between various branches of the state security services.

KOSHAROVSKY: *When did you hold that meeting?*

ZILBERG: If I'm not mistaken, it was at the very beginning of the fall of 1989. It was a very important meeting. We brought together all those in the national fronts who were responsible for cooperation among national groups so that they would work out a democratic national policy. It was purely our initiative. We sat together for three days. I must say that for a relatively long time all the national republics prevented the playing of the anti-Semitic card. They stood firm.

KOSHAROVSKY: *Was this also part of the preparations for the Vaad congress?*

ZILBERG: The Vaad had a committee for cooperation with national movements that was headed by Zisels.

The Vaad was nurtured by many sources. An important role in its creation was played by the battle-hardened old guard of the movement, which had already breached a purely Zionist framework, and by numerous perestroika groups.

Around the same time as the Riga roundtable, on May 25, 1989, the newly elected Congress of Peoples' Deputies opened in Moscow. That was the golden hour of perestroika, the height of hopes for democratic transformations and an improvement in living conditions in the country. The congress sessions were broadcast on television, and for the first time in Soviet history, the population was able to view the free discussion of democratically elected deputies. Hopes, however, were gradually replaced by anxiety: so many problems that had previously been swept under the carpet now became public knowledge. Some of them were purposely pumped up by forces opposed to perestroika. The work of the congress was accompanied by a feeling of growing chaos in the country, emptying store shelves, popular anti-Semitism, and interethnic conflicts at the periphery of the Soviet empire. Although Gorbachev managed on the whole to pursue a reform course, the aura of hope and expectation that had surrounded the start of his rule began to fade.

Centrifugal tendencies, which had long been developing latently and occasionally broke through to the surface in outbursts of popular dissatisfaction, began to threaten the integrity of the Socialist camp. Promising not to interfere in the sociopolitical processes in the Socialist countries, Gorbachev firmly adhered to his declared policy. Centrifugal tendencies also increased inside the empire itself. The preparations for the founding congress of the Vaad took place in the context of these events, which could not help but have an influence on the ideological debates of the founders.

The disagreements reflected not only the founders' varying personal stands but also the differences in the milieu in which they lived. Mikhail Chlenov was trying to establish a centralized, federative organization with its head office in Moscow and branches in the republics. Zisels and Zilberg sensed more keenly the centrifugal movement in their republics. Indeed, Zisels was one of those who not only firmly believed in independence for Ukraine but also did everything possible to facilitate it. Both Zisels and Zilberg categorically opposed centralizing leadership in Moscow. They proposed forming the Vaad as a confederation of autonomous organizations and giving the leadership only representative functions. They also insisted that a triumvirate of three cochairpersons head the organization. In the end, their viewpoint prevailed.

Another cluster of issues that provoked ardent arguments concerned the correlation between the Zionist and communal components of the organization's activity. All of the above-mentioned leaders favored a powerful Zionist component, but the organization also included many perestroika Jews who were still repelled and frightened by the very term "Zionism." Their opposition needed to be overcome. Although the activity in a legalist framework would entail constant contact and cooperation with the regime, it was not clear how the perestroika authorities would relate to the organization's Zionist activity. Moreover, some leaders suggested that the Vaad undertake only Zionist activity. Lev Gorodetsky, the leader of the Zionist organization and the Teachers' Union, proposed turning the Vaad into a committee on repatriation. When his viewpoint was rejected, he left the congress and withdrew from the Vaad's organizing committee. Moderate Zionists such as Zilberg and Zisels initiated the establishment of repatriation committees in the framework of the public organizations that participated in the founding of the Vaad. They were to serve as centers for consultation and be equipped with the appropriate printed material. Zisels also initiated the establishment of the Zionist Federation as a cofounder of the Vaad.

Although there were many disagreements, the issues on which there was relative unanimity were much weightier. People sensed an impending danger linked to the major changes in the country and the acute deterioration of the economic situation: sure signs of the approach of another "Time of Troubles" in Russia.[89] The Jews witnessed the greatly intensified activity of various extremist anti-Semitic groups that poured out onto the streets and squares of Soviet cities. Rumors of imminent pogroms spread already in 1988. The need to combat that evil provided a powerful stimulus to consolidate efforts.

Manifestations of anti-Semitism once again demonstrated to assimilated Soviet Jews that one could adopt the culture of the society in which they resided, accept its way of life, and successfully contribute to it, but at the same time remain mentally, visually, and spiritually an alien element in that milieu. Even establishment Jews who felt uncomfortable in the face of this vulgar anti-Semitism were drawn to their national roots. Many of them sensed that the best defense against anti-Semitism was not an attempt at complete spiritual mimicry of the dominant state model but a reliance on one's own national foundation. The interest in Jewish knowledge and the desire to see the restoration of sites for Jewish education and other communal institutions were also strong forces for unifying the community.

The founding congress of the Vaad took place in Moscow in the House of Cinema from December 18 to 22, 1989. Mikhail Chlenov described the scene: "It opened with a demonstration by Pamiat and Palestinians right in front of the doors. At the entrance, members of the Ukrainian (center-right national) movement Rukh that came from Kiev to protect us stood guard along with the police. It was December and freezing, and these scoundrels stood with their slogans, Palestinian flags, and cries: 'Down with the Yids!' Thus the Jews entered that elegant building."[90]

There were 414 delegates from seventy-seven cities, representing 204 organizations, along with guests from foreign countries, representatives from democratic and national movements in the USSR, and guests from various organizations in the USSR.[91] Representatives from Lishkat hakesher, the Joint, the WJC, the Jewish Agency, and other organizations also attended the founding congress of the Vaad.

The complete absence of representatives of the Soviet regime at the congress, who ignored their invitations, was indicative of the regime's position at that moment, which amounted to "wait and see." On the one hand, they did not want to give legitimacy to this independent gathering through their presence; but, on the other hand, they no longer dared to disrupt it as they had done several times in the past in the case of the Jewish Cultural Association. The authorities permitted Vladimir Mushinsky to rent a hall, arrange transportation, and reserve rooms for the hundreds of guests. Baruch Gur noted that the majority of foreign guests received entry visas with the approval of the Central Committee and the Foreign Ministry. Even representatives of the Jewish Agency (Sochnut), who insisted on receiving an invitation as an official delegation, received entry visas at the last minute.[92]

The congress adopted an impressive program, the intellectual foundation of which would have been the envy of many Western organizations, but its financial and organizational weakness soon became apparent. The Vaad did not have the funds to implement its program. In refusal, many things had been accomplished through pure enthusiasm, but that was no longer sufficient. There were expenses for transportation, offices, and representatives, not to mention the projects that the Vaad hoped to implement. The Joint's $200,000 grant to the Vaad in January 1990 enabled the organization to develop. The Vaad accepted the Jerusalem program, that is, it recognized the centrality of Israel in the Jewish world, which enabled it eventually to be accepted into the World Zionist Organization. Shmuel Zilberg explained the division of responsibilities among the three cochairpersons: "I was responsible for aliya: in the Vaad, it was called the Committee for Repatriation and Ties with Israel. Mika [Chlenov] wanted foreign ties and he received the post of foreign minister. Zisels handled communications with the republics and contacts with national movements."[93]

The Vaad was the peak that legalists attained while still linked to the Zionist movement. It turned out to be a stable organization resting on a durable ideological base. For the first two years, the regime hesitated to register the Vaad officially, but it did not hinder its functioning.

The Vaad survived the mass emigration from the USSR, the collapse of the Soviet Union, and the difficult years that followed. Its successors were the Vaad of Russia (founded in 1992) and the Vaad of Ukraine (founded in 1991). These two organizations continued to function and were recognized by the government authorities and worldwide. Mikhail Chlenov and Yosif Zisels became the permanent chairmen. Officially, the countrywide Vaad ceased to exist at the beginning of the twenty-first century, but, in fact, its meetings ended in 1996. In the post-Soviet countries, the Vaad's function as a unifying and coordinating body was taken over by the Euro-Asian Jewish Congress (EAJC).[94] Coordination among Jewish organizations from 1996 to 2002 was carried out at the level of personal contacts among the organizations' leaders. The third cochairman of the countrywide Vaad, Shmuel Zilberg, immigrated to Israel, where he became a professor at Hebrew University in the Chemistry Department. His replacement, Semyon Vaisman from Moldova, also immigrated to Israel and served as director of a museum in Ashdod.

Alexander Smukler looked back on what had been accomplished:[95]

SMUKLER: I give credit to Chlenov, who twenty years ago asserted that no matter how large the aliya, Jews would continue to live in the territories of the Soviet Union. Not foreseeing the collapse of the USSR, he began laying down the foundations for Jewish national life in Soviet perestroika conditions. He turned out to be right. I give credit also to Yosif Zisels, who solemnly believed that Ukraine would be independent. When he spoke to me about that in 1989, I thought he was crazy because it seemed so improbable, but what do you know—Ukraine became an independent state.

The Context of Mass Aliya

In 1990, 228,400 Jews left the USSR, of whom 183,400 arrived in Israel.[96] The high rate of aliya resulted from practically unimpeded emigration and the division of visa processing for the United States from visa processing for Israel. Starting on January 1, 1990, immigration to the United States was implemented via direct flights, and the processing of documents took place in Moscow based on invitations from direct relatives, in accordance with an annual quota of forty thousand visas for Jews and ten thousand for members of other Soviet nationalities. The process of submitting and reviewing requests for entry visas to the United States was rather lengthy, the quota was not that large, and the waiting period typically stretched to several years. At the same time, Israel, based on the Law of Return, automatically granted entry visas to Jews and family members up to the third generation. The growing chaos, economic distress, and fear that emigration might again be blocked impelled the majority of those who potentially would have preferred the United States not to wait and to move to where they were accepted: Israel. The extreme type of anti-Semitism seen in the late 1980s and early 1990s also enhanced the popularity of Israel as a destination. In 1990 emigration became practically free and was limited only by the technical possibilities of OVIR and the customs.

By the beginning of 1990, the number of people who had obtained invitations from Israel reached almost five hundred thousand. For them, departure from the USSR was the result of efforts that had been undertaken long before the empire's collapse or even at the first signs of the process; that is, it was a calculated step that had been prepared in advance. The mass of people who succumbed to the panic of the years between 1989 and the early 1990s left after the putsch of August 1991; subsequently, the level of departures declined twofold.

The rapidly changing situation in the USSR made it impossible to predict the final outcome of developments there. The first tremors of approaching conflicts appeared in 1988. In several republics, mass movements in support of perestroika arose one after the other. These turned into movements for expanding sovereignty at the expense of the central government and eventually into a striving for complete political independence.

The Baltic republics were at the forefront of this process. On August 23, 1989, the fiftieth anniversary of the signing of the Molotov-Ribbentrop Pact, the national fronts conducted a powerful demonstration protesting the forced annexation of the three Baltic republics to the USSR after the 1939 pact. In June 1988 a national front in support of perestroika arose in Belarus. In 1989 a movement to secede from the USSR arose in Georgia. In September 1989 the movement of Ukrainian national democrats—Rukh—was founded. The national fronts later took part in democratic elections to governing bodies and joined the ruling structures.

At the time, of course, no one thought that the Soviet Union, which possessed a first-class army and powerful policing services, could collapse like a house of cards. It seems probable that outside forces were not interested in such a rapid collapse of the Soviet Union because of the potential danger of unguarded nuclear weaponry. The events were perceived rather as an affliction of the transitional period, temporary troubled times, after which everything could be renewed in a more civilized and liberal form. Perhaps the Baltic republics were capable of gaining independence, but even that seemed unlikely.

Chlenov commented on the atmosphere of that time:[97]

KOSHAROVSKY: *You built the Vaad, a countrywide umbrella organization, while all that was occurring around you. I left in March 1989, and I had the feeling that things were rather stable. Just imagine—Pamiat! A bogeyman for the ordinary citizen that stimulated aliya.*

CHLENOV: I would say that you left in the last moments of stability. In 1990 the country was reduced to a state of complete ruin. It led to efforts in the West to save Russia. The concept of humanitarian help appeared. Panic truly was spreading, and in 1990 it reached its peak.

KOSHAROVSKY: *The people attained freedom and a free market appeared. Why the panic?*

CHLENOV: I've thought about this a lot. The panic occurred primarily in 1990 and during the entire period up to the putsch, that is, until August 1991. It arose because the customary state system began to break down. People who had been living in a totalitarian society began to understand that totalitarianism is not only oppression. It means everything depends on the regime: birth, death, work, food, security, education; in short, everything! In 1990 goods began to disappear from the stores and a black market developed. Right in front of the Bolshoi Theater, thousands of people were selling soap, matches, etc.—right on the street. Only some rusks and yeast remained in the stores; there were no goods. The authority was disappearing. At the same time, it seemed like everything depended on the black market, the underground. Cooperatives began to flourish. Some people started mixed enterprises with foreigners. The country began to open in the direction of the West but immediately afterward was closed from that side. The West stopped letting in Soviet citizens, and visa control became very strict. In 1990 the Jews already had the Vaad, but panic began, there was fear of pogroms, etc.

KOSHAROVSKY: *Do you mean panic because of Pamiat and other anti-Semitic organizations?*

CHLENOV: Not only because of Pamiat and not only panic among the Jews. I remember very well sending people to the Party's Municipal Committee (*gorkom*) to ask what it intended to do about this atmosphere of an impending pogrom. Our emissaries went there and were met by some bureaucrat who said, "Yes, there will be a pogrom, only not a Jewish one. It will be a pogrom against the Communists. Therefore, we invite you to join us: come and we'll defend ourselves together." Then I sent them to the Party's Municipal Executive Committee (*gorispolkom*). There they said, "Yes, you're right, there will be a pogrom, only not against Jews or Communists but against stores. We invite you to come and together we'll defend the groceries and warehouses," and so forth. That's how it was. In general, that great surge of emigration arose because the vast totalitarian country was writhing in convulsions. The regime became weak, ceased to protect or to control life and the country; it ceased to be the source of everything and that was frightening. People who a year earlier had refused to give their children permission to leave started hurrying themselves to flee to wherever they could obtain entry.

Russians, Germans, Ukrainians, and Greeks who were able to go somewhere hurried away. It was good for the Jews and Germans because they had somewhere to go.

KOSHAROVSKY: *Did they fear a savage Russian revolt?*

CHLENOV: Each person had his own fears. Overall, it was a reaction to the death of the totalitarian order. There was nothing to replace it. Crime and banditry appeared. Murders started and the unrestricted free press began to write about all this. Television began to show horrible things—here a murder, there a robbery.[98]

Chlenov described the context of mass emigration as seen from Moscow. The situation looked somewhat different in the hot spots that were the centers of separatist efforts.

Riga activist and cochairperson of the Vaad Shmuel Zilberg described that period from his perspective:[99]

KOSHAROVSKY: *What do you regard as the basic reason for the mass exodus of Jews from the Soviet Union?*

ZILBERG: I see it as one of the component parts of the disintegration of the empire. The Latvians went to their home in Latvia, the Armenians to Armenia, and the Jews had Israel. Few had either the strength or possibility in Latvia to prove that he or she was a Latvian Jew, and there was no special desire to do so. There were also people who remained in Riga, Moscow, and other places, but on the whole people got up and left. It was not, however, the result of the activity of the Sochnut, Lishkat hakesher, or Jewish activists. It was a result of the grandiose process of the disintegration of the empire.

One of the movement activists who received information from all over the Soviet Union was Alexander Smukler, the editor in chief of the *Informatsionnyi biulleten'* (Information Bulletin).

Smukler assessed the situation in retrospect:[100]

KOSHAROVSKY: *I know that you actively fought against Pamiat and similar organizations. Weren't you yourself afraid of them?*

SMUKLER: We were apprehensive and we continually discussed it. Moreover, there were cases when our names were mentioned in Pamiat leaflets. My name was frequently mentioned in connection with my position as head of the B'nai B'rith lodge in the USSR. There was a feeling that all this could turn into physical violence. Mashka, however, adopted the following position: Pamiat was created by the secret services, controlled and directed by them, and therefore physical violence was possible only with the secret service's approval. In other words, if they want to switch to repressions, a way to do so could be "by the hand of an anti-Semite." We seriously discussed whether we should hire guards for the Vaad office, but we did not consider that there was a real danger on the popular level.

KOSHAROVSKY: *The year 1990 was one of approaching catastrophe?*

SMUKLER: I didn't have a feeling of approaching catastrophe but rather one of fresh air.

KOSHAROVSKY: *Then the mass aliya was not a panicked flight but rather the realization of accumulated potential, including from the negative tendencies in the security sphere.*

SMUKLER: Let's not deceive ourselves. We interacted with rather high-ranking people, and we understood that Pamiat did not yet represent a danger. At the same time, we also used this card and played up the feeling of tension in order to stimulate aliya. If we are talking about Moscow or St. Petersburg, there were isolated anti-Semitic manifestations, especially at the cemeteries, and we utilized this information with all our might.

Mashka, after all, did not simply analyze the situation but also channeled events in a certain direction. There were many letters to various authoritative bodies and we publicized all of them. The bulletin appeared, there was a Jewish newspaper, and sometimes [the popular weekly] *Ogonek* published these letters. The Jewish public read these things. The empty store shelves and the hysteria about anti-Semitism played their role. Don't forget that in 1989 and 1990, the border opened a little. People were already able to travel to relatives in Israel, America, and so forth. Many paid visits and brought back so-called live letters, saying that one needn't fear leaving. Everything would be all right. These three things produced the avalanche.

Because of the collapse of the USSR, without leaving their homes the Jews unexpectedly found themselves in fifteen different states, each with its own national history, culture, and language. These states needed their own mythology that was radically different from that of the USSR. They required their own heroes, regarded in Soviet times as criminals because they had fought for national independence. The new states singled out local traitors and collaborationists, people who had been endowed with honor and glory by the Soviet regime. They cultivated the development of their own culture, which earlier had been woefully neglected. They now needed de-Russification in all areas of social life, as well as their own currency and their own army. The overwhelming majority of Jews, who had grown up with Russian culture, encountered complex problems of adaptation to the new conditions: their children now had to study in the local national language and the new pantheon of heroes often included those who had dishonored themselves by participation in anti-Semitic pogroms or cooperation with the Nazis during World War II. These changes occurred against the background of chaos, popular anti-Semitism, a lack of basic consumer products, the stupor of industrial enterprises, a sharp rise in unemployment, and other cataclysms connected to the disintegration of the empire. Cumulatively, these processes stimulated the massive emigration of Jews and their relatives from the former Soviet Union (FSU): 123,000 in 1992; 127,000 in 1993; and 116,000 in 1994. At the same time, this was significantly fewer than in the first two years of free emigration in 1990 and 1991, when 228,400 and 187,500, respectively, emigrated.[101]

As a rule, the newly formed states did not object to the emigration of the Jews. At first, emigration continued via Moscow, but it was clear that the logistics of processing and transporting Jews to Israel had to be organized from the capitals of the new states. Lishkat hakesher and the Sochnut quickly and effectively solved the problem. Whereas in 1991 Moscow was the sole dispatching point, by 1992 there were already eleven such sites. In 1993 there were fifteen, and by 1994 there were seventeen.[102] Lishkat hakesher, whose representatives were well acquainted with activists and local conditions, succeeded in obtaining the regimes' permission to open their offices. They took upon themselves consular functions such as verifying documents and issuing entry visas to Israel.

In almost all the states that were formed in the post-Soviet space, hot spots arose, at times developing into armed conflicts, including the Georgian-Abkhazian and Georgian-Ossetian conflicts in Georgia, the Nagorno-Karabakh conflict between Armenia and Azerbaijan, the Ossetian-Ingush and Chechen conflicts in Russia, and the Transdniestr conflict in Moldova. There was also a civil war in Tajikistan and clashes in the

Fergana Valley. The evacuation of repatriates to Israel from these conflict areas was a complex and difficult task. Lishkat hakesher generally undertook these operations. If circumstances permitted, its workers sometimes allowed Sochnut employees to join them.

For example, the war in Moldova began on June 19, 1992. The Russian-speaking areas of south and east Moldova seceded from Moldova and formed the Transdniestr Moldovan Republic with its capital in Tiraspol and the Gagauz Republic, which were not recognized by Moldova. The Joint, the Jewish Agency, and Lishkat hakesher collaborated to bring out Jews from the region, evacuating in total about eight thousand for immigration to Israel. Following the conflict, just around twelve hundred Jews remained in the region, one tenth of the number who lived there according to the census of 1989.[103]

Processes analogous to those in Moldova but with local differences occurred in other hot spots as well. Lishkat hakesher, the Sochnut, Joint, and local activists did everything possible to bring Jews out of danger zones as quickly as possible. The majority of those conflicts were not resolved, and from time to time they flared up again. The possibility of dangerous developments continued to threaten populations in those regions.

Having exceeded seventy thousand in 1989, emigration from the former Soviet Union did not go lower than one hundred thousand annually until 1997, declining in the following years. In 2004 just 10,100 people arrived in Israel from the former Soviet Union.[104] As of the early years of the twenty-first century, census figures showed just over 400,000 Jews remaining in the former Soviet Union, of whom 233,600 were in the Russian Federation and 104,300 in Ukraine.[105]

In the years of mass emigration, the overwhelming majority of Jews—more than 1,500,000 people—left the borders of the former Soviet Union. The majority of those who left—around 900,000—settled in Israel, comprising a significant percentage of the country's Jewish population.[106] If we look at total numbers of Jews and their non-Jewish relatives who left the FSU, we see that of 1,597,000 leaving between 1989 and 2005, more than 971,000 went to Israel, 324,000 went to the United States, and 218,200 went to Germany. Several tens of thousands settled in other countries.[107]

The exodus of Soviet Jews has now become part of world history. It was the largest exodus of Jews since the time of the exodus from Egypt. The exodus from the USSR—some call it the exodus from the Red Pharaoh—combined, on the one hand, the harsh realities of struggle and, on the other hand, a mystic feeling of reviving and fulfilling ancient prophecies. People felt the presence of some unknown force that aided the Jews in the unequal struggle with a mighty superpower. As in ancient Egypt, the Soviet Union received its "Egyptian plagues" for its refusal to release the Jews. Like ancient Egypt, it lost the fight and was punished for its many years of stubbornness.

The Jewish people as a whole played an active and generous role in the fate of Soviet Jewry. They put aside disagreements to unify for the cause. The victory of the exodus demonstrated the strength and worth of traditional Jewish values of brotherhood and mutual help in times of struggle and distress. The State of Israel played a most important role in this exodus, rousing Jewish communities for the struggle and coordinating efforts. During a period of more than thirty years, it supplied activists in the Soviet Union with the necessary elements for the struggle and for survival in refusal, and it mobilized Western democracies in their support. The aliya of almost a million people—including tens of thousands of engineers, doctors, teachers, scientists, and cultural figures—rewarded Israel for its efforts. Thanks to this aliya, Israel strengthened its position as a world leader in innovations and technological progress. This massive aliya reinforced the Jewish state demographically.

Many of the activists in the Jewish movement who participated in the struggle for aliya found that these were among the most intense and vivid years of their lives, lived at the limit of one's possibilities. The exodus could not have taken place without them, without their immeasurable courage and perseverance. Their protest letters, hunger strikes, and demonstrations aroused public opinion in the West. Their courage in the face of persecution, searches, interrogations, arrests, exile, forced psychiatric treatment, or difficult army service evoked waves of solidarity in the West. Their spiritual strength opposed the might of the totalitarian state. The Jewish people found the inner resources to unite for this struggle, and from this unequal battle they emerged victorious.

Appendixes

Notes

Bibliography

Index

APPENDIX A

Soviet and Post-Soviet Jewish Emigration

Year	Emigration	Olim	Dropouts
1968	231	231	—
1969	3,033	3,033	—
1970	999	999	—
1971	12,897	12,839	58
1972	31,903	31,652	251
1973	34,733	33,277	1,456
1974	20,767	16,888	3,879
1975	13,363	8,435	4,928
1976	14,254	7,250	7,004
1977	16,833	8,350	8,483
1978	28,956	12,090	16,866
1979	51,311	17,278	34,053
1980	21,648	7,570	14,078
1981	9,448	1,762	7,686
1982	2,692	731	1,961
1983	1,314	861	453
1984	896	340	556
1985	1,140	348	792
1986	904	201	703
1987	8,155	2,072	6,083
1988	18,961	2,173	16,788
1989	71,005	12,117	58,888
1990	228,400	183,400	45,000
1991	187,500	147,520	39,980[1]
1992	123,000[2]	65,100	57,900

Soviet and Post-Soviet Jewish Emigration *(Continued)*

Year	Emigration	Olim	Dropouts
1993	127,000	66,100	60,900
1994	116,000	68,100	47,900
1995	114,000	64,800	49,200
1996	106,000	59,000	47,000
1997	99,000	54,600	44,400
1998	83,000	46,000	37,000
1999	99,000	66,800	32,200
2000	79,000	50,800	28,200
2001	60,000	33,600	26,400
2002	44,000	18,500	25,500
2003	32,000	12,400	19,600
2004	25,000	10,100	14,900

Note: Emigration figures reflect the number of Jews who left the USSR in each year on the strength of invitations issued by Israel. *Olim* are those who went to Israel, while "dropouts" (*noshrim*) are those who went to other destinations, including the United States, Germany, and other countries.

[1]Figures up to 1991 match (with a couple of adjustments) the emigration figures in Yaacov Ro'i, "The Achievements of the Jewish Movement," table 3.1, "Exit, Aliya, and Dropping Out of Soviet Jews, 1968-91," in Ro'i, *The Jewish Movement*, 107.

Ro'i referred to the "Jewish Agency for Israel Report," 1993, which appeared in Yehuda Dominitz, "Israel's Immigration Policy and the Dropout Phenomenon," in *Russian Jews on Three Continents: Migration and Resettlement*, ed. Noah Lewin-Epstein, Yaacov Ro'i, and Paul Ritterband (London: Frank Cass, 1997), 119.

[2]Figures after 1991 come from table 13.6 in Mark Tolts, "Post-Soviet Jewish Demography, 1989–2004," *Revolution, Repression, and Revival: The Soviet Jewish Experience*, ed. Zvi Gitelman and Yaacov Ro'i (Lanham, MD: Rowman and Littlefield, 2007), 293. The figures are approximate, based on Hebrew Immigrant Aid Society (HIAS)-assisted emigrants. See also the figures in table 8, "Emigration of Jews and Their Non-Jewish Relatives from the FSU, 1989–2005," in Mark Tolts, "Population and Migration: Migration since World War I," *YIVO Encyclopedia of Jews in Eastern Europe*, 2010, accessed Mar. 16, 2015, http://www.yivo encyclopedia.org/article.aspx/Population_and_Migration/Migration_since_World_War_I.

APPENDIX B

Major Events and Anti-Zionist Trials

Prepared by Yuli Kosharovsky and Enid Wurtman with thanks to Pam Cohen and Jerry Goodman for their valuable contributions.

For an expanded chronology, see kosharovsky.com.

This chronology describes events in the history of Soviet Jews and the Jewish movement in the Soviet Union.

1917	Two Russian revolutions emancipate Russian Jews from a number of special anti-Jewish measures.
1919	Hebrew teaching is forbidden in Jewish schools by decision of the Ministry of Education.
1929	Nearly all Yiddish schools and cultural institutions outside of the Far East Jewish autonomous region Birobidzhan are closed.
1940	(June 16) During World War II, the Soviet Union invades and annexes Lithuania, Latvia, Estonia, and Bessarabia as part of its pact with Nazi Germany.
1941	(September 29–31) Massacre of 33,000 Jews of Kiev by the Nazis and their Ukrainian supporters takes place at nearby Babii Yar ravine.
1942	(April) The Jewish Anti-Fascist Committee (JAC) is created to help mobilize international support for the USSR during World War II.
1945	(May 9) Germany surrenders. By the end of World War II, nearly 30 million Soviet citizens, including 2.5 million Jews, have died.
1947	The Soviet Union's foreign minister, Andrei Gromyko, addresses the United Nations General Assembly and urges the partition of Palestine into a Jewish and an Arab state.

1948 The beginning of the period (1948–53) labeled the "Black Years" in Soviet Jewish history, during which Soviet authorities undertake the aggressive dismantling of the remaining Jewish institutions, including the Yiddish theater, newspapers, and journals.

1948 (January 12) The chairman of the Jewish Anti-Fascist Committee, Solomon Mikhoels, is killed by KGB agents on Stalin's order in a staged accident in Minsk. Within a year, the Yiddish theater is liquidated.

1948 (May 14) The Jewish People's Council in Palestine declares the establishment of the State of Israel.

1948 (October) Ambassador Golda Meir, head of an Israeli delegation to the USSR, visits the Moscow Choral Synagogue, attracting a crowd of some 50,000 Jews who greet her enthusiastically. The event causes concern among Soviet officials.

1948 (November 20) The Jewish Anti-Fascist Committee, the last vestige of organized Jewish cultural life, is dissolved and many of its leaders imprisoned. The Yiddish newspaper *Eynikeyt*, published by the committee, is closed.

1949 Anti-Zionist trials: Twelve people from the group Eynikeyt, a Zionist youth organization, in Zhmerinka, Kiev, Leningrad, and other cities are arrested and imprisoned for long terms in forced labor camps, including Meir Gelfond, Tatiana Kertsman, Alexander Khodorkovsky, Mikhail Spivak, Alexander Sukher, Elena Rakhlis, Efraim Volf, Liudmila Reznikov.

1949–51 Jews in the arts and sciences are targeted as anti-Soviet nationalists and "rootless cosmopolitans" sympathetic to the West. Key Jewish personalities in Birobidzhan are swept up in the campaign, and many are sent to prison or labor camps.

1950 Anti-Zionist trials in Moscow. Vitaly Svechinsky, Roman Brakhman, and Mikhail Margulis are sentenced to ten years of imprisonment.

1952 (August 12) Thirteen prominent Jewish writers, poets, scientists, and political figures associated with the Jewish Anti-Fascist Committee are executed.

1953 (January 13) Article in *Pravda* entitled "Dastardly Spies and Assassins in the Guise of Professors and Doctors" marks the beginning of the Doctors' Plot campaign accusing Jewish medical professionals of planning to kill Stalin and other officials, and of being "agents" of the American Jewish Joint Distribution Committee (JDC), an international social welfare agency.

1953 (March 5) Stalin dies three days after Purim. The trial of the Jewish medical professionals is cancelled.

1955 Arrests of Jewish activists connected to the Israeli Embassy in Moscow and their subsequent imprisonment: Moshe Brodsky: ten years of hard labor, reduced to six years upon appeal; Avraham Landman: one year; Ida Rozhansky: five years.

1956 Signing of Russian-Polish Repatriation Agreement, enabling Jews entitled to Polish citizenship to emigrate from the USSR to Warsaw en route to Israel. Nativ creates Bar, an international branch for mobilizing public opinion and lobbying political structures in the West in support of the Soviet Jewry struggle.

1956 (February 25) Nikita Khrushchev's secret speech denouncing the personality cult of Stalin, delivered at the Twentieth Communist Party Congress.

1957 (July–August) Sixth World Festival of Youth and Students in Moscow. Israeli delegation attracts Soviet Jews' interest.

1958 Arrests of Jewish activists connected to the Israeli Embassy and their subsequent imprisonment: Dora, Shimon, and Boris Podolsky; Tina Brodetsky; Evsei Drobovsky; and David Khavkin.

1958 Anatoly Rubin is arrested for Zionist activity and sentenced to six years in prison camps.

1961 (July) Campaign against economic crimes begins and lasts through March 1963. Convicted Jews disproportionately receive death penalties.

1963 Trofim Kichko's virulently anti-Semitic book *Judaism without Embellishment* is published in the USSR.

1965 Arrest and imprisonment of Mark Blum (Mordecai Lapid) in Riga for Zionist activities.

1966 Elie Wiesel's book *The Jews of Silence* is published, highlighting his encounters with Soviet Jews and the silence of Western Jews in the face of their plight.

1967 (June 5–10) Six-Day War. Israel's decisive victory in the Six-Day War arouses great pride and strong national sentiment among many Jews in the Soviet Union.

1967 (June 10) USSR severs diplomatic relations with Israel.

1967 (June 11) Yakov Kazakov (Kedmi) submits a written appeal to the USSR Supreme Soviet renouncing Soviet citizenship.

1968 (June 6) Presentation of Gromyko and Andropov to the Politburo with a proposal to allow limited emigration again.

1969 The underground All-Union Coordinating Committee (VKK) is created by Jewish activists in the Soviet Union.

1969 The underground Zionist movement initiates campaign of open appeals.

1969 (May 13–16) Trial in Kiev of Boris Kochubievsky. He is charged with slander against the Soviet regime and sentenced to three years of hard labor in prison camp. Afterward, arrests and trials of Jewish activists accelerate.

1969 (August 6) Eighteen Soviet Georgian Jewish families appeal to the United Nations concerning their right to leave the Soviet Union. Their appeal captures the attention of the media and advocates for Soviet Jews.

1970 (March 8) Thirty-nine Soviet Jews from different cities protest to the Soviet Foreign Ministry against the continuing anti-Israel and anti-Zionist campaign.

1970 (December 10) Human Rights Day. A Soviet Jewry Vigil is launched opposite the Soviet Embassy in Washington, DC. The vigil continues for twenty years.

1970 (December 15–25) The first Leningrad Trial of Jewish and non-Jewish defendants accused of "hijacking" an airplane to escape the Soviet Union and reach Israel. Defendants Mendel Bodnia, Izrail Zalmanson, Silva Zalmanson, Anatoly Altman, Leib Khnokh, Boris Penson, Vulf Zalmanson, Yosef Mendelevich, Aleksei Murzhenko, and Yuri Fedorov are convicted and sentenced to terms from four to fifteen years. Mark Dymshits and Eduard Kuznetsov receive the death sentence, which is commuted to fifteen years after strong international protests.

1971 (February 23–25) First World Conference on Soviet Jewry opens in Brussels.

1971 (May 11–20) Second Leningrad trial includes defendants Hillel Butman, Mikhail Kornblit, Lassal Kaminsky, Lev Iagman, Vladimir Mogilever, Solomon Dreizner, Lev Korenblit, Viktor Boguslavsky, and Viktor Shtilbans.

1971 (May 24–27) Trial of Arkady Shpilberg, Ruth Alexandrovich, Mikhail Shepshelovich, and Boris Maftser in Riga.

1971 (June 15–16) Trial of Valery Kukui in Sverdlovsk.

1971 (June 22) Trial of Reiza Palatnik in Odessa.

1971 (June 21–30) Trial of Anatoly Goldfeld, David Chernoglaz, Hillel Shur, Arkady Voloshin, Alexander Galperin, Gari Kizhner, Semyon Levit, Lazar Trakhtenberg, and David Rabinovich in Kishinev.

1971 (September 19) Trial of Emilia Trakhtenberg in Samarkand.

1971 (October 6–7) Trial of Boris Ozernikov-Yankelson in Leningrad.

1972 (May 22–30) President Richard M. Nixon is in Moscow for a summit meeting with Leonid Brezhnev. The subject of Soviet Jewry dominates press conferences.

1972 Anti-Zionist trials of Israel Brind (June 1) and the Vainman brothers (September 7) in Kharkov; of Yuri Pokh (June 17) and Grigory Berman (August 10) in Odessa; of Gabriel Shapiro (July 26), Mark Nashpits (August 2), and Ilia Gleizer (August 22) in Moscow; and of Vladimir Markman (August 9) in Sverdlovsk.

1972 (July 3) The Supreme Soviet of the USSR introduces a higher-education levy on would-be emigrants, ostensibly to recoup education costs.

1972 (September 25–26) Senator Henry "Scoop" Jackson publicly proposes legislation linking access to trade benefits for "non-market" (i.e., Communist) nations to liberalizing their emigration practices.

1973 (February 7) Congressman Charles Vanik cosponsors legislation in the House of Representatives similar to that introduced by Senator Jackson.

1973 Anti-Zionist trials of Yakov Iavor in Tashkent (January 14); of Lazar Lubarsky in Rostov (January 31); of Efim Potik in Brest (spring); of Nikolai Iavor in Leningrad (April 2); of Isaak Shkolnik in Vinnitsa (March 29–April 11); of Petr Pinkhasov in Derbent (October 13); of Alexander Feldman in Kiev (November 19); and of Leonid Zabelyshensky in Sverdlovsk (December 20).

1973 (March 20) After worldwide protests, the education tax is suspended.

1973 (June 16–25) Brezhnev visits the United States.

1973 (October 6–24) The Yom Kippur War.

1974 Anti-Zionist trials of Alexander Slinin in Kharkov (June); of Yuri and Anna Berkovsky in Novosibirsk (June 25); of Mikhail Leviev in Moscow (December 8); and of Mikhail Shtern in Vinnitsa (December 31).

1974 (June 27) President Richard Nixon's second visit to Moscow. Refuseniks are detained during the visit.

1974 (December 20) The Jackson-Vanik Amendment is approved by the US Congress.

1975 (January 3) US President Gerald M. Ford signs the Jackson-Vanik Amendment into law.

1975 (January 14) The Soviet Union repudiates the 1972 trade agreement with the United States in response to passage of the Jackson-Vanik Amendment.

1975 Anti-Zionist trials of Boris Tsitlenok and Mark Nashpits in Moscow (March 31); of Sender Levinson in Bendery (May 27); of Lev Roitburd in Odessa (May 17); of Yakov Vinarov in Kiev (August 15); of Isaak Iulitin in Leningrad (August 27); and of Alexander Silnitsky in Kharkov (November 18).

1975 (August 1) The Helsinki Final Act is signed.

1976 Anti-Zionist trials of Lidia Nisanov in Derbent (January 16); and of Avner Zavurov in Shakhrisabz (December 26).

1976 (February 17–19) The Second World Conference of Jewish Communities on Soviet Jewry in Brussels.

1976 (May 12) The Moscow Helsinki group is founded to promote the implementation of the Helsinki Accords.

1976 (December 21) The scheduled unofficial international symposium on Jewish culture in the USSR is blocked by Soviet authorities.

1977 (January 20) Soviet television premieres an anti-Zionist documentary, *Traders of Souls*, featuring Yosif Begun, Yuli Kosharovsky, Anatoly Sharansky, and Vladimir Slepak.

1977 (February 7) Members of the Moscow Helsinki group Alexander Ginzburg and Yuri Orlov are arrested.

1977 (March 15) Anatoly (Natan) Sharansky is arrested on charges of treason and spying for the United States.

1977 (June 1) Anti-Zionist trial of Yosif Begun in Moscow.

1978 Anti-Zionist trials of Vladimir Slepak and Ida Nudel (June 21), Maria Slepak (June 26), and Alexander Podrabinek (August 16) in Moscow; of Yakov Kandidov in Tashkent (March 3); of Grigory Goldstein in Tbilisi (March 29); of Semyon Shnirman in Zaporozhye (June 27); and of Mikhail Roiz in Kishinev (August 16).

1978 (July 14) Anatoly Sharansky is found guilty of espionage and treason and sentenced to three years in prison plus ten years in a forced labor camp.

1979 Anti-Zionist trials of Alexander Vilik in Volgograd (February 13); of Boris Kalendarev in Leningrad (May 14); and of Itskhak Rubinov in Derbent (October).

1979 (April 19) Five Prisoners of Zion are pardoned by the Soviet authorities and leave for Israel: Boris Penson, Anatoly Altman, Leib Khnokh, Hillel Butman, and Vulf Zalmanson.

1979 (April 27) Soviet dissidents and Jewish activists, including Mark Dymshits and Eduard Kuznetsov, are exchanged by the Soviets for two Soviet spies.

1979 (May) Authorities begin to halt emigration in provincial towns including Odessa, Tashkent, Kharkov, Minsk, and Kiev.

1979 (August) Intercity seminar for Hebrew teachers in Koktebel.

1979 (December 25) Soviet invasion of Afghanistan.

1980 Anti-Zionist trials of Leonid Volvovsky in Gorky (January); of Igor Guberman (March 11), Yosif Begun (August 23), Dmitry Shchiglik (September 19), and Alexander Vilig (September 26) in Moscow; of Amner Zavurov in Dushanbe (April 16); of Moisey Tonkonogy in Odessa (April 28); of Shmuel Rosenberg in Tashkent (June 2); of Moshe Zats in Chernovtsy (June 2); of Valery Pilnikov in Kiev (June 20); of Grigory Geishis in Leningrad (August 8); and of Semyon Shnirman in Zaporozhe (November 29).

1980 (July 19–August 3) The Olympic Games in Moscow are boycotted by fifty-six Western and Asian countries because of the Soviet invasion of Afghanistan.

1980 (October) The second intercity Hebrew teachers' seminar is held in Koktebel, Crimea. The seminar is attended by more than fifty teachers from nine cities.

1980 (November 11) The Conference on Security and Cooperation in Europe (CSCE) meets to review the Helsinki Final Act.

1980 (November 13) Arrest of Viktor Brailovsky inaugurates a crackdown on unofficial Jewish activities in USSR.

1981 (January) Moscow Hebrew teachers Yuli Kosharovsky, Alexander Kholmyansky, Yuli Edelstein, and Mikhail Kholmyansky begin the underground Cities Project to disseminate Hebrew instruction to provincial cities.

1981 (March 3) Soviet authorities put pressure on Hebrew teachers. Yuli Kosharovsky and Pavel Abramovich are threatened with arrest.

1981 (April 27) Soviet authorities prevent the holding of the cybernetics seminar organized by refusenik Professor Alexander Lerner in his apartment.

1981 Anti-Zionist trials of Kim Fridman (May 15), Vladimir Kislik (May 27), and Stanislav Zubko (July 22) in Kiev; of Viktor Brailovsky (June 18), Boris Chernobylsky (December 9), and Samuel Rombe (December 11) in Moscow; of Evgeny Lein in

Leningrad (August 6); of Osip Lokshin and Vladimir Tsukerman (September 22) in Kishinev; and of Alexander Paritsky in Kharkov (November 13).

1981 (May 27) President Reagan receives Avital Sharansky and Yosef Mendelevich, who was recently released from a Soviet prison after serving an eleven-year sentence.

1981 (September 2–8) The Third Moscow International Book Fair takes place with the participation of an Israeli delegation.

1982 Increasing pressure on Jewish activists and Hebrew teachers. Dozens of Hebrew teachers are summoned to the KGB and warned to stop teaching Hebrew or face arrests.

1982 Anti-Zionist trials: of Lev Shefer (April 6) and Vladimir Elchin (April 6) in Sverdlovsk; and of Felix Kochubievsky in Novosibirsk (October 12).

1982 (September 30) Professor Alexander Lerner and other Moscow refuseniks are warned by the KGB not to meet visitors from the West.

1982 (November 10) Soviet leader Leonid Brezhnev dies.

1983 Anti-Zionist trials: of Semyon Shnirman in Zaporozhe (February 14); of Valery Senderov (March 1); and of Yosif Begun—third trial (October 14) and Vladimir Albrekht (December 15) in Moscow.

1983 (March 15) Refusenik-scientist Yuri Tarnopolsky arrested in Kharkov.

1983 (March 15–17) The Third World Conference on Soviet Jewry is held in Jerusalem.

1983 (April 21) The Anti-Zionist Committee of the Soviet Public is formed in Moscow to combat Jewish cultural and emigration activities.

1983 (June 16) Yuri Andropov, former chief of the KGB, is appointed head of state.

1983 (November) Underground coordinating body of the Zionist movement called Mashka is founded in Moscow.

1984 (February) Death of Andropov. Konstantin Chernenko is appointed general secretary of the CPSU.

1984 Beginning of a new wave of arrests of Hebrew teachers and other Zionist Movement activists: arrests of Zakhar Zunshain in Riga (March 4); of Natalia Volshonok (May 17), Alexander Iakir (June 18), Alexander Kholmyansky (July 25), and Yuli Edelstein (September 4) in Moscow; of Yakov Levin (August 10) and Mark Nepomniashchy (October 12) in Odessa; of Yosif Berenshtein (November 12) in Kiev; of Nadezhda Fradkova (August 25) in Leningrad; of Yosif Zisels (October 19) in Chernovtsy; and others.

1985 Anti-Zionist trials: of Leonid Shraier (January 1) and Yosif Zisels (April 1) in Chernovtsy; of Anatoly Vershubsky (May 7) in Kiev; of Alexander Kholmyansky (February 1) and Vladimir Brodsky (August 15) in Moscow; of Mark Nepomniashchy (February 4) in Odessa; of Evgeny Aizenberg (June 6) in Kharkov; of Roald Zelichenok (August 8) in Leningrad; of Evgeny Koifman (September 17) in Dnepropetrovsk; and of Leonid Volvovsky (October 24) in Gorky.

1985 (March 11) Mikhail S. Gorbachev appointed general secretary of the Communist Party after the death of Konstantin Chernenko.

1985 (September) International Book Fair in Moscow with Israeli exposition.

1985 (November 19) The first summit meeting between Reagan and Gorbachev in Geneva.

1986 (February 11) Early release of Anatoly Sharansky from imprisonment.

1986 Anti-Zionist trials: of Vladimir Lifshits (March 19) in Leningrad; and of Betsalel Shalolashvili (April 21) and Aleksei Magarik (June 6) in Tbilisi. Many activists are arrested on a short-term basis.

1986 (October 11–12) The second summit between President Ronald Reagan and Soviet leader Mikhail Gorbachev takes place in Reykjavik.

1987 (February) Pardon and release of 140 dissidents.

1987 Early release of Prisoners of Zion: Roald Zelichenok (February 6); Yosif Begun (February 20); Zakhar Zunshain (March 6); Yosif

Berenshtein (March 16); Vladimir Lifshits (March 17); Valery Senderov (March 18); Yakov Levin (March 19); Leonid Volvovsky (March 20); Yuli Edelstein (May 5); and Aleksei Magarik (September 14).

1987 (December 6) On the eve of the first Reagan-Gorbachev summit meeting in the US capital, the Freedom Sunday March on Washington, DC, takes place. A record 250,000 people participate in the largest rally ever organized in the United States on behalf of a Jewish cause. The event marks the peak of the Soviet Jewry advocacy campaign in the United States.

1987 (December 7–10) Gorbachev-Reagan summit in Washington, DC.

1987 Developments in independent legal Jewish culture in Moscow: Museum of Jewish Culture (January 21); Friendship Society with Israel (July 10); Jewish Cultural Association (September 11); Sokol Jewish Library (September 14); Koretsky Jewish Library (September 21); Koretsky Record Library (October 11); Jewish Bibliophile Club (October 13); Mikhoels Cultural Center (October 20); and Cultural Society "Shalom" (October 28).

1987 Developments in independent legal Jewish culture elsewhere include the Society of Friends of Jewish Culture (Minsk, October 11); Jewish Historic and Ethnographic Society (Leningrad, November 8); and the Jewish Cultural Society (Kiev, December 4).

1987 (May 29–June 2) Reagan-Gorbachev summit in Moscow. Thirteen well-known refusenik families and a large group of Soviet dissidents are invited to a meeting with President Reagan in Moscow on June 1.

1987 (June 19) Israeli government organizes "direct" flights to Israel via Bucharest.

1988 Anti-Semitic organizations Pamiat (Memory), Otechestvo (Fatherland), and others strengthen their public anti-Semitic campaign in the form of demonstrations, meetings, and distribution of anti-Semitic materials.

1989 (January) The Soviet delegation at the meeting of the Conference on Security and Cooperation in Europe (CSCE) in Vienna approves the Final Declaration, which includes the Right to Leave and the Principle of Family Reunification.

1989 (February 12) Opening of the Solomon Mikhoels Cultural Center in Moscow.

1989 (December 18–21) The Congress of Jewish Organizations and Communities in the USSR is held in Moscow, establishing the Vaad, an umbrella organization of Jewish cultural bodies.

1991 (August 19–21) Unsuccessful attempt to overthrow Gorbachev's administration.

1991 (December 26) Dissolution of the Soviet Union, which is transformed later into the Commonwealth of Independent States (CIS).

Notes

Foreword

1. Larisa Bogoraz, "Do I Feel I Belong to the Jewish People?" in *I Am a Jew: Essays on Jewish Identity in the Soviet Union*, ed. Aleksander Voronel and Viktor Yakhot (New York: Academic Committee on Soviet Jewry and the Anti-Defamation League of B'nai B'rith, 1973), 63.

2. See chapter 4.

3. See chapter 2.

4. "Prisoners of Zion" was a term used in this context for people imprisoned in the Soviet Union because of their Zionist activity. A listing of such prisoners based on the album *Haaretz Nikneit Baisurim* [The Land Is Attained through Suffering] (Tel Aviv: Izdatel'stvo Organizatsii uznikov Siona iz SSSR, 1995) can be found on the website of the Association "Remember and Save," http://www.soviet-jews-exodus.com/English/POZ_s/POZ_En.shtml (accessed Feb. 14, 2016).

1. Soviet Jews: Making History

1. Yaacov Ro'i noted the upsurge in national energy and activity among Soviet Jews stimulated by the Six-Day War in his introduction to *The Jewish Movement in the Soviet Union*, ed. Yaacov Ro'i (Washington, DC: Woodrow Wilson Center, 2012, 6). See also Zvi Gitelman, "The Psychological and Political Consequences of the Six-Day War in the U.S.S.R.," in *The Six-Day War and World Jewry*, ed. Eli Lederhendler (Bethesda: Univ. Press of Maryland, 2000), 249ff.

2. In his detailed and highly readable account of the Western and Israeli campaign for Soviet Jewry, Gal Beckerman described the advent of "Am Yisrael Chai!" as a militant slogan, based on Meir Kahane's angry challenge to American Jews to do what they had not done during the Holocaust. Kahane had the words spray-painted on the walls of the TASS office and on the sides of an Aeroflot plane fuselage at Kennedy airport. See Beckerman's *When They Come for Us, We'll Be Gone. The Epic Struggle to Save Soviet Jewry* (New York: Houghton Mifflin Harcourt, 2010), 170, 231.

3. Pauline Peretz described the memory of the Holocaust with its attendant question about responsibility as being "the single most important factor" in mobilizing Western

Jewish communities on behalf of Soviet Jews apart from the central role of Israeli efforts to facilitate this engagement. See Peretz, *Let My People Go: The Transnational Politics of Jewish Emigration during the Cold War,* trans. Ethan Rundell (New Brunswick, NJ: Transaction Publishers, 2015), 93.

4. Natan Sharansky, a noted Jewish activist accused of espionage (see chapter 4 in this book), recalled in his memoirs a KGB officer's comment disparaging the mere "students and housewives" supporting him. He reflected that those students and housewives turned out to be "mightier than the KGB." See Sharansky, *Fear No Evil,* trans. Stefani Hoffman (New York: Vintage Books, 1989), 170.

5. Jonathan Frankel described Russian Jewry and their radical projects informed by social and secular messianism in his book *Prophecy and Politics: Socialism, Nationalism, and the Russian Jews, 1862–1917* (Cambridge, UK: Cambridge Univ. Press, 1981), 2.

6. Writing about the period of Russian Jewry covered by Jonathan Frankel, Benjamin Nathans cautioned that such dramatic causes were not the whole story. Russian Jews in that period also sought simply civic emancipation. See Nathans, *Beyond the Pale: The Jewish Encounter with Late Imperial Russia* (Berkeley: Univ. of California Press, 2002), 10.

7. Hasia Diner wrote about the pressure on American Jews to manifest loyalty in the Cold War era and shed "Socialist" labels. See Diner, *We Remember with Reverence and Love: American Jews and the Myth of Silence after the Holocaust, 1945–1962* (New York: New York Univ. Press, 2009), 287. At the same time, it was important to Soviet Jews and their supporters that they not seem "anti-Soviet." For discussion of this point, see Henry L. Feingold, *"Silent No More." Saving the Jews of Russia: The American Jewish Effort, 1967–1989* (Syracuse, NY: Syracuse Univ. Press, 2007), 76–77; and Peretz, *Let My People Go,* 80.

8. On Nativ, see chapter 3 of this book. Nehemiah Levanon published *HaKod "Nativ"* [Hebrew for The Code Name Is Nativ] (Tel Aviv: Am Oved) in 1995, shedding public light on the formerly clandestine bureau. In English, see Nehemiah Levanon, "Israel's Role in the Campaign," in *A Second Exodus: The American Movement to Free Soviet Jews,* ed. Murray Friedman and Albert D. Chernin (Hanover, NH: Brandeis Univ. Press, 1999), 70–83. Since Levanon's publications, a number of scholars have outlined the establishment of Nativ and its initiatives, including Gal Beckerman (*When They Come,* 50–55) and Pauline Peretz (*Let My People Go*), who detailed Nativ's efforts in establishing research centers and pursuing international lobbying and public relations.

9. Yuli Edelstein (Edelshtein), Speaker of the Israeli Knesset and former fellow activist, gave the eulogy at Kosharovsky's funeral in 2014. He described Kosharovsky as "the man behind the scenes, organizing the Hebrew teaching, the culture, and even the structure (though we dared not call it that) of our activities in Moscow. It's quite possible that without him, none of these things would have happened." The same might be said of this history—at least it would not have been done on this scale. Laura Bialis quoted Edelstein in her obituary "Yuli Kosharovsky, Soviet Jewry's 'Man Behind the Scenes,' Dies at

72," *The Forward*, Apr. 18, 2014, accessed Apr. 26, 2016, http://forward.com/news/196765/yuli-kosharovsky-soviet-jewrys-man-behind-the-scen/#ixzz45dKI0CwX.

10. See chapter 5 of this book.

11. Elie Wiesel's account of his trip to the Soviet Union, published originally in English in 1966, was *The Jews of Silence: A Personal Report on Soviet Jewry* (New York: Knopf, Doubleday Publishing Group, 2011). Almost two decades later, Martin Gilbert answered Wiesel's book with his own, entitled *Jews of Hope* (London: Macmillan, 1984). In addition, Theodore Bikel released an album of songs sung by Soviet Jews under the title *Silent No More* (N.p.: Star Record Co., 1971), and the phrase was used in the title of Feingold's book (*"Silent No More"*).

12. After Stalin's death on March 3, 1953, the administration of First Secretary Nikita Khrushchev oversaw a "thaw" in cultural politics and relations with the West. Khrushchev's "Secret Speech" on Stalin's crimes to a closed session of the Twentieth Party Congress on February 25, 1956, leaked out over the next few months to regular Soviet citizens and the Western press, fundamentally changing the atmosphere in the Soviet Union.

13. Ludmilla Alexeyeva, *Soviet Dissent: Contemporary Movements for National, Religious, and Human Rights*, trans. Carol Pearce and John Glad (Middletown, CT: Wesleyan Univ. Press, 1985), 274–77.

14. On the dissident resonances of Siniavsky's Jewish pseudonym, see Ann Komaromi, "Jewish Samizdat—Dissident Texts and the Dynamics of the Jewish Revival in the Soviet Union," in *The Jewish Movement*, ed. Yaacov Ro'i (Washington, DC: Woodrow Wilson Center, 2012), 278–79.

15. See Nikolai Arzhak, *This Is Moscow Speaking, and Other Stories*, trans. Stuart Hood, Harold Shukman, and John Richardson (London: Collins and Harvill, 1968).

16. From Vladimir Bukovsky's memoirs, *To Build a Castle—My Life as a Dissenter*, trans. Michael Scammell (New York: Viking Press, 1978), 140.

17. For a critical survey of the Hegelian philosophy of history and the conundrum it posed for colonized peoples (a conundrum not unlike that of Soviet citizens alienated from their official history), see Ranajit Guha, *History at the Limit of World-History* (New York: Columbia Univ. Press, 2002).

18. Irina Paperno discussed this phenomenon in *Stories of the Soviet Experience: Memoirs, Diaries, Dreams* (Ithaca, NY: Cornell Univ. Press, 2009), 14.

19. Voronel's memoirs, *Trepet iudeiskikh zabot* [The Tremor of Judaic Anxieties], originally circulated in samizdat in 1970. They were republished in *Evreiskii samizdat*, no. 12 (1977): 19–20.

20. Alexander Voronel, "Jewish Samizdat," in *Jewish Culture and Identity in the Soviet Union*, ed. Yaacov Ro'i and Avi Beker (New York: New York Univ. Press, 1991), 255–56.

21. In her study of Soviet Jewish memoirs, Stefani Hoffman assessed that Voronel most fully and theoretically expressed the need for Soviet Jews to confront their love of Russian

culture and to find a new "inner compass" in Jewish civilization. Hoffman, "Voices from the Inside: Jewish Activists' Memoirs, 1967–1989," in Ro'i, *The Jewish Movement*, 239.

22. Issues of the Russian-language samizdat journal *Evrei v SSSR* were reprinted in *Evreiskii samizdat* (Jerusalem), in various issues between no. 4 (1974) and no. 22 (1980). A few of these responses were translated in *I Am a Jew: Essays on Jewish Identity in the Soviet Union*, ed. Aleksander Voronel, Viktor Yakhot, and Moshe Decter (New York: Academic Committee on Soviet Jewry and the Anti-Defamation League of B'Nai B'rith, 1973).

23. Voronel, "Jewish Samizdat," 259.

24. See chapter 4 of this book.

25. Mikhail Zand delineated three broad groups of Soviet Jews, detailing factors influencing the preservation of Jewish knowledge and traditions among the group in the Baltic republics, the Moldavian Republic (Bessarabia), and Ukraine's Northern Bukovina; and among the non-Ashkenazic Jews of the Caucasus and Central Asia. The largest group of Jews in the central Russian territories had become much more assimilated. See Zand, "Fate, Civilization, Aliya," in *Search of Self: The Soviet Jewish Intelligentsia and the Exodus. A Collection of Articles*, ed. David Prital, trans. Stefani Hoffman (Jerusalem: Mount Scopus Publications, 1982), 23–34.

26. See Viktor Polsky's statement about the novel's impact on his mother (chapter 2 of this book). Leonard Schroeter was one of the first chroniclers to record the impact of the book on Soviet Jewish readers. See Schroeter, *The Last Exodus* (Seattle: Univ. of Washington Press, 1979), 64–65.

27. Larisa Bogoraz, for example, wrote in her response for the rubric "Who Am I?" (*Evrei v SSSR*) about her perception that Jewishness became more problematic during World War II. As people in the USSR then said, "Ivan is fighting for Abram, and Abram hurried off to hide in Tashkent." Bogoraz wrote about the shame she felt over being Jewish—a shame not changed by the fact that her Jewish friends and acquaintances came back from the war with marks of their service and sacrifice, one missing a leg, one with a crippled hand, and yet another with a shell splinter in his lungs. The Jews were still not like the Russians: "On the one hand, there was the heroic nation-liberator, on the other, merely a few decent young men." Bogoraz, "Do I Feel I Belong to the Jewish People?" (*I Am a Jew*, 61).

28. For example, the samizdat journal *Lietuviu archyvas* [Lithuanian Archive], no. 1 (1976) featured materials documenting the agreement between Germany and the USSR to divide up territories into respective spheres of influence.

29. From Birutė Burauskaitė, "The Unarmed Resistance (1954–1990)," in *Resistance to the Occupation of Lithuania: 1944–1990*, trans. Laima Junevičienė (Vilnius, Lithuania: Organisation Committee Frankfurt, 2002), 30–31.

30. Algirdas Landsbergis wrote about religious Lithuanian samizdat, "God's Whispers in a 'Godless' Literature," *Religion in Communist Lands* 14, no. 3 (1986): 262–67.

31. Stefani Hoffman wrote in detail about the periodical editions characteristic of the most mature "third" stage of Jewish samizdat, as well as the circulation of translations and

petitions characterizing earlier stages, in her article "Jewish Samizdat and the Rise of Jewish National Consciousness," in Ro'i and Beker, *Jewish Culture and Identity*, 88–111.

32. Based on data collected for database Soviet Samizdat Periodicals, compiled by Ann Komaromi, University of Toronto Libraries, 2011, http://samizdat.library.utoronto.ca.

33. In his memoirs, *Operatsiia svad'ba* [Operation Wedding] (Jerusalem: Tarbut, 1987), Mendelevich described his work on *Iton* and recounted the twelve years he was incarcerated for his role in the airplane hijacking plot (see chapter 2 of this book) before repatriation to Israel. Mendelevich's memoirs appeared in English as *Unbroken Spirit* (Jerusalem: Gefen, 2012).

34. The issue was reprinted in the series *Evreiskii samizdat* 1 (1974): 36–40.

35. Goricheva made these comments in her preface to selections from the ecumenical religious samizdat collection *Nadezhda* [Hope], edited by Zoia Krakhmalnikova, one of those intelligentsia of Jewish origin who embraced Russian Orthodoxy (in *Cry of the Spirit: Christian Testimonies from the Soviet Union*, ed. Tatiana Goricheva (London: Fount Paperbacks, 1989), 17. On Krakhmalnikova and her collection, see Judith Deutsch Kornblatt, *Doubly Chosen: Jewish Identity, the Soviet Intelligentsia, and the Russian Orthodox Church* (Madison: Univ. of Wisconsin Press, 2004), 53–55. Information on the religious-philosophical seminar hosted by Goricheva and Krivulin appeared in *Samizdat Leningrada, 1950-e–1980-e. Literaturnaia entsiklopediia*, ed. D. Ia. Severiukhin (Moscow: Novoe literaturnoe obozrenie, 2003), 445–47.

36. These authors of Jewish origin turned to biblical themes and the "world culture" they represented with famous predecessors such as Osip Mandelshtam and Boris Pasternak in mind. On the Petersburg school, sometimes treated as "Metarealism," sources include Mikhail Epstein's "A Catalogue of New Poetries," in *Russian Postmodernism: New Perspectives on Post-Soviet Culture*, ed. Mikhail Epstein, Alexander Genis, and Slobodanka Vladiv-Glover (New York: Berghahn Books, 1999), 105–12, 145–51; and A. A. Zhitenev, *Poeziia neomodernizma* (Saint Petersburg: INAPRESS, 2012), 9.

37. In his important samizdat novel *Pushkin House*, Andrei Bitov wryly evoked the Silver Age myth of the death of culture, associated with the end of Alexander Blok's life in 1921. The novel also featured a Jewish father figure, named Blank, a character who recalls James Joyce's character Leopold Bloom in the novel *Ulysses*.

38. The editorial foreword to the record of an "Evening in Memory of Aronzon" (1939–70) identified him as more influential than Brodsky; *37*, no. 12 (1977): 2, http://samizdatcollections.library.utoronto.ca/islandora/object/samizdat%3A5424#page/4/mode/1up. Aronzon's date of birth is given based on biographical information from L. L. Aronzon, *Sobranie proizvedenii*, 2 vols., ed. P. A. Kazarnovskii, I. S. Kukui, and V. I. Erl' (Saint Petersburg: Izdatel'stvo Ivana Limbakha, 2006).

39. Vladimir Toporov's study of the "Petersburg Text" in Russian literature is the classic reference on the subject. The study appears in V. N. Toporov, *Peterburgskii tekst russkoi literatury: Izbrannye trudy* (Saint Petersburg: Iskusstvo-SPB, 2003).

40. Beizer also noted the irony of the fates of Babel and his Cheka contact Moisei Uritsky, who both died young as a result of their revolutionary engagements. Beizer's text for the excursion appeared in *The Jews of St. Petersburg: Excursions through a Noble Past*, trans. Michael Sherbourne, ed. Martin Gilbert (Philadelphia: Jewish Publication Society, 1989), 56–57.

41. Joseph Brodsky's early poem "The Jewish Cemetery near Leningrad" ("Evreiskoe kladbishche okolo Leningrada," 1958) about that cemetery became well known in part because it was included in the early samizdat literary collection *Sintaksis* [Syntax], no. 1, 1959, compiled by rights activist Alexander Ginzburg and published abroad in the émigré journal *Grani* [Facets], no. 58, 1965.

42. This quote from the section of Mandelshtam's 1925 memoirs entitled "Judaic Chaos" can be found in *The Noise of Time: The Prose of Osip Mandelstam*, ed. Clarence Brown (Princeton, NJ: Princeton Univ. Press, 1965). Gregory Freidin treated Mandelshtam's uneasy attempts to assimilate into Russian society in a nuanced way in *A Coat of Many Colors: Osip Mandelstam and His Mythologies of Self-Presentation* (Berkeley: Univ. of California Press, 1988), 22. Beizer cited the passage in *The Jews of St. Petersburg*, 197. He explained that Abram Varshavsky settled in Petersburg in the 1860s and became known there as a distinguished philanthropist and public figure.

43. The name is spelled "Warshawski" in the English edition of Beizer's text (*The Jews of St. Petersburg*, 197).

44. A. Frenkel' and M. Ryvkin, "Pamiatniki i pamiat'," *VEK* (Vestnik evreiskoi kul'tury) (July–Aug. 1989), 23–25.

45. Elie Wiesel, *Souls on Fire: Portraits and Legends of Hasidic Masters* (New York: Random House, 1972), 81. The Russian samizdat translation done by Alexander Okun was probably based on the English edition rather than on Wiesel's original French text *Célébration Hassidique* (Paris: Seuil).

46. V. Dimshitz, "Dva puteshestviia po odnoi doroge," in *Istoriia evreev na Ukraine i v Belorussii*, ed. V. Dimshitz (St. Petersburg: Petersburg Jewish Univ., 1994), 8–11. These and other activists learned Yiddish and established places where Yiddish is now taught, including the Jewish community center on Rubinshtein Street in St. Petersburg (directed by Alexander Frankel) and the Jewish Studies Center at European University in that city.

47. See, for example, comments about the production network established by Vladimir Mushinsky (chapter 3 of this book).

48. From *Ivrit* 1 (1978), reprinted in *Evreiskii samizdat* 17 (1979): 74.

49. Benjamin Pinkus traced these attitudes and Stalin's harsher treatment of the question in *The Soviet Government and the Jews, 1948–1967: A Documented Study*, ed. Jonathan Frankel (Cambridge, UK: Cambridge Univ. Press, 1984), 11–12.

50. From *Ivrit*, no. 1, reprinted in *Evreiskii samizdat* 17 (1979): 74.

51. The Soviet press could not ignore the widespread popularity and inflammatory anti-Semitic rhetoric of the other (Russian nationalist) Pamiat (Pamyat) organization, which

rose to some prominence for a time during Perestroika. Soviet press coverage was summarized in the section on "Israel/Soviet Jewry" in *The Soviet Union and the Middle East: A Monthly Summary and News Analysis of the Soviet and East European Press* (Hebrew University) 13, no. 2 (1988): 12–15. The Russian nationalist organization Pamiat is discussed in chapter 5 of this book.

52. From Roginsky's interview for the Polish journal *Karta*, "Arsenii Borisovich Roginskii," hro.org.

53. Henry Jenkins wrote about epistemological changes precipitated by new media. For example, the new "knowledge communities" facilitated by new media complement the more traditional "expert paradigm." See Jenkins, *Convergence Culture: Where Old and New Media Collide* (New York: New York Univ. Press, 2006), 52.

54. Alexeyeva, *Soviet Dissent*, op. cit.

55. See http://kosharovsky.com. Plans to find an archival home for the collections of Yuli Kosharovsky and Enid Wurtman are in progress.

56. The collection of the Association "Zapomnim i sokhranim" (Remember and Save), many documents of which are accessible at http://www.soviet-jews-exodus.com/index.shtml, have gone to the Central Archive of the History of the Jewish People, Jerusalem.

57. Margarita Gimelshtein quoted refusenik Lev Furman: "This was all wonderful—our socializing, the Hebrew ulpans, friendship. But I am tired. I just want to work in my country. Rear children. Simply to live." From "Otkaz ob otkaze," *Otkaz i otkazniki. Leningrad, 80-e gody* (Leningrad: Samizdat, 1987), The Central Archives for the History of the Jewish People, Jerusalem, Collection of the Centre for Research and Documentation of East European Jewry, file 955, p. 193.

58. Significant new Russian Jewish populations appeared in North America and Western Europe. Very striking is the fact that by the mid-1990s, Israel had experienced a 14 percent increase in its Jewish population because of this immigration, according to Noah Lewin-Epstein, introduction to *Russian Jews on Three Continents: Migration and Resettlement*, ed. Noah Lewin-Epstein, Yaacov Ro'i, and Paul Ritterband (London: Frank Cass, 1997), 1.

2. Beginnings

1. Albert Yehoshua Gilboa, *The Black Years of Soviet Jewry, 1939–1953*, trans. from Hebrew by Yosef Shachter and Dov Ben-Abba (Boston: Little, Brown and Co., 1971).

2. Alexander Lerner, a prominent scientist and witness of those events who later became one of the leaders of the Zionist movement of the 1970s (see chapter 3 of this book), described the chilling effect this period had on Jewish professionals in all fields in his memoir, *A Change of Heart* (Rehovot, Israel: Balaban Publishers, 1992), 133.

3. Communist authorities did not admit to the executions and other repressions. Communists abroad did not discuss these events until after First Secretary of the Communist Party Nikita Khrushchev read a speech to a closed session of the Twentieth Party Congress in February 1956, denouncing Stalin's cult of personality and the excesses of his regime.

Full details became known only much later. See *Stalin's Secret Pogrom: The Postwar Inquisition of the Jewish Anti-Fascist Committee,* ed. Joshua Rubenstein and Vladimir P. Naumov, trans. Laura Esther Wolfson, with an introduction by Joshua Rubenstein (New Haven: Yale Univ. Press, 2001).

4. Eynikeyt was an unofficial group organized in 1945 on the basis of a Zhmerinka ghetto group that existed under the same name. Like other spontaneous Jewish youth groups formed after the war, Eynikeyt was not anti-Soviet, but participants of such groups were repressed for "anti-Soviet behavior and Jewish bourgeois nationalism." See Ludmilla Tsigelman, "The Impact of Ideological Changes in the USSR on Different Generations of the Soviet Jewish Intelligentsia," in *Jewish Culture and Identity in the Soviet Union,* ed. Yaacov Ro'i and Avi Beker (New York: New York Univ. Press, 1991), 50–51.

5. Meir Gelfond (1930–1985), born in Zhmerinka in the Vinnitsa region. Gelfond helped form the early youth Zionist group Eynikeyt in 1944. He was arrested with other group members in 1949 and spent more than five years incarcerated. Later, Gelfond studied at the Moscow Medical Institute and became a practicing cardiologist. He completed his PhD work on medical topics in 1968. Gelfond helped organize Jewish samizdat production and distribution in Moscow. He also offered medical help to Jewish activists and refuseniks until he immigrated to Israel in 1971.

6. Vitaly Svechinsky, interview with the author, Sept. 8, 2004. Svechinsky (b. 1931, Kamenets-Podolsk, Ukraine) grew up in Moscow. Arrested in 1950, he returned from the camps in 1955. He engaged in underground Zionist activity until 1967 and began an open struggle for repatriation in 1969. Svechinsky emigrated from the Soviet Union to Israel in 1971. Excerpts from Kosharovsky's interviews with activists presented in this book have been edited for concision and focus.

7. A "tenner" refers to a sentence of ten years, which was lighter than other sentences in the Stalin era.

8. Natan Zabara (1908–1975) was a Yiddish writer, imprisoned from 1950 to 1956, who became one of the first Hebrew teachers in Kiev following his release. His books included *Haint vert geboirn a velt* [Today the World Is Born, 1965], and an unfinished historical novel, "Hagalgal hahozer" [The Wheel of Eternity], 1970–75.

9. A *sharashka* is a prison research institute, made famous in Alexander Solzhenitsyn's books about life in the Gulag.

10. Yaacov Ro'i discussed these groups in *The Struggle for Soviet Jewish Emigration, 1948–1967* (Cambridge, UK: Cambridge Univ. Press, 1991), 61–62.

11. Ro'i, *The Struggle,* 62–63.

12. Ibid., 62.

13. "Sovetskii Soiuz. Evrei v Sovetskom Soiuze v 1953–67 gg." (The Soviet Union. Jews in the Soviet Union, 1953–67), in *Kratkaia evreiskaia entsiklopedia,* 11 vols. (Jerusalem: Keter, 1976–2005), 8:257, http://www.eleven.co.il/.

14. Ro'i, *The Struggle,* 261.

15. On this activity, see ibid., 276, 279.

16. Ro'i, *The Struggle*, 282–83.

17. David Khavkin, interview with the author, Sept. 8, 2004. Khavkin (1930, Moscow–2013) was arrested in 1958 for Zionist activity. After returning to Moscow in 1965, he became a leader of the early Zionists. Khavkin left for Israel in 1969.

18. Boris Podolsky made contact with the Israeli embassy to get materials on Israel, and he and his family, along with others, including Tina Brodetsky, facilitated the distribution of materials (Ro'i, *The Struggle*, 77, 281–82).

19. The 101-kilometer marker indicated the minimum distance outside of Moscow where former prisoners were allowed to reside.

20. Ro'i, *The Struggle*, 288.

21. German (Yirmiyahu) Branover (b. 1931, Riga), doctor of physics and math, emigrated from the USSR to Israel in 1972. He began studying Torah in the USSR and translated religious texts into Russian, which were published in Israel. In Israel Branover headed the Shamir Association of Religious Professionals from the USSR and its publishing house. He assisted the government in drawing up a plan of employment for *olim* from the USSR.

22. Ro'i, *The Struggle*, 289.

23. Ibid., 306–8.

24. *The Glass Cage* (1965) was a French film directed by Philippe Arthuys. The film about a kibbutz referred to here was probably the popular Israeli comedy *Sallah Shabati* (1964).

25. Ro'i, *The Struggle*, 290.

26. Sverdlovsk (formerly and currently Yekaterinburg) was the city Kosharovsky considered his hometown. The protests of 1970 were part of the more widespread and vigorous protests provoked by the Leningrad trial, described below.

27. Yuli Kosharovsky punctuated his history with personal reminiscences such as this one, keyed to the periods he described. Kosharovsky (1941–2014) was a Hebrew teacher and a leading organizer of Jewish activity in Moscow and other cities. Initially employed as an aviation engineer working at an institute where they developed guidance systems for nuclear missiles, Kosharovsky left that job and the secrecy it entailed in 1968. He applied for an exit visa in 1971. As an activist leader, Kosharovsky ran the Engineers' Seminar in Moscow. He systematized the teaching of Hebrew and set up various pedagogical and social activities for students and teachers of Hebrew. In the early 1980s Kosharovsky helped run a project to support Hebrew teaching to other Soviet cities. With other leading activists of the Jewish movement he set up the organizing committee Mashka in 1983, to collect information and coordinate and support activities for refuseniks. Kosharovsky repatriated to Israel in 1989 after spending eighteen years in refusal. Excerpts from Kosharovsky's personal recollections have been edited for concision and focus.

28. See below on the "Voices."

29. Shapiro's Hebrew-Russian dictionary was published as F. L. Shapiro, *Ivrit-russkii slovar'* (Moscow: Gosudarstvennoe izdatel'stvo inostrannykh i natsional'nykh slovarei, 1963).

30. *Iton* [Hebrew for Newspaper], nos. 1–2 (1970), was a samizdat journal created by the VKK (Vsesoiuznyi koordinatsionnyi komitet [All-Union Coordinating Committee]), the first of the underground Jewish periodicals.

31. Shlomo Kodesh's *Hasafa Haivrit* [Hebrew for Hebrew Language] (Jerusalem: Kiryat Sefer, 1963), was popular among Zionist activists in the 1960s. Kodesh wrote the book at the request of Shaul Avigur (of Nativ), who asked him to do a language textbook for Jews in the USSR. See Vera Yedidya, "The Struggle for the Study of Hebrew," in Ro'i and Beker, *Jewish Culture and Identity*, 164–65, notes 57 and 58.

32. Zvi Gitelman wrote, "Perhaps nowhere else in the Jewish Diaspora was the Six-Day War to have as revolutionary and long-lasting effect as it did in the Soviet Union. In the short term, the war galvanized a segment of Soviet Jewry to assert its identification with Israel and to reject the Soviet Union as hostile to Jews . . . [which] led logically to a demand for 'repatriation' to Israel and to the emergence of a dissident movement for Aliyah whose seeds had been scattered and planted long before." See Gitelman, "The Psychological and Political Consequences of the Six-Day War in the U.S.S.R.," in *The Six-Day War and World Jewry*, ed. Eli Lederhendler (Bethesda: Univ. Press of Maryland, 2000), 249.

33. Yosif Begun, interview with the author, Jan. 16, 2004. Begun (b. 1932, Moscow), applied for an exit visa in 1971. Begun taught Hebrew and distributed Jewish materials unofficially. He was arrested for these activities in 1977, 1978, and 1982. Begun immigrated to Israel in 1988.

34. Boris (later Baruch) Ainbinder, interview with the author, July 5, 2004. Ainbinder (b. 1940) applied for an exit visa in 1971, and left for Israel in 1973. Between those years he taught Hebrew, participated in protests, and helped communicate information about refuseniks to supporters in the West.

35. Yakov Kedmi, interview with the author, June 6, 2004. Kedmi (Kazakov) (b. 1947, Moscow) first renounced his Soviet citizenship in June 1967. He was allowed to leave for Israel in 1969. Kedmi subsequently worked on behalf of Soviet Jewry in Israel and was director of the Israeli bureau Nativ (on Nativ, see below) from 1992 to 1999.

36. The Soviet Union broke off diplomatic relations with Israel on June 10, 1967. The next day, June 11, was a Sunday. It may be that Kazakov wrote his letter renouncing Soviet citizenship on June 11, having learned of the break in diplomatic relations, and that he submitted it to the Supreme Soviet of the USSR one or two days later. That letter has not been found. However, having received no official reply, Kazakov composed a second letter on March 20, 1968, and that letter circulated in samizdat and was reprinted abroad.

37. OVIR (Otdel viz i registratsii) is the Soviet office that handled registration of foreign visitors and exit visas.

38. Kazakov's second letter, composed on March 20, 1968, was reported in the *Washington Post* on December 19, 1968 ("Jew Living in Moscow Hits Regime").

39. Yuri Galanskov (1939–1972) was sentenced in 1968 to seven years in labor camps in connection with rights activity including support of the writers Andrei Siniavsky and Yuli

Daniel, who had been arrested in 1965. Galanskov died of complications from a stomach ulcer while serving his term. The trials and sentences of Siniavsky, Daniel, and other rights defenders provoked domestic protests and an international outcry.

40. See chapter 4 on Sharansky's case.

41. Leonard Schroeter discussed the appeal in *The Last Exodus* (Jerusalem: Weidenfeld and Nicolson, 1974), 45.

42. From the *Khronika tekushchikh sobtyii* [Chronicle of Current Events], no. 6 (Feb. 28, 1969), www.memo.ru/history/diss/chr/index.htm. Find in English in *A Chronicle of Current Events*, nos. 1–15 (Zug, CH: Amnesty International Publications, 1978).

43. Boris Kochubievsky, interview with the author, June 2005. Kochubievsky (b. 1936, Kiev) was arrested in 1968 after protesting official Soviet silence about the destruction of Jews in World War II. Kochubievsky was released in 1971, and he went to Israel.

44. See Zand, "Fate, Civilization, Aliya," 23–34.

45. On August 6, 1969, eighteen Jewish families from Georgia wrote an appeal to the UN Commission on Human Rights. Israeli Prime Minister Golda Meir read the letter to the Knesset, and it was published in the West, where its emotional language had a strong impact. Gal Beckerman described the effect of the letter (*When They Come*, 121).

46. Benjamin Pinkus named Vitaly Svechinsky, Meir Gelfond, David Khavkin, Tina Brodetsky, and Izrail Mints among these early leaders. See Pinkus, *National Rebirth and Reestablishment* (Hebrew) (Beer-Sheva, Israel: Ben-Gurion Research Center, Ben-Gurion Univ. of the Negev Press, 1993), 265.

47. From the testimony of Eitan Finkelshtein, interview with the author, June 18, 2004. There were only two operating synagogues in Moscow: the Choral Synagogue in the center of town on Arkhipov Street and a small one in the area of Marina Roshcha. When the synagogue is not specified, the Choral Synagogue is meant.

Simeon Charny wrote that the first large gathering on the famous "hillock" (*gorka*) in the street in front of the Moscow Choral Synagogue by Jews who were not regular members of the community occurred on Simhat Torah in October 1958. Already at that time, a significant percentage of those who gathered were young people. KGB reports named L. B. Bershadsky as an organizer. Evidently from 1958 on, it became traditional for Moscow Jews to gather there on Simhat Torah. See Charny, "Judaism and the Jewish Movement" (Ro'i, *The Jewish Movement*, 314).

48. Schroeter, *The Last Exodus*, 91.

49. Vitaly Svechinsky, interview.

50. Nikolai Berdiaev's *Istoki i smysl russkogo kommunizma* [The Sources and Meaning of Russian Communism], written in 1937, appeared in English translation as *The Origin of Russian Communism*, trans. R. M. French (London: G. Bles, 1937). Another related work is *Russkaia ideia* [The Russian Idea], 1947. Berdiaev's works were difficult to obtain in the Soviet period.

51. Jabotinsky's *Feuilletons*, published in Russian in two collected editions (St. Petersburg, 1913; Berlin, 1922) were very popular in Jewish samizdat. Leonid Katsis discussed the

context and reception of the feuilletons in "Zhabotinskii—publitsist," in Vladimir (Zeev) Zhabotinskii, *Polnoe sobranie sochinenii v deviati tomakh* (Minsk: Met, 2008), vol. 2, book 1, 6–24.

52. Available as Leo Pinsker, "Auto-emancipation" [Autoemanzipation] (New York: National Education Department, Zionist Organization of America, 1948).

53. See chapter 1.

54. The above-mentioned people were all leading members of the Soviet rights movement, sometimes called the human rights movement and commonly called the democratic movement. On rights activists and other dissident groups, see Ludmilla Alexeyeva, *Soviet Dissent*.

55. Anatoly Iakobson (1935–1978) was one of the founders of the human rights bulletin *Khronika tekushchikh sobytii* [Chronicle of Current Events]. He left for Israel in September 1973 with his wife, Maia Ulanovsky, and son Alexander.

56. Vladimir Bukovsky (b. 1942) was one of those locked away in psychiatric institutions in order to silence their dissent. See his memoirs, *To Build a Castle—My Life as a Dissenter*, trans. Michael Scammell (New York: Viking Press, 1978). In 1976 Bukovsky was exchanged for a Chilean Communist prisoner and began living in the West.

57. Alexander (Alik) Ginzburg (1936–2002), Yuri Galanskov (1939–1972), Aleksei Dobrovolsky, and Vera Lashkov were arrested for compiling and distributing the samizdat White Book on the trial of Andrei Siniavsky and Yuli Daniel. Their 1968 trial was referred to as The Trial of the Four. On the trial and its effects mobilizing dissidents, see Alexeyeva, *Soviet Dissent*, 280.

58. Leonid Vasilev was a Russian dissident imprisoned in 1950 for anti-Soviet activity and released in 1956.

59. See the previous interview segment with Svechinsky for the note on Natan Zabara.

60. David Drabkin, interview with the author, Sept. 8, 2004. Drabkin (1923–2005) helped organize invitations from Israel for those who wanted to leave, and he translated Leon Uris's *Exodus*. He immigrated to Israel in 1971.

61. See Ro'i on the issue of economic crimes and Jews sentenced to death in the USSR for such crimes (*The Struggle*, 130–31, 138, 163–64).

62. A *heder* is a traditional primary school for religious Jewish boys.

63. *Elef Milim* [Hebrew for A Thousand Words], a four-volume textbook by Yosef Ben-Shefer and Aharon Rozen published in Israel in 1954–59, was widely used for informal Hebrew study in the Soviet Union during this period. It circulated in samizdat copies.

64. Vitaly Svechinsky, interview.

65. On these and other means for supporting activities, see Michael Beizer, "How the Movement Was Funded," in Ro'i, *The Jewish Movement*, 359–91.

66. Vitaly Svechinsky, interview.

67. The list of those who participated in *Iton* appeared in Benjamin Pinkus, "Soviet Jewish Self-Expression, 1945–1988," *Jews in Eastern Europe* 3, no. 25 (1994): 29.

68. Vitaly Svechinsky, interview.

69. Shimon Redlich wrote that "[t]he first wave of Jewish collective appeals started in the second half of 1969." Redlich surveyed the early period of appeals and petitions, including the stimulating effect of campaigns by rights activists on Jewish activists, in "Jewish Appeals in the USSR," *Soviet Jewish Affairs* 4, no. 2 (1974): 27.

70. See Hillel Butman, *From Leningrad to Jerusalem: The Gulag Way,* trans. Stefani Hoffman, ed. Carol Talpers (Berkeley, CA: Benmir Books, 1990), 145, 157–58.

71. Boris Morozov, ed., *Documents on Soviet Jewish Emigration* (London: Frank Cass, 1999), doc. 27, 113–15.

72. See Butman, *From Leningrad to Jerusalem,* 60.

73. Vitaly Svechinsky, interview. The reference is to the leading samizdat rights bulletin *Khronika tekushchikh sobytii* [Chronicle of Current Events].

74. Vitaly Svechinsky, interview.

75. Ten Moscow families had applied for exit visas and received refusal on the same day.

76. The Crimean Tatars had been fighting for the right to return to the Crimea from which they had been deported during World War II (see above). Their efforts received a boost when they began working with rights activists in 1968. See Alexeyeva, *Soviet Dissent,* 146.

77. In December 1964 Yuri Maltsev wrote a letter renouncing his Soviet citizenship because of his refusal to accept the official ideology. As a result, he was fired from his teaching position at Moscow State University. He subsequently wrote a number of other letters demanding an exit visa and protesting rights violations, and in 1969 he was forcibly hospitalized for psychiatric treatment. From the *Slovar' dissidentov* [Dictionary of Dissidents], forthcoming from the International Memorial Society, Moscow.

78. The "Trial of the Four"—see above.

79. See Andrei Amalrik's *Will the Soviet Union Survive until 1984?* (New York: Harper and Row, 1970); and *Involuntary Journey to Siberia* (New York: Harcourt, Brace, Jovanovich, 1970).

80. Chalidze put his name and address on his samizdat journal *Obshchestvennye problemy* [Social Problems], nos. 1–15, 1969–72.

81. This letter and others from Soviet Jews were published later in the Israeli series *Evrei i evreiskii narod. Petitsii, pis'ma i obrashcheniia evreev SSSR* [Jews and the Jewish People: Petitions, Letters and Appeals from the Jews of the USSR] 1 (1973): letter 21, 33–34. Hereafter: *Petitsii, pis'ma.*

82. Vitaly Svechinsky, interview.

83. Elina Bystritsky and Arkady Raikin were famous Soviet performers. General David Dragunsky was a famous war hero, later appointed head of the Anti-Zionist Committee of the Soviet Public.

84. Leonid Zamiatin, head of the Foreign Ministry Press Department 1962–70; from 1970 director-general of TASS.

85. Vitaly Svechinsky, interview.

86. Elie Wiesel, *The Jews of Silence. A Personal Report on Soviet Jewry* (New York: Holt, Rinehart and Winston, 1966).

87. Letters to officials in the USSR and abroad came from signatories in Leningrad and Moscow, and also from Belarus, Bukhara, Georgia, Latvia, Lithuania, Moldavia, Tashkent, Ukraine, the Ural region, and Siberia. For the period 1968–70, 300 letters were recorded, while the number grew to 366 letters for 1971 alone, and to 391 letters for 1973. See *Petitsii, pis'ma*, vols. 1–2 (1973), vols. 3–4 (1974), vol. 7 (1977).

88. See emigration figures in table 3.1, "Exit, Aliya, and Dropping Out of Soviet Jews, 1968–91," in Yaacov Ro'i, "The Achievements of the Jewish Movement" (Ro'i, *The Jewish Movement*, 107). Ro'i referred to the Jewish Agency for Israel Report, 1993, which appeared in Yehuda Dominitz, "Israel's Immigration Policy and the Dropout Phenomenon," in *Russian Jews on Three Continents: Migration and Resettlement*, ed. Noah Lewin-Epstein, Yaacov Ro'i, and Paul Ritterband (London: Frank Cass, 1997), 119.

89. Yaacov Ro'i provided an overview of the attempt to hijack an airplane, the arrests, the trial, and ensuing international protests in "Strategy and Tactics" (Ro'i, *The Jewish Movement*, 54–60).

90. On events associated with the escape plan and its consequences, see Butman, *From Leningrad to Jerusalem.*

91. Ibid., 120.

92. David Chernoglaz (Maayan), interview with the author, Feb. 28, 2007. Chernoglaz (b. 1939, Leningrad), a member of the VKK, was arrested in 1970 as part of the attempted airplane hijacking process. Chernoglaz served five years, and after his release in 1975, he immigrated to Israel.

93. Butman, *From Leningrad to Jerusalem*, 150.

94. Edward Kuznetsov, interview with the author, May 18, 2004. Kuznetsov (b. 1939, Moscow), arrested in 1961 for anti-Soviet activity and imprisoned for seven years, was one of the organizers of the attempted airplane hijacking in 1970. Kuznetsov's death sentence was commuted to fifteen years, and he was released in a prisoner exchange in 1979, after which he emigrated from the USSR to Israel.

95. In addition to the twelve mentioned previously, four other participants waited at Priozersk.

96. Kuznetsov talked about his time in prison and his decision to leave general rights activism in favour of Jewish activism in "Interview with Eduard Kuznetsov," *In Search of Self: The Soviet Jewish Intelligentsia and the Exodus. A Collection of Articles*, ed. David Prital (Jerusalem: Mount Scopus Publications, 1982), 95–107.

97. Morozov, *Documents*, document 17, 85.

98. Kosharovsky and Valery Kukui sent an open letter from Sverdlovsk addressed to the Soviet leaders Brezhnev and Podgorny and the Supreme Court of the USSR. It asserted that the sentence was "unjustifiably cruel and inhuman" and pointed out that the defendants

were motivated by the absence of legal means for departure and by "the Soviet authorities' failure to observe their own country's laws." Yuli Kosharovsky, personal archive.

99. The wedding of Ruth Aleksandrovich and Isai Averbukh finally took place a year later on November 15, 1971, after the couple arrived in Israel. WIZO, the worldwide women's Zionist organization, arranged a lavish wedding for them with more than a thousand guests, including Prime Minister Golda Meir, the head of the opposition Menachem Begin, and the legendary defense minister Moshe Dayan.

100. Aron (Arkady) Shpilberg, interview with the author, Mar. 5, 2007. Shpilberg (b. 1938, Leningrad) became involved with Jewish activity in 1966. In 1967 he moved to Riga, where he distributed Zionist materials. Arrested in 1970, he was sentenced to three years of imprisonment. Released in 1973, Shpilberg emigrated from the Soviet Union to Israel.

101. The Joint (American Jewish Joint Distribution Committee) is a Jewish philanthropic organization founded in 1914.

102. Morozov, *Documents*, 86–87.

103. Aron Shpilberg, interview.

104. Palatnik effectively communicated her concerns through open letters, and her case became a cause célèbre in the West, prompting the formation of the Jewish women's group "The 35s—The Women's Campaign for Soviet Jewry" in London in May 1971. The name of the group reflects the fact that Palatnik was arrested on her thirty-fifth birthday. Subsequently operating in a number of Western countries, members of "The 35s" were women who identified with a female Prisoner of Zion close in age to many of them. They dedicated their efforts to drawing attention to Palatnik's plight and the cause of Soviet Jewry.

105. An article entitled "Where Is the Land of Our Ancestors?" by E. Denisov appeared in the newspaper *Uralskii rabochii* [The Ural Worker] on February 21, 1971. The anti-Zionist article named Kukui and Kosharovsky. From Kosharovsky's personal archives.

3. Context and Strategies

1. Albert D. Chernin, "Making Soviet Jews an Issue: A History," in *A Second Exodus: The American Movement to Free Soviet Jews*, ed. Murray Friedman and Albert D. Chernin (Hanover, NH: Brandeis Univ. Press, 1999), 60. An account of the Brussels Conference appears also in Beckerman, *When They Come for Us*, 224–28.

2. Morozov, *Documents*, document 13, 65.

3. Viktor Polsky, interview with the author, Sept. 21, 2004. Viktor Polsky (1930, Moscow–2010) was an important leader of the movement in the early years. In 1974 he was framed for hitting a girl who attempted suicide by throwing herself under his car. When facts contradicting the official version of events appeared, authorities let Polsky off with a nominal fine and issued him and his family exit visas. The Polsky family repatriated to Israel.

4. A "free" diploma came without a specific work assignment, as opposed to the usual Soviet practice of assigning a place of work after graduation.

5. On Nativ, see chapter 1 and sidebar on p. 94.

6. Vladimir (Volodia) Slepak, interview with the author, Mar. 23, 2004. Slepak (1927–2015) was born in Moscow to a highly placed Communist family, and he spent his early childhood in China. Vladimir and his wife, Maria (Masha), applied for an exit visa in 1970. Their home was an important meeting place for activists and foreign visitors, and he was a leader of the Jewish movement. Slepak also became one of the founders of the Moscow Helsinki group together with democratic rights activists. In 1978 the Slepaks hung a banner from their balcony demanding the right to leave for Israel. For this Vladimir was exiled to Siberia. He continued his activity after returning in 1982, going on hunger strikes. Vladimir and his wife emigrated from the USSR to Israel in 1987.

7. In the Soviet educational system, after completion of institute studies, in order to receive the diploma it was necessary to prepare, write up, and defend a work project carried out at the assignment location.

8. The Komsomol was the CPSU youth organization designed to indoctrinate youth with Communist ideology.

9. Mark Blum became Mordecai Lapid in Israel.

10. Information about the Slepaks that could be used in Israel to issue a personalized invitation to come to Israel.

11. It was easier to obtain an exit visa if one had no access to classified information; having a high level of access often meant long years of refusal.

12. Nehemiah Levanon was head of Nativ (Lishkat hakesher) from 1970 to 1980.

13. Vladimir Prestin, interview with the author, Jan. 24, 2004. Vladimir Prestin (1934–2015), born in Leningrad, moved to Moscow after the war. He first applied for a visa in 1970. Prestin taught Hebrew, helped plan the 1976 Symposium on Jewish Culture, and participated in the production of Jewish samizdat. He was associated with the Cultural activists (*kulturniki*). Prestin left the USSR for Israel in 1988.

14. See Yuli Kosharovsky's biographical information in chapter 2 at the first segment of his "Personal Recollections."

15. Ilia Voitovetsky, interview with the author, May 27, 2004. Voitovetsky (1936–2015), born in the Vinnitsky oblast, went to Sverdlovsk to attend the Polytechnic Institute and subsequently began working at a closed research institute (an institute with special security considerations) designing submarine navigation systems. He applied for an exit visa in 1971 and received permission to leave at the end of that year. Voitovetsky immigrated to Israel.

16. The first department was a personnel office where KGB officers, the men in "black suits," might discuss issues with an employee, including threats to employment or proposals to cooperate with the security services.

17. Yuli's wife, Sonia, could not emigrate with him because at the time she needed to take care of her ill elderly mother.

18. Vladimir Aks (b. 1941, Kharkov) became an early Zionist activist in Sverdlovsk. He left for Israel in 1971. Aks provided an interview to the author on May 23, 2004.

19. Sverdlovsk was a "closed" city, that is, a city with special security considerations because of weapons manufacture, military installations, or nuclear facilities in the area.

20. Nora Kornblum was told by the authorities that she had to divorce Kosharovsky in order to obtain an exit visa. After her departure, Kosharovsky was able legally to live in her former apartment. From Kosharovsky's personal recollections.

21. Benjamin Pinkus calculated that 5,454 people signed petitions for emigration between 1969 and 1978, most of them between 1968 and 1973. He classified nearly three hundred people as "leaders" in the 1969–83 period, including eighty-seven who were put on trial. See Pinkus, *The Jews of the Soviet Union: The History of a National Minority* (Cambridge, UK: Cambridge Univ. Press, 1988), 312–14.

22. *Petitsii, pis'ma* 5 (1976): 11, 37–38.

23. See Ro'i, *The Jewish Movement*, table 3.1, 107.

24. *News Bulletin on Soviet Jewry* 211 (Dec. 2–Jan. 1, 1972). The bulletin was prepared by the Action Committee of Newcomers from the Soviet Union and edited by Ann Shenkar.

25. Colin Shindler, *Exit Visa, Détente, Human Rights and the Jewish Emigration Movement in the USSR* (London: Bachman and Turner, 1978), 20.

26. *News Bulletin on Soviet Jewry* 213 (Feb. 24–Mar. 12) and 215 (Apr. 8–May 3, 1972).

27. Shindler, *Exit Visa*, 18.

28. Benjamin Pinkus discussed the position of the Nixon administration in *National Rebirth*, 483.

29. Shindler, *Exit Visa*, 27.

30. In an open letter to the US Congress from Sept. 14, 1973, influential democratic dissident Andrei Sakharov argued that using legislation to make free emigration a "minimal condition" for the fulfillment of agreements made in the context of détente was appropriate. He urged the American Congress to assume its "historical responsibility before mankind." See "A Letter to the Congress of the United States" (Sept. 14, 1973) in *Sakharov Speaks* (London: Collins and Harvill, 1974), 211–15. William Korey discussed the influence of Sakharov's letter in "Jackson-Vanik: A 'Policy of Principle,'" in *A Second Exodus*, 97–98, 105.

31. Reported in "Aresty, obyski, doprosy" (Arrests, Searches, Interrogations), *Khronika tekushchikh sobytii* [Chronicle of Current Events] 27 (Oct. 15, 1972).

32. Shindler, *Exit Visa*, 41.

33. Excerpts of a record of the meeting of Mar. 20, 1973, were published in the post-Soviet era in *Novoe Vremia* 9 (1996), 42–44, which appeared in English in Morozov, *Documents*, 170–76.

34. Feingold detailed Secretary of State Henry Kissinger's resistance to the amendment. Aware of the threat it posed to the policy of détente, Kissinger insisted that "the best opportunity for emigration lay in an unofficial agreement" (*"Silent No More,"* 131).

35. Levanon, *HaKod "Nativ,"* 401.

36. See Slepak's comments above.

37. Reported in the article "Sovetskii Soiuz. Evrei v Sovetskom Soiuze v 1967–85 gg" (The Soviet Union. Jews in the Soviet Union 1967–1985), in *Kratkaia evreiskaia entsiklopedia*, vol. 8, 271.

38. The amendment sponsored by Senator Adlai E. Stevenson III, which was unrelated to the Jackson-Vanik Amendment and little known to Jewish organizations, promised to cap trade credits to the Soviet Union at $300 million for the next four years, significantly less than the $1 billion the Kremlin sought over the next three years within the context of most-favored-nation status. See analysis by Korey ("Jackson-Vanik," 110–11).

39. An ulpan (from the Hebrew for "studio" or "educational institution") is a center for intensive study of Hebrew and Jewish culture, mainly for adults. Ulpans facilitated the teaching of modern Hebrew in various countries and the integration of repatriated citizens in Israel. On the use of ulpans in the Soviet Union, see Vera Yedidya's "The Struggle for the Study of Hebrew," in Ro'i and Beker, *Jewish Culture and Identity*, 136–67. See also Ro'i on "Ulpanim" and Ari Volvovsky on "The Teaching and Study of Hebrew" in Ro'i, *The Jewish Movement*, 73–75; 344–55.

40. For example, on Feb. 22, 1972, twenty-two Hebrew teachers from several cities appealed to the chairman of the World Union for the Dissemination of Hebrew in a letter that identified a lack of textbooks and dictionaries as a principal obstacle facing those who wanted to study and teach Hebrew in the USSR. From *Petitsii, pis'ma* 5 (1976): 75–76.

41. Pavel Abramovich, interview with the author, May 19, 2007.

42. From Kosharovsky's personal recollections.

43. Begun's letter was recorded in *Petitsii, pis'ma* 6 (1976): 99–100.

44. Yosif Begun, interview.

45. Their letter can be found in *Petitsii, pis'ma* 5 (1976): 83–84.

46. Ari Volvovsky said that Moshe Palhan was "the first to develop a methodology for teaching Hebrew suited to the conditions prevalent in the Soviet Union and the needs of Soviet Jews." See Volvovsky, "The Teaching and Study of Hebrew" in Ro'i, *The Jewish Movement*, 338.

47. Mikhail Chlenov, interview with the author, Jan. 31, 2004. On Chlenov, see chapter 4.

48. Zeev Shakhnovsky, interview with the author, Feb. 27, 2006. Shakhnovsky (b. 1941, Moscow) applied for an exit visa in 1972. He taught Hebrew beginning in 1971 and became a leading figure in the religious renaissance associated with Chabad—on religious activity, see below. Shakhnovsky left for Israel in 1989.

49. Israel Palhan, interview with the author, July 22, 2004. Israel Palhan (b. 1945, Tomsk) immigrated to Israel in 1972.

50. Moshe Palhan, interview with the author, Aug. 7, 2004. Moshe Palhan (b. Ernst Trakhtenberg, 1939) spent his early years in Tomsk before the family returned to the Moscow area to live. Moshe started teaching Hebrew in 1968. He left for Israel in 1971.

51. Lea Trakhtman-Palhan was born in Ukraine in 1913 and immigrated with her family to Palestine in 1922. She was later expelled from Palestine by the mandatory authority as a member of the Palestine Communist Party.

52. Zeev Shakhnovsky, interview.

53. Sara Frenkel (Frankel) wrote for the Israeli press and worked at the radio station *Kol Yisrael* beginning in 1970, reporting on questions related to immigration and diaspora. Frenkel established regular phone contact with Soviet Jews and became one of the best-informed Israeli individuals on the topic. She joined Nativ and served as their emissary in New York from 1978 to 1983, becoming the first woman and the first Likud sympathizer working for the Bureau. See Pauline Peretz, *Le combat pour les juifs soviétiques. Washington-Moscou-Jérusalem 1953–1989* (Paris: Armand Colin, 2006), 266; and Pauline Peretz, "The Action of Nativ's Emissaries in the United States. A Trigger for the American Movement to Aid Soviet Jews, 1958–1974," trans. Julie Wayne and Pauline Peretz, *Bulletin du Centre de recherche français de Jérusalem* 14 (2004): 112–28, accessed Jan. 2, 2008, http://bcrfj.revues.org/document270.html.

54. Greville Janner, a British politician of Jewish origin, served as Labour MP from 1970 to 1997. He subsequently became a member of the House of Lords. Janner advocated on behalf of refuseniks in Parliament and maintained personal telephone connections with some of them.

55. The organization Haivrim (Aivrim) was established by Israel Palhan after he arrived in Israel in 1972, in order to send books in Hebrew by ordinary mail to recipients in the Soviet Union. See testimony by Dan Roginsky, below.

56. Boris Ainbinder, interview.

57. Michael Sherbourne, a schoolteacher in London who knew Russian and communicated extensively with Soviet Jewish activists in order to advocate for their rights, coined the English term "refusenik" in 1971 to translate the Russian *otkaznik*.

58. Dan Roginsky, interview with the author, Aug. 22, 2004. Roginsky (b. 1939, Moscow), a physicist with a PhD, applied for a visa in 1971. He became a Hebrew teacher and helped maintain contacts with Western supporters to transmit news about refuseniks. Roginsky participated in the scientific seminars led by Lerner and Voronel, and he was one of the seven scientists to go on a hunger strike in June 1973. Later that year, Roginsky left for Israel.

59. Alexander Lerner, *Change of Heart* (Minneapolis, MN: Lerner Publications, 1992), 192.

60. Alexander Voronel, interview with the author, Apr. 11, 2007. Voronel (b. 1931), a professor of physics and mathematical science, had been arrested as a youth in Cheliabinsk for distributing (non-Jewish) illegal leaflets. He was mobilized with democratic activists by the 1965 arrests of Siniavsky and Daniel. In the early 1970s he began working with Jewish activists. Voronel organized the first scientific seminar, facilitated the establishment

of a humanities seminar in which he also participated, and founded the samizdat journal *Evrei v SSSR* [Jews in the USSR], working as its first chief editor. In 1972 he and his wife, Nina Voronel (a writer), applied for exit visas, and they left for Israel in 1975. Nina Voronel described their life in *Bez prikras. Vospominaniia* (Moscow: Zakharov, 2003).

61. Voronel's autobiographical and philosophical work *Trepet iudeiskikh zabot* [The Tremor of Judaic Anxieties] appeared in the samizdat journal *Evrei v SSSR*, nos. 10–11. It later appeared in Israel, in Russian, as *Trepet zabot iudeiskikh* (Jerusalem: Stav, 1976).

62. The Committee of Concerned Scientists was an organization of American scientists who supported the struggle of refusenik scientists in the Soviet Union. Yuval Neeman was part of a Scientists' Committee for Soviet Jewry in Israel. Both committees were formed with the help of Nativ.

63. Mark Azbel, interview with the author, Mar. 26, 2006. Azbel (b. 1932, Kharkov), a doctor of physical and mathematical sciences, applied for an exit visa for the first time in 1972. He participated in the Collective Phenomena seminar and led it after Voronel's departure, serving also as editor for the samizdat journal *Evrei v SSSR*. Azbel left for Israel in 1977.

64. Mark Azbel described the logic of the timing in his book *Refusenik: Trapped in the Soviet Union* (Boston: Houghton Mifflin, 1981), 303.

65. *Jerusalem Post*, June 18, 2003.

66. Roginsky believed the hunger strike played a role in getting him a visa. Dan Roginsky, interview.

67. Azbel, *Refusenik*, 332.

68. Mark Azbel, interview.

69. Remarks condensed from Viktor Brailovsky's interview with Aba Taratuta, *Remember and Save*, http://www.soviet-jews-exodus.com.

70. Alexander Lerner, interview with the author, Feb. 24, 2004. Lerner (1913–2004), a member of the Academy of Sciences since the mid-1950s, had been director of the Institute of Control Problems. He applied for an exit visa for the first time in 1971. He worked with leading Jewish activists and established contact with Andrei Sakharov. Lerner knew English and had many contacts with foreign scientists. His seminar for refuseniks on control systems and the use of mathematical methods ran from 1972 to 1981. Lerner finally left the USSR for Israel in 1988.

71. Vitaly Rubin (1923–1981) graduated from the History Department (Chinese Division) of Moscow State University in 1951. He and his wife, Inna, were in refusal beginning in 1972. After the Rubins left for Israel in 1976, Arkady Mai ran the seminar.

72. Beginning in 1974, the seminar moved to Feliks Kandel's apartment. Kandel's larger, separate apartment in a writers' building with cultured neighbors was a more hospitable location for such gatherings.

73. The Hong Wei Bing (Red Guards) were active participants in the Cultural Revolution initiated by Mao Tse Tung in 1966. They consisted primarily of student youth who

carried out pogroms against those who followed the "wrong path." In 1969 the organization of Hong Wei Bing was dispersed and the participants were expelled to the provincial regions of China. Thanks to Soviet press reports, the term "Hong Wei Bing" (Hunveibiny) had currency in the USSR in the late 1960s and 1970s.

74. Mikhail Babel, interview with the author, May 2, 2006.

75. Leonid Tsypin, along with Alexander Lipavsky, publicly denounced Anatoly Sharansky for treason. Sharansky was arrested in March 1977.

76. Andrei Tverdokhlebov (1940–2011) was a physicist and prominent rights activist associated with the democratic movement. In 1970 Tverdokhlebov founded the Committee on Human Rights in the USSR along with Valery Chalidze and Andrei Sakharov.

77. Although Nudel and Slepak hung their banners the same day (June 1, 1978), they were tried separately. Both were convicted of "malicious hooliganism" and sentenced to four and five years in exile, respectively.

78. Valery Krizhak, interview with the author, Apr. 23, 2006. Krizhak (1939, Kiev) studied at the Moscow Auto-Mechanical Institute. He began studying Hebrew in 1970 and applied for an exit visa in 1971. Krizhak participated in demonstrations and helped form the Hong Wei Bing group. He and his family left for Israel in 1974.

79. Natan Sharansky, interview with the author, June 21, 2007. On Sharansky, see chapter 4.

80. Natalia Shtiglits (Stieglitz), later Avital Sharansky, married Anatoly Sharansky July 4, 1974, and left the next day on an exit visa due to expire shortly. She was highly effective campaigning around the world on his behalf until his release on February 11, 1986.

81. Natan Sharansky, interview.

82. Mikhail Grinberg, interview with the author, May 6, 2007. Grinberg (b. 1951), educated as a historian, became close to Chabad leaders and other Hasidic groups near Moscow beginning in 1969. By the 1980s he had taken a leading role in the religious community. Grinberg left for Israel in 1988, and in the 1990s he founded the publishing house Gesharim, which publishes literature about Judaism and other works in Russian.

83. Zeev Shakhnovsky, interview.

84. Ilia (Eliyahu) Essas, interview with the author, May 6, 2006. Essas (b. 1946, Vilnius) moved to Moscow in 1970. He applied for an exit visa in 1973. Essas helped refuseniks with religious matters and began to teach Torah in 1977. In 1983 he became ordained as a rabbi, the only Soviet Jew of his generation to be so ordained by Western rabbis. Essas also worked as an editor on the refusenik journals *Jews in the USSR* and *Tarbut*. He left for Israel in 1986.

85. Vladimir (Zeev) Dashevsky, interview with the author, May 7, 2006. Dashevsky (b. 1937, Poltava) received a doctorate in theoretical physics. He applied for an exit visa in 1977. His informal religious group took shape in 1979–80. In Israel in 1987 his group opened a center to support religious Zionism among Russian speakers. The center's name, "Mahanaim" (Two Camps), refers to Genesis 32:3, and the "two camps" of Moscow and Jerusalem. Dashevsky immigrated to Israel in 1990.

86. See Stefani Hoffman, "Jewish Samizdat and the Rise of Jewish National Consciousness," in Ro'i and Beker, *Jewish Culture and Identity*, 88–111. See also "Samizdat," *Kratkaia evreiskaia entsiklopedia*, vol. 7, 627–42.

87. The Library of Aliya (Biblioteka Aliia) was an Israeli publishing series created in 1972 by Nativ for books on Jewish topics in Russian. The series produced more than 250 books on the creation of the State of Israel, Jewish history, philosophy, and religion that were smuggled into the Soviet Union in the 1970s–80s.

88. The samizdat bulletin *Khronika tekushchikh sobytii* [Chronicle of Current Events], nos. 1–63, 1968–82, was the principal organ of the rights activists associated with the democratic movement in Moscow. It reported violations of human rights and independent activity throughout the Soviet Union; it was circulated widely and attracted international attention. Information on these titles is included in the database *Soviet Samizdat Periodicals*, compiled by Ann Komaromi (Toronto: Univ. of Toronto Libraries, 2011), http://samizdat.library.utoronto.ca.

89. Jewish samizdat journals produced prior to perestroika were reprinted in the series *Evreiskii Samizdat* (Jerusalem: Hebrew University—Center for Documentation of East European Jewry, 1971–92), 1–27. See also Ann Komaromi, "Jewish Samizdat—Dissident Texts and the Dynamics of the Jewish Revival in the Soviet Union," in Ro'i, *The Jewish Movement*, 273–303.

90. Matvei Chlenov, "Kul'turnicheskoe dvizhenie i zhurnal 'Nash ivrit,'" *Vestnik evreiskogo universiteta v Moskve* (Moscow-Jerusalem) 3, no. 10 (1995): 70–88.

91. Vitaly Svechinsky, interview.

92. Alexander Voronel, interview.

93. Viktor Brailovsky, interview with the author, May 17, 2007. Brailovsky (b. 1935) applied for a visa in 1972. As a refusenik, he helped organize and run a scientific seminar for refuseniks and became the last editor of the samizdat journal *Evrei v SSSR*. In 1980 Brailovsky was arrested for his work on the journal, imprisoned, and sentenced to five years of exile. Brailovsky was released in 1984, and he and his wife, Irina, left for Israel in 1987.

94. Father Alexander Men (1935–1990), a Russian Orthodox priest with Jewish origins, known for his ecumenical Christianity, became central to the general, informal, religious renaissance among Soviet intellectuals beginning in the 1960s.

95. Azbel emigrated in 1977.

96. Leonid (Ari) Volvovsky, interview with the author, Apr. 4, 2006. Leonid (Ari) Volvovsky (b. 1942, Gorky), a computer scientist with a doctorate, applied for an exit visa in 1974. Refused and fired from his job, he became a Hebrew teacher and organizer of Jewish cultural activities, participating in planning for the aborted symposium on Jewish culture in 1976 and the Hebrew week, March 1979. Volvovsky became religious and learned to do ritual slaughter, which he performed in Gorky. Arrested in 1985 on Article 190-1 for slander of the Soviet system, Volvovsky served time in the Lensk camp but was released early in 1987. He and his family arrived in Israel in 1988.

97. Vneshtorgbank (Foreign Trade Bank): at the time, the Soviet state had a monopoly and controlled all foreign trade and currency dealings.

98. Ida Nudel, interview with the author, Feb. 11, 2008. Nudel (b. 1931, Krasnoyarsk) applied for an exit visa in 1970. In Moscow she worked to help Prisoners of Zion by corresponding with them and writing on their behalf. She also coordinated material aid sent via prisoners' relatives. In 1978, at the same time as the Slepaks, Ida hung a banner from her apartment demanding an exit visa to Israel. She was arrested and sentenced to four years of internal exile. After release, unable to return to Moscow, Nudel settled in Bendery, Moldova. She was allowed to leave for Israel in 1987. Nudel's autobiography appeared as *A Hand in the Darkness: The Autobiography of a Refusenik,* trans. Stefani Hoffman (New York: Warner Books, 1990).

99. Dina Beilin, interview with the author, Jan. 20, 2008. Beilin (b. 1939), an engineer, applied for an exit visa in 1971 and left for Israel in 1978. In between those years she was active in the Jewish movement, notably keeping lists of refuseniks.

100. See chapter 4 on the Helsinki Final Act.

101. In September–October 1976, twelve activists, including Chernobylsky, Ahss, Slepak, and others, conducted a protest campaign against unjustified refusals. They wrote letters and organized a series of demonstrations in October at important government buildings. At the end of the October 18 demonstration, Nikolai Shchelokov, minister of the interior, promised to receive a delegation of refuseniks.

102. Sofia Kalistratov (1907–1989) was a well-known Moscow lawyer who defended many democratic dissidents. The assistance group formed on November 1, 1976. It included activists from the Jewish movement and observers from the Moscow Helsinki group (on the Helsinki groups, see chapter 4). Kalistratov became the consultant on legal issues for the assistance group.

4. Developments and Divisions

1. Robert C. Toth wrote an article publicizing the rift, "Split among Activist Soviet Jews Breaks into Open over Talks with U.S. Senators," *Los Angeles Times,* July 1 (1975), cited and discussed by Beckerman, *When They Come,* 323.

2. Alexander Lerner, interview.

3. Lerner, *A Change of Heart,* 188–90. As a prominent academician, Lerner had a larger apartment than most Soviet citizens, making it a more appropriate place for meetings with foreigners.

4. Vladimir Prestin, interview.

5. By 1978 the number of "dropouts" among Soviet Jews leaving the USSR for the West exceeded the number arriving in Israel. Yehuda Dominitz detailed the numbers and traced the ideological context for Israel's reaction in "Israel's Immigration Policy and the Dropout Phenomenon," in *Russian Jews on Three Continents: Migration and Resettlement,* ed. Noah Lewin-Epstein, Yaacov Ro'i, and Paul Ritterband (London: Frank Cass, 1997), 118.

6. Veniamin Fain, interview with the author, July 12, 2007. Fain (b. 1930, Kiev–2013), having attained the rank of professor in physics, began working near Moscow in the late 1960s. He attended the scientific seminars for refuseniks beginning in 1972 and applied for an exit visa in 1974. Fain led the group that was planning the 1976 symposium on Jewish culture. In 1977 he was allowed to leave the Soviet Union for Israel. Fain discussed the symposium in Benjamin Fain, "Background to the Present Jewish Cultural Movement in the Soviet Union," in Ro'i and Beker, *Jewish Culture and Identity in the Soviet Union*, 235–45. He also discussed Soviet Jewry and its issues in his book *Vera i razum* [Faith and Reason] (Jerusalem: Mahanaim, 2007), 218.

7. Alexander Lunts, interview with the author, Apr. 7, 2004. Lunts (b. 1924), a mathematician, applied for an exit visa in 1972 from Moscow. He became one of the leading Jewish activists, participating in Voronel's seminar and organizing protests. Lunts emigrated from the USSR to Israel in 1976.

8. Probably Viktor Ivanovich Alidin, chief of the Moscow City and Oblast KGB. Thanks to Yaacov Ro'i for this identification.

9. Mikhail Chlenov, interview with the author, Jan. 31, 2004. Chlenov (b. 1940, Moscow) earned a PhD in ethnography and published studies of Indonesian groups, Siberian peoples, and non-Ashkenazic Jewish groups in Soviet academic publications. Chlenov began participating in the Jewish movement in the early 1970s, becoming one of the leaders of the cultural wing, with a particular focus on developing an autonomous Jewish culture for those living in the USSR. He participated in the planning of the aborted 1976 symposium on Jewish culture and later, in 1989, established the independent organization the Vaad (the Committee), which brought together representatives of Jewish communities in various regions and republics of the Soviet Union and helped bridge the gap between the unofficial Jewish movement and legal Jewish culture.

10. Vladimir Prestin, interview.

11. Much to the surprise of democratic rights activists and other civil-society advocates, Soviet authorities published the full text of the Helsinki Accords in official newspapers in August 1975, providing legal grounds for a whole new set of challenges to Soviet violations of human rights, including the right to emigrate. Liudmila Alekseev referred to the era of rights activism beginning in 1976 as "the Helsinki Period" (Alexeyeva, *Soviet Dissent*, 335–36).

12. On the 1976 symposium on Jewish culture, see below.

13. A Purimspiel is a humorous dramatization of the events recounted in the Book of Esther. These plays performed on or around the festival of Purim are often satirical and topical.

14. Vladimir Prestin, interview.

15. Veniamin Fain, interview.

16. Fain referred to the fact that Solomon Mikhoels had been assassinated and other leaders of Soviet Jewish culture associated with the Jewish Anti-Fascist Committee were eliminated, many executed on August 12, 1952.

17. Mikhail Chlenov, interview.

18. A minyan (plural: minyanim) is a group of at least ten adult males who come together for prayer services. The term may refer to any such groups that assemble more or less regularly in members' homes.

19. Chlenov used the pseudonym Zubin in his work for the symposium.

20. Vladimir Prestin, interview.

21. Fain, *Vera i razum*, 229.

22. Ibid., 231.

23. Veniamin Fain, interview.

24. A list of reports prepared for the symposium appeared in *Evreiskii samizdat* 15 (1978): 20–23.

25. Leonid Volvovsky, interview.

26. Mikhail Chlenov, interview.

27. Vladimir Prestin, interview.

28. Mikhail Chlenov, interview.

29. Anatoly (Natan) Sharansky, interview with the author, June 21, 2007. Sharansky (b. 1948, Donetsk), after completing studies at the Moscow Physical-Technical Institute, took a job at the Oil and Gas Research Institute. Sharansky applied for an exit visa in 1973, and he began participating in Jewish refusenik demonstrations and signing letters. In 1976 he joined Andrei Sakharov and other democratic rights activists in founding the Moscow Helsinki group, and he took an active role in advocating and publicizing Jewish and other human rights issues. On March 15, 1977, Sharansky was arrested on charges of treason and anti-Soviet propaganda; subsequently he was convicted and sentenced to thirteen years in prisons and labor camps. While Sharansky was in the camps, his wife, Avital, who left for Israel right after their marriage in July 1974, campaigned actively for his release. Their case became a cause célèbre, and Sharansky was granted an early release on February 11, 1986, and sent to the West as part of a prisoner exchange. In Israel, Sharansky has remained an advocate for human rights. He has participated in Israeli politics, serving in the Knesset and at the ministerial level in Israeli governments. In 2009 he was appointed chairman of the Jewish Agency for Israel.

30. Martin Gilbert, *Shcharansky, Hero of Our Time* (London: Macmillan London, 1986), 156.

31. Gilbert, *Shcharansky*, 162–65.

32. From Kosharovsky's personal recollections.

33. Gilbert, *Shcharansky*, 172.

34. Anatoly Sharansky, interview.

35. Felix Roziner, *Anatolii Shcharanskii* (Jerusalem: Shamir, 1985), 152–53.

36. Lev Ulanovsky, interview with the author, probably Feb. 11, 2004. Ulanovsky (b. 1950, Moscow), graduate of the Moscow Institute of Physics and Technology, possessed mastery of several languages, including Hebrew, which he began to study long before

applying for an exit visa. A number of Ulanovsky's Hebrew students went on to become prominent teachers. Ulanovsky also hosted a Torah study circle. He left for Israel in 1979.

37. Anatoly Sharansky, interview.

38. Avital Sharansky.

39. The Lishka (Nativ) did not support Sharansky because they feared his activity could endanger the Jewish movement. See Alan M. Dershowitz, *Chutzpah* (Boston: Little, Brown and Co., 1991), 250–55.

40. Robert C. Toth's article appeared in the November 22, 1976, issue of the *Los Angeles Times*. On the friendship between Toth and Sharansky and the use of Toth's article to incriminate Sharansky, see Beckerman, *When They Come*, 331, 375–76.

41. On the trial, see Natan Sharansky, *Fear No Evil*, trans. Stefani Hoffman (New York: Random House, 1988), 224–25.

42. Dina Beilin, interview with the author, Feb. 7, 2008. Beilin (b. 1939), an engineer, applied for an exit visa in 1971. Beilin served as secretary for Lerner's seminar for refuseniks. She kept lists of refusenik information, helped support Jews who wanted to leave, and aided those arrested and imprisoned or exiled. Beilin left for Israel in 1978.

43. Sharansky, *Fear No Evil*, 244.

44. Ibid., 224–25.

45. See table 3.1, "Exit, Aliya, and Dropping Out of Soviet Jews, 1968–91," in Ro'i, *The Jewish Movement*, 107.

46. Lev Ulanovsky, interview.

47. In the Soviet Union, languages were studied in order to translate some of the West's technological, scientific, and cultural achievements into Russian. As contact with foreigners was not encouraged in the closed totalitarian state, conversational language was practically not taught. Instruction focused on grammar and the search for the equivalents of foreign expressions in Russian. Refusenik teachers, however, had different tasks and goals.

48. From Kosharovsky's personal recollections.

49. Mikhail Nudler, interview with the author, May 17, 2006. Nudler (b. 1946, Moscow) began teaching Hebrew in 1973. In the late 1970s he became actively involved in Jewish cultural activities, including organizing samizdat production, a cultural seminar, and the Ovrazhki program. Nudler left the USSR for Israel in 1980.

50. Vladimir Albrekht (b. 1933), a mathematician, participated in the rights movement and helped Jewish activists. He authored two influential samizdat works, "How to Be a Witness," and "How to Conduct Yourself during a Search." The first was very popular among various rights activists, refuseniks, and Jewish activists. Kosharovsky recalled that Albrekht participated in the work of refusenik legal seminars, delivered lectures, and made himself available for consultations with refuseniks. He was tried on December, 15, 1983, and sentenced to three years of imprisonment for "anti-Soviet agitation." Albrekht immigrated to the United States in 1988.

51. The following description of seminar activities comes from Aba Taratuta, interview with the author, May 30, 2007. Taratuta (b. 1935) and his wife, Ida, were leading activists in Leningrad who taught Hebrew and supported Jewish samizdat production, among other activities. They applied for an exit visa in 1973, only leaving for Israel at last in 1988. In Israel, Taratuta and friends collected materials for the Association "Remember and Save" [*Zapomnim i sokhranim*], which became a rich source on the Jewish national movement in general and Leningrad activities in particular. See http://www.soviet-jews-exodus.com.

52. Grigory Kanovich (b. 1934), interview with the author, June 4, 2007. Kanovich, a historian by training, became involved with general rights activism briefly, before turning his attention to Jewish activism. Prodded by the efforts of foreign visitors to educate Soviet Jews on Jewish topics, Kanovich decided to organize a seminar led by the Soviet Jews themselves. He emigrated from the USSR to Israel in March 1981.

53. An active participant in the Leningrad seminar on Jewish history and culture, Lein (b. 1935) analyzed numerous cases of refusal and transmitted his findings to the West. His daughter Nehama was subsequently beaten up on the street. It later became clear that it was done in order to "teach someone a lesson." See Lein's memoirs, *Lest We Forget* (Israel: Jerusalem Publishing Center, 1997), 75. On August 5, 1981, the Leningrad municipal court sentenced Lein to two years of *khimiya* (exile with forced labor) in the small Siberian city of Chernogorsk, six thousand kilometers from Leningrad (*Lest We Forget*, 42–44, 86).

54. Beizer's book *The Jews of St. Petersburg* (Philadelphia: Jewish Publication Society, 1989) appeared in English with a record of the excursions.

55. From Mikhail Beizer, interview with the author, Apr. 25, 2007. Mikhail Beizer (b. 1950, Leningrad) applied for an exit visa in 1979. Beizer led excursions around Jewish historical sites in Leningrad beginning in 1982. He directed a seminar on Jewish history and culture from 1982 to 1987, and he edited the samizdat collection LEA from 1983 to 1987. Beizer emigrated to Israel in 1987. He earned a doctorate in history at Hebrew University in 1996.

56. From Kosharovsky's personal recollections.

57. Mikhail Nudler, interview.

58. Roza Finkelberg, interview with the author, Mar. 30, 2005. Finkelberg (1956–2008) began participating in Jewish unofficial life in 1973. By 1979 she was writing Purimspiel scripts. Finkelberg applied for an exit visa in 1981. She helped organize part of the women's refusenik movement. Finkelberg and her husband, Evgeny, left for Israel in 1986. Part of the founding group of the Zionist Forum, she headed its department on Diaspora ties.

59. Pavel Abramovich, interview with the author, Aug. 22, 2008. Abramovich (b. 1939, Moscow) applied for an exit visa in 1971. He taught Hebrew and participated in the organization of many Jewish cultural activities, including the symposium on Jewish culture planned for 1976. Abramovich emigrated from the Soviet Union to Israel in 1988.

60. Lia Prestin (mother of Vladimir Prestin) wrote about her father and the dictionary he produced in her book *Slovar' zapreshchennogo iazyka: 125-letiiu F.L. Shapiro* (Minsk: MET, 2005).

61. See Ro'i, *The Jewish Movement,* table 3.1, 107.

62. Morozov, *Documents,* document 13, 65.

63. Yakov Kedmi (Kazakov), interview.

64. Mikhail Beizer, interview.

65. Vladimir Kislik, interview with the author, Feb. 19, 2004. Kislik (b. 1935, Kislovodsk) applied for an exit visa in 1973. He began teaching Hebrew and organized scientific and legal seminars in Kiev in the mid-1970s. Later he and his wife, Bella Gulko, ran a legal seminar in Moscow. Kislik was arrested in 1981 and sentenced to three years of forced labor. Kislik and his wife left for Israel in 1989.

66. Yuli Kosharovsky is speaking here. See biographical information at the first segment of "Personal Recollections."

67. "Chronicle of Events," *Soviet Jewish Affairs* (London) 12, no. 1 (1982): 102.

68. "Chronicle of Events," *Soviet Jewish Affairs* 11, no. 2 (1981): 98.

69. For a small fee, the organization Mosgorspravka offered press monitoring on a particular topic. Mushinsky subscribed to materials on Zionism and Israel and regularly received bundles of publications. Using the methodology employed by the journalism faculty of Moscow State University, he calculated the average number of publications around the country.

70. At least seven separate cases of KGB harassment of Hebrew teachers and students were reported for the period from October 1981 to June 1982, in the "Chronicle of Events," *Soviet Jewish Affairs* 12, no. 2 (1982): 86–102.

71. Kosharovsky recalled his own experience: he taught a Hebrew group each morning of the week and led a seminar in the evening. Beginning in mid-1981, he found himself being detained on the way to a lesson almost every week. He and his wife also began receiving phone calls at home with vague threats.

72. "Chronicle of Events," *Soviet Jewish Affairs* 11, no. 3 (1981): 98.

73. Numbers come from "Sovetskii Soiuz. Evrei v Sovetskom Soiuze v 1967–85 gg.," in *Kratkaia evreiskaia entsiklopediia,* vol. 8, 282.

74. Elena Bonner held this press conference on September 8, 1982. See the "Chronicle of Events," *Soviet Jewish Affairs* 13, no. 1 (1983): 100.

75. Beckerman, *When They Come,* 435.

76. Viktor Brailovsky, interview.

77. Parasitism (*tuneiadstvo*), or not holding officially registered employment, was treated as a crime in the Soviet Union. The authorities famously tried poet Joseph Brodsky on this charge in 1964.

78. Yosif Begun, interview with the author, Jan. 16, 2004. Begun (b. 1932, Moscow) began studying Hebrew and socializing with Zionists in the 1960s. He first applied for an

exit visa in 1971. Begun signed letters of protest, taught Hebrew, and produced and distributed Jewish samizdat. He was arrested and given significant terms three times: in 1977, 1978, and 1982. Released in 1987, Begun left for Israel in 1988.

79. Feingold, *"Silent No More,"* 228.

5. Legalization and Mass Aliya

1. See Ro'i, *The Jewish Movement*, table 3.1, 107.

2. "Chronicle of Events," *Soviet Jewish Affairs* 11, no. 2 (1981): 98.

3. "Chronicle of Events," *Soviet Jewish Affairs* 12, no. 3 (1982): 95–96.

4. Alexander Ioffe, interview with the author, Apr. 29, 2004. Ioffe (b. 1938, Leningrad) grew up in Moscow. A mathematician with a doctorate, Ioffe began attending refusenik seminars in 1972. He applied for a visa in 1976. Ioffe led Brailovsky's scientific seminar after Brailovsky's arrest in 1980, and he became a member of the Mashka coordinating group established in 1983. He received permission to emigrate at the end of 1987.

5. On the different religious streams among Jewish activists, "Chabad," "Aguda," and the Religious Zionist Movement, see chapter 3.

6. Pinhas Polonsky, interview with the author, June 6, 2011. Polonsky (b. 1958, Moscow) began to study Hebrew and Torah in the 1970s and applied for an exit visa in 1980. He became part of the religious community, associated with the religious Zionist movement. In addition to organizing courses on Judaism, Torah, and Talmud, Polonsky coordinated with Hebrew teachers to arrange Hebrew instruction for members of his community and provide access to Torah study for others. He also produced religious samizdat. After immigrating to Israel in 1987, Polonsky became editor in chief of the Mahanaim publishing house in Israel.

7. See the conversation in chapter 3 of this book with Vladimir Dashevsky, who was also involved with the establishment of Mahanaim in Israel.

8. Boris Berman, a professional philologist, discovered Torah in the 1970s, studied Hebrew and Aramaic independently, and began teaching Torah by the early 1980s. In popular lectures just outside of Moscow he introduced Judaism to writers, art critics, and directors. Berman left for Israel in 1988 and taught there until he was killed in an automobile accident in 1992.

9. Mikhail Khanin, interview with the author, Apr. 5, 2009. Khanin (b. 1947) studied philosophy at MGU and subsequently earned a PhD in sociology. He began teaching Hebrew in the late 1970s. Khanin also taught Judaism in the early 1980s and became a *sofer* (scribe), capable of writing ritual texts. He applied for an exit visa in 1981 and left the USSR for Israel in 1985.

10. Alexander (Ephraim) Kholmyansky, interview with the author, Apr. 14, 2004. Kholmyansky (b. 1950, Moscow) applied for an exit visa in 1978 and began teaching Hebrew in Moscow in that year. By the early 1980s, he began to implement his idea for an organized underground system to aid Hebrew teachers in other cities, the Cities Project. He

was arrested in 1984 and imprisoned until 1986, but he took up teaching Hebrew again after his release. Kholmyansky left for Israel in 1988. His memoirs appeared as Ephraim Kholmyansky, *Zvuchanie tishiny* [The Sound of Silence; in Hebrew: Kol hademama] (Jerusalem: N.p., 2007).

11. Zeev (Vladimir) Geizel, interview with the author, July 14, 2009. Geizel (b. 1958, Zhdanov, Ukraine) moved to Moscow in 1974 and studied math. By the early 1980s, Geizel taught Hebrew, produced Purimspiels, and organized other cultural activities. He joined the Cities Project in 1983 and helped run the project after Kholmyansky's arrest in 1984. Geizel became the first chairman of the Igud Hamorim, an unofficial organization of Hebrew teachers, before leaving the USSR for Israel in 1988.

12. On the Russian-language publishing series Biblioteka Aliya (Library of Aliya) produced in Israel, see chapter 3 of this book.

13. This title has not been found in the Biblioteka Aliya series. Perhaps Kholmyansky had in mind the book *Safed*, published by the Israel Tourism Administration in 1968, which might have been translated into Russian. On Leon Uris's *Exodus*, see chapter 2 of this book.

14. These books are available as *90 Minutes at Entebbe*, by William Stevenson, with material by Uri Dan (New York: Bantam Books, 1976); and Randolph S. Churchill and Winston S. Churchill, *The Six Day War* (Boston: Houghton Mifflin, 1967). Michael Elkin's book *Forged in Fury*, about the hunt for Nazi war criminals after the end of World War II, appeared in New York (Ballantine Books) in 1971.

15. Dov Kontorer, interview with the author, Feb. 1, 2010. Kontorer (b. 1963, Moscow) began to work with religious Jews in 1981, traveling to different cities on missions to support Jewish individuals in need of religious support or other types of aid. In 1984 he joined the Cities Project to help Hebrew teachers. Kontorer left the USSR in 1988.

16. Yuli Edelstein, interview with the author, Nov. 20, 2007. Edelstein (b. 1958, Chernovtsy) moved to Moscow in 1978. He first applied for an exit visa from Moscow in 1979. In 1977 Edelstein began studying Hebrew, quickly becoming an outstanding teacher; he was selected to train Hebrew teachers in other areas as part of the Cities Project. In 1983 Edelstein joined the organizational committee Mashka. Arrested in 1984 on trumped-up charges of narcotics possession, he served time until May 1987. In that year he left the USSR. In Israel Edelstein served as a Knesset member. In 2013 he was elected Speaker of the Knesset.

17. Mashka was an acronym from "Moadon le Shtia Kabira" (Hebrew). The unofficial group, which took shape in late 1983, functioned as a low-profile and relatively loosely structured executive committee, analyzing, directing, and supporting activities within the Jewish movement from 1983 until the late 1980s. Mashka was the first countrywide organizing committee since the VKK, which had been formed in August 1969 but disbanded in June 1970 after arrests (see chapter 2). While the VKK had involved representatives from a number of cities, Mashka was based in Moscow.

18. Anatoly Khazanov, interview with the author, Apr. 15, 2004. Khazanov (b. 1937, Moscow) earned a PhD in ethnography. He applied for an exit visa in 1980. Khazanov

helped form the Mashka committee and wrote their analytic reports. He also participated in the Jewish Cultural Association. Khazanov emigrated from the USSR in 1985.

19. On the Jewish Cultural Association, a founding congress of which was initially held in May 1988, see below.

20. Mikhail Chlenov, interview.

21. Chlenov probably had in mind the refuseniks' *Informatsionnyi biulleten' po voprosam evreiskoi repatriatsii i kul'tury* [Information Bulletin on Issues of Jewish Repatriation and Culture], which Smukler edited. Hereafter referred to as *Informatsionnyi biulleten'*.

22. On the Vaad, see below.

23. Viktor Fulmakht, interview with the author, no date. Fulmakht (b. 1945, Moscow) taught Hebrew beginning in 1974, and edited the samizdat journal *Evrei v sovremennom mire*. He also organized reproduction of copies of samizdat texts, including titles from the Biblioteka Aliya series and Hebrew teaching materials. He became part of the organizing committee Mashka. Fulmakht applied for an exit visa in 1978, and he immigrated to Israel in 1988.

24. The Anti-Zionist Committee of the Soviet Public, a propaganda initiative created by the Central Committee of the CPSU in March 1983, purported to represent the views of Soviet Jewish citizens. Led by General David Dragunsky, all members except Yuri Beliaev were Jewish. The Anti-Zionist Committee ceased its activity in the early 1990s.

25. See Sakharov's account of the conversation in his *Memoirs* (New York: Alfred A. Knopf, 1990), 615–16.

26. "Chronicle of Events," *Soviet Jewish Affairs* 17, no. 2 (1987): 92.

27. Ibid., 95.

28. "Chronicle of Events," *Soviet Jewish Affairs* 17, no. 3 (1987): 92.

29. Ibid., 94.

30. Ibid., 94–95.

31. Ro'i, *The Jewish Movement*, 67.

32. Wurtman, "Soviet Jewry."

33. "Chronicle of Events," *Soviet Jewish Affairs* 17, no. 3 (1987): 95.

34. Ibid., 97.

35. Elena Dubiansky, interview with the author on Apr. 6, 2011. Elena Dubiansky (b. 1946, Moscow) first applied for an exit visa in 1976. Dubiansky was one of the organizers of the group Jewish Women against Refusal (JEWAR) in the early 1980s (on JEWAR, see below). She participated in protests, circulated Jewish samizdat, and facilitated contacts between foreign supporters and refuseniks. Dubiansky left for Israel in 1988.

36. "Chronicle of Events," *Soviet Jewish Affairs* 17, no. 3 (1987): 94.

37. "Chronicle of Events," *Soviet Jewish Affairs* 18, no. 2 (1988): 95.

38. *Informatsionnyi biulleten'* 5 (1987): 3.

39. See the report of Kosharovsky's remarks to Reagan in "Doyen of refuseniks tells Reagan of plight of Soviet Jews," *Jerusalem Post*, June 2, 1988, 4. Further excerpts of

Kosharovsky's remarks appeared in Enid Wurtman's column, "A World without Refuseniks," *Jerusalem Post,* June 3, 1988, 8.

40. "Chronicle of Events," *Soviet Jewish Affairs* 17, no. 3 (1987): 97.

41. Members of the Poor Relatives group banded together to protest a common administrative reason for refusal: their dossiers lacked documents affirming that the exit visa applicants' relatives had no material claims on them. It was sometimes difficult to obtain such documents, even when legitimate material claims were unlikely. *Informatsionnyi biulleten'* 5 (1987): 14.

42. "Chronicle of Events," *Soviet Jewish Affairs* 18, no. 1 (1988): 100.

43. Ibid., 101.

44. "Chronicle of Events," *Soviet Jewish Affairs* 18, no. 2 (1988): 94.

45. *Informatsionnyi biulleten'* 5 (1987): 2.

46. Inna Uspensky, interview with the author, May 30, 2007. Inna (b. 1932), sister of the mathematician and refusenik Alexander Ioffe, and her husband Igor, were both trained as medical biologists. They began visiting refusenik seminars and signing letters of protest in the 1970s, although they did not apply for exit visas until 1979. The Uspenskys organized a medico-biological seminar (1983–89), and from 1985 they worked on getting medical help to refuseniks. The Uspenskys left for Israel in 1989.

47. Igor Uspensky (b. 1939), interview with the author, Feb. 8, 2010.

48. Alexander Smukler, interview with the author, Jan. 5, 2010. Smukler (Shmukler) (b. 1960, Moscow) applied for an exit visa in 1985. He began studying Hebrew in the late 1970s, and in the 1980s participated in samizdat networks, taking over editing the *Informatsionnyi biulleten'* in 1987. In 1987 Smukler also joined the organizational committee Mashka. He left the USSR in 1991.

49. Vladimir Kislik, interview.

50. *Informatsionnyi biulleten'* 16 (1988): 1–3.

51. *Informatsionnyi biulleten'* 21 (1988): 3.

52. Lev Gorodetsky, interview with the author, probably late 2000s, exact date unknown.

53. See Ro'i, *The Jewish Movement,* table 3.1, 107.

54. In a letter of January 2, 1987, to Soviet Prime Minister Nikolai Ryzhkov, more than eighty refuseniks objected to the emigration law that came into force January 1, requesting among other things that repatriation to one's historical homeland, rejoining one's national culture, and religious motives be considered valid reasons for emigration. "Chronicle of Events," *Soviet Jewish Affairs* 17, no. 2 (1987): 94–95.

55. Shoshana Cardin discussed this figure in her interview with the author, Aug. 11, 2004. Cardin was chairperson of the National Conference on Soviet Jewry from 1988 to 1992. In late 1990 she became the first woman head of the Conference of Presidents of Major American Jewish Organizations. Cardin participated in governmental discussions

of Jewish immigration to the United States and aliya. On the forty thousand slots for Soviet emigrants, see also Feingold, *"Silent No More,"* 287.

56. Yoel Florsheim cited a figure of 71,238 total emigrants from the Soviet Union in 1989. Of these, 12,277 went to Israel and 58,961 "dropped out" to go to other countries. See Florsheim's "Emigration of Jews from the Soviet Union in 1989," *Jews and Jewish Topics in the Soviet Union and Eastern Europe* 12 (1990): 23. For more on the context, see Anatoly Adamishin and Richard Schifter, *Human Rights, Perestroika, and the End of the Cold War* (Washington, DC: United States Institute of Peace, 2009).

57. Mark Kupovetsky, interview with the author, Apr. 4, 2011. Kupovetsky (b. 1955, Moscow), a historian and specialist in ethnic demography, was active in the Jewish movement beginning in 1979. He served as director of the Research Center of the Association of Jewish Studies and Jewish Culture from 1989 to 1991. Kupovetsky helped establish the Jewish University in Moscow in 1991, and in 1998 he became director of the Center for Bible Studies and Jewish Studies at the Russian State University for the Humanities.

58. Mark Kupovetsky, interview.

59. Based on Yosif Begun's unpublished memoirs.

60. Alexander Smukler, interview.

61. "Chronicle of Events," *Soviet Jewish Affairs* 18, no. 2 (1988): 97.

62. *Informatsionnyi biulleten'* 13 (1988): 1.

63. The Yakuza administrators reportedly used the leaflets as proof that the event might provoke disturbances, and therefore denied the Jewish group a permit to use the facility: "Anti-Semitism Greets Jews at Moscow Clubhouse," *Jerusalem Post*, June 1, 1988, 4.

64. Mikhail Chlenov, interview.

65. Vladimir Zhirinovsky (b. 1946) became leader of the first officially sanctioned opposition party in the USSR, the Liberal Democratic Party of Russia, in 1990. A provocative and theatrical politician, whose father was Jewish, Zhirinovsky channeled nationalist and other sentiments of the populace into an opposition that lacked long-term electoral credibility. Leaders of the Jewish movement assumed that Zhirinovsky joined the group founding the Shalom Jewish Cultural Society at the behest of the KGB.

66. *Informatsionnyi biulleten'* 22 (1988): 11–15.

67. "Chronicle of Events," *Soviet Jewish Affairs* 19, no. 1 (1989): 96.

68. "Chronicle of Events," *Soviet Jewish Affairs* 19, no. 2 (1989): 96, 98.

69. "Chronicle of Events," *Soviet Jewish Affairs* 20, no. 1 (1990): 93–97.

70. "Chronicle of Events," *Soviet Jewish Affairs* 18, no. 2 (1988): 97.

71. Ibid., 95–96.

72. Ibid., 97.

73. Shmuel Zilberg, interview with the author, Jan. 10, 2004. Zilberg (b. 1954, Starokonstantinov, Ukraine) studied chemistry at Moscow State University and earned a doctorate in the field. Zilberg wrote articles on Jewish topics for samizdat. In 1988 he helped organize

the Latvian Jewish Cultural Society in Riga and worked with Mikhail Chlenov and others to organize the Vaad.

74. "Chronicle of Events," *Soviet Jewish Affairs* 20, no. 1 (1990): 96.

75. Ibid., 97.

76. Ibid., 93.

77. Yosif Zisels, interview with the author, Jan. 15, 2004. Zisels (b. 1946) grew up in Chernovtsy. He completed studies at the Physics Department of Kishinev University. Zisels began participating in the Jewish and democratic movements in the early 1970s. In 1978 he joined the Ukrainian Helsinki group. In that year Zisels was arrested and sentenced to three years in a labor camp. In 1984 he was again sentenced to three years in a labor camp. In 1988 Zisels formed the first independent Jewish organization in the Ukrainian Soviet Republic in Chernovtsy, and in 1989 he helped establish the Soviet Vaad, becoming one of its cochairs.

78. "Chronicle of Events," *Soviet Jewish Affairs* 18, no. 1 (1987–88): 96.

79. "Chronicle of Events," *Soviet Jewish Affairs* 20, no. 1 (1989): 96.

80. Mikhail Chlenov, interview.

81. Yosif Zisels, interview.

82. The ORT (Obshchestvo remeslennogo truda), an international nonprofit Jewish organization, was originally founded in Russia in 1880.

83. Shmuel Zilberg, interview.

84. The document appeared in print as "Itogovyi dokument. Vsesoiuznogo kruglogo stola 'Problemy sovetskogo evreistva," *VEK* (*Vestnik evreiskoi kul'tury*) (Riga), July–Aug. 1989, 1–5.

85. Mikhail Chlenov, interview.

86. Viacheslav Chornovil (1937–1999) was a member of the Ukrainian Helsinki group and one of the first leaders of Rukh, the people's movement of Ukraine.

87. Zviad Gamsakhurdia (1939–1993) was a rights activist, cofounder of the Georgian Helsinki group, and the first president of post-Soviet Georgia.

88. Shmuel Zilberg, interview.

89. The "Time of Troubles" (*smutnoe vremia*) from 1598 to 1603 in Russia between the end of the Rurik Dynasty and the beginning of the Romanov Dynasty was marked by famine and foreign occupation. The period has been the subject of dramatic representation, including in Alexander Pushkin's *Boris Godunov* (also a play by Modest Mussorgsky) and in Mikhail Glinka's opera *Ivan Susanin*. The term therefore refers to dramatic social upheaval.

90. Mikhail Chlenov, interview.

91. *S"ezd evreiskikh organizatsii i obshchin SSR: Sb. materialov* [The Congress of Jewish Organizations and Communities of the USSR: A Collection of Materials] (Moscow, 1990), 3.

92. Baruch Gur-Gurevitz, *Open Gates: The Story Behind the Mass Immigration to Israel from the Soviet Union and Its Successor States*, trans. Naftali Greenwood (Jerusalem: Jewish Agency for Israel, 1996), 54.

93. Shmuel Zilberg, interview.

94. The EAJC was conceived by Chlenov in 1991.

95. Alexander Smukler, interview.

96. See Ro'i, *The Jewish Movement*, table 3.1, 107.

97. Mikhail Chlenov, interview.

98. In the Soviet era, the media was not allowed to report most major accidents or lurid crimes.

99. Shmuel Zilberg, interview.

100. Alexander Smukler, interview.

101. See table 13.6 in Mark Tolts, "Post-Soviet Jewish Demography, 1989–2004," in *Revolution, Repression, and Revival: The Soviet Jewish Experience,* ed. Zvi Gitelman and Yaacov Ro'i (Lanham, MD: Rowman and Littlefield, 2007), 293.

102. Gur, *Open Gates*, 156.

103. Semyon Vaisman, interview with the author, Jan. 24, 2004. Vaisman was a resident of Tiraspol and cochairman of the Vaad.

104. In 2004 a total of 25,000 Jews left the FSU. See table 13.6 in Tolts, "Post-Soviet Jewish Demography," 293.

105. See table 13.1 in Tolts, "Post-Soviet Jewish Demography," 285. These figures cover only "core" or self-identified Jews. The estimates of an "enlarged" Jewish population would be somewhat higher.

106. These numbers are based on table 14.4, "Jewish International Migration, by Major Areas of Origin and Destination . . . 1969–2000," and accompanying text, in Sergio Della Pergola, "The Demography of Post-Soviet Jewry: Global and Local Contexts," in Gitelman and Ro'i, *Revolution, Repression, and Revival*, 324. The number of olim including non-Jewish relatives was higher.

107. See table 8, "Emigration of Jews and Their Non-Jewish Relatives from the FSU, 1989–2005," in Mark Tolts, "Population and Migration: Migration since World War I," *YIVO Encyclopedia of Jews in Eastern Europe*, 2010, accessed Mar. 16, 2015, http://www.yivoencyclopedia.org/article.aspx/Population_and_Migration/Migration_since_World_War_I.

Bibliography

Adamishin, Anatoly, and Richard Schifter. *Human Rights, Perestroika, and the End of the Cold War.* Washington, DC: United States Institute of Peace, 2009.

Alexeyeva, Ludmilla. *Soviet Dissent: Contemporary Movements for National, Religious, and Human Rights.* Translated by Carol Pearce and John Glad. Middletown, CT: Wesleyan Univ. Press, 1985.

Amalrik, Andrei. *Involuntary Journey to Siberia.* Translated by Manya Harari and Max Hayward. New York: Harcourt, Brace, Jovanovich, 1970.

———. *Will the Soviet Union Survive until 1984?* New York: Harper and Row, 1970.

Aronzon, L. L. *Sobranie proizvedenii.* 2 vols. Edited by P. A. Kazarnovskii, I. S. Kukui, and V. I. Erl'. St. Petersburg: Izdatel'stvo Ivana Limbakha, 2006.

"Arsenii Borisovich Roginskii." Accessed Oct. 15, 2016. http://hro.org/node/5665.

Arzhak, Nikolai. *This Is Moscow Speaking, and Other Stories.* Translated by Stuart Hood, Harold Shukman, and John Richardson. London: Collins and Harvill, 1968.

Association "Remember and Save." Accessed Oct. 1, 2016. http://www.soviet-jews-exodus.com/English.

Association "Zapomnim i sokhranim" (Remember and Save). Accessed Oct. 1, 2016. http://www.soviet-jews-exodus.com/index.shtml.

Azbel, Mark. *Refusenik: Trapped in the Soviet Union.* Boston: Houghton Mifflin, 1981.

Beckerman, Gal. *When They Come for Us, We'll Be Gone. The Epic Struggle to Save Soviet Jewry.* New York: Houghton Mifflin Harcourt, 2010.

Beizer, Michael. "How the Movement Was Funded." In *The Jewish Movement in the Soviet Union*, edited by Yaacov Ro'i, 359–91. Washington, DC: Woodrow Wilson Center, 2012.

———. *The Jews of St. Petersburg: Excursions Through a Noble Past.* Translated by Michael Sherbourne and edited by Martin Gilbert. Philadelphia: Jewish Publication Society, 1989.

Berdyaev, Nicolas. *The Origin of Russian Communism.* Translated by R. M. French. London: G. Bles, 1937.

Bialis, Laura. "Yuli Kosharovsky, Soviet Jewry's 'Man Behind the Scenes,' Dies at 72." *Forward,* Apr. 18, 2014. Accessed Apr. 26, 2016. http://forward.com/news/196765/yuli-kosharovsky-soviet-jewrys-man-behind-the-scen/#ixzz45dKI0CwX.

Bikel, Theodore. *Silent No More.* N.p.: Star Record Co., 1971.

Bitov, Andrei. *Pushkin House.* Translated by Susan Brownsberger. Normal, IL: Dalkey Archive, 1998.

Bogoraz, Larisa. "Do I Feel I Belong to the Jewish People?" In *I Am a Jew: Essays on Jewish Identity in the Soviet Union,* edited by Aleksander Voronel, Viktor Yakhot, and Moshe Decter. New York: Academic Committee on Soviet Jewry and the Anti-Defamation League of B'nai B'rith, 1973.

Bukovsky, Vladimir. *To Build a Castle—My Life as a Dissenter.* Translated by Michael Scammell. New York: Viking Press, 1978.

Burauskaitė, Birutė. "The Unarmed Resistance (1954–1990)." In *Resistance to the Occupation of Lithuania: 1944–1990.* Translated by Laima Junevičienė. Vilnius, Lithuania: Organisation Committee Frankfurt, 2002.

Butman, Hillel. *From Leningrad to Jerusalem: The Gulag Way.* Translated by Stefani Hoffman and edited by Carol Talpers. Berkeley, CA: Benmir Books, 1990.

Charny, Simeon. "Judaism and the Jewish Movement." In *The Jewish Movement in the Soviet Union,* edited by Yaacov Ro'i. Washington, DC: Woodrow Wilson Center, 2012.

Chernin, Albert D. "Making Soviet Jews an Issue: A History." In *A Second Exodus: The American Movement to Free Soviet Jews,* edited by Murray Friedman and Albert D. Chernin. Hanover, NH: Brandeis Univ. Press, 1999.

Chlenov, Matvei. "Kul'turnicheskoe dvizhenie i zhurnal 'Nash ivrit.'" *Vestnik evreiskogo universiteta v Moskve* 3, no. 10 (1995): 70–88.

A Chronicle of Current Events, 1–15. Zug, Switzerland: Amnesty International Publications, 1978.

Churchill, Randolph S., and Winston S. Churchill. *The Six Day War.* Boston: Houghton Mifflin, 1967.

Della Pergola, Sergio. "The Demography of Post-Soviet Jewry: Global and Local Contexts." In *Revolution, Repression, and Revival: The Soviet Jewish Experience,* edited by Zvi Gitelman and Yaacov Ro'i. Lanham, MD: Rowman and Littlefield, 2007.

Dershowitz, Alan M. *Chutzpah.* Boston: Little, Brown and Co., 1991.

Dimshitz, V. "Dva puteshestviia po odnoi doroge." In *Istoriia evreev na Ukraine i v Belorussii*, edited by V. Dimshitz, 8–11. St. Petersburg: Petersburg Jewish Univ., 1994.

Diner, Hasia. *We Remember with Reverence and Love: American Jews and the Myth of Silence after the Holocaust, 1945–1962*. New York: New York Univ. Press, 2009.

Dolinin, V. E., B. I. Ivanov, B. V. Ostanin, and D. Ia. Severiukhin, eds. *Samizdat Leningrada, 1950-e–1980-e. Literaturnaia entsiklopediia*. Moscow: Novoe literaturnoe obozrenie, 2003.

Dominitz, Yehuda. "Israel's Immigration Policy and the Dropout Phenomenon." In *Russian Jews on Three Continents: Migration and Resettlement*, edited by Noah Lewin-Epstein, Yaacov Ro'i, and Paul Ritterband. London: Frank Cass, 1997.

Elkins, Michael. *Forged in Fury*. New York: Ballantine Books, 1971.

Epstein, Mikhail. "A Catalogue of New Poetries." In *Russian Postmodernism: New Perspectives on Post-Soviet Culture*, edited by Mikhail Epstein, Alexander Genis, and Slobodanka Vladiv-Glover. New York: Berghahn Books, 1999.

Evrei i evreiskii narod. Petitsii, pis'ma i obrashcheniia evreev SSSR (Jews and the Jewish People: Petitions, Letters and Appeals from the Jews of the USSR) 1–10 (1970–78). Centre for Research and Documentation of East European Jewry, Hebrew Univ. of Jerusalem.

Evreiskii samizdat 1–27 (1974–92). Centre for Research and Documentation of East European Jewry, Hebrew Univ. of Jerusalem.

Fain, Benjamin. "Background to the Present Jewish Cultural Movement in the Soviet Union." In *Jewish Culture and Identity in the Soviet Union*, edited by Yaacov Ro'i and Avi Beker, 235–45. New York: New York Univ. Press, 1991.

———. *Vera i razum* (Faith and Reason). Jerusalem: Mahanaim, 2007.

Feingold, Henry L. *"Silent No More." Saving the Jews of Russia: The American Jewish Effort, 1967–1989*. Syracuse, NY: Syracuse Univ. Press, 2007.

Florsheim, Yoel. "Emigration of Jews from the Soviet Union in 1989." *Jews and Jewish Topics in the Soviet Union and Eastern Europe* 12 (1990).

Frankel, Jonathan. *Prophecy and Politics: Socialism, Nationalism, and the Russian Jews, 1862–1917*. Cambridge, UK: Cambridge Univ. Press, 1981.

Freidin, Gregory. *A Coat of Many Colors: Osip Mandelstam and His Mythologies of Self-Presentation*. Berkeley: Univ. of California Press, 1988.

Frenkel', A., and M. Ryvkin. "Pamiatniki i pamiat'." *VEK* (*Vestnik evreiskoi kul'tury*), Riga, July–Aug. 1989, 23–25.

Friedman, Murray, and Albert D. Chernin, eds. *A Second Exodus: The American Movement to Free Soviet Jews*. Hanover, NH: Brandeis Univ. Press, 1999.

Gilbert, Martin. *Jews of Hope*. London: Macmillan, 1984.

———. *Shcharansky, Hero of Our Time*. London: Macmillan, 1986.

Gilboa, Albert Yehoshua. *The Black Years of Soviet Jewry, 1939–1953*. Translated from Hebrew by Yosef Shachter and Dov Ben-Abba. Boston: Little, Brown and Co., 1971.

Gimelshtein, Margarita. "Otkaz ob otkaze." In *Otkaz i otkazniki. Leningrad, 80-e gody*, edited by Margarita Gimelshtein. Leningrad: Samizdat, 1987. Copy at the Central Archives for the History of the Jewish People, Jerusalem. Collection of the Centre for Research and Documentation of East European Jewry, file 955.

Gitelman, Zvi. "The Psychological and Political Consequences of the Six-Day War in the U.S.S.R." In *The Six-Day War and World Jewry*, edited by Eli Lederhendler. Bethesda: Univ. Press of Maryland, 2000.

Goricheva, Tatiana. Preface to *Cry of the Spirit: Christian Testimonies from the Soviet Union*. Edited by Tatiana Goricheva. London: Fount Paperbacks, 1989.

Guha, Ranajit. *History at the Limit of World-History*. New York: Columbia Univ. Press, 2002.

Gur-Gurevitz, Baruch. *Open Gates: The Story Behind the Mass Immigration to Israel from the Soviet Union and Its Successor States*. Translated by Naftali Greenwood. Jerusalem: Jewish Agency for Israel, 1996.

Haaretz Nikneit Baisurim (The Land Is Attained through Suffering). Tel Aviv: Izdatel'stvo Organizatsii uznikov Siona iz SSSR, 1995.

Hoffman, Stefani. "Jewish Samizdat and the Rise of Jewish National Consciousness." In *Jewish Culture and Identity in the Soviet Union*, edited by Yaacov Ro'i and Avi Beker. New York: New York Univ. Press, 1991.

———. "Voices from the Inside: Jewish Activists' Memoirs, 1967–1989." In *The Jewish Movement in the Soviet Union*, edited by Yaacov Ro'i. Washington, DC: Woodrow Wilson Center, 2012.

"Itogovyi dokument. Vsesoiuznogo kruglogo stola 'Problemy sovetskogo evreistva." *VEK* (*Vestnik evreiskoi kul'tury*), Riga, July–Aug. 1989, 1–5.

Jenkins, Henry. *Convergence Culture: Where Old and New Media Collide*. New York: New York Univ. Press, 2006.

Kats, Leonid. "Zhabotinskii—publitsist." In *Polnoe sobranie sochinenii v deviati tomakh*, by Vladimir Zhabotinskii, vol. 2, bk. 1, 6–24. Minsk, Belarus: Met, 2008.

Kholmyansky, Ephraim. *Zvuchanie tishiny* (The Sound of Silence). Jerusalem: N.p., 2007.

Khronika tekushchikh sobtyii (Chronicle of Current Events), 1–63 (1968–82). Accessed Aug. 18, 2016. www.memo.ru/history/diss/chr/index.htm.

Komaromi, Ann. "Jewish Samizdat—Dissident Texts and the Dynamics of the Jewish Revival in the Soviet Union." In *The Jewish Movement in the Soviet Union*, edited by Yaacov Ro'i. Washington, DC: Woodrow Wilson Center, 2012.

———. *Soviet Samizdat Periodicals*. Toronto: Univ. of Toronto Libraries, 2011. Accessed Oct. 10, 2016. http://samizdat.library.utoronto.ca.

Korey, William. "Jackson-Vanik: A 'Policy of Principle.'" In *A Second Exodus: The American Movement to Free Soviet Jews*, edited by Murray Friedman and Albert D. Chernin. Hanover, NH: Brandeis Univ. Press, 1999.

Kornblatt, Judith Deutsch. *Doubly Chosen: Jewish Identity, the Soviet Intelligentsia, and the Russian Orthodox Church*. Madison: Univ. of Wisconsin Press, 2004.

Kosharovsky, Yuli. Electronic archives. Accessed Oct. 13, 2016. http://kosharovsky.com.

Kuznetsov, Edward. "Interview with Edward Kuznetsov." In *In Search of Self. The Soviet Jewish Intelligentsia and the Exodus: A Collection of Articles*, edited by David Prital, and translated by Stefani Hoffman, 95–107. Jerusalem: Mount Scopus Publications, 1982.

Landsbergis, Algirdas. "God's Whispers in a 'Godless' Literature." *Religion in Communist Lands* 14, no. 3 (1986): 262–67.

Lein, Evgeny. *Lest We Forget*. Jerusalem: Jerusalem Publishing Center, 1997.

Lerner, Alexander. *A Change of Heart*. Rehovot, Israel: Balaban Publishers, 1992.

Levanon, Nehemiah. *HaKod "Nativ"* (Hebrew) (The Code Name Is "Nativ"). Tel Aviv: Am Oved, 1995.

———. "Israel's Role in the Campaign." In *A Second Exodus: The American Movement to Free Soviet Jews*, edited by Murray Friedman and Albert D. Chernin, 70–83. Hanover, NH: Brandeis Univ. Press, 1999.

Lewin-Epstein, Noah. Introduction to *Russian Jews on Three Continents: Migration and Resettlement*, edited by Noah Lewin-Epstein, Yaacov Ro'i, and Paul Ritterband. London: Frank Cass, 1997.

Mandelstam, Osip. *The Noise of Time: The Prose of Osip Mandelstam*. Edited by Clarence Brown. Princeton, NJ: Princeton Univ. Press, 1965.

Mendelevich, Iosef [Yosef]. *Operatsiia svad'ba* (Operation Wedding). Jerusalem: Tarbut, 1987.

———. *Unbroken Spirit*. Jerusalem: Gefen, 2012.

Morozov, Boris, ed. *Documents on Soviet Jewish Emigration*. London: Frank Cass, 1999.

Nathans, Benjamin. *Beyond the Pale: The Jewish Encounter with Late Imperial Russia.* Berkeley: Univ. of California Press, 2002.

Nudel, Ida. *A Hand in the Darkness.* Translated by Stefani Hoffman. New York: Warner Books, 1990.

Paperno, Irina. *Stories of the Soviet Experience: Memoirs, Diaries, Dreams.* Ithaca, NY: Cornell Univ. Press, 2009.

Peretz, Pauline. "The Action of Nativ's Emissaries in the United States: A Trigger for the American Movement to Aid Soviet Jews, 1958–1974." Translated by Julie Wayne and Pauline Peretz. *Bulletin du Centre de recherche français de Jérusalem* 14 (2004): 112–28.

———. *Le combat pour les juifs soviétiques: Washington-Moscou-Jérusalem, 1953–1989.* Paris: Armand Colin, 2006.

———. *Let My People Go: The Transnational Politics of Jewish Emigration during the Cold War.* Translated by Ethan Rundell. New Brunswick, NJ: Transaction Publishers, 2015.

Pinkus, Benjamin. *The Jews of the Soviet Union: The History of a National Minority.* Cambridge, UK: Cambridge Univ. Press, 1988.

———. *The Soviet Government and the Jews, 1948–1967: A Documented Study.* Edited by Jonathan Frankel. Cambridge, UK: Cambridge Univ. Press, 1984.

———. "Soviet Jewish Self-Expression, 1945–1988." *Jews in Eastern Europe* 3, no. 25 (1994).

———. *Tehiyah u-tekumah le'umit: ha-Tsiyonut veha-tenu'ah ha-Tsiyonit bi-Verit-ha-Mo'atsot, 1947–1987* (National Rebirth and Reestablishment). Kiryat Sedeh Boker, Israel: Ben-Gurion Research Center, Ben-Gurion Univ. of the Negev Press, 1993.

Pinsker, Leo. "Auto-emancipation." New York: National Education Department, Zionist Organization of America, 1948.

Prestina, Lia. *Slovar' zapreshchennogo iazyka: 125-letiiu F. L. Shapiro.* Minsk, Belarus: MET, 2005.

Redlich, Shimon. "Jewish Appeals in the USSR." *Soviet Jewish Affairs* 4, no. 2 (1974).

Ro'i, Yaacov, ed. *The Jewish Movement in the Soviet Union.* Washington, DC: Woodrow Wilson Center, 2012.

———. *The Struggle for Soviet Jewish Emigration, 1948–1967.* Cambridge, UK: Cambridge Univ. Press, 1991.

Roziner, Felix. *Anatolii Shcharanskii.* Jerusalem: Shamir, 1985.

Rubenstein, Joshua, and Vladimir P. Naumov, eds. *Stalin's Secret Pogrom: The Postwar Inquisition of the Jewish Anti-Fascist Committee*. Translated by Laura Esther Wolfson. New Haven: Yale Univ. Press, 2001.

Sakharov, Andrei D. "A Letter to the Congress of the United States" (Sept. 14, 1973). In *Sakharov Speaks*, 211–15. London: Collins and Harvill, 1974.

———. *Memoirs*. New York: Alfred A. Knopf, 1990.

"Samizdat." In *Kratkaia evreiskaia entsiklopedia*. 11 vols., 7:627–42. Jerusalem: Keter, 1976–2005. Accessed Sept. 15, 2016. http://www.eleven.co.il/.

Schroeter, Leonard. *The Last Exodus*. Seattle: Univ. of Washington Press, 1979.

Shapiro, F. L. *Ivrit-russkii slovar'*. Moscow: Gosudarstvennoe izdatel'stvo inostrannykh i natsional'nykh slovarei, 1963.

Sharansky, Natan. *Fear No Evil*. Translated by Stefani Hoffman. New York: Vintage Books, 1989.

Shindler, Colin. *Exit Visa, Détente, Human Rights and the Jewish Emigration Movement in the USSR*. London: Bachman and Turner, 1978.

"Sovetskii Soiuz. Evrei v Sovetskom Soiuze v 1953–67 gg." (The Soviet Union. Jews in the Soviet Union, 1953–1967). In *Kratkaia evreiskaia entsiklopedia*. 11 vols., 8:257. Jerusalem: Keter, 1976–2005. Accessed Sept. 15, 2016. http://www.eleven.co.il/.

"Sovetskii Soiuz. Evrei v Sovetskom Soiuze v 1967–85 gg." In *Kratkaia evreiskaia entsiklopedia*, 11 vols., 8:282. Jerusalem: Keter, 1976–2005. Accessed Sept. 15, 2016. http://www.eleven.co.il/.

Soviet Jewish Affairs, vol. 1–21 (1971–91).

The Soviet Union and the Middle East. A Monthly Summary and News Analysis of the Soviet and East European Press. Jerusalem: Hebrew Univ., 1980–91.

Stevenson, William. *90 Minutes at Ėntebbe*. New York: Bantam Books, 1976.

S"ezd evreiskikh organizatsii i obshchin SSR: Sb. materialov (The Congress of Jewish Organizations and Communities of the USSR: A Collection of Materials). Moscow: N.p., 1990.

Tolts, Mark. "Population and Migration: Migration since World War I." *YIVO Encyclopedia of Jews in Eastern Europe*. Accessed Mar. 16, 2015. http://www.yivoencyclopedia.org/article.aspx/Population_and_Migration/Migration_since_World_War_I.

———. "Post-Soviet Jewish Demography, 1989–2004." In *Revolution, Repression, and Revival: The Soviet Jewish Experience*, edited by Zvi Gitelman and Yaacov Ro'i. Lanham, MD: Rowman and Littlefield, 2007.

Toporov, V. N. *Peterburgskii tekst russkoi literatury: Izbrannye trudy*. St. Petersburg: Iskusstvo-SPB, 2003.

Tsigelman, Liudmila. "The Impact of Ideological Changes in the USSR on Different Generations of the Soviet Jewish Intelligentsia." In *Jewish Culture and Identity in the Soviet Union*, edited by Yaacov Ro'i and Avi Beker. New York: New York Univ. Press, 1991.

Uris, Leon. *Exodus*. New York: Doubleday, 1958.

Volvovsky, Ari. "The Teaching and Study of Hebrew." In *The Jewish Movement in the Soviet Union*, edited by Yaacov Ro'i, 344–55. Washington, DC: Woodrow Wilson Center, 2012.

Voronel, Alexander [Aleksandr]. "Jewish Samizdat." In *Jewish Culture and Identity in the Soviet Union*. Edited by Yaacov Ro'i and Avi Beker. New York: New York Univ. Press, 1991.

———. "Trepet iudeiskikh zabot" (The Tremor of Judaic Anxieties). In *Evreiskii samizdat* 12 (1977): 14–56, 157–96.

Voronel, Aleksandr, Viktor Yakhot, and Moshe Decter, eds. *I Am a Jew: Essays on Jewish Identity in the Soviet Union*. New York: Academic Committee on Soviet Jewry and the Anti-Defamation League of B'nai B'rith, 1973.

Wiesel, Elie. *The Jews of Silence: A Personal Report on Soviet Jewry*. New York: Knopf, Doubleday, 2011.

———. *Souls on Fire: Portraits and Legends of Hasidic Masters*. New York: Random House, 1972.

Yedidya, Vera. "The Struggle for the Study of Hebrew." In *Jewish Culture and Identity in the Soviet Union*, edited by Yaacov Ro'i and Avi Beker. New York: New York Univ. Press, 1991.

Zand, Mikhail. "Fate, Civilization, Aliya." In *In Search of Self. The Soviet Jewish Intelligentsia and the Exodus: A Collection of Articles*, edited by David Prital, and translated by Stefani Hoffman. Jerusalem: Mount Scopus Publications, 1982.

Zhitenev, A. A. *Poeziia neomodernizma*. St. Petersburg: INAPRESS, 2012.

Index

Italic page numbers denote illustrations.

Yuli Kosharovsky (1941–2014) was born in the Ural region of central Russia. He became an active leader of the Jewish refusenik movement, and in 1989 he immigrated to Israel, where he continued to advocate for Jewish freedom.

Ann Komaromi is an associate professor of comparative literature at the University of Toronto. She is the author of *Uncensored: Samizdat Novels and the Quest for Autonomy in Soviet Dissidence.*

Stefani Hoffman is working as a freelance academic researcher, editor, and translator after her retirement from the Hebrew University of Jerusalem. She has published several articles on Soviet Jewry and translated the memoirs of outstanding Soviet Jewry activists such as Natan Sharansky, Ida Nudel, and Hillel Butman.